JOHN COLTRANE
and the Jazz Revolution *of the* 1960s

JOHN COLTRANE
and the Jazz Revolution *of the* 1960s

The expanded and revised second edition of
Black Nationalism and the Revolution in Music

by Frank Kofsky

PATHFINDER

New York   London   Montreal   Sydney

Copyright © 1970, 1998 by Pathfinder Press

ISBN 978-0-87348-857-0
Library of Congress Catalog Card Number 97-69548
Manufactured in the United States of America

Cover design: Susan Zárate
Cover photographs: John Coltrane/*Frank Kofsky*

First edition, 1970
Second revised edition, 1998
Ninth printing, 2017

Pathfinder
www.pathfinderpress.com
E-mail: pathfinder@pathfinderpress.com

To the memory of

JOHN COLTRANE AND MALCOLM X

✳

Contents

Preface and acknowledgments

I have no idea what is the world's record for the longest interval between the first and second editions of a book, but the twenty-seven years that separate the publication of *Black Nationalism and the Revolution in Music* from the appearance of this volume surely must be in the running. Given that such a lengthy delay is highly unusual to say the least, I think an explanation is in order. That explanation, however, inevitably involves an autobiographical excursion of some length, so the reader whose interest in the subject matter does not extend to the author may wish to skip these passages and go directly to the text itself.

To begin with, it was never my intent to allow more than a quarter century to elapse before bringing out a new edition of *Black Nationalism and the Revolution in Music*. My original idea was that I would overhaul the book and publish a substantially revised and expanded version sometime around the middle of the 1970s. That, at any rate, was my dream; circumstances dictated otherwise, though, as so frequently they do. Little did I think then that it would take decades, not years, before the dream became a reality.

It is not very often that I can claim to have anticipated the future—the numerous wrong predictions that litter the pages of this book should make that quite evident—but on at least one crucial occasion I did. The opening sentence of the preface to the first edition begins, "In a book by an academic (assuming that I manage to remain one in these perilous times until the moment of publication)," indicating that already as early as September 1969, when I wrote those words, I sensed that I would not have an easy time of it in my new position as a member of the history faculty at California State University, Sacramento. My premonition was better founded than even I suspected at the time. As it turned out, I would spend the greater part of the 1970s bringing grievance actions against this department—one every other year, on the average—in order to remain employed at Sacramento State and to receive the promotions due me. Matters came to a head when the History Department personnel committee sent me a letter notifying me that under no condition would it recommend me for tenure, and therefore this would be my last year at the university. Although the grounds the committee gave for reaching this decision included such weighty items as my having an unlisted telephone number (notwithstanding the fact that several tenured members of the department were no less guilty than I of this grave offense), probably the most important accusation—in any case, it headed the list—was that I was "unduly pro-black" in my "behavior and [my] grading."

I see I was prescient in another respect when I composed the preface to *Black Nationalism and the Revolution in Music*, for I also wrote then of "my indebtedness to the black people of this country" for "their invaluable, if unintended, assistance—in the streets of Watts, Detroit, Newark; at San Francisco State, Cornell, Howard." It was these same black people—including colleagues at the university, the Sacramento African-American community, and musicians from one end of the country to another—who came to my defense when I was most in need of it. Black faculty at Sacramento State openly threatened the members of the History Department with ostracism if the recommendation denying me tenure were allowed to stand. Local black leaders saw to it that newspaper and television journalists invaded the campus en masse to learn how it could happen that a white professor was being fired for being "unduly pro-black." Black musicians rallied to my side and offered to play benefit concerts to raise money for legal action, should that prove necessary.

Faced with this obviously unexpected wave of opposition, the History Department personnel committee beat a rapid retreat and sent me a second letter rescinding the first one and stating that I would obtain tenure as soon as my Ph.D. dissertation was accepted by the University of Pittsburgh. (Even at that, the department was not exactly gracious in defeat. Later that same year, when I presented a telegram from the History Department at the University of Pittsburgh certifying that I had completed all the requirements for the Ph.D. degree, a representative of the department at Sacramento sent an inquiry to the Dean of the Graduate School at Pittsburgh asking if the telegram was genuine!)

In some respects, though, my victory proved to be a Pyrrhic one. Although I did, thanks to the involvement of outraged African-Americans, manage to wrest tenure from the History Department, it was not long thereafter that I discovered I would no longer be permitted to teach the course in the history of African-American music that I myself had introduced into the curriculum. How odd, I thought, that the only person on this campus who had ever written a book on jazz—much less one translated in whole or in part into every major European language as well as Japanese—was now prevented from offering a class in that very specialty.

Ordinarily, if a student of mine were to write a sentence like the preceding one, I would scribble in large letters in the margin, "Don't use passive voice! *Who* did the 'preventing'?" In this case, however, the passive construction is unavoidable, for the simple reason that I could never locate anyone—and I took this issue all the way to the top officials of the university—who would assume responsibility for barring me from teaching the history of African-American music. The only thing that I knew for sure, as I bounced merrily from one administrator's office to the next, was that the chances of my ever being able to give this course again seemed more slender with each passing day. (And so matters still remain at the end of 1996.)

Coincidentally, at the same time these events were in motion, I was systematically being stripped of any opportunity to express myself in the jazz world itself. As early as 1966, for example, the editors of *down beat* gave a hint of what lay in store by publishing Leonard Feather's scurrilous attack on me *by name* and then (as I relate in the third section of chapter 3) refusing me so much as a single line by way of reply.[1] This incident was, I see in retrospect, the handwriting on the wall: as time went on, it grew increasingly difficult for me to find jazz-oriented publications willing to allow my writing entry to their pages. The climactic blow fell toward the end of the 1970s, in the form of a letter from J.R. Taylor, the assistant to critic Martin Williams at the Smithsonian Institution's jazz program, to the editors of the *Journal of Jazz Studies:*

APRIL 22, 1977

To the Editors:

I am afraid I can no longer tolerate professional association with a supposedly scholarly journal that traffics in the embarrassing and wholly self-serving likes of Frank Kofsky's [article] "Elvin Jones" (*Journal of Jazz Studies*, Fall 1976). This article—which despite my [name's] presence on the *Journal*'s masthead, appeared without my foreknowledge—brings to crisis a number of questions concerning the intentions and professional qualification of the *Journal*'s current editors, whose continuing overemphasis upon sociology and social history (even on topics of doubtful relevance to jazz) has evidently reached the point of indiscrimination and disregard for documented fact.

Please consider my resignation as editorial assistant effective immediately.

J.R. Taylor[2]

This undisguised effort at political censorship made my situation painfully obvious. The *Journal of Jazz Studies* was one of the last periodicals where I could expect my work to be evaluated on its merits. If the price the *Journal* was forced to pay for publishing me was loss of the Smithsonian's support, however, I was under no illusion that its editors would for long continue to accept my contributions. Authors, after all, are a dime a dozen; the backing of such a prestigious organization as the Smithsonian is far more valuable to an academic journal still struggling to establish itself and become solvent.

As a result of Taylor's letter, I was forced to do some hard stock-taking. Without meaning to be histrionic or flatter myself in any way, it struck me that in an odd kind of way my own career had come to parallel those of the most outspoken black musicians whose words I had quoted so freely in *Black Nationalism and the Revolution in Music*. Like them, I had made no secret of my views; also like them, it now appeared, I would not escape paying the penalty for espousing those views so openly. I suppose, too, that in its own way this experience enriched my understanding; hereafter I could describe from the inside, as it were, some of the consequences of taking an uncompromising stand in the suffocatingly narrow world of jazz criticism and scholarship.

Meanwhile, what of *Black Nationalism and the Revolution in Music*? Despite my desire to prepare a second edition of the book, as the 1970s wore on it also began to dawn on me that this goal was no longer realistic. I could, of course, continue beating my head on the same stone wall—but to what end? Unable to teach my class on African-American music, unable to publish any of the findings of my research, I had to ask myself if it was not time to look at the situation for what it was and begin considering a tactical retreat. In addition, the state university system recently had begun providing a smattering of time and money to encourage research, and there were some questions in my original field of specialization, the history of United States foreign relations, that had never ceased to intrigue me. If it was only too plain that I had no chance of obtaining either time or money to pursue my interest in jazz, it was still possible that I might have better luck in another area. With that in mind, I turned my energies to an investigation of the Truman administration's war scare of March and April 1948, and in due course (thanks to a great deal of timely financial and moral support from a wide variety of sources) managed to produce a book-length study of that subject.[3]

In the meantime, the historian's first principle—that the only constant in history is change—again asserted itself. With the coming of the 1990s, two new developments emerged. First was the increasingly widespread realization that the 1960s had been a golden age—conceivably the final one—in jazz. With that realization came renewed interest in the music of John Coltrane and the jazz revolution of the 1960s. Much to my initial surprise, I began receiving not only questions from students doing research on one or another aspect of what we at the time had called avant-garde jazz, but also a sprinkling of invitations to speak and write on the topic. The second development—the growth of the Internet and especially the World Wide Web—reinforced the first, as now people who shared an interest in Coltrane and the jazz revolution could make electronic connections with each other.

For me, I think the turning point arrived when I stumbled across a page on the World Wide Web that contained a version of my 1966 interview with John Coltrane (see chapter 13, below). If, I mused, there is this much curiosity about Coltrane and the jazz upheaval that his work catalyzed, perhaps . . . perhaps . . . perhaps now, after so much water had flowed under the bridge, it finally might be possible to see my old dream of publishing a new edition of *Black Nationalism and the Revolution in Music* brought to fruition.

I will spare the reader the intervening details. Suffice it to say that out from their box in the garage came the revisions I had begun too long before, and with them, my musty copies of *down beat* and other jazz magazines. Out, too, came the Coltrane recordings—now often on compact disc, of course—for a more intense scrutiny than I had given them in many a moon. Before I knew it, I was again fully immersed in the 1960s, which remain—as I imagine they always will—the headiest and most-heartening years of my adult life (an admission I make with no apologies whatsoever).

With that by way of introduction, I propose we look at the structure of this new volume in detail.

Revising a work like *Black Nationalism and the Revolution in Music*, I soon enough discovered, is easier said than done. The problem is that it—like all of my books, I suppose—falls between genres. In one respect, it is an attempt at a scholarly account of the jazz revolution of the 1960s. At the same time, however, it is—as I was compelled to recognize once I got down to the actual mechanics of revision—very much an *aspect* of that musical and intellectual insurgency: I wrote then, as I do now, as a partisan of (and in some respects, even a participant in) the jazz revolution. It has always been my conviction that partisanship and objectivity are not mutually exclusive. A student of history and politics need not keep his sympathies secret, in other words, so long as he does not allow them to color his investigation and findings.

All well and good, but this high-flown theorizing did not bring me any closer to answering the more mundane and practical question of how, after more than twenty-five years, I ought to go about revising a volume like *Black Nationalism and the Revolution in Music* without distorting the historical record. After considerable wrestling with the issue, however, I finally managed to devise what I consider a defensible solution: by wielding a very delicate scalpel, I think I have been able to differentiate those passages written primarily to advance the cause of the jazz revolution from those written primarily to analyze and explain it. The former I felt honor-bound to leave unaltered, for to change them would be to engage in the falsification of what is now, for better or worse, a historical document. The latter, in contrast, were entirely legitimate objects of revision. This approach, to be sure, is not perfect—what is?—but I do think it the best available compromise. Certainly it is superior to either of the alternatives: on the one hand, to leave the book as it was, thereby allowing its shortcomings to remain uncorrected, or, on the other, to take advantage of hindsight by depicting myself as possessing the kind of omniscience it has never yet been my lot to enjoy.

Accordingly, let me explain how I went about preparing a new edition of *Black Nationalism and the Revolution in Music*. To start with, I sought to *improve the writing*. For reasons we need not go into, my style in the first edition is needlessly verbose and convoluted. Granted that no one will ever mistake my prose for that of Ernest Hemingway, nonetheless, in this new edition I have sought to minimize the demands my writing makes on the reader's patience and indulgence.

Second, I have *revamped the organization* of the book. In some instances, as I will explain in detail momentarily, this has involved removing material from one chapter and either incorporating it elsewhere or converting it into a chapter in its own right. In addition, I have attempted to eliminate unnecessary repetition and to provide as many cross-references as possible. The latter, ideally, should permit a reader interested in, say, the effect of the soprano saxophone on John Coltrane's style to move fairly easily from the discussion of that topic in chapter 8 to others in chapters 9 and 13.

Third, I have added an *index*. The omission of this aid to the reader was bad enough in the original edition; in the current one, as bulky as it has become, it would be downright inexcusable.

Fourth, I have aimed at enhancing the *quality of the scholarship*. I am not quite so rash as to claim to have read every book and article on jazz published in the United States during the 1960s, but by the same token, I don't think I have fallen too far short of that mark. As a result, I have sharpened my understanding of certain key episodes, as should be most readily apparent in chapter 2, on Establishment harassment of the group of artists I call the forerunners—Sonny Rollins, Charles Mingus, Max Roach, and Abbey Lincoln; in chapter 3, on jazz critics and the musically and socially reactionary role of *down beat;* in chapter 5, on the ruling-class use of jazz as a means of waging the Cold War; and in chapter 8, on the varieties of critical hostility to the music of John Coltrane.

Fifth, I have markedly deepened the level of *musical analysis.* Not only does my examination of John Coltrane's influence on Albert Ayler in chapter 9 now rest on a far-more-firm foundation, but this same chapter also contains a fairly close analysis of Coltrane's musical development from his "sheets of sound" (more accurately, "three on one") period during the late 1950s to his "Giants Steps" period in 1959–1960 to his modal period from 1961 to 1966. For its part, chapter 10, which replaces the essay on Elvin Jones that was the weakest link in the first edition, is entirely new. It offers a general discussion of the reciprocal influence of Coltrane and Jones on each other, several transcriptions of Jones's style as an accompanist, and some theoretical suggestions about what made the rhythmic approach of Coltrane's various groups during his modal period unique. Chapter 11, also new, is an interview with Jones that complements those with McCoy Tyner (in chapter 12) and Coltrane (in chapter 13).

Sixth, I have *discarded* two full chapters because I did not feel I could do their subjects justice herein, especially if I wanted to keep this work at a manageable length. One of these is the original chapter 9, John Coltrane and the Revolution in Rock. I do not doubt the topic is a worthy one, but just because of that, it should be attacked by someone whose expertise in this area exceeds my own. (Given a new generation of jazz scholars, I suspect we will not have long to wait.) I have also had to delete, albeit not without misgivings, the original chapter 6, "The 'Jazz Club': An Adventure in Cockroach Capitalism." There are two reasons why I made this choice. One is that although the environment in all too many jazz nightclubs is sheer torture for musicians and audiences alike—which is, of course, what makes these "clubs" such an inviting target—it is mistaken to focus primarily on them when decisive economic power in the jazz world resides with the immensely larger recording companies and booking agencies. Accordingly, in view of the fact that I have written a companion volume, *Black Music, White Business: Illuminating the History and Political Economy of Jazz* (New York: Pathfinder Press, 1997), that documents how these white business institutions historically have exploited jazz artists, I reluctantly decided that I would have to refer the reader seeking further information to that work.

In summary, for the convenience of those who come to this book after having read *Black Nationalism and the Revolution in Music,* here is a schematic description of how the chapters in this volume relate to their predecessors in that one.

Chapter 1 derives from the original introduction, but I have expanded the introduction's discussion of certain topics, such as the reason why African-Americans predominate among jazz innovators, and moved others to different chapters altogether. Thus, both chapter 2, on the forerunners (Rollins, Mingus, Roach, Lincoln), as well as the reflections that open chapter 14, on Malcolm X, first saw the light of day as parts of the introduction.

Chapter 2, as I noted directly above, was part of section II of the old introduction; it is now both substantially longer and, more important, better researched.

Chapter 3, on jazz critics, is an enlarged version of the old chapter 1.

Chapter 4, on *Blues People* by LeRoi Jones (Amiri Baraka), is essentially unchanged from the old chapter 2.

Chapter 5, on ruling-class use of jazz as a means of winning Cold War cultural victories over the Soviet Union (while maintaining the music's second-class standing in the United States), has a much-fuller account of this issue than the old chapter 3 that it replaces.

Chapters 6, 7, and 8, on the jazz revolution and John Coltrane's leading role in it, correspond to the old chapters 4, 5, and 7, respectively. The first two differ from the originals relatively slightly; the last has new evidence on the critical condemnation of John Coltrane's innovations of the 1960s.

Chapter 9, on John Coltrane's sway over Albert Ayler, is vastly more ambitious, in terms of musical analysis, than its predecessor, the old chapter 8. It offers what is, so far as I am aware, the first detailed attempt to explain how Coltrane's search for a new style led him from his "three on one" ("sheets of sound") approach to his "Giant Steps" period and from there to an involvement with scales, modes, and motivic variation.

Chapter 10 is wholly new. It focuses on the way that Coltrane and Elvin Jones stimulated each other's artistic growth and on Jones's consummate skill as an accompanist (with several musical examples by way of illustration); it also advances some reflections on Coltrane's desire for a more densely polyrhythmic framework for improvisation.

Chapter 11, an interview with Elvin Jones, is also new.

Chapters 12 and 13 contain interviews with McCoy Tyner and John Coltrane, respectively, superseding old chapters 11 (Tyner) and 12 (Coltrane). Each has some new material, including excerpts from other interviews.

Chapter 14, on the thought of Malcolm X, combines portions of section IV of the original introduction with the old chapter 13.

There you have it. My hope is that readers who found some merit in *Black Nationalism and the Revolution in Music* will upon reflection conclude that the various improvements I have tried to incorporate in its successor make this later volume a much more readable, informative, provocative and, ultimately, enlightening effort. If they do, then perhaps the decades-long delay in publishing a second edition will not have been for naught after all.

✳

A note on how I have chosen to cite recordings. The speed at which jazz recordings come into and go out of print is too great for the unaided human eye to follow, as I learned to my dismay in trying to put my hands on the compact-disc version of the album, *John Coltrane "Live" at the Village Vanguard*. Catalogs stoutly assert that such a disc exists; record-store clerks, going by what they read in those catalogs, have even ordered it for me. In the end, however, to be able to carry out the microscopic analysis of "Chasin' the Trane" on which so much of the argument of chapter 9 rests, I had to borrow a copy of the disc from a kindhearted soul whom I "met" via the Internet. This experience in frustration convinced me that it would be absolutely pointless to cite recordings by their current designations, because those designations are no more likely to be lasting than any of their predecessors. Accordingly, the information I supply in citing a recording generally refers to the original release of that work. I am fully aware that in most cases this release is probably no longer in print—but then, as of this writing, neither is a version of *John Coltrane "Live" at the Village Vanguard*, regardless of what current catalogs may claim.

*

Like every author who has ever set pen to paper, I have incurred my share of moral and intellectual debts in the course of producing both editions of this book. It is a pleasure again to acknowledge both the encouragement and the useful criticism I received from Cliff and Julia Houdek in Los Angeles at the start of the 1960s, when I was still a fledgling author and this project was little more than a gleam in my eye. Later that decade, in Pittsburgh, Tom and Jeri McCormick spent endless late-night hours with me listening to recordings of the jazz avant garde, letting me try out my ideas on them, even accompanying me to New York to see what turned out to be John Coltrane's last public performance (in April 1967 at the Olatunji African Cultural Center in Harlem). Just to recall some of those wonderful experiences at two different times in two different cities is enough to suffuse me with a warm glow and remind me, should I ever lose sight of it, what a blessing dear friends can be.

Assistance of a different nature came from other sources. The Louis A. Rabinowitz Foundation of New York was kind enough to give me a research fellowship that allowed me to visit New York to interview approximately two dozen of the participants in the jazz revolution during 1966 and 1967.

I am also grateful, as I imagine goes without saying, for the unstinting help I have had over the last thirty-five years from almost every jazz musician with whom I have come in contact. I know that sometimes my questions must have been an intrusive nuisance, but the musicians put up

with them patiently and, little by little, helped me to overcome my initial naiveté and to repair the deficiencies in my
knowledge. I owe a special debt to John Coltrane himself in
this regard; it never fails to sadden me that I did not have
an opportunity to reciprocate his graciousness.

Relations between author and publisher, as any candid
author will attest, can all too easily turn troubled and con-
tentious. It therefore came as a great relief to discover that
Michael Baumann and his colleagues at Pathfinder Press
treat authors with respect and due regard for their often
tender sensibilities, a fact that made working together both
easy and enjoyable.

My obligations to the community of jazz musicians only
increased once I began to think about a new edition of *Black
Nationalism and the Revolution in Music*. Initially hesitant
and somewhat uncertain, the consistent support and even
urging I received from the musicians themselves soon over-
came my doubts. Indeed, I probably would have abandoned
this project in the early stages had I heard substantial objections from the musicians with whom I discussed it, but
I can honestly say that—much to my own amazement—I
received only the most favorable comments from them. That
fact alone convinced me I had some kind of responsibility—
to the music and the musicians—to proceed. In this connection, I must express my appreciation to three fine artists in
particular. The eagerness of San Francisco saxophonist Glenn
Spearman—who carries on the legacy of the 1960s that too
many others have abandoned—to have me finish the second
edition helped keep me at my desk when I might otherwise
have chosen to procrastinate. Pianist Matthew Goodheart,
another San Franciscan, was always available when I needed
him to transcribe a few measures, explain a chord sequence,
or verify the correctness of a musical interpretation. Bassist Arthur Davis—on whose talent and musical intelligence
Coltrane continued to draw until the end—supplied valuable

information that clarified my understanding of Coltrane's musical evolution at the start of the 1960s. I am delighted to have this opportunity to give thanks to all three.

Frank Kofsky
BENICIA, CALIFORNIA
NOVEMBER 1996

NOTES

1. See Leonard Feather, "Feather's Nest: A Plea for Less Critical Infighting, More Attention to the Music Itself," *down beat*, December 16, 1965, p. 13, and Frank Kofsky to the editor of *down beat*, unpublished letter of December 6, 1965.

2. This letter is in *The Journal of Jazz Studies*, IV:2 (Spring/Summer 1977), p. 102.

3. Frank Kofsky, *Harry S. Truman and the War Scare of 1948: A Successful Campaign to Deceive the Nation* (New York: St. Martin's Press, 1993; paper edition, 1995).

Part 1

Introduction

1

An invitation to the dance

A. Ideology and reality in jazz

The Negro musician is a reflection of the Negro people as a social phenomenon. His purpose ought to be to liberate America aesthetically and socially from its inhumanity. The inhumanity of the white American to the black American, as well as the inhumanity of the white American to the white American, is not basic to America and can be exorcised. I think the Negro people through the force of their struggles are the only hope of saving America, the political or cultural America.

Culturally, America is a backward country; Americans are backward. But jazz is American reality—total reality. . . . Some whites seem to think they have a right to jazz. Perhaps that's true, but they should feel thankful for jazz. It has been a gift that the Negro has given, but [whites] can't accept that—there are too many problems involved with the social and historical relationship of

the two peoples. It makes it difficult for them to accept
jazz and the Negro as its true innovator.

—ARCHIE SHEPP[1]

There is a curious dichotomy that reigns among white Americans. If they are in the jazz world proper, then they will tend to deny that, whatever else jazz may be, it is first and foremost a black art—an art created and nurtured by black people in this country out of the wealth of their historical experience. If, in contrast, they are not part of the jazz environment, white Americans will automatically and virtually without exception assume that jazz is black—though not an art—and therefore, though this may go unstated, worthy of no serious treatment or respect. Thus it is that (as I relate in more detail in chapter 4) the most celebrated elder statesman of the music, Duke Ellington, could be denied a Pulitzer Prize for music in 1966, at the very same time as his "triumphs" over Soviet poet Yevgeni Yevtushenko at the first World Festival of Negro Arts were being celebrated by Lloyd Garrison in the pages of the *New York Times*.[2]

In his book *The Crisis of the Negro Intellectual*, Harold Cruse examines this denial of a Pulitzer Prize for Ellington, and concludes, in rather restrained tones, that "here was an affront to the entire musical and cultural heritage of every Negro in America."[3] Affront though it may have been, it surely was not unique. Even now, for all of the supposedly greater acceptance of black art and culture this country is said to have achieved, only a single black musician, Ornette Coleman, has ever been the recipient of a Guggenheim Foundation award for his work in jazz. So far as the Anglo-Saxon-Protestant-dominated Establishment—that is, ruling class—is concerned, serious black art is beneath consideration.[4]

Though the refusal of the Establishment to support jazz on anything approaching the same level that it subsidizes, say, light opera, is indicative of its inherent narrowness and cultural provincialism, at least it has the virtue of candor. After all, the ruling class seems to be saying, jazz, when you come right down to it, is the music of blacks and belongs in whorehouses, bars, dives, and other appropriately debased surroundings. What would *we* want to have to do with a music like *that?*

If the class bias of such an attitude is reprehensible, the willingness to concede the black origins of the music called jazz is a distinct improvement over the position taken by the bulk of the white semi-literati in jazz. For the most part, these latter worthies have spent reservoirs of ink striving to convince their readers that jazz is "American" rather than black.[5] Of course, the American experience is undeniably a major component of the music; but it is an experience *as perceived by blacks* from a vantage point unique to them. To anyone not involved in grinding ideological axes, the point is probably obvious and needs little emphasis. That is just it: an enormous amount of what passes for writing on jazz stems from an ideological stance, the product of a false consciousness. The purpose of such writing is systematically to obscure, if not deny, the black roots of the music. As the saxophonist, poet, and playwright Archie Shepp observes in the passage at the start of this chapter, whites "can't accept" the fact that jazz "has been a gift that the Negro has given," because "there are too many problems involved with the social and historical relationship of the two peoples. It makes it difficult for them to accept jazz and the Negro as its true innovator."

The source of such difficulties is twofold. First, whites are generally unable to believe that blacks, as a people (as opposed to a handful of individual "geniuses," whose gifts are manifested primarily by their good taste in imitating whites), are capable of creating anything that is of durable value. Thus, even where black artistic achievements are acknowledged with one hand, as in the field of popular music, the concession is snatched back with the other by consigning the areas in question to the realm of the trivial and ephemeral. In this way, blacks can be recognized as creators while at the same time the significance of their creations can be denied.

Second, because of the realities of the social and economic structure of the jazz world, most whites involved in the business aspects of the music are extremely loath to describe matters as they actually stand. One of the earliest explanations of the causes of such ideological thinking, that by Marx and Engels in *The German Ideology*, remains unsurpassed to this day and is particularly germane here: "If in all ideology men and their relations appear upside-down as in a *camera obscura*, this phenomenon arises just as much from their historical life-process as the inversion of objects on the retina does from their physical life-process."[6] The "circumstances" in jazz are quite easy to comprehend. To quote Archie Shepp once more: "You own the music and we make it."[7] Presumably it is unnecessary to specify to whom the *you* and *we* refer.

In any case, it is whites who, with very minor exceptions, do indeed own the major economic institutions of the jazz world—the booking agencies, recording companies, nightclubs, festivals, magazines, radio stations, and so on. Blacks in the main own nothing but their own talent. Although that talent in some cases may suffice to secure an adequate livelihood—that is, one comparable to what a performer of European art music with comparable ability enjoys—more often it does not. Here an analogy may be useful. In its relation with a developing country (neocolony), a more advanced industrial nation (metropolis) will use its superior technology to ensure that economic exchanges between the two perpetuate the impoverishment of the former in order to benefit the latter. The metropolis employs its ownership of capital to generate more capital—that is, profits. The neo-colony, possessing nothing to exchange save its raw materials, natural resources and the labor-power of its citizens, has its capital slowly drained away to the metropolis. Just so does the situation stand in jazz. Black musicians, and some whites as well, toil not primarily for themselves, but to enrich those who own the means of production and distribution I enumerated above.[8]

Is it any wonder, then, that this state of affairs goes unrecognized in the literature of jazz? To ask for matters to be otherwise would be equivalent to asking North American economists to conclude, for instance, that the pattern of U.S. capital investment in Latin America works to retard rather than stimulate economic growth there. It is very difficult for those who live off the labor-power of others to perceive the exploitation inherent in such a situation. It is even more difficult, apparently, for those who serve as ideologues and publicists for the owners of capital to arrive at this recognition. If we are to believe their paid representatives, investments by the Rockefellers and Mellons in Latin American petroleum resources are actually philanthropic endeavors undertaken for the betterment of the indigenous population. By the same line of reasoning, it follows that the activity of white-owned businesses in an art created by blacks is least of all for the sake of the profits that just happen to accrue, but is, as everyone ought to know, a form of charity motivated by disinterested love of the arts and the spirit of noblesse oblige.

Or so things appear, to invoke the metaphor of Marx and Engels, "upside down as in a *camera obscura*" in the ideological picture of jazz drawn by its principal authors and periodicals. The reality, of course, is nowhere near so sublime. Here and there an occasional black musician will be able to transcend the obstacles that are a permanent feature of the jazz milieu and attract a sufficiently large following to control the conditions of his or her employment. Such artists, however, are rare exceptions to the rule. On the whole, the vocation of jazz musician is a doubly perilous one and its practitioners labor under multiple disadvantages: because they are artists in a country with only the shallowest traditions of supporting its own artists, and because they are black in a society that views blacks with not-very-well-disguised disdain.

But very little of these matters manages to trickle its way into print, and the reasons are scarcely esoteric. At bottom, they stem from the situation summarized by Archie Shepp: "You own the music and we make it." Part of the ownership Shepp refers to extends to what Marx and Engels term "the means of mental production," as these pertain to jazz. As the authors of *The German Ideology* explain:

> The ideas of the ruling class are in every epoch the ruling ideas. . . . The class which has the means of material production at its disposal, consequently also controls the means of mental production, so that the ideas of those who lack the means of mental production are on the whole subject to it. The ruling ideas are nothing more than the ideal expression of the dominant material relations. . . .
>
> The division of labor . . . one of the chief forces of history up till now, manifests itself also in the ruling class as the division of mental and material labor, so that inside this class one part appears as the thinkers of the class (its active, conceptive ideologists, who make the formation of the illusions of the class about itself their chief source of livelihood).[9]

What Marx and Engels have written about the ruling class as a whole—that, because of the division of labor, some of its members play the role of "active ideologists," while others, the "active members," are practical people of affairs—applies to the microscopic world of jazz as well. Here, the first group goes by the name of *jazz critics.*

As a number of the essays that follow this introduction attempt to deal in some depth with the modus operandi of the jazz critic, we need only the most summary description at this point. Let it suffice that until very recently almost all of the best-known American critics have been anti-radical white men who support the main features of the social status quo and who have made "perfecting of the illusion . . . their chief source of livelihood."* That is to say, a major (if not *the* major) responsibility of the jazz critic, linked as he is to the white owners of the jazz business by ties of economics, color, and social viewpoint, is to obscure prevailing social relations in this milieu. Because the most glaring reality of jazz society is that of black creation versus white control, that relationship is also the one most urgently in need of having its nakedness concealed behind ideological fig leaves.

To illustrate why this matter is one of such high priority, we need only to consider an analogy. Imagine the repercussions were North American corporations openly to admit that the effect of their overseas economic activity is to promote stagnation, resource-depletion, and pollution, rather than growth and a higher standard of living, in developing nations. Clearly, such an admission would be little short of an across-the-board invitation for the expropriation of U.S. firms around the globe.

Though the sums of money involved in jazz businesses are, obviously, insignificant by comparison, the logic of the situation is similar. If it is undeniable that a relatively small handful of black individuals do benefit from white

---

* To date, all the leading white ideologues in jazz have been white men, so I hope I may be exonerated of charges of male chauvinism if I use the pronouns *he* and *his* with reference to them.

business investments in the colonial economy of jazz, it is hardly open to question that the black community as a whole would be far better off were it in a position to control one of its leading resources, the talents of its people. Under the existing circumstances, however, this is an impossibility. Like Peruvian copper or Chilean nitrates, the "raw material" of jazz—musical artistry—is dumped on a glutted market, where the price it can command is relatively low; whereas those who dispose of the "finished product"—recording companies, festival promoters, bookers and agencies, nightclub owners—are, by virtue of their entrenched domination of the processes of production and distribution, able to take the lion's share of the profits.*

Norman Granz, to cite a not unusual case, managed to amass a world-renowned collection of contemporary art largely from promoting concerts and from producing recordings of saxophonist Charlie Parker; critic Leonard Feather established himself as a leading authority on the music of Parker and his contemporaries by being among the first writers to recognize its brilliance, and he parlayed this achievement into a position of syndicated preeminence in the field of jazz journalism. Meanwhile, however, Parker himself died the death of a penniless drug addict. His career was extraordinary for incredible bursts of creativity; its ending was all too commonplace. Those who find nothing perturbing in the juxtaposition of the circumstances of Parker's demise and the enrichment of those white business figures whose paths intersected his are no doubt among those who will be wholly surprised when one fine day the continent of Latin America follows the example

---

* I refer the reader to chapters 1–4 of my study *Black Music, White Business: Illuminating the History and Political Economy of Jazz* (New York: Pathfinder Press, 1997) for a more detailed exploration of this subject.

of Southeast Asia and erupts into revolutionary flames. Their astonishment may be genuine, but their sense of social justice—if that is not an outmoded concept—could do with some sharpening.

In any event, to return to our white jazz ideologue, one of his principal assignments, particularly in recent years, has been in one way or another to disguise the nature of the social relationships that determine the distribution of rewards reaped from jazz. Much of the time, of course, he will be dealing in aesthetic judgments—in which he will almost invariably exhibit European rather than African-American cultural preferences—and not with social issues. Yet as the tide of black-nationalist sentiment has continued to swell in the nation's ghettos, the attack against "outside" ownership and control of jazz production and distribution has steadily increased in intensity. Consequently, these jazz ideologues have to some degree been forced onto the defensive and compelled to offer explanations purporting to demonstrate that the status quo in jazz is beneficent rather than exploitative. Their arguments, though they may differ in detail, fall into three main categories:

1. Jazz is not primarily a black or African-American art, inasmuch as "anyone" can learn to play it.

2. Blacks themselves do not support jazz, or at least certain kinds of jazz—a contention often advanced when the writer wishes to discredit certain styles, schools, and the like.

3. Jazz has no particular social content; specifically, it in no way pertains more closely to black experiences, modes of perception, sensibilities, and so on, than it does to white. At its most vulgar, this argument is condensed into the assertion that jazz is not "protest music," that black jazz musicians are either unwilling or unable to concern themselves with social issues, unless manipulated

into doing so by some diabolical white puppetmaster behind the scenes. The racism implicit in such an approach
ought to be so palpable to everyone save its formulators
as not to require further comment.

Although I treat the critics at length in chapters 2 and 3
and elsewhere below, these tenets of white critical dogma
contain some points of sufficient importance to merit consideration here.

B. "Anyone" can learn to play jazz—or, how asking the wrong question leads to a meaningless answer

There is probably a certain amount of truth in the postu-
late that "anyone" can learn to play jazz—about as much as
there is in the assertion that "anyone" with some musical
ability can *davin* in Yiddish as a cantor, can sing flamenco
songs in the *cante hondo* style, can learn Indian ceremo-
nial dances or Irish sea chanties or Japanese Koto music or
what have you. To be sure, one need not be born Jewish and
raised in an Orthodox home to be a good cantor; but it is a
striking fact that there aren't very many Gentile daviners
of distinction.

As the foregoing paragraph suggests, perhaps the best way
of putting this touching article of faith in perspective is by
analyzing an analogous proposition in a different artistic
field. Rather than focusing on jazz, therefore, let us for the
moment look instead at symphonic music. In a very abstract
and general sense, it is no doubt the case that "anyone" can
write, or play, or conduct a symphony. But when we descend
from the Mount Olympus of abstraction to the mundane
terrain of concrete reality, what we find is completely different. For all intents and purposes, the symphony is entirely
a phenomenon of European origins—and if we care to be
utterly blunt about it, Central and Eastern European at that.
For all of the work of Franck, Elgar, Britten, Vaughn Wil-

liams, Ives, Copland, Bernstein, and the like, the history of this musical genre would not be significantly different if all the symphonies written by composers born west of the Rhine had been destroyed before publication. Nor is the story much different when it comes to conductors and performers. Even though the symphonic form is now well over two hundred years old and symphonic recordings have circulated around the globe for almost a century, the number of performers and, to an even greater degree, conductors of the first rank who are not of European descent is minuscule (there are, in fact, all of two such conductors, Seiji Ozawa of the Boston Symphony and Zubin Mehta of the Israeli Philharmonic—and some people would object to the inclusion of Mehta).

Is it, then, "racist" or otherwise intellectually impermissible to refer to the symphony as a European art form? Most assuredly not. The symphony was born in a (Central) European cultural environment, it flourished in that environment, it reflects the ethos of that environment—how many times has one seen Beethoven held up as a representative of European romanticism or Mahler's music treated as a specimen of Europe's fin de siècle decadence and ennui?—and, not surprisingly, its most eminent exponents, from Mozart and Haydn to Mahler and Shostakovich, have sprung from its soil.

Indeed, given the almost total domination of the writing, playing, and conducting of the symphonic literature by (Central and Eastern) Europeans, only a fool or lunatic would argue that this art is anything but European in nature. But exactly the same considerations apply to jazz. If we were to conduct a similar "thought experiment" by asking ourselves to what degree contemporary jazz would be changed had there never been any white jazz musicians, the answer would be quick in coming: hardly at all. On one instrument after another, the jazz tradition has been defined exclusively by a series of black artists; only in a single, solitary instance, in fact, has a white artist—pianist Bill Evans—left a lasting mark on the music that followed him.*

Understanding the reasons for the undeniable preponderance of black performers in jazz will permit us to evaluate the notion that "anyone" can play this music. Before an aspiring novice can become even a somewhat-competent jazz improviser, of course, he or she must first gain control over an instrument. But that is simply a beginning—a prerequisite, as it were. To progress further—to arrive at the point where it is honestly possible to call oneself a *jazz musician*—a performer must develop a unique personal style, the individual components of which include the *sound* the performer coaxes from the instrument and the *rhythmic phrasing, melodic construction,* and *harmonic approach* he or she employs. In all of these areas, the beginning jazz improviser has little choice but to look to black music in general and jazz in specific for guidance and models.

The necessity for reliance on black predecessors is most apparent with those instruments—including two of those most important in contemporary jazz, the saxophone and the drum set—for which European popular and art musics offer few, if any, useful precedents. Except for the concert- and marching-band repertoire, there is little music even written for the saxophone, and to play the instrument in the style of a marching or concert band in a jazz setting would be to court ostracism. Insofar as there is a history of saxophone and drum-set virtuosity, in fact, it is a fair statement that jazz artists originally established, and continue to define, the standards of excellence. But even with instruments more widely used in European music—the trumpet, say, and the

---

* Notwithstanding all the rhetoric about the "King of Swing," Benny Goodman's influence on jazz was quite transient, and, accordingly, his instrument, the clarinet, is almost totally absent from small-group improvised jazz after 1950.

trombone—black musicians from the outset have created their own characteristic modes of expression; one thinks here of the growls, cries, moans, and other guttural inflections that early brass performers like Bubber Miley and Joe ("Tricky Sam") Nanton pioneered. Thus, far from black musicians being able to draw on white models, the lines of influence in reality have flowed in exactly the other directions. It is a commonplace, for instance, that American symphonic trumpeters differ from their European counterparts because of the strong influence of Louis Armstrong in the sound of the former. The story is similar in white American popular music, where singers and instrumentalists alike are much more likely to have black models than the reverse.

If there is a case to be made for European influences in jazz, one would expect to find the strongest supporting evidence with respect to that quintessentially European instrument, the equal-tempered piano. To be sure, the work of black jazz pianists such as Art Tatum and Oscar Peterson has been shaped by European ideas of tone and attack, but that is only one aspect of jazz pianism, and not necessarily the most influential at that. The opposing school of jazz pianists—first exemplified by anonymous turn-of-the-century juke-joint performers, then by boogie-woogie musicians like Meade ("Lux") Lewis, Albert Ammons, and Pinetop Smith, and finally by Thelonious Monk, McCoy Tyner, and Cecil Taylor— tend to treat the instrument in a more African fashion, as if it were a marimba, by emphasizing its percussive possibilities at least as much as its melodic and harmonic ones.[*]

---

[*] Significantly enough in this context, some dictionaries suggest an African derivation for the words "boogie-woogie": "Possibly from Black West African English (Sierra Leone) *bogi(-bogi)*, to dance; possibly akin to Hausa *buga*, to beat drums." See entry for "boogie-woogie," *The American Heritage Talking Dictionary* on CD-ROM (Cambridge, MA: Softkey International, 1994).

Likewise for the handling of rhythm in jazz. Elsewhere I devote considerable space to an analysis of how the African-American community makes use of games and dances to imbue its young people with a sophisticated appreciation of both subtle variations in rhythm and rhythmic improvisation.[10] Although such games and dances may have existed in pre-industrial Europe, they have no counterpart in any contemporary society of European descent. From the standpoint of promoting the development of jazz musicianship, it would be hard to exaggerate the importance of the training in sensing fine rhythmic distinctions that the black community affords its youth. In chapter 10, as a case in point, I argue at length that the ability of the John Coltrane quartet of the early 1960s to create what I call rhythmic displacement by maintaining one pulse while simultaneously articulating a pattern of accents that implies a different one is central to the polyrhythmic feeling that was the hallmark of this group. (Although I cannot explore the topic further here, it is at least conceivable that rhythmic displacement of this type is also the basis for that still-unexplained aspect of the most memorable jazz improvisations, "swing.") It stands to reason that the more familiar one has become with rhythmic complexity in one's youth, the more readily one will be able to engage in elaborate manipulations of rhythm as an adult.

Hence in many respects, expressing oneself in jazz is not unlike expressing oneself in a second language: the earlier one starts, all other things being equal, the more readily one learns and more idiomatically one speaks. The analogy is especially pertinent to the construction of rhythmic-melodic lines, for jazz performers shape their melodies in highly characteristic ways that are unique to that genre: one can listen to European folk and art music from now until hell freezes over without hearing anything that in the least resembles four measures of blues improvisation by Charlie Parker or John Coltrane. In jazz as in French, or Cantonese, one betrays one's "foreign" origins by putting the accent in the wrong place (a rhythmic error) and/or by mispronouncing the words (an error in the choice of timbre and/or inflection). If the best way to acquire the ability to speak another language like a native is by being submerged from a young age in a culture in which that language is employed, it should come as no surprise that black musicians have never been displaced from their preeminent position in jazz. A youth who grows to maturity in one of the nation's ghettos has been continuously immersed in the various streams of African-American music from infancy (just as a youth raised in nineteenth-century Vienna would have been immersed in symphonic music and opera). From the standpoint of becoming a topflight jazz soloist, a person raised in this environment has an inestimable cultural advantage over his or her white counterparts, who have not enjoyed anything like the same exposure to this rich musical fare. (This situation could change with the next generation of white jazz musicians, whose listening habits are, thanks to the cheap portable radio and phonograph record, probably more catholic and closer to that of their black cohorts than has been true heretofore.) If there is always the possibility that an author can develop as a major voice in a second language, it is nonetheless true that only a handful in the history of literature have been able to accomplish the feat. Why should we expect the outcome with jazz to be any different?

We can throw the African-American nature of jazz into even sharper relief, moreover, by pushing the analogy between absorbing the jazz tradition and mastering a second language a step further. To learn to understand, speak, and perhaps write in a second language with reasonable facility is difficult, but by no means impossible. To become a genuinely creative and original prose stylist in an acquired tongue, though, is an achievement of an entirely different order, and the number of writers who have managed to pull it off is, as I suggested in the preceding paragraph, minute. We should bear in mind in this context that when we refer to the literature of any country or region, it is ordinarily the most creative figures, the seminal innovators, of whom we speak; competence, however praiseworthy in itself, does not, and can not, define a viable standard of excellence. The same logic is directly relevant to jazz. There are (and have been) innumerable musicians in jazz whose competence is beyond question; without such performers to perpetuate it, nothing resembling contemporary jazz could have been born, much less survived. Yet for all their importance, their contributions have been different *in kind* from those of the artists whose names immediately leap to our tongues when we think of the music's foremost creative figures over the years: Louis Armstrong, Duke Ellington, Coleman Hawkins, Lester Young, Charlie Parker, Dizzy Gillespie, Thelonious Monk, Miles Davis, Charles Mingus, Max Roach, John Coltrane, Ornette Coleman, Cecil Taylor. The difference lies in this, that the latter artists are the ones whose works *define* the basic contours that the music will follow thereafter, while the former are those who will not so much innovate as assimilate, and then elaborate on the innovations of others. Jazz, in short, like any area of human endeavor, has its foot soldiers as well as its generals. Both, needless to say, are necessary if the music is to endure and develop.

For all of that, it cannot be denied that the innovators, by definition, are the artists who give the music its direction, propelling it forward by devising new styles when existing ones have become threadbare through overuse. It does *not* follow from this that the rank and file are entirely passive and play no role in the evolution of jazz styles. On the contrary, it is this rank and file that, collectively, exerts what amounts to a veto power over the innovators. Those innovations that large numbers of the rank and file adopt and incorporate into their work are the ones that will persist;

those that the community of jazz musicians consistently rejects will ultimately end on the discard heap.

To earn a niche as an artist of lasting significance therefore requires more than simple "originality"; it demands as well that, in the long run—which sometimes may be very long indeed—the artist's original ideas meet with a favorable response from the body of jazz musicians as a whole, so that they may be added to existing approaches to improvisation. Dave Brubeck, to mention one example, is certainly unique in his approach to the piano, but unlike the no-less-unique Thelonious Monk, his style has never been sufficiently compelling to produce a "school" of musicians whose playing can be unequivocally traced back to him. As a result, one can assert with some confidence after fifteen years that Brubeck is an occasionally interesting but essentially minor figure in the development of jazz piano. His style will go with him to the grave, and future histories of jazz, when they are written, will relegate his name to the footnotes.

How does the foregoing bear on the question of the black origins and nature of jazz? The answer is that if we were to compile the names of the ten or twenty-five or fifty most significant jazz artists—those whose ideas have had the greatest influence on successive generations of performers—the color of such a list would be overwhelmingly black. The number of white musicians who have made a permanent contribution to the tradition of jazz—as opposed to exploring what turns out to be a musical blind alley, in the fashion of Dave Brubeck—is remarkably small. More than likely, one could count them on one's fingers. Of unquestioned importance are the aforementioned pianist Bill Evans and the late bassist Scott LaFaro. Depending on how tightly one wishes to draw the line, a good case could be made for the inclusion of such popular but essentially uninfluential performers as trumpeter Bix Beiderbecke, trombonist Jack Teagarden, clarinetist Benny Goodman, saxophonist Stan Getz, drummer Mel Lewis, and bassist Charlie Haden, none of whom have inspired numerous disciples. If we want to be extremely generous, we could add the names of clarinetists Artie Shaw and Pee Wee Russell, trombonist Frank Rosolino, and band-leaders Woody Herman and Stan Kenton. In sum, a baker's dozen—not exactly a multitude. And even if we double the number, on the assumption that we may have overlooked some noteworthy musicians, the figure is still comparatively tiny. It is probably safe to state that there have been more black innovators of consequence on any two instruments we might choose at random—trumpet and trombone, say—than there have been whites on all instruments put together.

The overwhelming prevalence of black innovators in jazz can easily be related to our earlier "second language" anal-ogy. Just as it is far more likely that a French rather than an English novelist will be the author of some potent new departure in French letters, so we can expect that the major revolutionary developments in jazz—abrupt discontinuities in accepted styles of improvisation—will flow from the hands and instruments of blacks. Ghetto blacks, if you will, "speak jazz" (or blues or gospel music) as their "native tongue" much as Italians "speak opera" and Viennese "speak symphony"; whereas for most whites, jazz is a "language" that must be acquired, often only with a great deal of painful effort and highly disciplined study.

Now consider the difference in situation of two young musicians, one black, one white, in their late teen years—at a time, that is, when most innovators are nearing their cre-ative peak (John Coltrane, whose greatest innovations came after the age of thirty, is a striking exception in this regard). The black youth, having unconsciously absorbed much of the jazz tradition as part of his culture, can take this tradi-tion more or less for granted in launching a musical career and also can, as a result, dedicate all of his or her energies and talents to elaborating a personal style—one that may be revolutionary in its impact on contemporary artists. The white youth, in contrast, must devote his or her efforts not so much to becoming a unique voice, but to the necessarily prior problems of simply mastering the jazz vernacular, of *acquiring* the tradition. The first musician thus finds the way open to becoming an innovator; the second may be satisfied to achieve something beyond run-of-the-mill competence.

It is essentially for this reason that most whites who enter the jazz world do so as imitators of black innovators. As yet unprepared to aspire to innovation themselves, they are content if they can produce credible facsimiles of their artistic mentors. Possibly the clearest illustration of this phenomenon came in the 1940s and 1950s, in the form of a "school" of white saxophonists who drew their inspiration from Lester Young. Their number was formidable, including Bill Perkins (in many ways the most impressive of the lot), Stan Getz, Zoot Sims, Al Cohn, Jimmy Giuffre, Allan Eager, Herbie Steward, Brew Moore, Serge Chaloff (a baritone saxophonist who was nonetheless heavily dependent on Young for his approach), and probably others whose names escape me. Aside from Perkins and perhaps Getz and Chaloff, none of these performers could be said to be original or innovative in any meaningful sense of those words. Their major achievement was that of perpetuating the style of Young after its creator himself had passed from the scene.

Apparently, the immense effort required to master the intricacies of a single jazz style—or, to broaden the perspective, a single artistic style—is so great as to force a kind of commitment-for-life from the artist. It is as if he or she has said, "Having invested all my psychological resources in learning this particular style, I have exhausted my artistic capital and cannot push myself further." At any rate, such a hypothesis accounts for the fact that, once having become fluent in a jazz idiom, most white musicians do not move beyond that point to become innovators, but continue with their initial style for the remainder of their careers.

For that matter, black jazz musicians who are innovators seldom make more than a sole great contribution in their lifetimes. This development usually comes early in their careers—typically, shortly before or during their early twenties—and after that they simply continue to follow in the same path.[11] Again, it seems as if by virtue of having invested immense psychic energy in producing an innovative style, the artist has become wedded to it and is simply incapable of going further. Thus, although black jazz performers may *in general* be more innovative than white, there is also a fundamental similarity between the two, in that once a musician arrives at a style, whether original or derivative, in the majority of cases he or she finds it impossible to abandon it in favor of a newer, more revolutionary one.

The number of musicians of either color who have been able to generate more than a single innovation, or even modify their mature style, is, as we would anticipate, truly insignificant: Miles Davis, John Coltrane, Coleman Hawkins, and perhaps Sonny Rollins and Pee Wee Russell, are the only ones whose names come to mind. In contrast, the number of innovators whose names are identified with a single stylistic innovation is much longer: Louis Armstrong, Lester Young, Dizzy Gillespie, Charlie Parker (up to his premature death at thirty-four in 1955), Thelonious Monk, Bud Powell, J.J. Johnson, Charles Mingus, Max Roach, McCoy Tyner, Elvin Jones, Roy Eldridge, Cootie Williams, Bubber Miley, Jelly Roll Morton, Kenny Clarke, Juan Tizol, Tricky Sam Nanton, and so on—one could add another twenty or thirty names with no trouble whatsoever, but I believe the point is already incontestable.

There is one other consideration that also helps explain why black artists have been the predominant innovators in jazz. Let us, as we did above, reflect upon the situation of two youths of comparable talent and intelligence, one black and living in the inner city, one white and living in a typical suburb. For the black youth, becoming a jazz musician, like becoming a professional athlete, appears to offer at least the possibility—regardless of how remote—of escaping the grinding poverty and oppression of the ghetto. Put it another way: an ambitious, sensitive and intelligent African-American growing up in the 1950s has all too few ways of making his or her mark. A career in jazz—unlike most of the avenues open to ghetto youth—at least holds out the tantalizing prospect of someday seeing one's picture on the cover of *Time* or having one's comments dutifully recorded for posterity in the pages of *Playboy*.[12]

Now think about the white youth. To begin with, he or she has an essentially unlimited array of professions—medicine, law, science or engineering, teaching, business, journalism, and heaven only knows what else—from which to pick, virtually any of which promises to be more lucrative and less onerous than that of performing jazz. Even if this young person ultimately rejects all these better-paid and more-secure fields for a career in music, moreover, he or she still has opportunities denied to black musicians of equal ability. Symphony orchestras, for example, which provide relatively well-compensated and stable livelihoods for their members, are notoriously difficult for black musicians to penetrate; the same is only slightly less true of the recording studios, where earnings are even greater yet.*

---

* Bassist Arthur Davis, who worked on numerous occasions with John Coltrane during the early 1960s, uses the word "sickening" to characterize the discrimination against black musicians in high-paying positions outside of jazz: "I am denied the opportunity to play in a symphony orchestra . . . to play in a staff orchestra or any other jobs that have dignity. I have more than ample qualifications. There are less than five non-whites in all the symphonies [in New York City]. We took a survey. There are NO Afro-Americans on any of the steamship lines or any . . . of the society orchestras. . . . I could write a book of incidents. They

The chief consequences of this state of affairs, it seems to me, are two. First, there will be many white youth who have the potential to become superior jazz performers, but who nonetheless select a different profession because of the rigors and sparse returns that are the lot of all save a handful of jazz artists. Hence even if the distribution of musical aptitude and intellectual capacity is the same on both sides of the color line, it will still be true that the *proportion* of young people who are both capable of outstanding achievement in jazz *and* who choose to enter that field will be greater in the black community than in the white.

Second and related, precisely because of the absence of opportunities elsewhere, *commitment* to jazz probably runs higher among black than among white musicians. A white musician who grows weary of the sacrifices that a career in jazz demands can always seek musical employment in other areas, especially the recording studios. Or abandon music altogether, for that matter, inasmuch as a white person with a bent for engineering, say, or business, usually can change careers in midstream without encountering insuperable difficulties (having spent nearly a decade in one profession before leaving it for another, I speak from experience). For a black performer, in contrast, the alternatives to jazz are likely to be much less appealing. When J.J. Johnson was unable to support himself in jazz during the early 1950s, he had to seek work in the post office; faced with a similar plight twenty years later, pianist McCoy Tyner ended up driving a taxicab in Manhattan. In a letter to *down beat* in 1966, the eminent theoretician and composer George Russell recounted the "dreary subway trips to Macy's or scrubbing floors or washing dishes in a Harlem, Bronx, or Brooklyn luncheonette" that kept him alive when his income from jazz could

---

are definitely intent on keeping [black] people out of secure prestige work." Letter to the author, August 10, 1962.

not. "Until last year," he added, "I held a membership card in Local 1199, Retail Drug Workers' Union of New York." One suspects that before enduring the kind of punishing conditions that Russell—who was then at the zenith of his creative powers—experienced, most white musicians of his stature would have long since packed it in, forsaking jazz for more-promising terrain.*[13]

For the final word in this discussion, it will be useful to turn to a totally unrelated area. In his study of epoch-making innovations in science, Thomas S. Kuhn calls attention to two characteristic facts about those who originate them: (1) they generally are young at the time that they produce their greatest work; (2) only rarely are they ever able to devise a second, equally revolutionary contribution to their particular field.[14] Kuhn explains the latter finding by hypothesizing that once a novel scientific "system"—such as the Newtonian system of celestial mechanics of the eighteenth century—has been proposed and accepted, the scientists who subscribed to its predecessor transfer all their loyalty to the new orthodoxy. It then becomes, in the fullest sense of the word, unthinkable for them to question this orthodoxy, inasmuch as, having staked their careers on its being correct, they have now a tremendous psychological and professional investment in it.

Yet members of the *next* generation of scientists will not share that investment; they will have been educated (perhaps *indoctrinated* is more accurate) in the new orthodoxy, which, because of the nature of science teaching, they will accept as "natural" and "self-evident." Indeed, initially they may conceive of this intellectual system as the only *possible* way of

---

* Which is exactly the strategy pursued by countless cool and West Coast jazz musicians when, beginning in the late 1950s, the popularity of those two genres plunged precipitously. See the next section of this chapter for additional details.

viewing the natural universe, notwithstanding the fact that their predecessors had to wage a prolonged mental struggle before they could bring themselves to embrace it. Having no particular personal stake in the prevailing system, members of the new generation of scientists will be less emotionally involved in it and, as a result, more likely to see its short-comings—especially while they are still young, with little to lose and the possibility of a brilliant career to be gained from taking risks. (Thus, Kuhn's first finding, the youthfulness of scientific innovators.) To this generation or one of its successors, accordingly, will fall the task of demolishing the new orthodoxy and replacing it with yet a newer one—which, of course, will in due time suffer a similar fate.

The scientists who undermined Newtonian physics—Planck, Bohr, Einstein—were all trained in that mode of thought and, at least at the outset of their careers, considered themselves its stalwart adherents; similarly, those who overthrew Bohr's model of subatomic physics had it force-fed to them as undergraduates. And so on, down to the present day of "strange" particles, unified field theories, chaos theory, string theory, and the remaining arcana of contemporary physics. One could equally well construct the same argument for other sciences, as, for example, chemistry, where the phlogiston explanation of chemical reactions was done in by investigators originally schooled in its soundness.

The parallel with jazz—or, as I have tried to imply throughout, any art—is not difficult to discern. An African-American born around 1940 in a metropolitan ghetto in the North, for instance, will imbibe jazz of the bebop period as effortlessly as a baby does the proverbial mother's milk; it will be for this young person what Newtonian mechanics was for an eighteenth-century astronomer. If he or she then decides to become a jazz musician and elects to tackle the problem of working out an original style, bebop will of necessity be the music to transcend. It will be too commonplace, too tame, too devoid of excitement, too lacking in the unexpected, too uninspiring—it will be what "everyone is playing." Only someone utterly lacking in musical ambition would be content to aim at nothing more than a recapitulation of bebop without seeking to extend it, develop it—and in the end, perhaps, subvert it.

For the white youth of the same age, however, the situation will be entirely different. Where bebop for the black has become banal and a bit of a bore, in the case of the white it will arrive as a tremendous awakening—novel, exotic, provocative. The youth's whole being will be thrown into trying to cope with this music's strange cadences, phrases, and rhythms, originally so outlandish. If the black musician will not rest until the sound of Charlie Parker's virtuosity has been expunged from the mind's ear, the white will be satisfied only after acquiring the ability to produce a plausible facsimile of Parker's style, which has posed the most absorbing and demanding artistic challenge of his or her entire career.

In the preceding paragraphs I have argued for the view that jazz not only sprang originally from black roots, but that because of the segregated nature of American society, in which white and black youth develop largely along separate economic, cultural, and psychological lines, it has to this moment remained tied to these roots and gives no evidence of being about to change. Only if we understand the black origins of the music will we be able to make any sense out of the postwar evolution of jazz or to account for the early eruption of black nationalism in all its myriad forms within the world of jazz performers and listeners.

C. From bebop to hard bop: the Black community and support for jazz

It is not the consciousness of men that determines their existence, but their social existence determines their consciousness. At a certain stage of development, the material productive forces of society come into conflict with the existing relations of production, or—this merely expresses the same thing in legal terms—with the property relations within the framework of which they have operated hitherto. From forms of development of the productive forces these relations turn into their fetters. Then begins an era of social revolution. The changes in the economic foundation lead sooner or later to the transformation of the whole immense superstructure. In studying such transformations, it is always necessary to distinguish between the material transformation of the economic conditions of production, which can be determined with the precision of natural science, and the legal, political, religious, artistic, or philosophic—in short, ideological forms in which men become conscious of this conflict and fight it out.

—KARL MARX[15]

The thesis that black people do not support jazz comprises the second argument of those guardians of orthodoxy, the ideologically fixated white jazz critics.[16] To attempt to refute it with numbers would be a tedious and probably ultimately hopeless task. To begin with, no reliable statistics—on record sales, nightclub patronage, concert and festival attendance, and the like—exist, so far as I know. And even if such figures were available, what, indeed, would they prove? If, for example, the amount of money spent on jazz recordings is higher for whites on a per capita basis than for blacks, does this indicate that whites are more likely than blacks to purchase (and enjoy) jazz albums? Or that pernicious and persistent differentials in income prevent blacks from indulging their musical tastes as freely as whites and that black people compensate for their lower incomes by sharing recordings more widely? If, as happens to be the case, Shelly's Manne-

Hole, in the midst of white Hollywood, draws a higher proportion of its customers from the white rather than the black community,[17] are we to conclude that jazz must therefore be more popular with whites? Or could it be that the combination of an alien location, exorbitant admission prices, and other charges conspire to keep away not only the black but the young of all colors?

We will, then, leave vulgar empiricism to the vulgar empiricists of all persuasions, and instead approach the issue from another perspective altogether. Prior to embarking on that analysis, however, let me note parenthetically that anyone on a university campus with a sizable black student population will not need elaborate calculations to be convinced that jazz does without doubt have the emotional support of the young black generation. Wherever Black Studies courses are being undertaken, jazz is (at long last) quickly being incorporated into the curriculum. Our jazz critics may remain obdurate, but the history of the next few decades ought to settle the question of the relationship between the black community and jazz once for all.

Rather than straining futilely to obtain a breakdown by color of such items as jazz-record purchases and concert and nightclub attendance, therefore, I propose to investigate the relationship between blacks and jazz by a brief and very schematic consideration of some turning points in the social history of the music since World War II. This survey will show, I believe, that the only way in which we can comprehend the evolution of the music is on the assumption of an intimate and persistent symbiosis between it and the community out of which it is continuously being reborn. Such an overview will in no sense be "a history of jazz"; I lack both the space and the will for a project of that magnitude. What I want to call attention to instead is the way in which jazz has evolved roughly in synchrony with the most important developments in the black ghetto.

There is in international jurisprudence the concept of dual citizenship, whereby a child born to parents not living in their native land has the citizenship both of the parents and of the country of his or her own birth. In a certain sense African-Americans can lay claim to a kind of dual citizenship of their own: they are *in* the country, but not always *of* it.[18] They are, more than any other ethnic group save perhaps the Native American (Indian), Spanish-speaking, and the Asian-American, heir to a culture that is uniquely their own and thus at least partially hidden from whites.[19] By virtue of this "dual citizenship," black people often respond not only to events that shake and move the rest of the country, but also to those that barely even register with the white population. Among the most obvious recent examples has been the gaining of independence during the 1960s by the former colonial states of Africa—something that, as Harold R. Isaacs has revealed, had profound psychological and political consequences in the ghetto, though white America was only subliminally aware of it.[20] The assassinations of Medgar Evers, Malcolm X, and Martin Luther King, Jr., patently carried vastly different implications for blacks than whites; it is also probable that while whites perceived the assassination of the two Kennedy brothers as a tragedy, blacks viewed it as a tragedy *and* a direct blow at themselves.

If the position of black people in this society is anomalous—they are both in and not in white society and culture—that of the black jazz musician is multiply so. Conceivably the single most acute contradiction experienced by the jazz performer is that of being simultaneously the object of adulation by the jazz-loving public—including a sizable number of whites[21]—and the object of something that, at its extreme, approaches contempt by those white business executives who control the most desirable economic opportunities.[22] It is not unusual for a jazz musician to return home after an evening of applause to, say, a rat-infested hovel in New York's

Harlem or East Village. The abrupt transition from being a celebrated artist to being a penniless and persistently exploited commodity is, of course, at the root of Archie Shepp's observation, "You own the music and we make it."

That indignity, however, is not the sole one to which the black musician is exposed. He or she must also watch as less talented but more palatable white imitators and popularizers—a line that extends from the earliest white minstrels who performed in blackface to Paul Whiteman, Benny Goodman, Frankie Laine, Al Jolson, Elvis Presley, the Rolling Stones, and others too numerous to mention—reap the financial benefits of black innovations. Finally, as often occurs with artists (as opposed to entertainers), an innovative jazz musician may on occasion "get ahead of" the public. This fact means that even though the black community can in the long run be expected to provide sustenance for jazz, the long run may prove in certain cases to be precisely the artist's most creative years. All of these processes interact in such a way to expose the black musician to a maximum of insecurity and isolation, and they naturally cause his or her alienation to run continuously at a very high pitch. For such a performer must cope not merely with being black, or being an artist, or even being an artist who happens to be black, but with the almost insuperable obstacle of attempting to define oneself as a black artist practicing a black-based art in a country that is deathly afraid of both its artists and its blacks. That jazz musicians, confronted with this hostile situation, have sometimes sought refuge in various narcotics is not to be wondered; the marvel is that there are many who have not succumbed entirely to this form of escapism. Nonetheless, a destructive and inhumane environment will eventually take its toll in one form or another. The two most influential figures in the jazz of the second half of the twentieth century, Charlie Parker and John Coltrane, were both dead before their forty-first birthday.

It may well be that the best vaccine against early death from the cumulative effects of a dehumanizing, racist environment is political consciousness and action aimed at undermining the status quo. Such, at any rate, is suggested by authors as different as the pacifist Albert Camus (in *The Rebel*) and the revolutionary Frantz Fanon (in *A Dying Colonialism*).[23] In any case, it should be readily apparent to any honest and reasonably sensitive observer that a substratum of black resentment, as I hope to demonstrate, has been an integral aspect of the jazz world almost from the outset. The reasons for this are anything but complex or obscure, and ultimately they all pivot about the central contradiction of black creation versus white control. The fact that black musicians can at one and the same time be lionized and callously used serves to make the jazz milieu a most explosive one, and the black artist a likely candidate for conversion to some form of black nationalism (or other radicalism).

In making this statement, I certainly am not suggesting that all jazz musicians, now or at any time in the past, have been militant and outspoken black nationalists. Such a proposition would be historically wrong on two counts: first, it ignores the way in which nationalism in the ghetto waxes and wanes in response to changes in the political economy of the United States and the world; second, it neglects the very serious economic reprisals to which all but a sprinkling of jazz musicians would leave themselves open were they to declare themselves in favor of black nationalism, separatism, or any other radical ideology. What I do assert, however, are two other theses: (1) that at least since the late 1930s, a certain residue of proto-nationalist thinking, sometimes inchoate and scarcely articulated as such, has been present in jazz, even to the point of influencing the timing and the direction of stylistic innovations; and (2) that in recent times it has been the jazz musicians who, of any identifiable group of African-Americans, have been the first to be converted and to espouse the tenets of black nationalism.

The last point needs particular emphasis. By the end of the 1960s, we have already witnessed nationalist-minded protests by black entertainers, amateur and professional athletes, students, and even that most conservative, apathetic, and essentially apolitical group, academics. That and the prevalence, especially among the young, of certain cultural gestures rooted in nationalism ("natural" hairdos, African *dashikis*) has led whites to take nationalism—or at least its trappings—for granted among blacks, and to assume that beneath every "natural" head of hair there lurks a cortex brimming with nationalist ideology. Besides being mistaken, these assumptions mask the fact (which I must here again insist upon) that nationalist ideas first gained wide currency within the realm of jazz. There should be nothing surprising in this, for in no other sphere is the disparity between the level of black achievement and the lack of appropriate white recognition, in social and economic terms, as gross as in jazz; nowhere else, that is, is a black person venerated as an artist of the greatest creative stature at precisely the same moment as he or she is being pushed into the gutter as a nigger.*

So jazz musicians have ample cause for being particularly susceptible to the seductive strains of black nationalism. To

---

* Actually, and not merely in metaphor. A few years ago, the trumpeter Miles Davis was spending an intermission walking outside the New York nightclub where he was in the midst of an engagement when, without provocation, a white policeman began beating him over the head with his club. Similarly, the pianist-composer Cecil Taylor was on his way home from a concert when he was set upon by a gang of young white thugs, who injured his hands so badly that he could not play for some weeks. What would have been the reaction had these brutalities been inflicted on, for instance, Leonard Bernstein—or for that matter, Lawrence Welk? Beside the pain and injury of the beating itself, there is the further humiliation in the white public's indifference to the event. After all, it wasn't as if a white person had been attacked, was it?

say that much, however, still leaves unanswered the question of why the appeal of black nationalism has not been uniformly great during every phase of jazz's history, but instead has fluctuated sharply. To arrive at an answer will require that we go beyond the confines of the jazz world itself to consider its relationship with ghetto society.

The history of jazz (or art), as I have been at pains to underline, cannot be written—other than very superficially—as aesthetic history alone; we are, rather, compelled to regard the music as one aspect of the social history of black people in America. Adopting this approach immediately disposes of such notions as "black people themselves do not support jazz"—dilapidated, impoverished theses whose effect at best would be to deny credit to a people for their achievement in the face of monumental obstacles.

Ideas, Marx observed, have no independent history of their own; only *people* have history. The same applies to jazz, music in general, or any art: its history does not exist apart from that of the men and women who create it. An elementary point, the reader may demur; but if so, one that appears to have eluded the great majority of white jazz critics. For that reason, and at the risk of being redundant, I advance the idea once more: we cannot permit ourselves the luxury of speaking of the history of jazz while at the same time divorcing it from the social biographies of those who made the music and those who, at each phase in its evolution, responded to it.

To illustrate this principle, it will be helpful to consider how the fate of jazz has been inextricably bound up with that of the black ghetto that nurtures it, using the period from 1940 to 1970 as, so to speak, our laboratory.

Just as the United States was poised on the edge of World War II, a new generation of young black innovators was assembling in New York to perfect their novel methods of improvisation. The names of these musicians are by now familiar to anyone with more than a passing acquaintance with the music: Charlie Parker (alto saxophone), Dizzy Gillespie (trumpet), Thelonious Monk and Bud Powell (piano), Max Roach and Kenny Clarke (drums). Before much time had elapsed, there was also a second line of bebop (as the new music came to be called) performers—Miles Davis, Fats Navarro, and Howard McGhee (trumpet), J.J. Johnson (trombone), Dexter Gordon and Wardell Gray (tenor saxophone), Charles Mingus (bass), and others. Meanwhile, the United States had entered the war, with a variety of consequences for jazz. Among other things, the war was able to accomplish what Franklin Roosevelt's New Deal, bound as it was by the rules of the game of private-ownership capitalism, could not: the pall of a dozen years of depression finally lifted. For blacks, this meant an acceleration of the trend propelling them out of the South, into the cities and, temporarily at least, into the ranks of the industrial workforce. The orders for war production that got the wheels of industry turning and, thanks to a shortage of labor, brought blacks into the factories (usually only in menial capacities, however)[24] also put money into their pockets.

Although some of this money undoubtedly was spent on music and other arts, prior to 1945 or 1946 the new bebop style did not have much dissemination beyond New York. A wartime shortage of shellac, reinforced by a year and one-half strike by the American Federation of Musicians, led to a concentration of what phonograph-record production there was on jukebox hits, with a drastic cutback in recordings of jazz, rhythm-and-blues and all other forms of black music. As a result, for four or five years a relatively small group of jazz artists was at work polishing the novel bebop style while cut off from a national audience via the normal channel of record sales. It is not very surprising, therefore, that by the time the war came to an end, a gap had begun to open between the radically new bebop performers, no-

tably Parker and Gillespie, and the lay jazz public. For that
matter, even some young black musicians who had spent
the war years abroad in uniform later confessed to being
taken aback the first few times they were confronted with
the seemingly "crazy" procedures (musical and otherwise)
of the bebop musicians.

However serious and deep this split between artist and
community, it was on the way to being healed when the inevitable postwar economic downturn overtook the country,
starting in the second half of 1948 and lasting until almost
the middle of 1950.[25] (At that time, recall, the Cold War had
not yet been fully institutionalized as a means of subsidiz-
ing giant corporations and thereby preserving capitalism.)[26]
Ultimately, a war in Korea that appears to have been deliberately prolonged by the administration of Harry S. Truman
would provide the customary means of staving off economic
stagnation and rescuing capitalism once again.[27] But before
that could happen, the slump had made grave inroads into
the support that the black community was able to give to
jazz. Traditionally last hired and first fired, when economic
stagnation began to hit in 1948—and in not a few cases, even
before—blacks were driven out of many of the positions in
industry they had occupied during the war; these losses were
for the most part never reversed, even after the economy
began to recuperate in the wake of the Korean War. In this
way jazz in general and bebop in particular were deprived of
a critical portion of their public at what was clearly a crucial
moment for the latter; and bebop, thus enfeebled, was forced
underground. (Even a summary reading of the jazz press
from the late forties bears eloquent witness to the sudden
demise of both big-band swing and bebop in the number of
ballrooms abruptly forced to close their doors.) Bebop never
got beyond the status of a nascent movement. A few more
years of prosperity would in all probability have been decisive for its survival. Without those years, it was reduced

almost to the level of a cult, and many of its most famous practitioners fell from sight (as was true, for example, of J.J. Johnson, who, as I noted earlier, went to work for the post office, and Thelonious Monk).

When the economic revival finally commenced, moreover, the country was in a far different state of mind than it had been in the late forties. It is only with the greatest trepidation that a prudent historian dares generalize about such nebulous entities as "the national mood." Nonetheless, it should be quite evident that the fearful, even paranoid days of the early Cold War period (roughly, from the inception of Truman's proto-McCarthy loyalty oath program for federal employees in March 1947 to the end of Eisenhower's first term) were not such as to provide a very hospitable environment for the unabashedly emotional music that was bebop. Though highly sophisticated, bop was nevertheless an art of raw electric energy; to flourish, it required an audience that could appreciate its naked passion and uninhibited romanticism. Such an audience, however, was not easily come by in jazz, any more than it was in literature or painting, during these years. It was as if, to speak metaphorically, the national obsession with "the Communist menace" had paralyzed all of the country's creative wellsprings, draining energy away from any serious concern with the arts, politics, and meaningful intellectual or spiritual endeavors in general.

To document this contention would be, if not impossible, extremely difficult; but that is a task that we may safely leave for the empiricists. To anyone who has lived through, or even read the newspapers of, that era—whose best-remembered public figures are, on the one hand, Harry Truman, Dwight Eisenhower, John Foster Dulles, Joseph McCarthy and Norman Vincent Peale, and on the other, Julius and Ethel Rosenberg—the contention will not demand additional evidence.

The jazz style that began to emerge as bebop went under

was entirely in keeping with the character of the epoch. Even the name of the style itself—*cool*—reflected the change. It would never have occurred to anyone who knew the music to refer to bebop as "cool," for it was above all an art of engagement, with the feelings of the performers, especially its symbolic leader, Charlie Parker, out in the open for all to see. As a style, cool was quite the opposite; it was the quintessence of individual *dis*engagement. To hear the difference, simply compare a solo by the father of bebop trumpet-playing, Dizzy Gillespie, to one from the cool period by the then-idolized but now out-of-favor trumpeter Chet Baker. Where Gillespie roams the entire instrument, plays at the top and bottom of its range, is not afraid to be triple fortissimo as the context demands, packs his solos full of flurries of rapidly cascading short notes, and is generally eloquent in a florid, full-blooded manner, Baker's approach is smooth to the point of blandness and almost completely devoid of excitement. He eschews both loud notes and high ones, his phrasing is mostly legato, with relatively few short or staccato notes and many long ones, so that the overall effect is one of "pretty" but relatively vapid music. By virtue of what he has excluded from his playing—high notes, loud notes, biting attacks, and the like—Baker is compelled to convey his ideas with a very limited, even constricted emotional palette. It is theater with all the passions politely expunged, painting with all the vivid tones forgone. Naturally, such music has no lasting appeal. There are still many collectors who continue to enjoy Louis Armstrong's Hot Five and Hot Seven recordings from the late 1920s, but no one, to my knowledge, who now listens to cool jazz of the early 1950s.

The cool period in jazz was dominated by white musicians. The only prominent black performer to be involved in it was Miles Davis, and Davis himself repudiated the style when, in the mid–1950s, he began to evolve in the direction of a more loose, emotional, blues-rooted music that paid explicit deference to the black foundations of jazz. With the single exception of Davis, the individuals who led the cool movement were white and, save in a few cases, are now in complete obscurity so far as jazz is concerned. In its own way, by the force of negative example, the cool years can tell us something about the nature of jazz: first, that it cannot remove itself too far from the experience of the ghetto and still retain its vitality; second, that whites in the main cannot bring to bear the necessary resources, either musically or socially, to sustain the music and conceive fruitful and lasting innovations.

In one way, it is useful to look at cool jazz as a musical counterpart to the Beat literary movement. Both celebrated the virtues of passivity and withdrawal—we would today call it *dropping out*—over those of active resistance. To display fervent emotion within either a cool or beat setting was at once to brand oneself as hopelessly square. And so it is no accident that when Beats were gathered in their pads, cool music, rather than bebop, rhythm-and-blues, or rock-and-roll, provided the musical backdrop. Both Beat literature and cool music have to be seen as the only form of rebellion—that of disaffiliation, as opposed to direct confrontation with the status quo—available to alienated young whites during the first (and worst) years of the Cold War. (Alienation, of course, ran at high-tide for both Beats and followers of cool jazz, and their circles to some degree overlapped.) Later, when blacks had begun to mount a more direct attack on Cold War society, Beats and cool jazz fell by the wayside. Beats yielded to student radicals, civil rights workers, black nationalists, hippies, yippies, and so on; cool, to various forms of black revivalism within music, a development I will discuss presently.

Besides being a musical parallel to Beat literature, however, cool jazz also represented a more or less conscious attempt to "whiten" the music, to bleach away its African-American roots. As I will bring out in the following section, one of the driving forces behind the search for a new mode of expression that culminated in bebop was to devise a music that "they" couldn't play; in this way would the question of white ownership versus black creation be addressed. The search was largely successful, for initially, at least, there were very few whites able to cope with the intricacies of bebop. That being so, it shouldn't be especially astonishing that, after a stagnant economy had driven black jazz musicians from the scene and the playing as well as the control of jazz had come to lie in the lap of whites, it was not long before white, or European, values began to take priority over black, or African, ones. By this I certainly do not mean that any white musician was ever so reckless as to proclaim—or even to consciously formulate—the goal of replacing black values with white ones. What I do mean, though, is that the cool period saw an attempt by white musicians to divorce jazz from its historical black moorings and transform it into a music with which they felt more at ease. Usually, the attempt proceeded under the guise of making the music more "legitimate," which translated as "respectable to white middle-class audiences," which in turn translated as "more like European art music."

The center for these bleaching efforts was California, mostly Los Angeles, to a lesser extent the San Francisco Bay area. In New York, although jazz activity was at a low ebb, record companies such as Prestige, Savoy, Blue Note, Bethlehem, and others continued releasing occasional albums by black artists whose roots were in bebop, and these musicians still dominated that particular niche, minuscule as it might be. On the West Coast, contrariwise, the soil was essentially virginal, the only established jazz activity at that point revolving around white Dixieland bands. (Contemporary Records, one of the companies formed to record cool jazz in Los Angeles, was in fact an offshoot of a Dixieland recording company, Good Time Jazz.) Hence in California whites did not have to deal with the problem of dispossessing a well-entrenched phalanx of black bebop musicians, for the simple reason that such musicians were here relatively few in number, much less well known than their counterparts in New York, and had little access to the principal recording companies.

The white musicians involved in California cool jazz—which later came to be called, with more precision but less evocativeness, West Coast jazz—came from a variety of backgrounds. Many of them—Shelly Manne, Shorty Rogers, Art Pepper, Bud Shank, Bill Holman, Bob Cooper, Conte Candoli, Lenny Niehaus, Bill Perkins, Frank Rosolino, to name a few—settled in Southern California after lengthy service in one or another of the bands of Stan Kenton, himself devoted to "dignifying" jazz by steering it in the direction of second-rate contemporary European music. Others—Jimmy Giuffre, Stan Getz, Zoot Sims, Herbie Steward—came from one of Woody Herman's "Herds." Still others, like Gerry Mulligan, were expatriates from the East Coast or, like Chet Baker, Dave Brubeck, Jack Montrose and Bob Gordon, were indigenous musicians without much previous reputation. As of the late 1960s, only a small fraction of these musicians are in any significant way connected to the jazz world. Those who have not been able to find a safe, if uncreative, haven in the Hollywood recording studios have, with only few exceptions (Brubeck, Mulligan, Paul Desmond, Getz, Baker), become, in Orwell's phrase, unpersons so far as the jazz audience is concerned.

At the peak of their popularity in the mid-fifties, though, cool and/or West Coast white musicians bid fair to shape all succeeding jazz in their likeness. (There were also, of course, black musicians in California, but they were almost entirely excluded from the cool movement and consequently "didn't count.") These were the years that Chet Baker, for example, triumphed over both his black model, Miles Davis, and Dizzy Gillespie in the various "critics" polls.[28]

What nearly all the cool musicians had in common, especially in California, was some training in European art ("classical") music, and an intense desire—born equally, one supposes, out of a longing for higher social standing and feelings of inadequacy (perhaps from working in an "inferior" art, perhaps from not measuring up to standards established by black performers, perhaps from both)—to make jazz more like it. The music of Dave Brubeck, with its truly heavy-handed allusions to Baroque counterpoint, is a particularly glaring instance in point, because Brubeck has never made any secret of the fact that he wanted to "classicize" jazz.* In the early days of his popularity, much was made of Brubeck's studies with French composer Darius Milhaud—as if this conferred some special qualifications to determine the future of jazz. But Brubeck was not alone. Shorty Rogers and Jimmy Giuffre—every one of their album jackets made it a point to mention this—were "studying" with Dr. Wesley La Violette, whoever the good doctor may be. And so it went. No self-respecting white musician could afford to be caught not "studying" with some European musician, theorist, or composer. How much relevance all of this study had for the creation of jazz is, to be charitable, dubious. But it was part and parcel of the times, and woe indeed to that cool or West Coast musician so indiscreet as to violate the code.

---

* Ironically, Cecil Taylor and Bill Evans, the pianists who have brought off the most skillful wedding of European and African-American musics—albeit in vastly different ways—have done so without any of the attendant ballyhoo lavished on Brubeck. Taylor, in fact, has led a borderline existence just this side of total poverty throughout the 1960s, while Brubeck, naturally, is a person of considerable wealth. But Taylor is black and his music has great depth, whereas Brubeck . . . but why even bother finishing the sentence?

As a result, never before or since has such a plethora of fugues, concerti, divertimentos, rondos, and the like, inundated jazz. How these works sold, if they ever did sell, what audiences bought them, who listened to them—these are riddles of the Sphinx. Before a decade had elapsed, the great bulk of the white cool and West Coast music of that era had become unendurable; I very much doubt that I am the only person to have disposed of nearly all my collection of records from that particular era. In all likelihood, those who still count themselves lovers of jazz have done the same, for the only conceivable value most works of this provenance might now possess has less to do with music than with nostalgia (assuming that anyone could possibly yearn for such a cramped and ugly time).

The history of cool and West Coast jazz demonstrates with surpassing clarity what happens to the music when it becomes the plaything of middle-class whites with huge appetites for the trappings of status and legitimacy. If there has been no other period when control of the musical aspects of jazz has been vested so completely in white hands, so also has there been no other period of such uniform and wholesale artistic bankruptcy. It does not require occult powers to detect the relationship between the two. The conclusion is inescapable: whites, as late as the 1950s, did not have the social, cultural, and musical wherewithal to infuse jazz with sufficient vitality to enable it to survive, much less develop. By implication, this conclusion demonstrates the correctness of our earlier thesis, that innovation in jazz is indeed rooted in the black community.

The sine qua non for white domination of jazz performance and composition was black non-participation. As soon as blacks were, as a by-product of the uneven and sporadic economic recovery after the Korean War, once more able to enter the jazz marketplace both as creators and consumers, this development further undermined, and ultimately demolished altogether, the already shaky white preeminence of the cool and West Coast years.

The name jazz journalists gave to the style that first challenged and then replaced cool and West Coast jazz was *hard bop*; later, it would be known as *funky*, and after that, *soul*. While not especially elegant, the first title was apt, for it highlighted the fact that the new black music of the mid-1950s was for the most part based on bebop, but that there was a new component—a new *hardness*—as well. The sources of this distinguishing feature of hard bop were twofold; investigation of them sheds a great deal of light on the nature of how stylistic change in jazz ordinarily comes to pass.

Viewed as strictly a movement among musicians—which it was not—hard bop amounted to a black rebellion against the bleaching tendencies of the cool and West Coast whites. As such, it tended deliberately to lay particular stress on the contemporary fundamentals of urban black music, in the form of blues and gospel songs.

In this respect, perhaps the clarion call of the hard bop movement was Miles Davis's version of "Walkin'," recorded April 29, 1954.[29] For our purposes, there are two features of interest about this recording. First, "Walkin' " is a 12-measure blues. The blues form, whose African-American origins no one has yet had the temerity to deny, is one of the simplest harmonic structures of jazz, and accordingly, it is among those most conducive to heartfelt improvisation. Traditionally, in fact, the index of a jazz musician's prowess has been the ability to play movingly (not to be confused with sentimentally) on the blues "changes" (chord sequence). In choosing a blues as the basis for his manifesto, therefore, Davis—who, remember, was himself initially a leading figure in the cool movement—implicitly made clear his rejection of the cool aesthetic. For cool musicians, like the majority of white would-be improvers of jazz—Stan Kenton is probably the most notorious case in point—were not especially fond of the open emotionalism of the blues. Instead, they prized complexity of structure over fervor in performance, and tended to relegate individual improvisation to a very distant second place after compositional complexity, which latter often involved "advanced" harmonies, counterpoint, polyphony, and so on.*

---

* As a general rule, innovative black jazz artists such as Charlie Parker and John Coltrane have been most concerned to find ways of heightening the emotional intensity of the music, especially the improvised portions, whereas whites who aspire towards the role of innovation—Don Ellis, say, or Stan Kenton—lean toward the notion of enhancing jazz by incorporating *new technical devices* into the music *as ends in themselves.* This latter tendency is particularly noticeable during the cool period, not only in the borrowing of forms identified with European music, but also in the use of several instruments—flute, oboe, English horn, French horn, cello—that are only rarely associated with jazz but that occupy a prominent place in European music. Of these instruments, the flute alone has found a permanent niche as an instrument suitable for jazz improvisation.

As for the primacy of written form over improvised content, consider the composition "Circling the Blues" by saxophonist Lenny Niehaus, a better-than-run-of-the-mill West Coast performer. Niehaus wrote "Circling the Blues" in the standard blues format, but with one difference: at the end of each 12-measure chorus, the harmony modulates not back to the tonic chord (I) as in an ordinary blues, but to the subdominant (IV), until the entire cycle of 12 (major) key signatures has been traversed (for instance, F to B-flat to E-flat to A-flat, and so on). Niehaus, as quoted in the album notes, was inordinately proud of this achievement. That he impeded the fluidity of improvisation by imposing this artifice on his soloists—some of the sharp keys (such as A, E, and B) are quite awkward for the saxophone and brass instruments—seemed not to bother him in the least, if, in fact, it even crossed his mind. Thus, typically, was uninhibited communication of feeling sacrificed on the altar of pseudo-"serious" posturing during the cool era.

Nor did that strain of thought end with the demise of cool styles. To the degree that jazz musicians have found work in the southern California recording studios, their ranks are overwhelmingly white. It is a striking fact that these performers continue to be obsessed with formal devices and technique for the sake of technique (for example, playing

Second, the very title itself, "Walkin'," was a sharp slap at the arid, insipid, Eurocentric-cool way of thinking, with its welter of too-clever fugues, canons, sonatas, and what have you. The contrast between the unpretentious "Walkin' " and the straining-to-be-genteel of, say, the "Divertimento in C Minor for Three Reeds" is patent. Then, too, it was "Walkin' " rather than "Walking"—that is, the self-conscious use of ghetto argot as a manifestation of cultural-nationalist pride in one's black roots. So that between the playing—Davis used as soloists such masterful blues improvisers as vibraharpist Milt Jackson, tenor saxophonist Lucky Thompson, and the musician who most nearly personified the entire hard-bop movement, pianist Horace Silver—and the title, the extent of Davis's breakaway from the sterility of cool–West Coast convention could hardly be more marked.

But though hard bop was a revolt of black musicians against the alien sensibility of cool, it was considerably more than that alone. In retrospect, it seems highly unlikely that the hard-bop movement could ever have come about without a simultaneous upheaval in the black community—an upheaval that hard bop both reflected and manifested in musical form. I am thinking, in the first instance, of the earliest stirrings of the contemporary black liberation movement—the suit brought by the National Association for the Advancement

---

in unusual time signatures such as 11/17) at the expense of expressivity, hence their improvising is still too often weak and unpersuasive by comparison with what contemporary black innovators—Cecil Taylor, Pharoah Sanders, Albert Ayler, Ornette Coleman, Don Cherry, John Coltrane—are producing. On occasion, I have had an opportunity to observe these musicians as they watched some of their black avant-garde counterparts. Their reaction mingled incredulity and ill-concealed race- and class-based derision in roughly equal parts. The notion that jazz could actually be played *like that*—with so much forcefulness and so little ersatz refinement—seemingly had never penetrated their skulls. More's the pity.

of Colored People (NAACP) in *Brown v. Board of Education* (decided by the U. S. Supreme Court in 1954), the Montgomery, Alabama, bus boycott and the debut of Martin Luther King, Jr. (1956), the Little Rock, Arkansas, school-integration conflict (1957), and so on. By helping to shatter whatever habits of apathy and accommodation to inferior treatment may have existed previously, these monumental events drove black people to redefine their very concept of self.[30]

Because of all the contradictions of their position in society, it was virtually inevitable that black jazz musicians would react first and most strongly to the efforts of African-Americans to free themselves from the historic shackles of racist subjugation. Initially, that reaction took the form of a renewed pride in the black roots of jazz, the blues, and the gospel music of black evangelical churches. Later, as the liberation movement grew in size and scope and developed greater consciousness, this pride and the assertion of black-based values began to be voiced more explicitly and the symbolism, such as that in Miles Davis's "Walkin'," became less difficult to decipher.

This burgeoning movement was probably the major social force impinging on the consciousness of black jazz musicians in the mid-1950s, and it is, as I have said, unthinkable that the hard-bop repudiation of cool jazz could have taken place in its absence. Be that as it may, however, it was not the only influence impelling blacks to revise their worldviews and act accordingly. In the interest of historical completeness, therefore, let me at least mention some of the other developments agitating the nation's ghettos. The parallel movement of the African peoples for the ending of formal colonialism—even though in most cases colonialism's demise left the mechanism of neocolonial exploitation intact—had a profound impact on the way in which American blacks perceived themselves. In jazz, as we shall see, the winning of independence by African states early on played an important role in fueling the hard-bop rejection of Eurocentric-cool aesthetics; it can be traced, for instance, in the numerous references to Africa that begin to appear in the titles of black musicians' compositions after 1954.

Less dramatic but still of great significance was the continuing trend for blacks to move from the rural, agrarian South to urban centers in the North, West and, sometimes, within the South itself. Besides the cultural shock involved in such abrupt transitions, there were further frustrations and disappointments in realizing that the supposedly liberal North and West had methods and means for keeping black people "in their place." The anguish to which such realizations gave rise showed up in jazz as another force driving blacks in a nationalist direction.

Related to the latter is the cautionary note of the distinguished Belgian economist Ernest Mandel that, in seeking to understand the growth of black nationalism, "we must not overlook the objective stimuli that have grown out of the inner development of American capitalism itself." Mandel, of course, is not concerned specifically with events in the realm of African-American jazz, but his words have the greatest relevance nonetheless. Pointing to the "rapid decline in the number of unskilled jobs in American industry" as the "nexus that binds the growing Negro revolt, especially the revolt of Negro youth, to the general socioeconomic framework of American capitalism," he goes on to observe that

> the long . . . boom [after the Korean War] and the explosive progress in agricultural productivity were the first factors in the massive urbanization and the proletarianization of the African-Americans: The Northern ghettos grew by leaps and bounds. Today, the average rate of unemployment among the black population is double what it is among the white population, and the average rate among youth is double what it is among adults, so

that the average among the black youth is nearly four times the general average in the country. Up to 15 or 20 percent of young black workers are unemployed: This is a percentage analogous to that of the Great Depression. It is sufficient to look at these figures to understand the social and material origin of the black revolt.[31]

When one considers Mandel's remarks in light of the fact that the newest black performers are themselves always drawn from among the young, it seems a reasonable conclusion that the concerns of black youth, including those arising from structural trends within the U.S. political economy, will sooner or later find an outlet in the most recent styles—and especially important, *changes* of style—in jazz.

As indeed was the case, although this was not sufficiently appreciated at the time, in the transition from cool to hard bop and its successors. If the movement away from cool to more affirmatively black styles in jazz was spearheaded at first by Miles Davis, and later pianist Horace Silver and drummer Art Blakey, all of whom by the mid-1950s had attained the status of veterans, in the first ranks of the revolt were also numerous younger musicians from the principal Northern urban centers: trumpeters Clifford Brown (Wilmington, Delaware, and Philadelphia), Lee Morgan (Philadelphia), and Donald Byrd (Detroit); saxophonists Sonny Rollins (New York) and John Coltrane (Philadelphia); bassists Wilbur Ware (Chicago), Doug Watkins and Paul Chambers (both Detroit); pianists Tommy Flanagan (Detroit), Mal Waldron and Wynton Kelly (both New York). Either born in these Northern ghettos or taken there at a young age, the consciousness of these young performers, it is now clear, would be different in kind from that of an earlier wave of black musicians who had emigrated from the South and Southwest. Like the generation of avant-garde musicians who followed them in the 1960s, the young black performers of the late

1950s were highly literate, both musically and politically. That they chose to simplify the framework of jazz from the overly formalized, effete and mannered conventions of the cool–West Coast period stemmed not from any inability to master those conventions, but from a fundamental refusal to concede that the game was worth the candle. Accordingly, they chose instead to formulate a new set of stylistic guidelines that combined some of the complexity of bebop with a heightened emphasis on the black basics, blues and gospel music.

Although it is not my intention to write a history of jazz criticism, I cannot do justice to my topic without some attention to the critical response to hard bop, for this response illustrates the massive gap between the sensibility of the ghetto and that of the respectability-loving, implacably white-middle-class mentality that continues to hold sway in writing about jazz. It seems probable that *any* change from cool would have met with condemnation: jazz critics, no less than others, prefer the reassurance of the familiar to the risk of the untried, value stability above change, and seek to protect their investment in acquiring expertise against any threat to such hard-won hegemony. Particularly interesting in this instance, however, was the nature of the critical response. Without saying so in so many words—for there are some ideas too dangerous to voice—the critics attacked the hard boppers for deviating from white or European standards in the direction of African-American ones.*

---

* This same feature is also present in the avant-garde revolution associated with John Coltrane, Ornette Coleman, Cecil Taylor, and others, as I attempt to bring out at several places in this volume (most notably, chapters 6–9). Critics widely and repeatedly denigrated the innovations of Coltrane, Coleman, and their followers as "anti-jazz," out-of-tune and aimless meanderings, deplorable lapses of taste, and the like. In sum, these accusations meant only that European values (of timbre, of adherence to the equal-tempered scale, of white-middle-class propriety

Inasmuch as saxophone players have been in the vanguard of every major development in jazz since the bebop revolution of the early 1940s, it is not surprising that saxophonists, particularly Sonny Rollins and John Coltrane, bore the brunt of the critical onslaught. Both Rollins and Coltrane (whom the critics usually linked in any case) were continually summoned before the high tribunals for their alleged "harsh" or "bad" or "honking" tones. Implicit here was the doubly untenable assumption that there is something in jazz than can be specified as a "good" or "pleasant" tone, and that the critics are gifted above ordinary mortals in being privy to the knowledge of what constitutes such goodness, pleasantness, and so forth.

Both parts of this assumption, needless to say, would have been highly suspect had they ever been articulated. That was just it: they never were. Silence on this score prevailed in large part because the critics did not have even sense enough to recognize that their assumptions were only that, nothing more, and therefore hardly worthy of adoption without first being subjected to a rigorous examination. The notion that there is a single standard of goodness in art is, after all, hardly likely to find many adherents among those knowledgeable about the tumultuous history of the arts in the West since the Renaissance; fewer still are about to subscribe to the notion that the critical dogma of the moment should be swallowed whole as if it held the key to Eternal Enlightenment. And if this is true of European art, where major stylistic changes take place perhaps once every generation, how

---

and decorum) were being sacrificed to the development of indigenous African-American ones. Such a development, however, inevitably ran afoul of the bias of the critics, as manifested by their persistent assertion that pianist Thelonious Monk plays "wrong" notes and their preference for facile but shallow European-oriented performers (pianist Oscar Peterson, saxophonist Stan Getz) over more profound non-European-oriented improvisers (Monk, John Coltrane).

much more must one insist on a measure of critical caution in jazz, where a given style may hold sway for as little as five or ten years before yielding to its successor?[32] Not that these considerations in the least fazed the critics of the 1950s, who continued virtually as one to insist on the illegitimacy of the playing of Rollins and Coltrane, until a mass shift in popular tastes simply forced many of them to give way. (Interestingly enough, a number of them at that point dropped into oblivion, along with the cool–West Coast heroes they had persisted in championing until the very end.)

At the base of the critical rejection of hard bop was, as I suggested above, that music's deviation from white-defined, Europe-oriented, standards of timbre, inflection, attack, and the like, as these had been defined during the preceding cool period. Some of the reviews of hard-bop saxophonists especially made this criterion almost embarrassingly clear. Thus, Nat Hentoff could write as late as 1957 that

> Coltrane's tone is often strident at the edges [a debatable assertion] and rarely appears to sustain a legato softness, as [white-cool saxophonist Stan] Getz can.
>
> Coltrane has a feeling for variegated moods, but his tone doesn't yet display enough range and control of coloration when he expresses gentler, more complex feelings. Another horn—a gentler trumpeter, say—would have helped complement the not always attractive Coltrane sound.[33]

In other words, the "often strident" and "not always attractive" Coltrane—and, by implication, his hard-bop brethren as well—could not convey subtlety, complexity, gentleness, softness. Certainly no racist overtones here!

In similar fashion, Whitney Balliett, for decades the arbiter in matters jazz at the *New Yorker*, heaped great praise on Bill Perkins, a white tenor saxophonist much in vogue during the mid-1950s, ostensibly because in Perkins's work "there is none of the hair-pulling, the bad tone or the ugliness that is now a growing mode largely in New York among the work of the hard-bopsters like Sonny Rollins, Hank Mobley and J.R. Montrose [*sic*]."[34] Balliett was too well mannered to remark that New York was exactly where black musicians had remained in the saddle during the cool–West Coast years, but the thrust of his comment probably was not lost on his readers, least of all the jazz musicians among them.

Finally, by way of teasing out the racist bias inherent in the critical opposition to hard-bop and funky styles, in 1958 Bill Coss, the editor of *Metronome*, then the second-largest jazz periodical, condemned what he called "creeping sentimentalism" and "propaganda"—always a favorite term of opprobrium among white critics hostile to the latest form of black music—in hard bop and funky jazz. In the course of this denunciation, Coss quoted with evident relish the censorious comment of another white critic apropos one member of a funky group: "He doesn't really fit in with this group; he doesn't hate enough." Coss continued by explaining that although hate was not "the only emotion that funky music is purveying . . . there is a limited scope in the emotional content of the music and *hate is one of the major ones*" (my emphasis).[35]

To the critical mind, evidently, hard bop sinned not merely because it had moved beyond an earlier style, but because it had rejected a white aesthetic stance for a black one. Critics or no, however, the hard-bop revolt against the tepidity of cool and West Coast jazz could not be contained. As cool grew increasingly inbred and bland, its inability to produce music of any emotional substance emerged with ever-greater clarity, especially in comparison to the infinitely more demonstrative and muscular hard-bop style. The result was not long in doubt. Some cool musicians attempted to swim with the new tide, but most were unable to change course successfully; in any event, the massive shift in taste heralded by Miles Davis's "Walkin' " in 1954 soon made it clear that all but a few cool performers had fallen permanently from public favor. A decade and one-half later, almost the only cool figure of major stature to retain a sizable following is Stan Getz—and even he has revamped his approach to incorporate some of the ideas of saxophonists John Coltrane and Sonny Rollins. The other cool performers have for the most part either left music altogether or retreated into the economically secure but musically trite haven of the recording studios.

The subsequent evolution of hard bop is highly instructive from the standpoint of our effort to lay bare the nature of the connection between jazz and the black community. The name *hard bop*, to begin with, was probably not that of the black musicians themselves, but of some reviewer or writer of notes for the jackets of recordings faced with the problem of understanding a new and not necessarily welcome style. The artists themselves, in contrast, had a variety of titles for the new style, the first of which was *funky*. Right here we commence, as it were, to have our noses rubbed in the black roots of the anti-cool revolt. Funky is a piece of African-American slang; at its most fundamental, it means dirty, smelly, with particular reference to odors said (by blacks and whites) to be found especially in the ghetto.[36] But African-Americans, as possessors of a separate culture they wish to defend from the depredations of a hostile environment, have long since perfected the art of remaking the English language into a new dialect that (for a while, at any rate) serves their needs exclusively.

In this way, for instance, black musicians had earlier subverted the word bad into its dialectical opposite, a term of approbation: "Man, that cat is *bad!*" In its jazz usage, funky, obviously, represented an extension of this tradition. To describe a musician as funky—that is, unwashed, repellent—

meant that this particular individual is worse (hence better) than just *bad*—he or she is . . . *funky*. But beyond this, funky was a uniquely *black* idiom; like many words and phrases from another tongue (such as *chozzerei, schlemiel, mensch,* and *mazel tov* in Yiddish) it has no precise equivalent in standard English. To call a composition, a passage, or a performer funky, therefore, is not only to offer praise in general, but is a means of lauding the object of praise for its specifically black qualities. A black musician might admire, say, one of Mahler's symphonies; she might even enthuse over the composer as "a bad cat"; but it is highly doubtful that it would ever occur to her to refer to any of the music as funky. That particular term would in all cases be reserved for artists who were expressing their ideas in a particularly African-American idiom. The fact that the black artists who comprised the first wave of the anti-cool revolt chose to call their style of playing funky is thus of the greatest significance. It immediately proclaimed: "Look! This is *our* music—a product arising from *our* experience, and only our experience." Black audiences did not have to have the new connotation of the word explained to them; they knew, or could feel readily enough, what the musicians were striving to convey. White audiences, by contrast, were another matter entirely, as the profusion of articles in the jazz press devoted to explicating "funk"—the word and the style—bore eloquent testimony.

Funky, in its turn, was succeeded by *soul* as the obligatory name for post-cool black music. In no sense, however, should this process of simple replacement be regarded as a repudiation, as hard bop and funky had been a repudiation of cool. Rather, two other social forces were at work in bringing about the change. There is, first of all, even under ordinary circumstances, a fairly rapid turnover rate in ghetto argot. Black urban culture highly esteems verbal agility and certain other forms of public display; nothing could be a clearer demonstration of squareness than the use of yesterday's hip phrase (or dance or article of clothing) today. One consequence is the continuous obsolescence of a portion of the spoken idiom of the ghetto, especially that of the jazz musician, who, as an acknowledged shaper of ghetto taste, is looked to as a source of new styles, both musical and otherwise.[37]

Besides this built-in search for innovation, words describing styles in jazz, or in any area of popular culture, are particularly subject to rapid debasement, as first the media, and then the merchandisers, ferret out such terms and quickly convert them to catch-phrases and then into obnoxious, grating clichés. As album after album with "funky" somewhere in the title was released, the more sensitive musicians naturally began to recoil from use of the word, until it died an early—and by that time wholly unmourned—death. (Like "cool" however, "funk" and "funky" would enjoy a revival after sufficient time had passed.) Such linguistic overkill is hardly unique to jazz, however. More recently, we have watched as words from the vocabulary of the so-called youth culture have traveled the path from birth to death at an accelerated speed, as witness, for example, the rapid demise of *folk-rock, psychedelic, groovy, far out,* and numerous other relics of the Age of Aquarius. In any event, faced with the lightning-like preemption of "funky" by the recording companies, black musicians responded by moving to "soul" to describe what was in essence the same style.

There can scarcely be any doubt—especially not after the 1960s—that "soul" in some loose but inclusive way refers to the African-American experience, and in that sense differs little from "funky" as a descriptive term. After all, have we not observed that in every urban insurrection of the 1960s, black business-owners have written the words "soul brother" in large letters on the windows of their establishments in order to have them spared by the insurgents? And in the magazines devoted to chronicling the vagaries of the entertainment industry—*Billboard, Variety, Cash Box*—the phrase "soul music" serves as a euphemism for popular music performed by black artists (or their white imitators).[38]

These considerations (to which one readily could add others) make it plain that soul and funky were, in jazz circles, essentially synonymous. The only significant difference I can discern is that soul seems to have come into general use from the African-American church (it can be found quite frequently, for example, in the rhetoric of Martin Luther King), and as such was sometimes employed by musicians who wished to make explicit reference to the musical traditions of that church (as when, for instance, bassist Charles Mingus entitled a composition depicting a prayer meeting in a black working-class church, "Better Git It in Your Soul"). In the main, however, jazz musicians invoked the word "soul" to demarcate a music that was black in sensibility and point of origin. Numerous were the musicians during the late 1950s who emphatically declared in the pages of the jazz press that only those who "had soul" could play in the soul style, and that these were "soul brothers" or "soul sisters"—a thinly veiled assertion that the most authentic jazz stylists were black. (The assertion had to be made in this concealed, Aesopian form, of course, because of the hostility of the white journalists, critics, editors, and publishers to any more-overt claim.)

One should bear in mind that the funky-soul trend in jazz was occurring in synchrony with the intensification of what was then called the civil-rights movement—and that in all probability the latter was, as I explained at the start of this section, the most important single development in bringing about the funky-soul rebellion against cool and West Coast styles. The easiest way to demonstrate the truth of this proposition, and also at the same time to elucidate the continuity between funky and soul jazz, is to consider a representative selection of titles bestowed by black artists on their creations. What we shall see is that, taken en masse, these titles are strong evidence for the growth of (to use a phrase from a slightly later time) cultural nationalism among black people. Though not explicitly either nationalist or political in nature, such works attest nonetheless to the rising pride in blackness of African-American jazz artists. For convenience, and not altogether arbitrarily, I have grouped the titles into two classifications.

1. *African-American themes:* I include under this heading all compositions that deal with anything specifically and uniquely black, whether pertaining to the African-American religious experience (examples: "The Sermon," "The Preacher," "Right Down Front"), manifestos of cultural pride ("Bronze Dance," "Black Diamond," "Dis Hyeah" ["this here" in the dialect of the streets]), references to black history ("Work Song," intended to suggest the singing of convicts or slaves), panegyrics to leaders in the movement for black liberation (Max Roach's composition "Garvey's Ghost"),* and so on. What I want to emphasize with particular force is that I could find very few if any titles of this nature prior to 1954 or 1955, and even after that date there are only a handful of instances—fewer than a dozen in total—in which white musicians coined or recorded similar titles. There seemed

---

* Which earned for its composer the following critical encomium: "Roach's search for racial heroes has led him into some strange positions: . . . 'Garvey's Ghost' is heroic and grandiose in conception and feeling, giving rise to a picture oddly at variance with what is known [to whom?] of his 'leadership.'" Evidently, the position of white jazz critic carries with it the prerogative of evaluating not only a black artist's music, but also the titles of the artist's compositions and the political philosophy to which the artist subscribes. See Pete Welding, review of Max Roach, *Percussion Bitter Sweet* (Impulse 8), in *down beat Jazz Record Reviews* (hereafter, *dbJRR*), vol. 7, ed. Don DeMicheal (Chicago: Maher Publishing, 1963), p. 146.

to be, in other words, an unspoken consensus that titles containing words such as "funky" and "soul," titles that dealt with the African-American church, and titles alluding to some particular aspect of the black experience were off limits to whites.*

A partial listing of such titles, obtained from surveying the jazz press for the five years between 1957 and 1961, would include, in addition to the foregoing, the following: "Moanin' " (the prayer of a black worshipper); "Justice" (a play on the title of the popular song "Just You, Just Me" = just *us* [blacks] = justice; also, an obvious "protest" theme, as in the Nation of Islam [Black Muslim] rallying cry, "Freedom, Justice and Equality"); "Original Faubus Fables"; "Filthy McNasty" (who is clearly very funky); "Doin' the Thing" (argot); "Soultrane" (dedicated to John Coltrane); "Cook-in'" (a black musicians' term for swinging); "Plenty, Plenty Soul"; "Sermonette" (in a black church); "Barrel of Funk"; "Ezzthetic" (written

---

* To the degree that funk, soul, and other related themes were the exclusive preserve of black musicians, to that degree would they—for once—possess an economic advantage over their white counterparts. If funk or soul were indeed the essence of jazz, and if only blacks were privy to experiences enabling them to express funk and soul authoritatively, then clearly white musicians would be rendered largely superfluous. Such considerations, consciously or otherwise, surely must have played a part in sustaining the funk-and-soul phenomenon. But perhaps white musicians had a secret weapon of their own! Many white cool musicians—Stan Getz, Barney Kessel, Bud Shank, Herbie Mann, Shorty Rogers, Cal Tjader, Laurindo Almeida, Charlie Byrd—barred by definition from the ranks of the funk-soul school, seemingly sought to recapture lost ground with a music in which whites *could* participate, the bossa nova. Interestingly enough in the light of this suggestion of a tacit conflict between African-American funk-soul and white bossa nova, almost no black musicians performed in the latter style during the first phase of its popularity (the sole exception I can recall is Cannonball Adderley). It was not until several years had passed that sizable numbers of black musicians began composing and performing pieces in the bossa nova idiom.

for a black culture hero, prizefighter Ezzard Charles); "Talk that Talk" (speak in black argot); "Big Hunk of Funk"; "No Smokin'" (meaning its opposite, smokin' = cookin' = swinging); "Soulville"; "Home Cookin'" (a play on words; see entry for "Cookin', " above); "Funk Oats"; "Dat Dere" (= "that there"; see the entry for "Dis Hyeah," above); "Them Dirty [= funky] Blues" (that is, a characteristically black way of playing the blues); "Waltz de Funk"; "Head Shakin'" (what one does when listening to soul jazz); "Funk Mama"; "Amen" (church); "Free" (what blacks most want to be); "It's Time" (for liberation); "Little Brother Soul" (= little soul brother); "In a Funky Groove"; "Workin' " (= cookin'); "Down Home" (in the South; also, a funky way of playing); "Opus de Funk"; "Soul Junction"; "Soul Me"; "The Message" (analogous to "The Sermon"); "Sister Salvation" (church); "Wednesday Night Prayer Meeting"; "Cryin' Blues"; "My Jelly Roll Soul"; "Blue Soul"; "Blue Funk"; "Sumphin'" (= something); "Somethin' Else" (what black people and their music are); "Callin' All Cats"; "You Gotta Dig [study] It to Dig [understand] It"; "Dig Dis" (ghetto vernacular); "Soul Station"; "Big Fat Mama" (a particular type of black woman); "Soul Searchin'"; "Sister Sadie" (a member of the church, whence springs the custom of addressing women as "sister," men as "brother"); "The Nitty Gritty" (argot); "Soul Sister" (related to "Sister Sadie," above); "Soul Brother"; "Soul Meeting"; "The Prophet" (the Honorable Elijah Muhammad, head of the Nation of Islam); "Miss Ann" (archtypical wife of Mr. Charlie, an important, or self-important, white man, as in James Baldwin's play, *Blues for Mr. Charlie*); "Yes, I'll Be Ready" (for freedom; described by the reviewer as "another one of those gospel-inspired numbers"); "Black Groove"; "Like Church" (music); "Funk Underneath"; "Sack Full of Soul"; "Filet of Soul"; "Hog Callin' Blues"; "Devil Women" (voodoo survivals); "Ecclusiastics" (church); "Hip to It" (black vernacular); "Con Alma" (Spanish for "with soul"); "Bowl of Soul" (to be consumed, presumably, with filet of soul); "Ribs an' Chips" (soul food).

2. *African themes:* In addition to conferring on their works names that in some way or other connoted African-American culture, many black musicians also made their ethnic pride explicit by using African-derived titles. In this connection, there are two points to note. First, the strong pro-African orientation of black jazz musicians, beginning in the early 1950s with saxophonist Sonny Rollins's composition "Airegin", became visible long before that of the black community as a whole. (Typical of the intellectual musician's aversion to the obvious, Rollins made his point obliquely by spelling the inspiration for his piece backwards.) The same is true of African-American cultural consciousness in general. Second, there never emerged an African "school" of playing in the same way that there was a funky-soul school, nor was there ever any particular vogue for jazz pieces with African titles, hence a musician who chose such a title for a composition or album had no reason to expect material rewards from the choice; consequently, there are no legitimate grounds for objecting to the use of these titles as an index to the growth of nationalist feelings among black musicians.

The first such "African" title that I am aware of is, as I mentioned above, Rollins's "Airegin" (note also in this context that Rollins, like John Coltrane, was recorded through the intervention of Miles Davis and was, with Davis and Coltrane, among those at the head of the hard-bop movement). Other titles from the years 1957–1961 include: "Ritual" (according to the reviewer, "a vividly presented [Art] Blakey composition, based on his knowledge of African tribal music";* "Dakar"; "Tanganyika Strut"; "Africa"; "African

---

* The review continues: "On the track preceding it, Blakey speaks for two minutes on the African origins and inspiration for the composition. Then he digs in." Don Gold, review of Art Blakey, *Ritual: The Jazz Messengers* (Pacific Jazz M–402), in *dbJRR*, vol. 2, ed. Tracy, p. 24.

Lady"; "Bantu"; "Uhuru" (freedom); "Kwanza"; "Kucheza Blues"; "African Violets"; "Katanga"; "Dahomey Dance"; "Message from Kenya"; "Man From South Africa" (Nobel Laureate Albert Luthuli); "Effendi"; "African Waltz." As with compositions whose names refer to African-American themes, the frequency of African-inspired titles roughly increases with time after 1955.

All the selections with African-American and African titles bear witness to the growth of what is now conventionally called cultural nationalism among black people. They demonstrate, that is, the increasing sense of cultural self-awareness and pride in their heritage of African-Americans since the middle of the 1950s. As such, however, this new awareness and pride are not inherently political in nature; they do not intrinsically demand a radical restructuring of the society—a separate black state, say, or collective ownership by black people of all the economic resources within their communities. Cultural nationalism of this stripe may indeed go no further than the fashionable slogan, "black is beautiful."

In jazz, it is possible to discern with some precision the cresting of the cultural-nationalist wave around 1961–1962, with a pair of suites: pianist Randy Weston's *Uhuru Afrika: Freedom Africa* (1961) and saxophonist Oliver Nelson's *Afro/ American Sketches* (1962).[39] Both works were essentially celebratory; the former was described by one white critic as "just a warmly felt tribute to the new African nations by African-American musicians,"* the latter was a musical version of African-American history from the time of slavery and before (titles of the individual sections included

* White readers were no doubt further reassured to learn "there is no racism of any kind involved here"—as if anyone save a white jazz critic might have suspected there were! See Ira Gitler, review of Randy Weston, *Uhuru Afrika*, in *dbJRR*, vol. 7, ed. DeMicheal, p. 190.

"Message"; "Jungleaire"; "Emancipation Blues"; "There's a Yearnin'"; "Going Up North"; "Disillusioned"; "Freedom Dance").

Beyond this point it was not possible to go—at least not in a purely cultural-nationalist vein. Once it has been proclaimed that black is truly beautiful, the pinnacle of cultural nationalism has been reached; there is nothing more to do save to repeat the message—and no message can bear more than a certain amount of repetition—or to move on to something new. The majority of the jazz musicians contemporary with Randy Weston and Oliver Nelson had no other message to offer; and after *Uhuru Afrika* and *Afro/American Sketches*, it began to become evident that the cultural-nationalist, black-is-beautiful approach had yielded about all of which it was capable. The result, predictably enough, was an impasse in musical and—not coincidentally—social and political terms. Soul and funk recordings continued to appear, but by 1962 or thereabouts, the spontaneity and vitality of funk-soul had been pretty thoroughly exhausted through overuse.

It remained for a younger group of black jazz artists to break the impasse by moving beyond simple affirmation of black values to *negation*. Negation, Herbert Marcuse has shown in his classic study of Hegel and Marx,[40] is at the root of the dialectical method; regardless of whether the young black jazz performers of the 1960s were conscious dialecticians (and some were), negation of the status quo—in music and society alike—was their starting point. Inasmuch as a detailed examination of that double negation is the focus of what is to follow, there is no need for me to go into it now.

In order not to leave readers with a mistaken impression, however, I should note that even as cultural nationalism held sway, there were attempts by established musicians to get past its limitations, to devise a new and more viable musical-political synthesis. These musicians—drummer Max Roach

88 / PARTPART 1: INTRODUCTIONINTRODUCTION

and his wife at the time, singer Abbey Lincoln, saxophonist Sonny Rollins, bassist Charles Mingus—are among the
sources of spiritual inspiration for the current generation
of innovators. They stand in relation to the young radicals
of the late 1960s—Archie Shepp, Albert Ayler, and Pharoah
Sanders, among others—as a foretaste of things to come. I
will recount their attempt to challenge the status quo in
jazz in chapter 2.

Meanwhile, there remains the question of how we are
to interpret the spread of political-nationalist ideas among
young black jazz artists. To put this matter in its correct perspective, I maintain, we must view it against a backdrop of
nationalism's steady growth in the ghetto, as illustrated by
the increasing appeal of the Nation of Islam prior to the split
between Elijah Muhammad and Malcolm X, the immediate
support for the latter's Organization of African-American
Unity up until the time of his assassination, the formation of
an all-black Freedom Now Party for the 1964 elections, and
most recently, the steady swell of membership in the Black
Panther Party, notwithstanding the utterly vicious and violent repression directed against it by local police forces and
the Federal Bureau of Investigation. If I have not gone into
detail regarding these events, it is because I have assumed
they are well enough known to the reader. In any case, it
would be well to keep them in mind as a kind of historical
counterpoint to the narrative that follows this introductory
chapter, for in my view there is no other way of arriving
at a full understanding of why both cultural and political
nationalist ideologies flourished so dramatically within the
hothouse environment of jazz.

This last point is directly relevant to the purpose of this
section of the introduction: to establish that the black community offers physical and moral support for jazz. I have not
sought to "prove" this thesis in any quantitative way, because, as I explained at the outset, my intuition tells me that

such attempts are inherently fallible, hence futile. Instead, I have sought to demonstrate the existence of an intimate relationship between the black community and the much smaller jazz milieu, a relationship that exerts its influence on jazz by helping to shape the course and timing of that music's development aesthetically, socially, politically. Having surveyed the unprecedented upsurge of cultural-nationalist ideas in jazz following the release of Miles Davis's recording of "Walkin' " in 1954, it seems clear on the face of it that to deny the two-way flow between the jazz world and the black ghetto would leave us at a total loss when it comes to explaining this sudden explosion of nationalist sentiment. On that statement I am prepared to rest my case.

D. No social content in jazz? Tell it to Charlie Parker

If they don't own us, they push us off the scene. Jazz is big business to the white man and you can't move without him. We just work-ants. He owns the magazines, [booking] agencies, record companies and all the joints that sell jazz to the public. If you won't sell out and you try to fight they won't hire you and they give a bad picture of you with that false publicity.

—CHARLES MINGUS[41]

Jazz has no particular social content; specifically, it in no way pertains more closely to black experiences, modes of perception, sensibilities, than it does to white. Jazz is not "protest music" and black jazz musicians have lacked either the will or the ability to concern themselves with social issues.

These propositions comprise the final argument in the Revealed Wisdom that guides most white jazz critics in the discharge of their craft. But how could anyone possibly uphold such positions, the reader well may be asking, in light of the unmistakable African-American foundations of funky and soul jazz. The usual bit of sleight of hand to which jazz critics resort to get around this objection involves conceding this point for the immediate post-cool years—after all, the musicians themselves had proclaimed the black roots of funky and soul styles too emphatically to deny—only to retract it more vigorously for all other periods in jazz's history.

To be sure, not every era in jazz has been as overtly nationalist as was that of the late 1950s and early 1960s. Nevertheless, there is, as I argued in the preceding section, an intimate process of cross-pollination that takes place between jazz and the black community, the net effect of which ensures that both the music and the musicians will either anticipate or at the very least reflect the mood, concerns, and aspirations of the ghetto. It is just this thesis that white jazz critics go out of their way to reject.

Consider, by way of illustration, what one member of the white-critical fraternity, Ira Gitler, wrote during the course of a heated exchange between us on the subject of the relationship between black nationalism and jazz. Bear in mind, however, that there is nothing unique about Gitler's views; if we were to substitute for his name that of almost any other prominent white critic—Leonard Feather, Gene Lees, Don DeMicheal, Martin Williams, John S. Wilson, Willis Conover, Bill Coss—the outcome would not be significantly different. Indeed, as I will bring out, once Gitler came under attack, Feather himself almost immediately sought to ride to his rescue by committing himself in print to essentially the same position his comrade-in-arms espoused.*

---

* See the next chapter for an account of how Feather, Gitler, Lees, De-Micheal, Coss, and various of their colleagues joined forces to suppress nationalist ideas advanced by Max Roach, Abbey Lincoln, Charles Mingus and other dissident jazz artists.

One of the issues in this dispute was that of the correct historical interpretation of the bebop revolution of the 1940s. It is my contention that there were social as well as purely musical forces underlying the attempt of bebop artists to overturn the reigning swing style, as exemplified by the title of a Charlie Parker blues of the period, "Now's the Time."[42] To buttress the argument that there were "obvious social implications" in the bebop movement, I sought to bring out that this revolt against swing took place during World War II, an extraordinarily tumultuous time for African-Americans. It was in these years, I remarked, that black workers organized for a massive March on Washington for equal employment opportunities; that the "Double-V campaign," for victory over racism at home as well as abroad, began; that insurrections erupted in Harlem and Detroit; that "innumerable clashes both on and off the military posts" broke out when black servicemen and -women protested Jim Crow treatment;[43] that a work stoppage of black Seabees compelled the U.S. government to halt its dissemination of racist propaganda ("yellow-bellied Japs") aimed at whipping up popular support for the war in the Pacific;[44] that African-Americans participated in the formation of the United Nations in the hope that it would intervene in the struggle against racism in the United States, the Union of South Africa, and elsewhere—all these and other, similar events, I noted, were contemporaneous with the genesis of bebop. It was precisely such developments that more recently have led Richard M. Dalfiume to conclude:

The search for a "watershed" in recent Negro history ends at the years that comprised World War II, 1939–1945. James Baldwin has written of this period: "The treatment accorded the Negro during the Second World War marks, for me, a turning point in the Negro's relation to America. To put it briefly, and some-what too simply, a certain respect for white Americans faded." Writing during World War II, Gunnar Myrdal predicted that the war would act as a "stimulant" to Negro protest, and he felt that "there is bound to be a redefinition of the Negro's status in America as a result of this War." [The black sociologist] E. Franklin Frazier states that World War II marked the point where "The Negro was no longer willing to accept discrimination in employment and in housing without protest." Charles E. Silberman writes that the war was a "turning point" in American race relations, in which "the seeds of the protest movements of the 1950s and 1960s were sown."[45]

Faced with this mountain of evidence, one might suppose that Ira Gitler would be willing to concede that a social interpretation of the bebop revolution—and of Charlie Parker's purpose in entitling his composition "Now's the Time"—might not be wholly without merit. Instead, Gitler simply refused to acknowledge the relevance of this—or any—evidence: "I deny the 'obvious social implication.' The title refers to the music and the 'now' was the time for the people to dig it."[46] Gitler himself, moreover, was soon enough reinforced by his ideological alter ego, Leonard Feather, whose abstract and chaste account of the bebop revolution ended with the sweeping assertion that "neither in the sounds produced by Gillespie, Parker and [drummer] Kenny Clarke and their contemporaries, or [sic] in the titles or the arrangements, is there a relation to the brutal conditions that persisted through the bebop years."[47]

Now it is not outside the pale of possibility that the title of Parker's piece did have the meaning that Gitler (and, by implication, Feather) assigned to it; but if so, that meaning was secondary to the one I have suggested—or so I have been assured by every black musician with whom I have ever discussed the question (most often, such musicians respond to my reading of either Gitler's or Feather's statement by bursting into incredulous laughter). For the truth of the matter, as the eminent British economic historian E.J. Hobsbawm (writing pseudonymously as Francis Newton) has observed, is that "race relations" is "a factor in the coloured jazz musician's life which has steadily grown in *conscious* importance" (my emphasis). "No bar of coloured jazz," he continues, "has ever made sense to those who do not understand the Negro's reaction to oppression." Especially was this the case after the 1930s, when the "political awakening of all the oppressed and underprivileged . . . put a new tone" into the black musician's instrument: "open resentment." As a result, "from the late thirties the coloured jazz musician became increasingly ambitious, both to establish his superiority over the white musician . . . and to raise the status of his music. . . ."[48]

For the reasons supplied by Hobsbawm, there can be little question among serious students of the music that jazz has ineluctably (and increasingly) functioned not solely as music, but also as a vehicle for voicing outraged protest at the oppression of African-Americans as a people and the specific exploitation to which jazz musicians, as black artists, have been perpetually subjected *in an art of their own creation.* Nor is there much room to doubt, Gitler and Feather to the contrary notwithstanding, that the "open resentment" of which Hobsbawm writes was an important consideration in bringing about the bebop revolution of the 1940s. A black bebop musician thus confided in the German critic Joachim Ernst Berendt:

You see, we need music; we've always needed a music— our own. We have nothing else. Our writers write like the whites, our painters paint like them, our philosophers think like them. Only our musicians don't play like the whites. So we created a music for ourselves. When we had it—the old type of jazz—the whites came, and they liked it and imitated it. Pretty soon it was no longer our music. . . .

You see, as soon as we have a music, the white man comes and imitates it. We've now had jazz for fifty years, and in all those fifty years there has been not a single white man, perhaps leaving aside Bix [Beiderbecke], who has had an idea. Only the coloured men have ideas. But if you see who's got the famous names, they're all white.

What can we do? We must go on inventing something new all the time. When we have it, the whites will take it from us, and we have to start all over again. It is as though we were being hunted.[49]

There is, then, no reason whatsoever why we should not view the social aspect of bebop as a manifesto of rebellious black musicians unwilling to submit to further exploitation. Unfortunately, at the time of its origins this manifesto had to be proclaimed primarily in musical terms and its social implications left tacit—a situation that later allowed Ira Gitler and Leonard Feather to maintain that the title "Now's the Time" had only musical significance to its author. But until very recently, as the quotation from Charles Mingus at the start of this section indicates, black artists who attempted to act overtly against the oppressive conditions confronting either themselves or their people had to contend at the minimum with powerful efforts to force them into silence (the next chapter contains an extensive discussion of such efforts, not least as they were brought to bear against Mingus himself). My own inquiries fully confirm Mingus's point of view. Thus, Bob Thiele, who produced John Coltrane's recordings for Impulse Records between 1961 and 1967 and whose career in music spans several decades, told me:

> Through the years, as I've listened to music and collected records, I think it's a very simple deduction that the music is Negro music to begin with; and for these guys [critics] to write about the music as though it's an American music, that everybody plays equally, and that we all love one another and we're all brothers—to me, really, that's a lot of horseshit. I mean, I read critics even today in 1968 who say that in the old days, the Negro musicians were never unhappy and they didn't complain about the social conditions in the country, I think they forget that in those days it just wasn't done. A Negro musician just couldn't come out and say, "Hey! the situation stinks."[50]

Consequently, black musicians learned to resort to subterfuges—*bad* meaning "good," say, or *funky* meaning "fine"—to disguise their true sentiments.

Nonetheless, young African-American performers of the late 1930s had witnessed the fate of the black bands of that decade and had resolved that theirs would be different. Leslie B. Rout, Jr., explains that the career of black leader-composer-arranger Fletcher Henderson was paradigmatic in this regard:

> As early as 1928, this bandleader had worked out the basis of the jazz style known as Swing. By the early thirties he had assembled an outstanding aggregation—but it was still a black orchestra. A compromise of sorts resulted: Benny Goodman became the "King of Swing"—everywhere except in Harlem and other urban ghettos—and Fletcher Henderson became his chief arranger.

The swing bandwagon had ample room for the white orchestras of Glenn Miller, Tommy and Jimmy Dorsey, Artie

Shaw, Woody Herman, and others, despite the fact that, in
Rout's words, "black powerhouse battalions led by Count
Basie, Chick Webb and Jimmy Lunceford . . . played better
jazz" while earning "less than half as much as their white
counterparts."[51] One-half a century later, the obvious injustice of this state of affairs continues to rankle black musicians, such as drummer Art Blakey, who had lived through
the era:

> My contention is, is to give the people credit who brought
> forth the idea. . . . They never give them credit for it. . . .
> They turn around and they name Paul Whiteman the
> King of Swing [Jazz], and the only way he could swing is
> from a rope. I didn't think that was fair. Then they turn
> around and name Benny Goodman the King of Swing,
> and he's playing Fletcher Henderson's arrangements
> note for note. I could walk into Benny Goodman's band
> and play every arrangement they had, because Smack
> [Henderson] did it—it's Smack's music. He didn't get
> the credit for it, see, and that's what hurt. And he died
> a pauper—up in Harlem—and it hurt. And I didn't understand why that could be.[52]

Nor did the occasional hiring of black musicians by white
band-leaders such as Goodman materially improve the situation; instead, it served only to generate "increased black
discontent, because from the [black musician's] point of view,
acceptance into white orchestras demonstrated how badly
black swingsters were needed! Why, then, be satisfied with
a few crumbs, while 'Whitey' took cake?" Why indeed? The
logical move for black performers—especially appropriate by
the early 1940s, since "Swing had then passed its inventive
peak"—was "the creation of a jazz form that whites could
not play! Ideally, this would insure for black jazzmen the
recognition they craved, plus a lion's share of the profits."[53]

Hence one inescapably concludes that indignation fed by watching impotently as the economic rewards from black innovations went to enlarge white bank accounts helped catalyze the revolt against swing style and propelled the most imaginative and discontented young African-Americans of that day into the bebop camp.[54]

But more than concerns over dollars and cents—despite the undeniable importance of the latter—fueled the black breakaway from swing. All of the biographical information about Charlie Parker—the central figure in the bebop revolution and easily its most fertile musical imagination—show him to have been an impassioned, at times almost reckless enemy of racism in every manifestation. There is no black jazz musician of the period, in fact, who exhibited a stronger, more intense or outspoken antipathy than he to the color prejudice that pervades American society.

Whether Parker's associates—including drummer Max Roach and bassist Charles Mingus, whom we will encounter in chapter 2 in their roles as precursors of the black-nationalist movement in jazz during the 1960s—followed the saxophonist's lead or arrived at their own essentially identical conclusions independently, the truth is that this hatred of racism (as we can now observe quite clearly in the careers of Roach and Mingus) was one shared by virtually all of the bebop vanguard. Indeed, in doing research for these pages, it suddenly struck me that many of the positions or actions later taken by Roach or Mingus well may have had their roots in the apprenticeships they served in various of Parker's groups; there were countless incidents in Parker's own life that, if one did not know better, read as if they could have befallen Mingus. Nor was Mingus the only person touched by "Bird," to give Parker his jazz sobriquet. Among the more than eighty people Robert Reisner interviewed for the writing of *Bird: The Legend of Charlie Parker*, a remarkable number chose to relate one or another instance of the saxophonist's lifelong battle against white racism.[55]

Conceivably, Parker was simply incapable of doing anything by half-measures. But regardless of whether that or some other facet of his personality was responsible, it is quite clear that he did not blink at the risk of losing his life in order to demonstrate his adamant refusal to submit to racist treatment. Two illustrations suffice. On one Arkansas night in 1943, an unarmed Parker faced down and forced into retreat a white thug who, wielding a beer bottle, had just put a gash that required stitches in the head of Dizzy Gillespie.[56]

The following year, Parker was working in St. Louis in the big band of singer Billy Eckstine; the group was playing at a so-called black-and-tan cabaret that employed only black performers, but served only white patrons. When the management refused to let the musicians enter the front door or associate with the clientele, Parker's response exemplified his brilliant, unorthodox cast of mind. While the other musicians were relaxing during an intermission, Parker went to them one by one and asked for the glass from which each had been drinking, and at the end of his rounds broke all of the glasses at once. The "explanation" he offered to the incredulous proprietor was that he was sure the cabaret would not wish to serve its regular customers from a vessel "contaminated" (Parker's word, quoted by drummer Art Blakey) by the lips of a black person. The owner, a notorious St. Louis gangster—a combination of professions, alas, all too common in jazz—arrived in the midst of this amazing performance and was only narrowly dissuaded from doing violence to Parker. But the latter was so incensed at racist assaults on his human dignity that he was oblivious to the danger he courted in venting the hostility and resentment these insults inspired.[57]

Hampton Hawes, a Los Angeles pianist who often worked with Parker when he performed on the West Coast, was one of many young black musicians who looked to the saxophonist for both musical and political inspiration. Parker, Hawes would recall,

> had it all together in music and in life. A jazz musician makes a total commitment, which is himself, his attitude, his sound, his story, and the way he lives. . . . He talked to us about things I wasn't to read until years later in books by Malcolm X and [Eldridge] Cleaver. *I heard all that in his music.* Bird was a deeply frustrated man. . . . Bird felt deeply about the black-white split. He was the first jazz musician I met who understood what was happening to his people. He couldn't come up with an answer. So he stayed high. *His only outlet was his music.* [All italics mine.][58]

Such was the person who, I remind the reader, had as his disciples every imaginative and ambitious young black artist then active in jazz (Hampton Hawes being a representative instance in point). Can any honest soul find it conceivable that the music of someone with Parker's intense sensitivity to racist affronts would not somehow reflect its creator's mentality? Is it possible to believe, as Ira Gitler, Leonard Feather, and the others who espouse their ideology would have us do, that this tormented, volatile, and supremely *expressive* black genius did not imbue his music—titles and all—with his most-profound sentiments? To have suppressed them would have gone against the grain of Parker's philosophy, which he crystallized in a neat aphorism that is probably the most-quoted of any of his remarks: "Music is your own experience, your thoughts, your wisdom. If you don't live it, it won't come out of your horn."[59] All I am maintaining is that Parker (whom no one has ever accused of hypocrisy) meant exactly what he said: the music of an inventive jazz musician should—nay, *must*—be a distillation of that person's thoughts, wisdom and, above all, life and experience. It was this same philosophy that Parker bequeathed to his legion of followers, Max Roach and Charles Mingus not least among them.

For all of the hopes and dreams of Parker and his contemporaries, bebop was unable to liberate the black jazz artist from the burdens of exploitation by white business, nor could it for long prevent the inevitable copying of the style by those white musicians for whom imitation was indeed the highest form of flattery. For one thing, as I explained earlier, the economic decline of the late 1940s made it impossible for black bebop performers—regardless of how complex or daunting their improvisations, how adamant their social stance—to consolidate their initial advantage; and by the time the Korean War kicked economic recovery into high gear, bebop had been prematurely dethroned by the new cool style. The advent of the funky and soul styles was, at least in part, a renewed attempt—and a much more overt one, at that—to establish a lasting black monopoly in jazz. But notwithstanding its greater explicitness, the funky-soul approach was never entirely successful, though it may well have altered the distribution of rewards within jazz for a short time.*

It is not hard to grasp why funk and soul failed to be more effective; I have alluded to some of the reasons al-

---

* Ironically, many of the white cool musicians driven out of jazz by the onset of funk and soul probably take home greater incomes from the recording and movie studios than ever they did from jazz performance per se. Black musicians, in contrast, as I noted in previous sections of this chapter, never had the studios to cushion their fall when the economy and bebop collapsed simultaneously toward the close of the 1940s. Even as late as the 1970s, for that matter, only a tiny handful have gained admission to the much-prized studio work. All of which only goes to underline how convenient it is to inhabit a white skin in this society.

ready. There were, as we have seen, intrinsic limitations of the funk-soul movement stemming directly from its cultural-nationalist assumptions. That is to say, the implicit logic of the funk and soul styles was to go past the point of mere self-affirmation ("black is beautiful") toward overt action aimed at negating the musical and social status quo. Taking that next step, however, was beyond the resources of the funk and soul musicians; consequently, as I relate in succeeding chapters, it fell to the next wave of black innovators, many of whom are explicitly nationalist in a *political* sense, to accomplish that task.* Meanwhile, the efforts of funky and soul performers to maintain their styles in vogue indefinitely were doomed to come to naught, as their

---

* Inasmuch as the conventional wisdom holds that radical black nationalism means nothing more than "Hate whitey!" and that the new jazz is therefore merely a form of "hate music"—an accusation white critics began rehearsing at least as early as Bill Coss's contention in 1958 that "hate is one of the major emotions" in "funky music" (*Metronome*, March 1958, p. 13)—one must emphatically state that the new-music groups, which are generally the most nationalistically inspired, are also the most integrated. To be specific, the ensembles of Cecil Taylor, Archie Shepp, Marion Brown, Albert Ayler, and Ornette Coleman— certainly among the leading figures in this idiom—usually have at least one white member. The analogy for more-conventional jazz would be if the groups of, say, Miles Davis, Dizzy Gillespie, Cannonball Adderley, Thelonious Monk, and Horace Silver had one white member apiece, something that ordinarily is not the case (although Gillespie, Davis, and Adderley have on occasion hired white musicians). Here one sees the difference between the political nationalism of the new musicians and the cultural nationalism of the funky-soul rebellion against cool. Hence even as the Archie Shepps and Cecil Taylors are being pilloried for their supposed racial biases—I have myself heard them denounced on this score by white recording-company executives, nightclub owners, journalists, and others of that ilk—the integrated nature of their groups is conveniently ignored. The real offense of these artists, we have to conclude, is not the racism with which they have been charged, but their temerity in protesting exploitation and degradation. *That,* truly, is the unpardonable sin.

music gradually ran the gamut from innovation to painful cliché. Funk and soul jazz, once a breath of fresh air following the preciousness of the cool period, ultimately turned cloying. By its nadir, around 1962–63, the jazz public was understandably avid for a change.

Then, too, it would be quite naive to think that any given set of purely *musical* innovations could emancipate black musicians from the grip of white-business domination. To bring about a change of that magnitude would need not only an aesthetic revolution, but a social upheaval as well. Because funky and soul performers never devised any social or political plan of action, however, they left the existing distribution of power undisturbed; which meant, of course, that there was no permanent redistribution of economic rewards.

To be sure, the advent of funky-soul styles may have caused some white musicians to desert jazz, and even may have created a modicum of additional work for black artists. But one should not exaggerate the extent of such gains. Tastes in jazz are notoriously idiosyncratic: even if Dave Brubeck were never to play another engagement, it is extremely doubtful that all of his followers would shift their allegiance to, say, Thelonious Monk. The point is that, regardless of what many black musicians may believe, their disadvantaged position is less due to competition from white performers—few white jazz musicians, after all, have earnings in the same league as those of Miles Davis—than from the fact that ownership of the leading economic institutions of jazz is vested in the hands of entrepreneurs whose preeminent goal is not the enhancement of the art but the taking of a profit. And this situation is certain to continue so long as the artists do not themselves exert control over the nightclubs, booking agencies, recording companies and, in short, the terms of their collective employment. This contradiction the exponents of soul and funk never fully faced, whereas, by contrast, several avant-garde artists, Cecil Taylor and Bill Dixon most notably, have sought to organize musicians' cooperatives to circumvent the traditional white-business channels. Consequently, and not surprisingly, the aspirations of funky and soul musicians were at best partially and briefly fulfilled. Their liberation remained incomplete.

The purpose of this section of my introductory essay has been to illustrate the persistent presence of a social content—a *black* content—within jazz. Contrary to what the white critical consensus has claimed, such a content has been a permanent feature of the music since the 1930s, if not before. More than that. From the repeated attempts of black musicians to assert their primacy in an art of their own making, we can easily see the continuity that links the bebop period, the hard-bop-funky-soul period after 1955, and the present avant-garde period. That such efforts have not been more explicit or visible cannot be interpreted, as most white critics have done, as the absence of discontent with the prevailing situation. Rather, the muted, symbolic, or indirect nature of black protest within jazz, as the earlier comments of both Charles Mingus and Bob Thiele should remind us, springs directly out of the economic conditions that shape the jazz world—conditions that persist to this very day.

For the plain reality is that *there has never been anything like sufficient employment in jazz to provide work for all the musicians who want to perform.* It is as simple as that. Jazz musicians, the black ones especially, have always been forced to sell their services in a buyer's market. The most famous groups and individual artists ordinarily can secure as much work as they want; their problem is that they are unable to play every engagement offered them. But there probably are fewer than a dozen or so groups in this category (and even that number may be wildly optimistic). The typical jazz musician, on the other hand, is in no such privileged position. He or she takes such work as presents itself and, if not exactly grateful, is at least relieved to have it; it certainly is an improvement over sorting mail at the post office, an all-too-frequent alternative. The implications of this state of affairs should be obvious, particularly to any student of labor history. It is common knowledge that to organize a union is a near-impossibility during a period of high unemployment—and for black jazz artists as a whole, it has almost always been the Great Depression (the years of World War II *may* have been somewhat of an exception).[60]

As a result, black jazz musicians have concluded that they must be extremely guarded in their utterances if they are to survive, let alone flourish. All such a musician need do is let it be suspected that he or she is not quite orthodox in some way, and poof! a career gone up in smoke. Miles Davis or Thelonious Monk may enjoy success sufficient to be beyond fear of reprisals—but that won't help our hapless musician in the least. For once the entrepreneurial Powers That Be have decided that a black performer is unemployable, unemployable he or she becomes and unemployable he or she remains (the aborted career of Paul Robeson is illustrative). In all likelihood, this process of being transformed into an Orwellian unperson accounts for the abrupt decline in the fortunes of Max Roach and Charles Mingus—bad niggers both—during the late 1960s, and it is as certain as anything can be that it underlies the all-but-complete dearth of the new music in the established jazz nightclubs, such as Shelly's Manne-Hole in Hollywood.* The constant dread of perma-

---

* Archie Shepp played an engagement in this "hole" in the spring of 1966. Leonard Feather, who reviewed the saxophonist on that occasion, initially wrote that his music "must be taken seriously even by those of us who do not fully understand it." Subsequently, however, when confronted by none other than Shelly Manne himself and "accused . . . of writing a hypocritical review," the critic pled guilty: "I suppose he was right." See Leonard Feather, "Music," *Cavalier,* December 1966, p. 16. As this incident demonstrates only too well, it is the opposition of members of the white Establishment in jazz such as Manne, and

nent unemployment—as it is, the great majority of jazz musicians already spend too much time without work—is enough to make all but the most stalwart radicals cautious and equivocal in their public statements.

I have witnessed this phenomenon often enough firsthand. A black musician will accost me: "Hey, man, I dug your piece on X_____ Y_____. That was really telling it like it is!" Fine. May I quote him on this matter? "Well, man . . . you know how it is." If I didn't know before, by the fifth or sixth such episode, I am no longer in ignorance. Or again, I am tape-recording an interview on the subject of black nationalism and the jazz avant-garde. The subject of the interview is uneasy. He mumbles; he looks at his watch; he shuffles his feet; he becomes palpably anxious and uncomfortable. Finally, it emerges: "Look, man, I told this dude I'd meet him uptown. . . ." These are not invented anecdotes; neither are they isolated events. I could supply the names—but why impose further hardships? Doubtless the participants will recognize themselves should they happen to read these pages. I merely wish to have it understood why the continual undercurrent of protest in jazz has historically been advanced in a highly cryptic, al-

---

not the lack of a potential audience, that keeps the artists who play the new music unemployed. As Bob Thiele observes, "You know, we all try to be realistic and the only reason you make records is to sell records, and Coltrane happened to sell an awful lot of records. Most of the musicians in the new movement happen to sell records, too. I don't say that they sell in the quantities that Coltrane sold, but they do sell records and there is a market for them, not only in the United States but all over the world" (quoted in Kofsky, "The New Wave," p. 8). As the former head of Impulse Records (the jazz subsidiary of ABC Records), the producer of John Coltrane's recordings between 1961 and 1967, and someone with unsurpassed experience in the making and marketing of recordings by avant-garde black musicians, Thiele's qualifications to speak on this point are hardly open to question.

lusive, even Aesopian form.* After all, black people have
been speaking to white in riddles ever since slavery, when
"Steal Away to Jesus" signaled the impending departure of
a slave via the Underground Railroad. Have we any reason
for believing things are substantially different now, or that
the treatment of black jazz musicians has been so generous as to exempt them from the constraints felt by other
African-Americans?

It behooves us not to lose sight of the fact that the forces
of racial oppression are both so immense and so completely
irrational in their operation as to render insignificant most
isolated individual attempts to resist them. Given that truth,
it would be quite foolish, and much too simplistic, to expect
that all protest against such forces would be rational, explicit,
and political (especially so when protest movements among
whites, such as contemporary Protestant fundamentalist agi-
tation against sex education and the teaching of evolution,
are hardly models of sweet reason). Indeed, the history of
black literature in the United States ought to remind us that
protest against racism can at times assume forms so diverse,
or even bizarre, that one needs considerable psychological
insight to comprehend that it is protest we are observing.
Out of his frustration at seeing himself forever trapped in
the quasi-slavery of the ghetto, for instance, Bigger Thomas,
the protagonist of Richard Wright's novel, *Native Son*, kills
a young white woman who has sought to aid him.[61]

More recently, Eldridge Cleaver tells us in *Soul on Ice* of
his career as a rapist of white women—an obsession that,
inspired by impulses similar to those of Bigger Thomas,
brought him perilously close to recapitulating the latter's
fate as well. James Baldwin in his fiction and especially his

---

* As, for example, when Charlie Parker chose to title his blues "Now's
the Time" instead of "Double-V," or Sonny Rollins decided that his
composition would bear the name "Airegin" rather than "Nigeria."

essays, and Ralph Ellison in *The Invisible Man* have described some of the other ways in which efforts at coping with and overcoming white racism have resulted in various kinds of neuroses (or even psychoses) among blacks.[62] And the psychological literature, of course, is filled with examples (including those I cited earlier in notes 23 and 30). Resistance to racism, therefore, cannot be understood in any narrow, mechanistic fashion. Seen in this light, Marcus Garvey's slogan of "Back to Africa" was at least as much a repudiation of a racist United States as it was an affirmation of Africa.

In like fashion, we would do best to interpret the widespread use of addictive narcotics by musicians of the bebop generation as yet another kind of anti-racist protest—the flight from a hellish reality into an anxiety-free and non-racist, albeit drug-induced, nirvana. One of Charlie Parker's biographers suggests, as a case in point, that the saxophonist's use of heroin, alcohol, and other drugs

> allayed the pressure he suffered from the lack of steady work, the public indifference to his music, his contradictory, indeed ridiculous role—a creative artist composing and improvising in a night club. Drugs screened off the greasy spoon restaurants and cheap rooming houses with their unswept stairs and malodorous hall toilets. . . . Heroin became his staff of life. The monkey on his back kept the outside world off it.[63]

It would be interesting to know, would it not, whether any of these considerations has ever managed to force its way into the minds of those white critics who are so shamefully eager to divorce the music from its social environment and to deny the existence of a history of either implicit or explicit protest within jazz.

In any event, given the circumstances under which they are compelled to create, it has taken considerable courage for

black musicians such as Cecil Taylor, Bill Dixon, and Archie
Shepp to have spoken out for truth and against injustice—
and not just once, but repeatedly.[64] Naturally, their careers
have suffered because of it—of that there can be no doubt.
At the moment, we can only hope that someday, in some
perhaps brighter future, this country will have become
sufficiently humane to offer a partial and very inadequate
compensation for the damage it has inflicted by according
these prophets a semblance of the honor that they, and those
like them, so richly deserve. How much better, though, if it
were possible to do so now!

NOTES

1. Archie Shepp quoted in LeRoi Jones, "Voice from the Avant
Garde: Archie Shepp," *down beat*, January 14, 1965, p. 36.
2. Lloyd Garrison, "Soviet Poets Fail to Capture Dakar: Duke Ellington the Winner in Propaganda Skirmish," *New York Times* on
April 30, 1966, p. 31. Garrison specifically informed his readers that
Yevtushenko was in Dakar "not just to project the Soviet Union's
poetic image. He had been urgently summoned from Moscow to do
for Soviet propaganda what Duke Ellington had done for the Americans when he played before packed and cheering audiences during
Dakar's first World Festival of the Negro Arts."
3. Harold Cruse, *The Crisis of the Negro Intellectual: From Its
Origins to the Present* (New York: Apollo Editions, 1968), p. 107;
see also pp. 107–09.
4. As E. Digby Baltzell demonstrates in his study of *The Protestant Establishment*, (New York: Random House, 1964), Jews are
hardly more welcome than blacks within the innermost sancta of
the ruling class. It is also noteworthy in this context that in those
cities, such as Los Angeles, that saw a vast outpouring of ruling-
class money following a black insurrection in the late 1960s, little
or none of it went to benefit jazz or, for that matter, any form of
black music. Although artists' and writers' workshops are within

the bounds of genteel acceptability, art forms like jazz, in which a black sensibility operates on its own terms and within its own self-defined limits, clearly are not so blessed.

5. See, as a case in point, James Lincoln Collier, *The Saga of Jazz: A History* (New York: Henry Holt, 1995).

6. Karl Marx and Frederick Engels, "The German Ideology," in *Collected Works* (Moscow: Progress Publishers, 1976), vol. 5, p. 36.

7. Archie Shepp, "An Artist Speaks Bluntly," *down beat*, December 15, 1965, p. 42.

8. I explore this situation in much greater depth in chapters 1–4 of the companion volume to this one, *Black Music, White Business: Illuminating the History and Political Economy of Jazz* (New York: Pathfinder Press, 1997).

9. "German Ideology," p. 59. To avoid misrepresentation, it is mandatory to insist that, like Marx and Engels, I have been speaking in general terms, and that all generalities about the material universe admit of certain isolated exceptions.

10. See chapter 7 in Kofsky, *Black Music, White Business*.

11. Charlie Parker, for example, had attained his mature style by the time he became a member of the Jay McShann band at age eighteen. Drummer Anthony Williams was a year younger and pianist McCoy Tyner a year older when, at the start of the 1960s, these two musicians joined the groups led by Miles Davis and John Coltrane, respectively. The late trumpeter Lee Morgan played in Dizzy Gillespie's large ensemble when he was still only eighteen. Such a list is virtually endless. The following are only a few of the innovative musicians who were actively performing and recording with top-flight jazz units while still younger than twenty-five: trumpeters Clifford Brown (with Art Blakey, Max Roach), Freddie Hubbard (with Blakey), Booker Little (with Roach), Charles Tolliver (with Jackie McLean), Don Cherry (with Ornette Coleman); saxophonist Archie Shepp; pianists Keith Jarrett (with Charles Lloyd) and Herbie Hancock (with Miles Davis); bassists Paul Chambers (with Davis), Scott LaFaro (with Bill Evans), Eddie Gomez (with Evans), Charlie Haden (with Coleman), Chuck Israels (recorded with ad hoc Cecil Taylor group that included John Coltrane), Reggie Workman (with John Coltrane); vibraharpist Bobby Hutcherson. Gunther Schuller

also points out that in 1933, when Fletcher Henderson took his first group into the recording studio, the *average* age of its members was 22; see *Early Jazz: Its Roots and Musical Development* (New York: Oxford University Press, 1968), p. 254. In the Southwest, "where musicians tended to begin professional life at the age of fourteen or fifteen" (p. 301), it was not unusual for a jazz performer's style to be fully formed before the age of twenty, Charlie Parker being a conspicuous case in point.

12. As was the case with Thelonious Monk and Miles Davis, respectively, in the early 1960s.

13. George Russell, "Popular Delusions and the Madness of Crowds: A Letter from George Russell," *down beat,* April 7, 1966, p. 14; I discuss this letter and the circumstances surrounding it in more detail in chapter 3.

14. Thomas S. Kuhn, *The Structure of Scientific Revolutions* (Chicago: University of Chicago Press, 1964).

15. Karl Marx, "A Contribution to the Critique of Political Economy," in *Collected Works*, vol. 29, p. 263.

16. Thus the dean of this school, Leonard Feather, writes of the new black music of John Coltrane, Cecil Taylor, Archie Shepp, and others, that "what little support" it enjoys "comes from whites; it's not liked in the black community." See "Prestige [Records] Retains Its Independence," *Los Angeles Times*, February 17, 1969, part IV, p. 22. Feather's contention is remarkably similar to that of his colleague and sometimes-employee, Ira Gitler, that the "audience" for the New Black Music—"and a limited one at that—consists mainly of young Caucasians and not their Negro counterparts"; Ira Gitler, "Ira Gitler to Frank Kofsky," letter to the editor, *Jazz*, July 1965, p. 6. Gitler was an assistant to Leonard Feather in compiling *The Encyclopedia of Jazz*, 2nd. rev. ed. (New York: Horizon Press, 1960), according to information on pp. 5–6, and is listed as Feather's co-author of *The Encyclopedia of Jazz in the Seventies* (New York: Horizon Press, 1976).

17. "For the past couple of years [prior to 1969] problems have beset the Manne-Hole. Black patronage inexplicably fell off." Leonard Feather, "Manne-Hole Man Urges Jazz Boost," *Los Angeles Times*, May 12, 1969, part IV, p. 22. Feather to the contrary notwithstand-

ing, there is nothing whatsoever "inexplicable" about the unwillingness of black people to contribute a portion of their hard-earned
incomes to Shelly Manne's well-named "Hole."

18. After these words were already in print in the first edition of
this book, I realized with some chagrin that my metaphor of "dual
citizenship" was merely a restatement of W.E.B. Du Bois's much earlier concept of "the veil" that separates African-Americans from the
white majority; see, for example, Du Bois, *The Souls of Black Folk*, in
Three Negro Classics (New York: Avon Books, 1965), pp. 214–15.

19. Of course, each distinct ethnic or religious group has retained
certain fragments of a culture, but the culture of blacks appears to
be much more intact—a difference in kind rather than degree—
than that of all but the most recent immigrants.

20. See Harold R. Isaacs, *The New World of Negro Americans*,
(New York: Viking Press, 1964).

21. For example, whenever a certain noted black trumpeter performs at the Village Vanguard in New York, the narrow corridor
between the kitchen, where the musicians ordinarily spend their
breaks, and the main room is lined with young white women. As
he returns from the kitchen to resume playing, he makes a point of
bestowing a lingering caress on the posterior of each of those waiting in attendance. The latter can then return to their tables to boast
of their exploits to their less-daring sisters.

22. I treat this contempt in chapters 3 and 4 of *Black Music,
White Business*.

23. See Albert Camus, *The Rebel: An Essay on Man in Revolt*,
rev. trans. Anthony Bower (New York: Knopf, 1971); Frantz Fanon,
Studies in a Dying Colonialism, trans. Haakon Chevalier (New
York: Monthly Review Press, 1965).

24. In building the B–29 bomber during the Second World War,
for instance, the policy of so-called private industry—utterly dependent on payments by the taxpayers that guaranteed a fixed rate
of profits—was to insist that "[f]ew women rose to management,
supervisory, or skilled positions" and that "few African-Americans
were hired except for janitorial or other such work." See Jacob Vander
Meulen, *Building the B–29* (Washington and London: Smithsonian
Institution Press, 1995), pp. 42, 84.

25. As Fred L. Block has noted, "Unemployment averaged 5.9 percent in 1949 and reached a peak of 7.6 percent in February 1950." See Fred L. Block, *The Origins of International Economic Disorder: A Study of United States International Monetary Policy from World War II to the Present* (Berkeley: University of California Press, 1977), p. 93.

26. On which subject see Frank Kofsky, *Harry S. Truman and the War Scare of 1948: A Successful Campaign to Deceive the Nation*, paper ed. (New York: St. Martin's Press, 1995), chapter 8.

27. I argue in an in-progress work that prolonging the Korean War afforded the Truman administration a most welcome opportunity to overcome the persistent trade imbalance ("dollar gap") that since 1945 had frightened the American ruling class with the specter of a return to the depression economy of the 1930s. Eradicating the dollar gap was the sine qua non for maintaining high levels of exports by American multinational industrial and agricultural corporations, and hence for perpetuating U.S. control of the economic and military resources of such dangerous potential industrial competitors and military rivals as West Germany and Japan. Among the mechanisms the Truman administration used to eliminate the dollar gap were *offshore military procurement*—purchases of civilian goods manufactured in Western Europe and Japan by the U.S. Department of Defense—and the *stockpiling of raw materials* (such as tin and rubber) purchased from developing countries (such as Malaysia) that in turn spent the dollars thus earned in Western Europe and/or Japan. On the first of these, see William S. Borden, *The Pacific Alliance: United States Foreign Economic Trade Policy and Japanese Trade Recovery, 1947–1955* (Madison: University of Wisconsin Press, 1984), and "Keynesianism and Military Spending, 1950–1960," a paper read at a conference on Rethinking the Cold War, October 17–20, 1991, at the University of Wisconsin, Madison; on the second, see Andrew J. Rotter, *The Path to Vietnam: Origins of the American Commitment to Southeast Asia* (Ithaca, N.Y.: Cornell University Press, 1987).

28. In the eight years between 1953, when it began, and 1960, white instrumentalists took the top position in the *down beat* critics poll roughly one-half the time; white musicians held first place in seven categories: trombonist Bill Harris (two years); alto saxophon-

ist Lee Konitz (two years); tenor saxophonist Stan Getz (five years); baritone saxophonist Gerry Mulligan (three years); clarinetists Tony Scott (four years), Buddy DeFranco (three years) and Benny Goodman (one year); guitarists Barney Kessel (two years), Jimmy Raney (two years) and Tal Farlow (two years); drummer Buddy Rich (two years). From 1960 to 1966, in contrast, only four white performers were able to win in any of their respective categories: Gerry Mulligan (baritone saxophone), Bill Evans (piano), Jim Hall (guitar), and Pee Wee Russell (clarinet), the last instrument by this time having become marginal in contemporary jazz. Aside from these four exceptions, white artists had been largely dislodged from the top positions in such polls by the 1960s.

White preponderance in polls conducted among the readers of *down beat* during the 1950s (1951–1960, inclusive) was even more pronounced: trumpeters Maynard Ferguson (three years) and Chet Baker (two years); alto saxophonist Paul Desmond (five years); tenor saxophonist Stan Getz (every year); baritone saxophonist Gerry Mulligan (seven years); guitarists Barney Kessel (three years), Les Paul (three years), Billy Bauer (two years) and Johnny Smith (two years); clarinetists Buddy DeFranco (six years), Tony Scott (three years) and Jimmy Giuffre (one year); bassist Eddie Safranski (three years); drummers Shelly Manne (six years) and Gene Krupa (one year); small-band leaders George Shearing (three years) and Dave Brubeck (three years); big-band leader Stan Kenton (five years). See "*down beat* Readers and International Jazz Critics Polls," in *down beat Music '67*, ed. Don DeMicheal (Chicago: Maher Publications, 1967), pp. 41–46.

29. See "Walkin'," Miles Davis, *Miles Davis All-Stars* (Prestige 7076).

30. On which see Abram Kardiner and Lionel Ovesey, *The Mark of Oppression: Explorations in the Personality of the American Negro* (Cleveland: World, 1951), and William H. Grier and Price M. Cobbs, *Black Rage* (New York: Basic Books, 1968).

31. Ernest Mandel, "Contradictions: Where Is America Going?" *Hard Times*, June 2–9, 1969, p. 1.

32. Because, among other reasons, the technology for the production and mass distribution of the phonograph record makes

feasible more-rapid and widespread dissemination of artistic innovations than was possible, until very recently, in the arts of painting (whose works are more costly to reproduce well), sculpture (which is very difficult to reproduce at all), literature (which requires translation to achieve international currency), theatre (which resembles literature), and so forth.

33. Nat Hentoff, review of Tadd Dameron and John Coltrane, *Mating Call* (Prestige 7070), in *down beat Jazz Record Reviews* (hereafter, *db-JRR*), vol. 2, ed. Jack Tracy (Chicago: Maher Publishing, 1958), p. 51.

34. Whitney Balliett, notes to John Lewis, Bill Perkins, and others, *Grand Encounter: 2° East/3° West* (Pacific Jazz 1217). The "hard-bopster" Balliett actually had in mind was J.R. Monterose; the writer had confused Monterose with a different tenor saxophonist, Jack Montrose, whose playing, ironically, embodied all the most anemic tendencies of the West Coast musicians. It is unfortunate for such a fine musician as Bill Perkins that Balliett saw fit to drag him in as a stick with which to beat the accursed hard boppers.

35. Bill Coss, "Small Band in Transition," *Metronome*, March 1958, p. 13. Coss, we shall see in the next chapter, was an ardent participant in *down beat*'s campaign to crush black-nationalist thinking in jazz at the start of the 1960s.

36. According to *The American Heritage Talking Dictionary* on CD-ROM, *funky* is first recorded in 1784 in a reference to musty, old, moldy cheese. *Funky* then developed the sense "smelling strong or bad," which could be used to describe body odor. But *funky* was applied to jazz, too—a usage explained in 1959 by one F. Newton [Eric Hobsbawm] in *The Jazz Scene*: "Critics are on the search for something a little more like the old, original, passion-laden blues: the trade-name which has been suggested for it is 'funky' (literally: 'smelly,' i.e., symbolizing the return from the upper atmosphere to the physical, down-to-earth reality)." *Funky* comes from the earlier noun *funk*, which meant "a strong smell or stink." This noun can probably be traced back to the Latin word *fumus*, "smoke."

37. Miles Davis, for instance, has long been a sartorial trendsetter. Fashions that he inaugurates will soon begin to appear on other musicians, even spilling over into the consumption habits of

youths who are not black. The revival of the double-breasted suit in the 1960s is an excellent case in point: the first such suit I saw worn in that decade draped the figure of the trumpeter during an engagement in San Francisco.

38. The earlier phrase—"race music"—made up in candor what it lacked in subtlety.

39. Randy Weston, *Uhuru Afrika: Freedom Africa* (Roulette 65001); Oliver Nelson, *Afro/American Sketches* (Prestige 7225).

40. Herbert Marcuse, *Reason and Revolution: Hegel and the Rise of Social Theory* (Boston: Beacon Press, 1960).

41. Charles Mingus, ostensibly quoting the short-lived trumpeter Fats Navarro, *Beneath the Underdog: His World as Composed by Mingus* (New York: Bantam Books, 1972), p. 151.

42. There are several versions of this piece, presumably in the same sequence in which they were recorded originally, on Charlie Parker, *The Charlie Parker Story* (Savoy 12079). I don't believe it merely coincidental that Sonny Rollins, whose own foray into the rhetoric of protest I describe in chapter 2, chose to record this composition—and to give the album containing it the same title—during 1964, the year in which the nation's ghettos began to explode and the civil rights movement started to veer in a black-nationalist direction. See Sonny Rollins, *Now's the Time* (MGM 2927).

43. John Hope Franklin, *From Slavery to Freedom: A History of American Negroes*, 2nd rev. ed. (New York: Knopf, 1956), p. 574; see also Franklin's entire chapter 29, "Fighting for the Four Freedoms," pp. 560–90.

44. See on this topic John W. Dower, *War Without Mercy: Race and Power in the Pacific War* (New York: Pantheon, 1986).

45. Richard M. Dalfiume, "The 'Forgotten Years' of the Negro Revolution," in *The Negro in Depression and War: Prelude to Revolution, 1930–1945*, ed. Bernard Sternsher (Chicago: Quadrangle, 1969), p. 299; footnotes in original omitted. Dalfiume's article (pp. 298–315) documents in detail what objective students of the black music of the period have long known—see, for instance, LeRoi Jones, *Blues People: Negro Music in White America* (New York: William Morrow, 1963), pp. 175–202—and is well worth studying. Also useful is the bibliography that Sternsher has compiled for his volume. Dalfiume's thesis

finds further support in a statement from Harold Cruse: "The years between the day I entered the army, and the war's end in 1945, marked the end of an era for Harlem," although "it took a while to understand that World War II represented a very abrupt break, a switchover in the continuity of Harlem traditions." *Crisis*, p. 15.

46. Ira Gitler, "Ira Gitler to Frank Kofsky," letter to the editor in *Jazz*, July 1965, pp. 6–7. The debate over the role and significance of black nationalism in jazz was conducted (with a few exceptions that I will also cite) in the letters column of *Jazz* from the middle of 1965 to the end of 1966. Participating on the side of the negative in addition to Gitler were, among others, critic Martin Williams, director of jazz programming for the United States Information Agency–Voice of America complex Willis Conover, Gene Lees, and Prestige Records producer Don Schlitten, *versus* myself for the affirmative. See "Don Schlitten to Frank Kofsky," *Jazz*, July 1965, p. 7; "Frank Kofsky to Ira Gitler," *Jazz*, September 1965, p. 5; "Martin Williams to Frank Kofsky," *Jazz*, September 1965, pp. 5–6; "Frank Kofsky to Martin Williams," *Jazz*, October 1965, p. 6; "Frank Kofsky to Willis Conover," *Jazz*, November 1965, pp. 6–8; "Ira Gitler to Frank Kofsky," *Jazz*, November 1965, pp. 8–9; "Ira Gitler to [Nat] Hentoff," letter to the editor, *down beat*, September 9, 1965, p. 8 (this is a very important source); Kofsky, "A Reply to My Critics," *Jazz*, January 1966, p. 6; Williams, "The Bystander," *down beat*, June 30, 1966, p. 12; Kofsky, letter to the editor, *Jazz*, October 1966, p. 6, and review of Archie Shepp, *On This Night* (Impulse 97), *Jazz*, November 1966, p. 31, note.

47. Leonard Feather, "Whatever Happened to Beauty—Or, Who Wants Pleasant Music?" in *down beat Music '67*, p. 21.

48. Francis Newton, *The Jazz Scene* (Harmondsworth, Middlesex: Penguin, 1961), pp. 203–205.

49. J.E. Berendt, *Das Jazzbuch*, quoted in Newton, *The Jazz Scene*, p. 205. Note that Hobsbawm (Newton) and Berendt are European, rather than white North American writers. It is thus probably no mere coincidence that they are more perceptive regarding the social origins of jazz, for Europe has long led the United States in producing writers capable of analyzing jazz from either a social or musical standpoint (see, as examples of the latter, the works of André Hodeir and Wilfrid Mellers). Note also Hobsbawm's point apropos

bebop, that "an even more obvious form of revolt against inferiority, which a leading group of the new [bebop] players shared with other Northern big-city Negroes, was mass conversion to Mohammedanism. The new music was played, among others, by Abdullah ibn Buhaina (Art Blakey, the drummer), Sahib Shabab (Edmund Gregory, alto [saxophone]), Abdul Hamid (McKinley [Kenny] Dorham, trumpet . . .), Liaquat Ali Salaam (Kenny Clarke [the first bop drummer]), Ibrahim ibn Ismail (Walter Bishop, Jr., piano) and other sons of the Prophet. . . ." (*The Jazz Scene*, p. 207).

The poet Langston Hughes had his folk character Jesse B. Simple explain bebop as follows:

"Re-Bop certainly sounds like scat to me," I insisted.

"No," said Simple, "Daddy-o, you are wrong. Besides, it was not Re-Bop. It is Be-Bop."

"What's the difference," I asked, "between Re and Be?"

"A lot," said Simple. "Re-Bop was an imitation like most of the white boys play. Be-Bop is the real thing like the colored boys play. . . .

"You must not know where Bop comes from," said Simple, astonished at my ignorance.

"I do not know," I said. "Where?"

"From the police," said Simple.

"What do you mean, from the police?"

"From the police beating Negroes' heads," said Simple. "Every time a cop hits a Negro with his billy club, that old club says, 'BOP! BOP! . . . BE-BOP! . . . MOP! . . . BOP!'

"That Negro hollers, 'Ooool-ya-koo [a Dizzy Gillespie "scat" phrase]! Ou-o-o!'

"Old Cop just keeps on, 'MOP! MOP! . . . BEBOP! . . . MOP!' That's where Be-Bop came from, beaten right out of some Negro's head into them horns and saxophones and piano keys that plays it."

See *The Best of Simple* (New York: Hill and Wang, 1961), pp. 117–18; reprinted by permission of Hill and Wang, Inc.

50. Quoted in Frank Kofsky, "The New Wave: Bob Thiele Talks to Frank Kofsky about John Coltrane," *Coda*, May 1968, p. 4. Creed Taylor produced Coltrane's first recording for Impulse, *Africa/Brass* (Impulse 6), then left the company and was succeeded by Thiele, who remained until after Coltrane's death in 1967.

51. Leslie B. Rout, Jr., "Reflections on the Evolution of Post-War Jazz," *Negro Digest*, February, 1969, pp. 92–93.

52. Art Blakey quoted in Wayne Enstice and Paul Rubin, *Jazz Spoken Here: Conversations with 22 Musicians* (Baton Rouge: Louisiana State University Press, 1992), p. 23

53. Rout, "Reflections," pp. 92–93.

54. Which may be why the subsequent longing for a never-realized "return of the big bands" seems a peculiarly white form of nostalgia, not entirely dissimilar to the Dixieland "revival" of the 1940s. In many respect at opposite poles from the proud, defiant black bebop artists, swing musicians may have been more socially acceptable to a largely white public; that is to say, this public may have viewed black swing performers as relatively more willing to "stay in their place."

55. See as representative examples the narratives of Teddy Blume and Duke Jordan in Robert G. Reisner, *Bird: The Legend of Charlie Parker* (New York: Citadel, 1962), pp. 61–62 and 126, respectively; this work remains, in my opinion, the single most valuable source on Parker. Charles Mingus told Reisner that he "loved the man [Parker] so much" that he "couldn't stand seeing what he was do-ing to himself" through use of heroin and alcohol. As part of an attempt to shake him out of these addictions, Mingus on one oc-casion abruptly confronted Parker with the words, "Bird, you are more than our leader, you are a leader of the Negro race. Don't set a bad example" (pp. 151–52). The effort, of course, ultimately, and not unexpectedly, proved futile.

56. Ross Russell, *Bird Lives! The High Life and Hard Times of Charlie (Yardbird) Parker* (New York: Charterhouse, 1973), pp. 151–52; see also pp. 96, 118, 140–41, 209 for more material on Parker's overt resistance to racism. In spite of having been published more than a decade after Reisner's study, Russell's volume adds disappointingly little to what we know from the former, apart from some bootless

pseudo-psychoanalytical speculations and an unfailing fixation on the lurid. Its subject deserves better.

57. Art Blakey's description of this incident is in Reisner, *Bird,* p. 51; see also Russell, *Bird Lives,* pp. 159–60.

58. Hawes quoted in Russell, *Bird Lives,* p. 324.

59. Quoted, for instance, in Reisner, *Bird,* p. 27.

60. I explore these implications in greater depth in the first chapter of *Black Music, White Business.*

61. Richard Wright, *Native Son* (New York: Harper & Row, 1966).

62. See Eldridge Cleaver, *Soul on Ice* (New York: Dell, 1968), pp. 3–17; Ralph Ellison, *The Invisible Man* (New York: Signet Books, 1952).

63. Russell, *Bird Lives,* pp. 140–41.

64. Even at that, speaking out isn't always so easy. Bill Dixon, who, with Taylor and Shepp, is easily twice as literate as most professors I know—Dixon and Shepp, appropriately enough, have since *become* academicians themselves—states that "both *down beat* and the old *Metronome* rejected articles that I'd written"; see his article, "Bill Dixon," *Sounds and Fury,* July–August 1965, p. 39. Writer Robert Levin similarly relates that an article of his on the Jazz Composers Guild for *down beat* had some remarks of Cecil Taylor on the subject of organizing black musicians removed, supposedly on the grounds that Taylor's words "veered away from the subject of the Guild"! See "Some Observations on the State of the Scene," *loc. cit.,* p. 6. Archie Shepp, too, reports an attempt in 1965 by Don DeMicheal, the *down beat* editor responsible for traducing Levin's story on the Jazz Composers Guild, to persuade the saxophonist to excise certain favorable references to Ho Chi Minh and Fidel Castro from an article he had written for the publication; see the partial transcript of a discussion among Archie Shepp, Cecil Taylor, Rahsaan Roland Kirk, and others, "Point of Contact," in Don DeMicheal, ed., *down beat Music '66* (Chicago: Maher Publications, 1966), p. 110. I examine the issue of political censorship by jazz magazines at some length in chapter 3.

Part 2

The society, the critic

2

The forerunners resist establishment repression, 1958–1963

This chapter recounts the efforts of four black artists—saxophonist Sonny Rollins, composer and bassist Charles Mingus, and drummer and composer Max Roach, acting in conjunction with his former wife, singer Abbey Lincoln—to take and hold positions on the role of black people and black artists in U.S. society that went beyond what was acceptable to the jazz Establishment in the late 1950s and early 1960s. In all three cases (treating that of Roach and Abbey Lincoln together), the Establishment reacted with utmost rapidity by trying to choke off these impermissible ideas at the source; and in the two most serious cases, moreover, attempts at suppression were accompanied by tactics designed to ostracize, intimidate, and "black-bait" the recipients.[*]

---

[*] By analogy with red-baiting, which strives to discredit certain concepts by attributing "Communist" origins to them, black-baiting aims at the same ends by accusing individuals of being "professional Negroes," "Crow Jim," "black supremacists," et cetera, and by denouncing their

Having already made mention of the white Establishment in jazz, it will be useful if, by way of further clarification, I say a bit more on the subject. I use the phrase "the jazz Establishment" to refer to those individuals who own everything worth owning—with the possible exception of the instruments of the musicians themselves—in this particular artistic arena. The term, in other words, denotes the booking agents, concert and festival promoters, recording company executives, radio-station and nightclub owners, musical instrument manufacturers and, not least, editors and publishers who, collectively, control the political economy of jazz. The mechanism for exerting this control is one of admirable simplicity: members of the jazz Establishment can force the great majority of artists to abide by the Establishment's unwritten rules merely by denying the opportunity to perform in public and/or to have their music recorded and distributed to those few stubborn souls who violate the code.

Consider, by way of illustration, the fate of Abbey Lincoln, one of the four individuals who, at the start of the 1960s, espoused political ideas that the jazz Establishment considered dangerously heretical. Much in demand as a performer prior to 1962, when her infection with the malignancy of black nationalism at the hands of her husband, Max Roach, caused her to be mercilessly castigated in the pages of *down beat*, Abbey Lincoln witnessed her career in music plummet into obscurity immediately thereafter. Almost two full decades would elapse before any recording company in the United States would again consent to release an album of her singing. Power to control whether individuals can find employment is power indeed. The jazz Establishment does not lack for it, as Abbey Lincoln can readily attest.[1]

---

ideas as "racism-in-reverse," "self-segregation," "anti-Caucasian prejudice," and the like. All of these endearments, or their near-equivalents, will figure in the discussion that follows.

Mention of *down beat* in the preceding paragraph leads to a second point regarding the jazz Establishment: its ideology is disseminated—and, if necessary, departures from that ideology are condemned—primarily by this publication. Started in the 1930s as a magazine devoted to popular music, by the postwar period *down beat* had evolved into a periodical whose focus was almost exclusively on jazz. Because of both its relative size and its longevity in a field where the quick demise is an almost-universal rule, *down beat*'s influence in the world of jazz is preeminent. From 1961 to his death in 1967, for example, John Coltrane's several dozen recordings for Impulse Records were produced by Bob Thiele. Faced with the kind of exceedingly destructive criticism from *down beat* that I will treat in greater detail below, Thiele at one point during his association with Coltrane was sufficiently shaken that he urged the artist to beat a tactical retreat and make three complete albums of more conventional material. "Yes," the executive later explained, these recordings

> were all my ideas and John Coltrane accepted them. . . . In those days, what *down beat* said with respect to sales of records wrongly affected record people. . . . Here I was, working for a record company and concerned about how well our records would sell, and we have a [*down beat*] critic [Ira Gitler] who comes along and says John Coltrane's records are windy, flat and need editing, et cetera, or whatever he said. I have done my best to forget what he ever said, but at the time he registered, and I figured we had better go in and see if we can get John to do some melodic things, do some standard tunes. . . . [S]o in a way, it was my idea through Ira Gitler, if you get the message.[2]

That *down beat* was able to sway so notoriously resolute an artist as John Coltrane to the point where he was willing to modify his style and repertoire even temporarily offers potent testimony to the weight that this magazine's words carry in the narrow confines of jazz.

To complete these preliminary observations, we need to understand at least some of the numerous connections that bind *down beat* to the jazz Establishment, rendering the former into what can accurately be regarded as the house organ of the latter. In the late 1950s and early 1960s as now, *down beat* was dependent on its largest advertisers, the manufacturers of musical instruments and recordings, for the bulk of its revenues.[3] The link between the magazine and the larger U.S. jazz festivals, booking agents, and so on, is more subtle but no less real. Senior editors, for instance, regularly sit on the boards of directors of these festivals, serve as masters of ceremonies at them, and receive fees for essays that appear in their printed programs. Not infrequently, a *down beat* representative will take the opportunity that a festival stage provides to present an award from the magazine to one or more of the musicians performing there. Nor is it out of the ordinary for the festival's management to pay for all or part of the expenses for food and lodging for a *down beat* staff member in attendance, supposedly to "review" the musical proceedings, at one of these resort-and-vacation areas.[4] In innumerable ways great and small, then, the editors of this periodical come to look at matters from a perspective that is essentially identical with that of the festival executives, concert promoters, booking agents, and others of that ilk. An attack on one, as we shall shortly observe from the hysterical diatribes launched by the magazine's editors against Charles Mingus, Max Roach, and Abbey Lincoln, is invariably perceived as an attack on all.

And never more so than when the attack raises the question of the black origins and creation of jazz as music *versus* the white domination of jazz as business. For what unites the diverse members of the jazz Establishment above all else is precisely the awareness that the leading innovators of jazz have always been black, whereas ownership of the music—of the places where it can be played, that is, and of the channels through which it is distributed—has always gone to enrich whites. If this is the dirty little secret—the fundamental contradiction, if you will—on which the political economy of jazz ultimately rests, it is the unspoken but no less fervent desire of the jazz Establishment that things remain just as they are: the more secret, the better.

From which it follows, of course, that an artist who threatens to disclose that secret, who even dares to allude to it in public, is asking for trouble. And this is true, moreover, regardless of how innocuous or veiled the intimation. For that matter, some members of the jazz Establishment are so apprehensive about the precarious equilibrium that enables them to enjoy their wealth and power that they oppose on principle the slightest hint by any jazz musician, under any circumstance whatsoever, that this might not be the best of all possible worlds for black people in general and/or the artist himself in particular.

With that thought we arrive at the case of Sonny Rollins. In 1958, the saxophonist recorded an album on the Riverside label entitled *Freedom Suite,* one entire side of which was entirely taken up by the composition of that name. The front cover of the album, presumably in keeping with the motif of freedom, displayed a medium-sized (3 5/8 inch by 4 5/8 inch) photograph of Rollins's face and unclothed upper torso, as if he were posing to have a bust of himself sculpted. On the reverse side of the album jacket, set in a black-bordered box, was a 53–word statement (that I will reproduce in full momentarily), in which the saxophonist sought to point out, in relatively bland and unexceptionable language, that although Afro-American contributions were at the base of this country's popular culture, black people themselves were still "being persecuted and repressed." These two sentences by Rollins, however, were all but overwhelmed by the notes to the album—a virtual sea of equivocations and circumlocutions taking up about 1,500 words and almost three entire columns of print—by one of Riverside's two owners, Orrin Keepnews. As if that were not enough, moreover, shortly after its release, the *Freedom Suite* recording was mysteriously withdrawn from the Riverside catalog with no further explanation volunteered—only to reappear after a brief interval with a new album jacket and a new name, *Shadow Waltz*. Inasmuch as "Shadow Waltz" was the title of the second shortest of the five selections on the album—four minutes, eight seconds, compared to the more than nineteen minutes of "Freedom Suite"—I am sure that I was not the only spectator who found these goings-on baffling, to say the least.

Through an unanticipated stroke of good luck, I had an opportunity to suggest in the notes to yet a third release of an album containing Sonny Rollins's "Freedom Suite"—one that improved upon its immediate predecessor by bearing the name the composer had all along intended—that the original owners of Riverside had regarded the cover and title of the first *Freedom Suite* recording as too controversial and inflammatory, and had therefore quickly pulled it off the market, reissuing the same selections under the designation *Shadow Waltz* once the initial furor had died down.[5] A subsequent chance meeting with Orrin Keepnews afforded me an opportunity to verify my hypothesis. Keepnews claimed that my interpretation was not correct. *Freedom Suite* had been withdrawn solely because it was not selling well, he maintained, and it was re-released subsequently as *Shadow Waltz* in hopes that it would do better in the new format.[6]

Insofar as concerns his *conscious* motivation, I am, of course, unable to offer conclusive evidence that would refute Keepnews's claim. It is well known, however, that the conscious motive for an action is not necessarily the sole one, nor even the most important; it is also a commonplace that people frequently speak and act without full awareness of the underlying reasons that have driven them to do so. What is more, having spent some three decades as a practicing historian specializing in exploring the contradiction between the public rhetoric and private sentiments of high government officials, I think I have developed a fairly reliable intuition in these matters.[7] Accordingly, I continue to believe that my initial explanation of why the first recording of *Freedom Suite* was deleted from the Riverside catalog is probably the correct one. I also contend that, for a variety of reasons, it would be awkward and embarrassing for Orrin Keepnews, the surviving owner of the original Riverside operation, were he in any way forced to concede this point—even, perhaps, to himself.* In view of these circumstances, one can hardly expect him to come forward of his own volition and make an open confession of culpability. Such things simply do not happen in the real world inhabited by hardheaded jazz businessmen.

Even without such a confession, however, there is more than enough evidence from other sources to suggest what was Keepnews's own state of mind when he and his partner released the initial version of *Freedom Suite*. It is surely significant, to begin with, that no other instance of a Riverside album being given the treatment visited upon *Freedom Suite* has ever come to light, nor has there ever been another Sonny Rollins recording, regardless of label—and his music has appeared on at least half a dozen—to be removed from circulation so abruptly. These facts strongly suggest that

---

* Such an admission, especially if made publicly, would certainly exacerbate Keepnews's relations with such highly political black jazz musicians as McCoy Tyner and Joe Henderson—to say nothing of Rollins himself—whose more recent albums he has produced for Fantasy/Prestige/Milestone Records.

the decision to recall *Freedom Suite* involved considerations much more convoluted than the simple bookkeeper's reasoning that Keepnews later invoked by way of justification.

Second, it is instructive to contrast the statement that Sonny Rollins prepared for the album jacket of the *Freedom Suite* recording with excerpts from the notes that Keepnews wrote to accompany Rollins's terse remarks. A juxtaposition of the two reveals more than a little about Keepnews's reaction to the modest Rollins manifesto. The latter, quoted in full, reads: "America is deeply rooted in Negro culture: Its colloquialisms, its humor, its music. How ironic that the Negro, who more than any other people can claim America's culture as his own, is being persecuted and repressed, that the Negro, who has exemplified the humanities in his very existence, is being rewarded with inhumanity."

Rollins's declaration is quite straightforward and, in the thinking of most people at any rate, would seem to make it amply clear what his purpose was in titling his composition "Freedom Suite." Nonetheless, Keepnews went to some lengths to "explain" that Rollins didn't really mean it after all, ladies and gentleman, and no one should get nervous just because a black musician had seen fit to refer to the persecution and repression of his people on the back of an album cover. That the suite was about freedom even Keepnews had to acknowledge, but he made sure to couple that concession with the first of many evasions: "just as that one word itself means many things, so does its application here have many facets." Keepnews continued with a second masterful stroke, a passage as vague and meaningless as it was slippery and euphemistic: "In one sense, then, the reference is to the musical freedom of this unusual combination of composition and improvisation; in another it is to physical and moral freedom, to the presence and absence of it in Sonny's own life and in the way of life of other Americans to whom he feels a relationship." Presumably, those "other Americans" to whom Rollins "feels a relationship"—one looks in vain for the slightest trace of candor here—were, like the artist himself, black. But having thus ventured up to the water's edge, Keepnews immediately thereafter scurried back, denying out of one side of his mouth what he had just hinted from the other: "This is not a piece *about* Emmett Till, or Little Rock, or Harlem, or the peculiar local election laws of Georgia or Louisiana. . . ." And so on.

While the choice between the interpretation proffered by Keepnews and the one I have advanced must, of course, reside with the reader, I would be remiss if I did not point out the aftermath of this incident: given Keepnews's pusillanimous sabotage from above of the saxophonist's clearly proclaimed intentions, it was perhaps not altogether surprising that *Freedom Suite* turned out to be Sonny Rollins's last recording for Riverside.[8]

Unlike the case with Sonny Rollins, there was no single dramatic event that highlighted bassist Charles Mingus's collision with the white Establishment in jazz. There were, rather, a whole series of running conflicts, some of them quite explosive indeed, between Mingus and the self-appointed representatives of this Establishment. As was also true of Max Roach, whom I will discuss next, Mingus's various groups were a haven for young jazz iconoclasts—Eric Dolphy, John Handy, Rahsaan Roland Kirk, Booker Ervin, Joe Farrell, Jackie McLean, and J.R. Monterose, among the reed players; brass instrumentalists Ted Curson, Richard Williams and Jimmy Knepper; pianists Jaki Byard, Horace Parlan, Roland Hanna, Mal Waldron, and Paul Bley; and drummer Dannie Richmond, to mention only some—most of whom have since gone on (or, like Eric Dolphy, would have gone on had they lived) to illustrious careers. Yet it was not because of his musical daring that Mingus fell afoul of The Powers That Be. His heterodoxy in music could be tolerated, albeit sometimes uneasily; what could not was his insistence

on obtaining a full measure of equity for black people—
starting, logically enough, with Charles Mingus. Even in
the late 1950s, the bassist had gained a reputation among
critics for being anti-white,[9] and I myself, along with what
I assume to be other white writers, have been the recipient
of letters from him whose contents and style could only be
described as blistering.[10]

Until the 1960s, however, Mingus seems to have confined
himself entirely to verbal protests.* But the late 1950s and
early 1960s, as I argue throughout this volume, witnessed
a new determination among black musicians, and Mingus
was bound to be in the forefront of those affected. Thus it
was that a group of dissident black musicians led by Min-

---

* One aspect of these verbal protests was Mingus's smuggling of Aesopian allegories against racism and white-supremacist ideology into
the notes to his recording. Thus, his composition "Pithecanthropus
Erectus" (on the album of the same name, Atlantic 1237)

> depicts musically my conception of the modern counterpart of the
> first man to stand erect—how proud he was, considering himself
> the "first" to ascend from all fours, pounding his chest and preach-
> ing his superiority over the mammals still in a prone position.
> Overcome with self-esteem, he goes out to rule the world, if not
> the universe, but both his own failure to realize the inevitable
> emancipation of those he sought to enslave, and his greed in at-
> tempting to stand on a false security, deny him not only the right
> of ever being a man, but finally destroy him completely.

One doesn't require the services of a cryptographer to decipher the
fable.

Similarly, Mingus's composition "Haitian Fight Song" could just as
well be called "Afro-American Fight Song."

> . . . My solo in it is a deeply concentrated one. I can't play it right
> unless I'm thinking about prejudice and hate and persecution, and
> how unfair it is. There's sadness in it, but also determination. And
> it usually ends with my feeling: "I told them! I hope somebody
> heard me" [quoted in the notes to Charles Mingus, *The Clown:
> The Charles Mingus Jazz Workshop* (Atlantic 1260)].

gus and drummer Max Roach in July 1960 undertook the presentation of a musicians' festival to run in direct competition with the Newport Jazz Festival—an operation as deferential to non-jazz entertainers like Frank Sinatra as it was hostile to innovative figures like Mingus, Eric Dolphy, and Ornette Coleman.

The response of the jazz press was predictable. That year, the editor of *down beat*, Gene Lees, happened to be in attendance at the Newport Festival. Even Lees himself had to acknowledge that Mingus had for the past several years yielded to the pleas of festival officials and played "for them cheap, on the grounds that they were just starting. . . . As the years went by and the festival grew commercially more successful, Mingus continued playing the event but, he said, always for meager remuneration. Why wasn't he getting the money other groups were commanding?" The question was a good one, and most fair-minded, dispassionate observers probably would have agreed that it deserved pursuing, especially as Mingus was then the premier bass virtuoso in jazz.

Ah, but that is not how the journalistic minions of the white jazz Establishment think. Lees's outraged polemic against the musicians' counter-festival was almost apoplectic in tone and drenched in vitriol, with Mingus singled out for particular abuse. Twice in his article on the Newport events, for example, Lees implied that the bassist was afflicted with delusions: "Somehow, Mingus saw in the festival a symbol of all those forces opposing him, keeping him from his rightful recognition. . . . Somehow, Mingus seemed to think, Newport was to blame for all his troubles [so] he decided to start his own Newport festival."

Never one to hesitate to assume the White Man's Burden, Lees also took it on his own to lecture Mingus—in the most patronizing manner possible, of course—regarding the sacred nature of the ground rules in a capitalist politi-

cal economy: "Mingus apparently could not understand that
the law of supply and demand, as deplorable as it may be,
operates as inexorably in art as it does in business. A writer
who is in demand can command excellent deals; one who is
not is forced to take what he can get. . . . The same is true
in painting—and in jazz." In similar fashion, Lees airily
dismissed, without so much as a pretense of an impartial
investigation, Mingus's even more serious "charge that the
regular Newport festival was Jim Crow." In every conceivable way, Lees made it evident that in his eyes the matter
was as simple as black and white: Mingus, the black artist,
was completely in the wrong and probably deranged in the
bargain; Newport, the white-owned, white-operated jazz
festival, was innocent of all accusations and as pure as the
proverbial driven snow.[11]

The musicians' counter-festival led by Charles Mingus
and Max Roach at Newport in July 1960 was of signal importance for two reasons. On the one hand, Gene Lees's savage
and senseless attack on Mingus—of which there was much
more yet to come—illustrated the fate that might befall a
black jazz musician who refused to accept exploitation and/
or white-liberal racism with passivity. On the other, though,
the ability of this group of black musicians to produce a successful festival of their own evidently boosted the morale
of the participants. More than that, the counter-festival
brought together and cemented an alliance between the
most resolute activists of the bebop revolution, Max Roach
and Charles Mingus, and like-minded younger black artists,
such as saxophonist Ornette Coleman, who would assume
leading roles in the next upheaval in jazz, then just a speck
on the horizon. This alliance took on formal structure in
a new organization, the Jazz Artists Guild, established as
an outgrowth of the counter-festival.[12] Although the Guild
proved to be relatively short-lived, those who are familiar
with developments in the jazz world later in the 1960s will

doubtless recognize in it the precursor of the Jazz Composers Guild organized by Bill Dixon, Cecil Taylor, Archie Shepp and others midway through that same decade. The result was to assure that the work begun by one generation would be continued by the next.[13]

The other consequence of the musician's counter-festival at Newport—Gene Lees's vendetta against Charles Mingus— was of a distinctly uglier nature. A few weeks after the initial assault, Lees returned to the anti-Mingus offensive with redoubled vigor, this time using his prerogatives as an editor in an attempt to throw the full weight of *down beat* into the fray. Although Mingus was nowhere mentioned by name, it is clear both from the general context of Lees's harangue (published fewer than eight weeks after his account of the Newport events) and from internal evidence that the bassist was the primary target of these venomous fulminations.

The subject of this second splenetic outburst, which was even more hysterical and vituperative than its predecessor, was "prejudiced Negroes," with whom the editor had "lost patience." It was, Lees maintained, these biased blacks who were to blame for the "melancholy phenomenon of discrimination against white musicians." By discrimination, it developed, Lees did not have in mind the exclusion of white musicians from employment opportunities, but rather what he termed an "anti-Caucasian feeling [that] manifests itself in a tendency to belittle the playing of white musicians on grounds that they 'just don't swing.'" It was impossible for Lees to conceive that there could be any rational, factual basis for such a statement: "No matter how you slice it, that's racism." The coup de grâce, patently aimed at Charles Mingus and those who shared his beliefs, was unleashed in a stream of language that, even by Lees's standards, was unusually inflamed: "I'm getting tired of hearing certain Negro musicians, *obviously paranoiac*, claim that white musicians have stolen from the Negro and given nothing—almost as tired as I am of the views of Herman Talmadge and his ilk [my emphasis]. The playing of some of the cruder funk-merchants shows the impoverishment that can occur when separatism is sought."[14]

This parting shot—like most of the editorial, for that matter—was a complete *non sequitur*. Isn't it indeed the case, as I have sought to establish in chapter 1 on the basis of incontrovertible evidence, that the great majority of white (and other non-African-American) musicians are of necessity *compelled* to "steal" (the choice of verbs is Lees's, not mine) their fundamental inspiration and approach from black performers if they hope to master the music?[15] Is there, in reality, any *other* source on which they can draw, any other models on which to pattern themselves, so far as jazz is concerned? And does it, then, make the least bit of sense to equate—as Lees was so quick to do—musicians who point out these elementary facts of life with die-hard segregationists such as "Herman Talmadge and his ilk"?

As for "the cruder funk-merchants" allegedly illustrating the "impoverishment that can occur when separatism is sought," this concept is so ridiculously tangled and confused as to be near-impossible to unsnarl. Insofar as there were any black musicians then espousing "separatism," none of them could by any stretch of the imagination have been lumped with the "cruder funk-merchants," a reference that I assume Lees meant to apply to such musicians as pianists Les McCann and Ramsey Lewis, the Three Sounds group, and the like. The very popular "funk-merchants," for their part, were at the crest of their drawing power at the time, performing for, and selling records to, sizable black and white audiences; accordingly, they manifested only the greatest public indifference towards separatism, political black nationalism, overt protest movements, or any other -ism that threatened to "separate" them from their large and integrated followings. To mix the two groups in this fashion, was, from the standpoint of logic, completely impermissible. But then, logic, like truth, was an early casualty once Lees had launched himself on his holy crusade against those "prejudiced Negroes."

What made Lees's polemics especially reprehensible, however, was not just the eagerness of their author to play fast and loose with matters of both fact and reason, great though it was. Even more serious, in my opinion, was his evident willingness to allow racist practices that actually were (or are) directed at black musicians to go unchallenged, instead devoting the energies of himself and the magazine over which he presided to lunatic flailings at such chimeras as "prejudiced Negroes," "obviously paranoiac" black musicians, and "anti-Caucasian feelings." At the same moment that Lees was inveighing against these monumental evils, Southern audiences were still segregated by color; integrated groups were being denied Southern bookings; black musicians and performers of less than premier ("star") rank were excluded from first-class accommodations when playing many Northern cities (Las Vegas was a prime offender in this regard); television, film, and radio studio employment continued to be almost entirely closed to black artists, as were positions in symphony orchestras; and the list could be extended with little effort. All of these practices were, by any rational standard, monstrous injustices whose abolition, already long overdue, ought to have been made *the* order of the day. Yet when *down beat*, under Lees's leadership, ultimately did get around to an article on "Jazz in Hollywood Studios," there was not even a hint of these studios' ubiquitous discrimination against black artists and composers, and the word "Negro" (much less "black") was nowhere to be found therein.[16] To Gene Lees, and to those who controlled *down beat*, it was patently more important to hammer away in print at those black musicians whose deportment showed even the slightest trace of "getting out of line"—the line, naturally, being defined by *down beat*—than it was to combat segregation, discrimination, and other forms of white racism.

This point was underlined once more when, shortly after the appearance of Lees's second thrust at Mingus & Company, Leonard Feather undertook to survey "The Racial Undercurrent" in the *down beat* yearbook edited by Lees. Just as *down beat* was the most influential magazine in the world of jazz, Leonard Feather, through his syndicated newspaper column, was probably the most widely read author. Hence on the off chance that some members of the jazz public had failed to absorb Lees's previous messages, Feather—who has consistently distinguished himself by his zeal to campaign against any and all forms of black nationalism—threw his prestige into the fray in order to discredit the dangerous desperadoes who dared to espouse such views.

Feather's "Racial Undercurrent" article bore all the usual hallmarks of *down beat*'s earlier pronouncements, including the familiar assertion (printed in large type above the body of the article) that "in recent times an equally disturbing factor has emerged—discrimination against the white jazz man."[17] No white jazz musician had been, say, denied employment in a New York or Hollywood studio due to an insufficiency of skin pigmentation, but this alleged "discrimination against the white jazz man" was "equally disturbing" nonetheless—at least to Gene Lees.

And to Leonard Feather as well, to judge from his comments. Firmly aligning himself with his colleague, Feather proceeded directly to the point:

The Negro musician's increased sensitivity [to racism] has led to his finding refuge at times in less desirable solutions. In the last year or two, as Gene Lees reported in a *down beat* editorial Oct. 13, 1960, there has been an alarming upsurge of anti-white prejudice. Much of this feeling has found its outlet in the conversion of Negro

THE FORERUNNERS RESIST REPRESSION / 139

musicians to Islam, symbolically a repudiation of the white man's culture and religion. . . .

Not only that, Feather charged, but black nationalists had given "unmistakable evidence of anti-Semitism as well as anti-white hatred." Yet if an "increased sensitivity" to racist affronts and oppression was at bottom the cause of the "alarming upsurge of anti-white prejudice" that he claimed to be able to discern, Feather's proposed solution was notable for the lack of attention it paid to that cause. Rather than treat the disease, the critic preferred instead to focus on the symptom: "It seems to me," Feather wrote, "that what jazz, and society in general, could use at this critical point in history is less black nationalism. . . . The nationalistic movement has in it too much that is reminiscent of Marcus Garvey's back-to-Africa campaign of the 1920s, a form of voluntary self-Jim-Crowing [!] that accomplished nothing but a widening of the breaches."[18]

What was the effect of all of these preachments and proclamations on one of their primary targets, bassist Charles Mingus? My own estimate is that, as I trust the following paragraphs on the work of Max Roach and Abbey Lincoln will demonstrate, those black musicians who were disgruntled with their situation in jazz were not intimidated into silence by the pressures that Establishment propagandists like Lees and Feather brought to bear. Mingus himself, at any rate, does not appear to have been shaken in his determination to accept nothing less than his due, as he conceived it. Not too long after this barrage from the guns of the doyens of white jazz criticism, and in spite of renewed attacks on him in the jazz press,[19] Mingus established a company to sell albums of his own music so that he would no longer have to suffer the fate of a powerless black pawn in the white-controlled jazz-recording game.[20] And then—Mingus disappeared.

In his fictionalized autobiography ("some names . . . have

been changed and some of the characters and incidents are fictitious"), *Beneath the Underdog*, Mingus has Fats Navarro—a trumpet player of the bebop era who, perhaps significantly, had died at a very young age and was therefore unable to suffer reprisals *or* to contradict the bassist—say, "They shut you up and cheat you on the count of your record sales and if you go along they tell the world you a real genius. But if you don't . . . they put out the word you're a troublemaker, like they did me. Then if some honest club owner tries to get hold of you to book you, they tell [the owner] you're not available or you don't draw or you'll tear up the joint like you was a gorilla. And you won't hear nothing about it except by accident."[21]

Was this what had happened to Mingus himself? As could have been anticipated, the jazz press, which supposedly had the responsibility for turning up an answer, displayed not the least glimmer of interest in pursuing the question (evidently, *down beat*'s editors considered Mingus "news" only when they could sniff scandal in the offing). In 1969, however, with as little warning as when he had vanished, Mingus suddenly turned up and again began performing in public—and, by a bit of good fortune, I was able to put the question to him directly during that great rarity, an engagement on the West Coast (San Francisco, October 1969). In our conversation, Mingus repeatedly came back in particular to the booking agents as those whose ill will had kept him from working. One thus surmises that the bitter but not inaccurate description of conditions in jazz for black musicians that Mingus attributes to Fats Navarro probably owes as much to the former as the latter; it is, I suspect, a leaf directly out of the book of Mingus's own interrupted career. The interruptions, like the withdrawal of Sonny Rollins's *Freedom Suite* from circulation by Riverside Records and the harassments inflicted upon Max Roach and Abbey Lincoln by white critics (a subject I will discuss directly below), have for years stood—as they were no doubt intended to stand—as a series of object lessons for any black musician so rash as to voice a nationalist or other radical ideology, so foolhardy as to contend in public that the white Establishment rules through anything less than Divine Right.

Max Roach is the link that connects the three sides of the triangle Rollins-Mingus-Roach. It was in the quintet co-led by Roach and the late trumpeter Clifford Brown that Sonny Rollins first rose to national prominence as a saxophone innovator of significance; it may have been in this group as well that Rollins was encouraged to continue thinking in the direction that ultimately led to the ideas expressed in—and on the cover of—his *Freedom Suite* album; and it is probably not mere coincidence that the drummer Rollins chose to accompany him in recording the suite was none other than Max Roach. Roach also collaborated with Charles Mingus—the two men had known each other since their youthful days as pioneers in the development of bebop—in organizing the 1960 musicians' counter-festival at Newport and thereafter in the formation of the Jazz Artists Guild. At the time the single most unabashedly radical black nationalist in jazz, Max Roach was the common thread binding together this triumvirate of earliest overtly active rebels against white domination within and without the realm of music.

Thereafter, however, aside from a very occasional recording, Roach, much like Charles Mingus, was missing from the jazz circuit during the late 1960s and most of the 1970s—again, with no explanation either sought or offered by the jazz press. It is reasonable to infer that much of the responsibility for this state of affairs lies with the white-critical response to a pair of recordings that Roach and singer Abbey Lincoln, then husband and wife, made for the Candid label at the start of the 1960s. Release of these two albums—*We Insist! The Freedom Now Suite* (1960), followed by a record under Abbey Lincoln's name, *Straight Ahead* (1961)[22]—surely marks a turning point in the historical evolution of political black nationalism in jazz, for both espoused something close to what was at the time the dominant strain of that ideology, the separatist philosophy of Elijah Muhammad and the Nation of Islam. (Rumors circulated that Roach and Lincoln were members of the Nation, but to my knowledge these were never confirmed.) So explosive, indeed, were they that while all the other albums recorded by the now-defunct Candid firm were re-released during the early 1970s, it took a full two decades before the U.S. recording industry was able to work up sufficient courage to issue *We Insist!* a second time. By then, of course, its status was that of a classic (a development to which I like to think the discussion of this electrifying work in chapter 1 of the first edition of this book made some small contribution).

The aftermath of these recordings was a genuine tempest in a teapot, a "scandal" whose proportions were sufficient to rock the provincial world of jazz—or rather, the provincial world of its white critics—from one end to the other. For just as Charles Mingus in 1960 and subsequently had sought to translate the sentiments expressed by Sonny Rollins on the notes to *Freedom Suite* into concrete deeds, Roach and Lincoln were now attempting to make explicit the political nationalist thinking that was implicit in Mingus's own protest activities. The white counteroffensive against this manifest growth of black-nationalist ideas in jazz was led, predictably, by *down beat*. More specifically, at the head of the anti-black-nationalist parade marched the magazine's new editor, Don DeMicheal, and one of its principal writers, Ira Gitler, whose views can nearly always be assumed to be identical with those of his frequent employer, Leonard Feather.[23] By way of further reinforcement, Feather himself, who, at the behest of *down beat*'s editors had struck the final blow against Charles Mingus in the magazine's previous anti-nationalism crusade, performed a similar service at the close of this one as well. It bears reemphasizing at this point that the amount of space and energy wasted by *down beat* in its effort to suppress black nationalism in jazz by denouncing it as "Crow Jim," "reverse racism," and the like, greatly exceeded that ever devoted to any of the social evils that actually did plague the music, such as the myriad types of discriminatory treatment to which black musicians are continually subjected.

The opening salvo in *down beat*'s anti-nationalist campaign was unleashed by Ira Gitler, in the guise of a review of Abbey Lincoln's *Straight Ahead* recording. Here, Gitler charged the singer with being "misguided and naive," and asserted that her "only trouble is that she has become a 'professional Negro'"—whatever that might be. "Pride in one's heritage is one thing," pontificated Gitler, in tones reminiscent of *down beat*'s previous resident white missionary to the Afro-Americans, Gene Lees, "but *we* don't need the Elijah Muhammed [*sic*] type of thinking in jazz" (emphasis added). Gitler didn't feel it worth the trouble to define just who this "we" might be.[24]

Round Two consisted of an inquisitorial panel convoked by *down beat* in an effort to browbeat or intimidate the heretics into a recantation. The composition of the panel alone suffices to suggest the intentions of its sponsors: arrayed against the two isolated black artists, Max Roach and Abbey Lincoln, were no fewer than six white males—four critics, including, in addition to Gitler, the editor and associate editor of *down beat* (Don DeMicheal and Bill Coss, respectively), and two white musicians (trumpeter Don Ellis, pianist and composer Lalo Schifrin).[25]

Max Roach attempted at the outset to turn the tables on his assailants by arguing that, in the words of *down beat*, "it was one of the roles of the jazz magazines to make people aware of bad conditions in jazz instead of 'tearing up individual artists.'" Significantly, if not surprisingly, that thoughtful observation was simply ignored by the white participants, and the editors of *down beat* found it so little worthy of note that this portion of the discussion was excised from the published transcript altogether.[26] From this inauspicious beginning, matters rapidly degenerated into the usual series of accusations howled at outspoken black nationalists by Establishment attorneys within jazz. Gitler defended the contents of his review, again asserting that Abbey Lincoln "was leaning too much on her Negritude in this album."[27] Don DeMicheal objected to Abbey Lincoln's characterization of all art as propaganda ("I don't believe this") and disagreed even more strenuously with Max Roach's statistically unassailable statement, "if a guy wants a *good* jazz player, nine times out of ten he stands a better chance of getting him from the black population than from the white *because of exposure*" (second emphasis mine).[28] Don Ellis, also seemingly affronted by such a notion, tried to discredit Roach and Lincoln with the charge "you are giving ammunition to the whole thing of racial prejudice."[29] This brought Ira Gitler back to one of his most abiding preoccupations—the white jazz musician. "[A] lot of young Negro guys," he alleged, without offering evidence, "won't buy [a white musician's] records *because he's white*" (my emphasis).[30] Don Ellis took the opportunity this opening provided to return to the fray riding *his* hobby-horse. Claiming to be "in full agreement, of course," with "the Negro position . . . that everybody should have equal rights," he nonetheless insisted that "the best way, I think, for all of us that are concerned about this problem is to ignore the differences as much as possible."[31]

By this time, it had become apparent that additional exchanges would be futile. No agreement could possibly emerge from such a non-meeting of the minds; at one point, in fact, the discussion had almost broken down completely over the question of what to do in the event that an armed black-white conflict appeared imminent. Even with their numerical advantage of three to one, it turned out that this assemblage of white critics and musicians, with its reliance on the most threadbare and cliché-ridden arguments (for example, Nat Hentoff's platitude, "All prejudice is bad"),[32] had been unable to break the resolve of Max Roach and Abbey Lincoln. In that sense, although the debate itself was inconclusive, it represented a triumph of sorts for Roach and Lincoln: they were not cowed; they would not capitulate by repudiating their previous statements and beliefs. With no resolution in sight, Bill Coss—another *down beat* editor and the writer who, in 1958, had declared that "hate" was one of the "major" components of earlier funky and soul-jazz styles—took it upon himself to end the impasse by finding the appropriately trite note on which to adjourn: "Integration, I would imagine, means not exchanging rights, but just clasping hands."[33]

It fell to Leonard Feather, however, to get in the final word, just as he had in the earlier *down beat* witch-hunt aimed at Charles Mingus in 1960–1961. For this purpose he and yet a fourth *down beat* editor, John Tynan, arranged for a second panel discussion, entitled—in deference to Feather's sensibilities one imagines—"The Need for Racial Unity in Jazz."[34] In one respect, at any rate, this parley, held early in 1963, was an improvement on its predecessor: black participants now were outnumbered only two to one.

Feather's opening remarks, which were substantially the same as his closing remarks, convey the thrust of the proceedings. Summarizing the earlier *down beat* arraignment of Roach and Lincoln, the critic maintained that the "basic problem raised originally was that of the relationship of jazz to race—the extent to which jazz has to be the product of one race." He then took advantage of the absence of his opponents to misrepresent their views: "The feeling of Max [Roach] and Abbey [Lincoln] seemed to be that jazz, having been created by the Negro, was a Negro preserve, and

the white musician in effect was an intruder or interloper."
Feather's "hope," in contrast, was that the panelists would
"show today . . . that this is becoming less and less the case, as
time goes by. . . ."[35] With the conclusion thus announced at
the outset, it should astonish absolutely no one that, following six pages of closely printed and bland discussion, Feather
unfurled his proclamation of victory: "I don't think jazz is,
or is ever likely to be, a private club in which there are any
intruders"—thereby refuting a contention that nobody had
advanced.[36] Nearly a decade later, with black-nationalist sentiments in jazz running at high tide, Feather could be found
still dispensing the same tired nostrums and dogmas.[37]

I trust it hardly need be said that virtually all the vast
expanse of verbiage lavished on this topic by Feather, Gitler,
down beat, and other white critics was the utmost rubbish.
Black people, whether musicians or otherwise, had given no
indication of a desire to subjugate or oppress whites on the
basis of color—and even if they had, it was obvious to anyone whose thought processes were not hopelessly deranged
that they lacked the power to carry out any such designs
and were not about to obtain it at any time in the near future. It is certainly revealing that for all of their anguished
laments and anxious hand-wringing over "Crow Jim" and
the like, the editors of *down beat* never managed to unearth
a single case in which a white musician had been the victim
of discrimination by being refused employment, for instance,
on the basis of color.

But to rebut the indictment brought by *down beat* against
Roach and Lincoln in this fashion is to dignify spurious
charges by investing them with a patina of rationality they
certainly do not possess. In point of fact, what the editorial
staff of *down beat* reacted to was less the *substance* of the
Roach-Lincoln manifestoes than their mere *existence.* From
that standpoint, it was irrelevant whether what the two nationalists had said was true or false, racist or non-racist, sane

or crazy. What mattered was rather that the pair themselves be suppressed or, at the very least, discredited—again, as had been the case with Charles Mingus—for the benefit of those black musicians who just might be rash enough to harbor similar heretical tendencies of their own. In one sense, these tactics of vilification could be said to have succeeded: as I remarked earlier, the careers of Roach and Lincoln slid into a long decline as the 1960s and '70s wore on. In another sense, though, this approach was bound to fall short. The spread of radical political ideas, especially those associated with black nationalism, was not—and could not be—so easily stemmed.

What is more, *down beat* was compelled to concede as much, at least tacitly. As nationalist and other radical ideologies became both more widely accepted and more openly proclaimed by jazz musicians during the later years of the 1960s, the magazine's efforts at beating back this high tide of dissent turned increasingly shrill and frenzied. At one point in 1966, for instance, the editors even went to the extraordinary length of recruiting a *black* writer—one of the handful ever to grace its pages—to fulminate against nationalist ideas (see the next chapter for details). When it soon became apparent that such ritual denunciations could no longer be relied upon to ostracize the advocates of nationalism, the magazine then made a short-lived and halfhearted attempt at control through co-optation by opening its columns to two of the principal spokesmen for the nationalist and avant-garde movements in jazz, A.B. Spellman and LeRoi Jones. As one might expect, however, this improbable marriage of convenience did not last long—most likely, the prose of Spellman and Jones proved too strong for the stomachs of those in charge at *down beat*. As a result, the editors were forced to the unwelcome conclusion that neither their traditional approach nor any more sophisticated methods they had been able to devise were about to put an end to the currents of nationalism and radicalism that were sweeping through the ranks of jazz artists.

Faced with this realization, the editors of *down beat* embarked on their most drastic step yet: late in the 1960s, they simply began to turn their back on jazz entirely, to undertake a flirtation with rock and other varieties of popular music instead. It was as if these executives were saying: "Very well, then, if jazz musicians insist on being so unreasonable, so perverse as to challenge the status quo, we will retaliate by investing our resources in newer, and more profitable, fields." In this way, *down beat* underwent a transformation from a jazz-oriented magazine to one that dealt with jazz only as one form of popular music among many.

The managers and editors of *down beat* no doubt rationalized such a grim departure on both political and economic grounds. First of all, it was quite clear that jazz musicians, the newest crop in particular, were, like black people themselves, becoming extremely, shall we say, *unmanageable*. Second, the market for popular music—and by extension, for magazines treating popular music—was enormously greater than that for jazz. So leave jazz to the mau-maus and the maniacs—we're going where the *real* money is! Such appears to be the reasoning that held sway at *down beat*, as its editors and executives found themselves less and less able to control events in jazz in the style to which they had long since become accustomed.

Naturally, the shift in emphasis at *down beat* was never total, for a decision to abandon jazz altogether would have risked losing the old readership before a new one was securely in place. But the change could hardly have been more dramatic for all of that. Where *down beat* during the past two decades had been a magazine in which popular music of any type was regarded with a barely concealed sneer, by the end of the 1960s its pages were replete with features on white rockers, soul music, blues, and almost any other kind

THE FORERUNNERS RESIST REPRESSION / 149

of popular music that was not jazz.

A canny maneuver, to be sure—but did it succeed? The answer to that question cannot be a simple yes or no. In economic terms, *down beat*'s move into the journalism of popular music has to be judged a qualified failure. Because the senior members of its staff were wholly out of touch with young people—*all* young people, not merely politically aware blacks—there was no chance that it would be able to make substantial inroads in this new arena against the competition offered by *Rolling Stone* and other periodicals of that nature. Therefore, although *down beat* sought to "broaden"—more accurately, to dilute—its musical coverage, the size of its audience did not even begin to grow apace.

Politically, in contrast, the decision to de-emphasize jazz seems at first to have borne the desired fruit. Both within and without the world of jazz, the forces of nationalism and radicalism began to wane as the 1960s turned the corner into the 1970s. The editors of *down beat* were also aided in their efforts at regaining control by the deaths of John Coltrane and Albert Ayler towards the close of the earlier decade; these tragic events deprived the avant garde of much of its leadership and central focus (a point upon which I expand in chapter 9). Through these developments, the ground was gradually prepared for *down beat*'s resumption of its old role as the arbiter of musical and political acceptability within jazz. Accordingly, as the 1970s progressed, jazz little by little regained its paramount position in the magazine. Indeed, by the onset of the 1980s, a superficial examination would suggest that, aside from the inclusion of an occasional bit of profanity, little had changed at *down beat* in a generation.

But such a conclusion would be eminently mistaken. Although *down beat* had mounted all the weapons at its command in an attempt to maintain its dominance during the 1960s, it was ultimately forced to concede defeat. That the magazine was later able to reassert its supremacy once again is not the result of any of the steps its editors took so much as it is the product of a general movement to the political right during the 1970s.

Yet the grievances that have always fueled black-nationalist protest in jazz have not ceased to exist: black people are still the objects of oppression in the United States, and jazz, an art that is still in the main the creation of black musicians, has never ceased to reward its white owners disproportionately.[38] So long as these conditions persist, the "triumph" of the jazz Establishment and its various propaganda organs will remain inherently fragile and unstable. The present may well be a period of political quiescence—but change is the only constant in history. If no one was able to predict the furious radical and black-nationalist insurgencies of the 1960s, by the same token no one can guarantee that, in one form or another, they will not erupt again.

NOTES

1. Some of the singer's own comments on this score can be found in Frank Kofsky, "Abbey Lincoln," *Radio Free Jazz* (February 1977).

2. Frank Kofsky, "The New Wave: Bob Thiele Talks to Frank Kofsky," *Coda*, VIII:7 (May–June 1968), p. 4.

3. An issue of *down beat* chosen at random from 1962 (March 29) shows about one-third of its 56 pages given over to advertising, as opposed to roughly 40 percent of the 72 pages of an issue from 20 years later (April 1981, also randomly selected). Overall, the number of changes over the ensuing twenty years are small and insignificant: more advertisements for guitars and fewer for brass instruments, slightly more advertisements for instructional methods and courses, and so forth.

4. Though I was told by an official of the Monterey Jazz Festival of a brief falling-out between *down beat* and the festival board over the question of whether the board should also be held responsible

for the not-inconsiderable bar bill amassed by one especially thirsty *down beat* correspondent.

5. See the notes to Sonny Rollins: *Freedom Suite* (ABC/Riverside 3010). After going through bankruptcy proceedings, the Riverside catalog was purchased during the late 1960s by ABC Records, which then commenced re-releasing the best Riverside recordings from the 1950s and early 1960s; this edition of "Freedom Suite" was part of that (now out-of-print) series of ABC reissues. *The Freedom Suite Plus* (Milestone 47007), released in 1973, was the fourth incarnation of this same recording.

6. Interview with Orrin Keepnews, Berkeley, California, April 27, 1973.

7. See by way of illustration my study, *Harry S. Truman and the War Scare of 1948: A Successful Campaign to Deceive the Nation* (New York: St. Martin's Press, 1993; paper edition, 1995). Honesty compels me to say in this regard that the *quality* of bullshit is, not surprisingly, much higher in the upper reaches of the Truman administration than anything the picayune jazz-recording industry has to offer. Orrin Keepnews, in other words, can hardly hold a candle to the likes of Dean Acheson or Averell Harriman.

8. Both Sonny Rollins's statement and Orrin Keepnews's notes are on the jacket of the original *Freedom Suite* album (Riverside 12–258), out of print virtually from the moment of its birth.

9. As a case in point, here is a typical rag-bag of gossip about Mingus, dispensed by a former editor of *down beat*—that gossip magazine *par excellence*—during the period of Mingus's most overt opposition to the white jazz Establishment: "A critic who received one of Mingus's infamous phone calls got an unlisted number, began judo lessons and took to carrying a blackjack. . . . Another writer was offered a punch in the mouth after he wrote an unfavorable review. *[D]own beat* editors regularly received long, outraged letters and strange telegrams from Mingus, who at various times offered to buy the magazine, break the editor's neck," and so on, ad nauseam. See Don DeMicheal, notes to Charles Mingus, *Better Git It in Your Soul* (Columbia 30628); DeMicheal, as we will observe, was instrumental in the purge directed against Max Roach. Such scurrilous blather, which is still, I am afraid, far too representa-

tive (DeMicheal was writing for an album released in 1972), tells us much more about the light-mindedness of its purveyors than it does about Mingus.

10. For example: "You dont know mother fucker so quit writing. . . . White little unknowing boy, no black man chooses jazz [as I had maintained in a *down beat* review], when the white man ties up all other music with cliques, mafia, and unions that are biased to black's, there's nothing left, for us but jazz. Fuck *Jazz*, it is the same sick meaning as Negro in a so called free world society of the white mans America, Negro meaning second class citizen and third and none in some cases, and jazz meaning the same thing considering the position the black musician is forced to work under when he performs music even if its what's left over. . . . Jazz means Jim Crow music. That Agents, critics, managers, record companies, everybody but the cotton picking musician share profit from; or did you think Billy Holiday, Pres [Lester Young], Bird [Charlie Parker], Fats Waller, Jelly Roll Morton, Jimmy Lunceford, Sid Catlett died rolling in their money. Even before they died if they didn't make that next gig, they'd go hungry. . . ." Charles Mingus to Frank Kofsky, no date. Mingus began his letter to me on the same sheet of paper as mine to him of March 18, 1962. Earlier, on February 25, 1962, he sent to *down beat* a letter to me in reference to my review of a recording by another jazz artist, and the magazine forwarded a copy of that letter to me. Based on this sequence of exchanges, I surmise that his second letter to me probably dates from March or April 1962.

11. All of the quotations are from Lees's article, "Newport: The Trouble," *down beat*, August 18, 1960, p. 21. Lees's reportage, if such it can be called—in view of his ill-concealed biases, *editorializing* would be the more precise term—was woefully slipshod and of less than professional caliber; he was manifestly so preoccupied with laying down the law to Charles Mingus that he could scarcely be bothered looking into any of the latter's allegations. Nonetheless, musicians, some of whom are quite famous, have continued to lodge similar accusations against the Newport Jazz Festival, as the following report shows: "A word should be said about the negative aspects of Newport [in 1972]. Miles Davis refused to play, charging

that an exploitation of musicians was taking place and that younger black musicians were excluded." And just to make clear how little has changed, this writer added: "A counter-festival was organized where many of these younger players played." Shades of Newport 1960! See Sy Johnson, "Jazz Swallows the Big Apple," *Changes,* September 1972, p. 24.

12. Lees, "Newport: The Trouble," p. 44.

13. One is also struck especially by certain pronounced parallels between Mingus and Ornette Coleman. Both artists did not hesitate to protest vocally when they encountered what they considered racist and/or exploitative treatment by white business elements in jazz; both dropped—or were forced—out of sight for a number of years rather than submit to conditions they perceived as degrading; both had to overcome countless business-created obstacles in seeking to bring black art-music to a wider public.

14. Gene Lees, "Afterthoughts," *down beat,* October 13, 1960, p. 53.

15. I also elaborate on this point at considerable length in chapter 7 of *Black Music, White Business: Illuminating the Political Economy and History of Jazz* (New York: Pathfinder Press, 1997).

16. See John Tynan, "Jazz in Hollywood Studios," *down beat,* March 1, 1962, pp. 14–15. Note that even twenty years later, black musicians still found themselves compelled to form organizations such as Musicians United to Stop Exclusion (MUSE) in order to break down racist barriers that keep them from work in the Hollywood studios. See "MUSE Ponders Prejudice," *down beat,* June 1981, p. 14.

17. See the prefatory note (most likely by Gene Lees) to Leonard Feather, "The Racial Undercurrent," *down beat Music '61,* ed. Gene Lees (Chicago: Maher Publications, n.d., but probably 1961), p. 44.

18. Feather, "Racial Undercurrent," pp. 45–46. Like Lees, Feather put much greater effort into advocating "less black nationalism" than into calling for "less white racism."

19. See, for example, "Mingus Sharply Criticized for European Tour Behavior," *down beat,* June 18, 1964, p. 10; and Mingus's rejoinder, "Mingus in Europe, Pt. II—Or Get It Straight," *down beat,* July 16, 1964, pp. 11–12. As these sources further illustrate, the white

jazz press has never hesitated for a second—least of all to determine the truth—when there is a chance to print some particularly juicy rumor about Mingus. As it happens, however, the European performances for which Mingus was allegedly "sharply criticized" were, by some marvelous coincidence, also recorded, in which form they won three European prizes for the bassist. See the notes to Mingus, *The Great Concert of Charles Mingus* (Prestige 34001).

20. A two-record album, *Mingus at Monterey* (Mingus JWS 001, 002), is the only release by Mingus's company known to me. An earlier firm co-owned by Mingus, Debut Records, apparently went bankrupt.

21. Charles Mingus with Nel King, ed., *Beneath the Underdog: His World as Composed by Mingus* (New York: Bantam Books, 1972), p. 151; the quotation in parenthesis, "some names . . . are fictitious," appears in extremely minute print on the penultimate unnumbered page before p. 1. Mingus has Navarro add (p. 151): "But if you behave, boy, you'll get booked—except for less than the white cats that copy your playing and likely either the agent or owner'll pocket the difference." Compare the similarities of this entire passage with Mingus to Kofsky (excerpted above in note 10) and the bassist's notes to *Mingus at Monterey* (cited in full in the preceding note).

22. See Abbey Lincoln, *Straight Ahead* (Candid 8015); Max Roach, *We Insist! The Freedom Now Suite* (Candid 8002). As an instance of how developments in jazz often anticipate those in the black community at large, note that the subtitle of the first Roach-Lincoln recording, *Freedom Now*, became the name of a black-nationalist political party in 1964; note also the common theme of "freedom" in the titles of recordings by Sonny Rollins and the Roach-Lincoln duo.

23. Even though there tends to be a rough correspondence among the views of most white jazz critics, I was amazed to discover, during the course of my research, the degree of convergence—sometimes extending even to the choice of words—between the ideas of Leonard Feather and those of Ira Gitler. By and large it is accurate to say that, as their remarks during the offensive against Roach and Lincoln demonstrate, the transcendent concern of Feather and

Gitler, who were associated in the preparation of all three editions of the former's *Encyclopedia of Jazz*, is to safeguard the position of whites—as musicians, critics, and business figures—in jazz. To this end, they have repeatedly argued that jazz has never been, is not now, and never will be black music (see, for instance, the words of Feather cited below in note 37). Meanwhile, seemingly indifferent to the inconsistency if not outright hypocrisy involved, they have simultaneously contended that the new black music cannot be considered a valid and integral part of the jazz tradition because it appeals primarily to whites!—an objection the two publicists never cared to raise when it might have been most germane, during the period of cool–West Coast jazz in the 1950s. Similarly, as part of their overall ideology, both are also intent on denying any social interpretation of the history of jazz; in particular, they resolutely strive to suppress the ample evidence that points toward a social interpretation of the bebop revolution of the 1940s. Finally, as I attempt to make clear later in this volume, Feather and Gitler share honors as the most doggedly persistent foes of the jazz avant garde led by John Coltrane and other black artists of that persuasion.

24. This review is reprinted as a preface to the transcript of a discussion by Roach, Lincoln, Gitler, DeMicheal, and others, "Racial Prejudice in Jazz," Part I, *down beat*, March 15, 1962, p. 21; the circumstances of that discussion are described in the text. The review was originally published in *down beat*, November 9, 1961, pp. 35–36.

25. For a partial transcript of this discussion, see Roach, Lincoln, Gitler, DeMicheal and others, "Racial Prejudice in Jazz," Part I, *down beat*, March 15, 1962, pp. 20–26; "Racial Prejudice in Jazz," Part II, *down beat*, March 29, 1962, pp. 22–25. From the places where omissions occur in this transcript, it appears that the editors of *down beat* made a point of withholding from publication the most telling comments of Roach and Lincoln. When political opponents meet at the negotiating table, in other words, who actually said what is of less consequence than who takes physical possession of the minutes.

26. "Racial Prejudice," Part I, p. 21.

27. *Ibid.*, p. 23.

28. *Ibid.*, pp. 24–25.

29. *Ibid.*, p. 26.

30. "Racial Prejudice in Jazz," Part II, p. 22.

31. *Ibid.*, pp. 24–25.

32. *Ibid.*, p. 24. Hentoff's position at the time was, characteristically, ambiguous and equivocal. In this discussion, he occasionally offered a tepid defense of Roach and Lincoln, but not long before he had written for *Harper's Magazine*—in the best *down beat*–approved anti-black-nationalism style—an article whose contents are fully conveyed by the title: "Race Prejudice in Jazz: It Works Both Ways" (*Harper's Magazine*, June 1959, pp. 72–77). I examine Hentoff's ambivalence about social radicalism and black nationalism in more detail in chapter 1 of *Black Music, White Business*. The subject of armed hostilities between blacks and whites was broached by Max Roach, "Racial Prejudice in Jazz," Part II, p. 25.

33. "Racial Prejudice in Jazz," Part II, p. 25; for Coss's interpretation of funky jazz, see his article, "Small Band in Transition," *Metronome*, March 1958, p. 13.

34. Feather, Tynan, and others, "The Need for Racial Unity in Jazz: A Panel Discussion," *down beat*, April 11, 1963, pp. 16–21.

35. *Ibid.*, p. 16; brackets in original.

36. *Ibid.*, p. 21.

37. In 1971, a firm named Black Jazz Records began operations in Los Angeles. Feather's response to this development was to denigrate the company, especially its slogan, "Jazz is black and must be kept that way." In his nationally syndicated column the critic "deplore[d] the separatist attitude it represented," because of his supposed "reluctan[ce] to see any art form become the private preserve of black or white or any other people." Feather has yet to evidence such tender concern over the fact that the *profits* from jazz have all along been very nearly the "private preserve" of white entrepreneurs and executives, however. See "For Blacks Only Approach: Separatist View of Jazz," *Los Angeles Times* dispatch reprinted in the *San Francisco Chronicle*, November 30, 1971, p. 39.

38. A subject that I examine in much greater depth in the first four chapters of *Black Music, White Business*.

3

Critiquing the critics

A. The state of jazz criticism

I don't know, by any stretch of the imagination, how the music I heard that night could be called musical. . . . I think we're getting away from musical values that have been established for centuries.

—IRA GITLER[1]

Art is a means of communication. But it doesn't try to communicate anguish, horror, hate and war, it tries to communicate beauty. . . .

[In] art we're trying to create out of the havoc of living and of the world something beautiful. . . .

What I'm saying is that, when the form and the content [of art] is [sic] thrown out, the end result has to be beautiful.

—DON SCHLITTEN[2]

[T]here was a time I kind of froze up on those people at down beat. *I felt that there was something there that wasn't—I felt that they were letting their weakness direct their actions, which I didn't feel they should have. . . . I couldn't believe it, you know, it just seemed so pre-posterous. It was so ridiculous, man, that's what bugs me. It was absolutely ridiculous, because they made it appear that we didn't even know the first thing about music—the first thing. And there we were, really try-ing to push things off.*

—JOHN COLTRANE[3]

It is becoming increasingly clear that most of those who call themselves jazz critics do so despite some large and lam-entable defects in their preparation. Here I have in mind not merely the question of an extensive technical knowledge of music. Such knowledge offers no guarantee that its possessor will use it to enhance the public's musical understanding and appreciation; and by the same token, a lack of musical expertise need not prevent a critic from making a percep-tive appraisal of a given body of work or an artist's style. No one, after all, demands that the art critic also be a successful painter nor a literary critic a successful novelist.

But if a musical background is not absolutely essential to the critic's craft, it does not follow that there are *no* particu-larly relevant skills the would-be critic should have. Quite the contrary: one can think of numerous ways of improving the education of critics. If all critics possessed at least some grounding in the theory of aesthetics, to take one example, it might be possible for them to avoid much of the lack of clarity and repetitiousness that typify their discussions. At the very minimum, it might then be feasible to arrive at some meaningful definitions of terms and a rough consensus as to what constitutes the canons of taste in each historical era of the music.

To this one may object—rightly, in my opinion—that a magazine such as *down beat*, which is representative of its species, is not a suitable vehicle for weighty philosophical treatises better left to the academic journals. Even so, however, there are still countless other valuable services that we might legitimately expect an alert, insightful critic to perform. What comes to mind first concerns the continuing Negro social revolution and the simultaneous and related aesthetic revolution taking place in jazz. Now it should be obvious to an observer with even the most rudimentary sociological intuition that these revolutions are interconnected and interdependent. That is to say, rejection of the conventions of bebop, which the younger generation of jazz musicians perceives as unnecessarily restrictive, is a reflection of the same social forces that have led this country's urban ghettos to repudiate the values of white middle-class America. But although this may be the case, do not anticipate seeing it discussed in the pages of any "jazz" magazine. Such topics (save as they crop up in the laconic asides of a LeRoi Jones, an A.B. Spellman, or a Robert Levin) are too far outside the pale to be admitted to the parochial universe of jazz journalism.

Any seeming exceptions all turn out on closer examination to be of the kind that confirm the rule: a 1962 panel discussion sponsored by *down beat* in which, as we saw in the previous chapter, drummer Max Roach and singer Abbey Lincoln were put on trial by a group of white jazz critics unalterably hostile to, and evidently incapable of understanding, black nationalism; a disparaging article on "soul" in jazz—by a white writer, naturally—two years earlier in the same magazine;[4] and so on, ad nauseam et infinitum. By no stretch of the imagination can we regard these occasional discussions of jazz and race as an acceptable substitute for a consistent policy of diligent and objective inquiry unmarred by dogmatic preconceptions. And in point of fact, not a single jazz periodical has made an effort to meet this most elementary responsibility to its readership by presenting a broad analysis of the effect on jazz of social changes among African-Americans.

For that matter, are there more than two or three white writers who have bothered even to *try* to transcend their indoctrination and subjective prejudices to the point where black nationalism becomes something more intelligible than the "reverse Jim Crow" to which it is so ubiquitously equated (and thus dismissed) by the white critical fraternity? Merely to raise the question is to answer it. Judging by the gross manhandling and ludicrous distortions to which LeRoi Jones's ground-breaking book, *Blues People*,[5] was subjected by reviewers in the jazz press, such writers are too thoroughly enslaved by their conditioning and insecurities as white interlopers in a predominantly black arena to recognize reality—even when it glares up at them from the printed page.

That this state of affairs prevails is, as the phrase goes, not accidental. For one thing, consider the existing institutional restraints. How many jazz magazines—or magazines of any sort, so far as that goes—are willing to jeopardize a portion of their advertising revenues by undertaking a dispassionate appraisal of black nationalism as it pertains to jazz? (To point out the probable consequences of printing "radical" material, by the way, is not to indulge in any "conspiracy theory" of history. That advertisers exert control over the contents of a periodical, albeit through subtle and often indirect channels, is one of the fixed first principles of the publishing business. Not that such control is all that necessary: the vast majority of publishers have never distinguished themselves by marked tendencies toward unorthodoxy on questions of "race relations," economic policy, or anything else.)

But the matter only begins at the publisher's desk, it does not end there; one must also take into account the jazz critic him—or (more rarely) herself. In order to formulate the kind of sociological analysis of jazz and its ties to the African-American community that I have been discussing, the rank-and-file critic would have to be a vastly different animal. The fact that such an analysis would require a certain irreducible minimum exposure to the social sciences—my preference is for a combination of history and sociology—in itself suffices to disqualify easily four-fifths of the practicing jazz critics.

One of the areas in which our understanding of the sociology of jazz is most deficient is that bearing on the critics. From what we do know, however, it is probably a safe generalization that the majority of established critics—those whose names are recognized by the literate public at large—have come to the field not from a background in social science or even the humanities, but from advertising. Indeed, many may lack even that degree of professional preparation—may, in other words, be hangers-on and hustlers (or, in the evocative Yiddish term, *luftmenschen*—those who support themselves on air alone). Their outlook, therefore, *at best* tends most often to be the provincial and narrowly circumscribed one of the journalist, and the white-male journalist at that. What such critics are missing in the way of training, whether musical, philosophical, or sociological, they attempt to compensate for with raw enthusiasm, usually without even being aware of their shortcomings. Any glimmerings of their personal inadequacies (as non-musicians, for example, or as whites in a field dominated by blacks) that threaten to emerge into consciousness they readily suppress; their corresponding insecurities they then dissipate through a strident display of self-importance and officiousness, the less the inner certainty, the more forceful the assertion of prerogatives.[6]

But even if jazz critics were to be recruited from the ranks of history and sociology Ph.D.'s, because of the peculiar relationship to the recording industry in which most of them stand—a relationship not duplicated in any of the other arts—the situation would not be materially altered. For the fundamental and inescapable point of departure from which any investigation of jazz critics and criticism must proceed is that the majority of those who bear the name of critic do not, strictly speaking, deserve the title.

Arguments about *the* correct definition of criticism, like attempts to find the line of demarcation between art and non-art, are legion, but on one thing probably all sides would agree: the critic should be free to arrive at his or her judgments without being coerced, overtly or otherwise, by influences external to the work of art per se. Yet this condition, which—let me stress it again—is the basic prerequisite of all artistic criticism, is not even remotely approached where jazz is concerned.

More than likely, the ordinary jazz devotee has never given much thought to how a critic goes about procuring a livelihood. If a person's name appears often enough in the "right" magazines or on the jackets of enough recordings, that suffices to establish his or her legitimacy. Hence it is all the more essential to make the point explicitly that *only a very small fraction of the individuals (mostly white men) known as "critics" derive the major portion of their income from criticism; the remainder are, in one fashion or another, dependent for their livelihood on the recording industry.* The distinction between a critic and an employee of the recording industry is elementary. The absence in actual practice of this distinction results in a number of consequences, all of which have one thing in common—a pernicious effect on the practice of jazz criticism and, if I may say so, on the lives of jazz musicians themselves.

The truth of this assertion readily emerges from an examination of the way in which all but a privileged few jazz critics earn their keep, and the pivotal role that economic reliance on recording companies plays in shaping their views.

Within the United States only a *very* small minority of the best-known jazz critics make their livings primarily by writing aesthetic commentary. Included in this tiny group might be, say, columnists such as Whitney Balliett of the *New Yorker*, the permanent editorial staff of *down beat*, and so on. Clearly, the number of positions that allow one to survive by writing jazz criticism (or, more broadly, criticism of popular music) is severely limited. Those U.S. newspapers that retain a jazz columnist *on full salary* probably can be counted on one's fingers; likewise for the high-paying slick magazines. The corollary is that less fortunate writers—that is, the vast majority—must seek other means of support if they hope to continue in the role of critic. Here is where the recording companies enter the picture.

That such a state of affairs actually exists and is not merely the product of an overheated Marxist imagination is quite clear from the testimony of Stanley Dance, a generally middle-of-the-road commentator whose views, socially as well as musically, are far removed from my own. Beginning with the observation that where jazz is concerned, there is "a slight conflict" with the dictionary definition of a critic as "a professional reviewer," Dance remarks that "few jazz critics are truly professional. The art or industry cannot support them at a professional level. Few can make a living writing jazz criticism only." Similarly, this author decries the fact that "there are simply not enough work opportunities" for jazz critics: "Apart from this country's two syndicated columnists and a handful of magazine editors," he notes, "it is difficult to think of more than a dozen persons *through the world* [my emphasis] who exist solely by writing about jazz."[7]

Dance is indisputably correct, as I had the opportunity to discover firsthand as part of my education in the ways of the world during the late 1960s. I was at that time seeking work as a university professor, from which political considerations—openly invoked as such by countless interviewers to "justify" their rejection of my application—persistently barred me (hence my skepticism about "academic freedom" as conventionally understood and practiced in American universities). As a result, I had no choice but to attempt to support myself as a freelance writer and photographer. If I had ever harbored any illusions about the standard of living I would enjoy as a jazz critic, these years were more than sufficient to dispel them. I doubt that my combined earnings from reviews, essays and other critical efforts amounted to a *total* of $1,000 (roughly $6,000 in 1990s' dollars) for the entire three-year period between 1967 and 1970. I am thus able to affirm unambiguously, on the basis of evidence I accumulated as a reluctant participant-observer, that nine times (or more) out of ten, jazz criticism can be only a sideline, not a true vocation. The consequences for the practice of such criticism are, as I will bring out more fully below, dismal. It may well be considerations of this nature that have prompted so many jazz writers—Nat Hentoff and Ralph Gleason are among those whose names spring to mind—ultimately to renounce jazz criticism for greener fields.

In my own case, to continue in the autobiographical vein, I was forced to turn for employment to the recording industry, which is far and away the most common stratagem of would-be critics. At the very least, working for a recording company as a publicist or, more rarely, a producer, allows one to keep body and soul together—more than can be said (save in a few extraordinary cases) for the writing of criticism—and also provides some proximity to the music itself. And if the truth be known, just as the de facto political masters of the United States are drawn from the ranks of the corporate rich, to whose folds these bankers, lawyers and business executives periodically return,[8] so do the leading "critics" shuffle back and forth from positions in the recording industry. Hence even the best-paid writers, such as Leonard Feather, Nat Hentoff, and

Ralph Gleason, have from time to time found it either necessary or desirable to supplement their presumably insufficient income from criticism by accepting employment as producers or publicity agents with one or more recording firms (Feather with Metrojazz and others as a producer, and with Liberty-United Artists-Blue Note, the Newport Jazz Festival, and the like, as publicist; Hentoff with Candid as a producer; Gleason with Fantasy-Prestige-Milestone as a publicist).

Most aspiring critics, however, cannot realistically hope to enter the recording industry at an executive level; instead, they begin as writers of "liner notes"—that is to say, prose from which any hint of controversy has been diligently excised—for the jackets of recordings. Though this is lowly stuff, to be sure, it is nonetheless incomparably more lucrative than composing criticism. In 1962, for example, a single record review for *down beat* earned its author the princely sum of $4. In that same era, the minimum payment for a set of album notes was in the neighborhood of $75, while the top dogs in the jazz Establishment could on occasion command as much as two or three times that amount—the presumption being, of course, that the critic's famous name on the jacket sells more copies of the record within. It does not take the mental apparatus of a Nobel laureate in physics to perceive the blatant moral: between $4 on the one hand and $75, $100, or $200 on the other, there cannot be much hesitation.*[9]

---

* In this connection, a remark by Stanley Dance is certainly apropos: "The chief purpose of the critic in the eye of the [recording] 'industry' is praise and promotion. 'If you can't say anything nice,' it enjoins, 'don't say anything at all.' Praise and promotion are what it wants, more than health, and it exerts its subtle pressures to get them. The critic resists as best he can, or according to his nature." "Please Take It Seriously," in *down beat Music '65*, ed. Don DeMicheal (Chicago: Maher Publications, 1965), p. 41.

Naturally, the more "industry" employment a critic accepts, the more difficult it becomes not to be swayed by its "subtle pressure."

But what ludicrous incongruities this arrangement creates! No one would ever dream of having the interested publishers vote to select the outstanding novel of the year, yet somehow it is permissible for individuals who—like Leonard Feather, Ira Gitler, and Nat Hentoff—sustain themselves primarily through serving recording companies as publicists or producers to vote in the International Jazz Critics Poll that *down beat* conducts each year. Worse still, reflect on the situation in which a reviewer confronts a mediocre album issued by a company that also frequently hires him to write liner notes. Who can believe that Our Critic will not think long and hard about the consequences of giving this recording low marks? Even supposing that he dares brave the wrath of his employer on this one occasion, won't he be still more cautious the next time the identical dilemma presents itself?

Or again, take the case in which a given artist moves from one recording company to another, as almost every one of the best known performers in jazz has done at some point. (Miles Davis, Thelonious Monk, John Coltrane, and Sonny Rollins, for example, all had recording contracts with at least three different firms over the course of their careers.) To make matters *interesting*, shall we say, a critic who often works for one of these companies—call it A—draws an assignment to review a new album by this artist released by company B. The critic may want to praise this recording on the B label to the skies—may, indeed, think it far eclipses anything the artist ever has done for company A—but to speak his mind could mean that A's executives will be less inclined to throw well-paying jobs his way.

And so it goes. To believe that these conflicts of interest, and others like them, do not influence the judgment of jazz critics requires a greater degree of innocence or naiveté—I am not sure just which—than I, for one, am able to muster.

We can, as it happens, observe one of the clearest examples of how critics tailor their views in accordance with the wishes of their recording-company employers from an incident that began in 1962, when a few white writers unleashed a splenetic tirade denouncing the embryonic jazz revolution—then represented by John Coltrane, Ornette Coleman, Cecil Taylor, and the late Eric Dolphy—as "anti-jazz," a term these critics never bothered to define, but one whose pejorative connotation was unmistakable to even the most casual reader. Although Leonard Feather did not himself issue the original indictment, he lost no time endorsing in the pages of *down beat* the views of those who did.[10]

For all of that, before much time had elapsed commentary by the selfsame Leonard Feather began turning up on the covers of recordings by several prominent members of the avant garde. In one instance, he even had the temerity to pen the notes of an album memorializing Eric Dolphy, who, as I noted above, was one of the principal targets of the critic's "anti-jazz" calumny; in others, Feather supplied notes for recordings by two of Coltrane's key collaborators, drummer Elvin Jones and pianist McCoy Tyner, not to mention Coltrane's widow, Alice Coltrane. So ridiculous has this situation become, in fact, that his remarks can now even be discovered on albums by Ornette Coleman, who, with Coltrane and Dolphy, was the other principal target of the "anti-jazz" assault. It remains only for Feather to provide notes for the works of Albert Ayler, Archie Shepp, and Pharoah Sanders (who did, in fact, perform on the Alice Coltrane recording that Feather annotated) to extend this absurdity to the ultimate—and no doubt this feat, too, the ubiquitous author will soon accomplish.[11]

What accounts for such a striking reversal? Feather himself is of less than no help in resolving the mystery. Not only has he refused to explain his change of position, but he is not even willing to acknowledge that he ever held the views he so adamantly proclaimed in 1961. Thus, under the entry for "John Coltrane" in his *Encyclopedia of Jazz for the Sixties*, Feather writes of "some critics who attacked his [Coltrane's] use of harsh, human sounds and his often excessively long solos as 'honking and bleating' and 'anti-jazz.'"[12] *Some critics!* Can you believe the man having the sheer gall to conceal his own culpability so baldly? Deceitfulness and *chutzpah* that flagrant ought to be made punishable by a fine, with a jail sentence thrown in for good measure.

As Feather is clearly not about to enlighten us about his abrupt conversion to the side of the angels, of necessity we are left to our own devices. The most plausible interpretation—nay, the *only* plausible interpretation—is that during the period since the publication of his first "anti-jazz" polemics, there has occurred a large enough shift in the tastes of the jazz public to make it profitable for several recording companies to release albums by avant-garde performers. Blue Note Records, one of the firms that has moved aggressively into this new terrain, coincidentally happens to be a frequent employer of Leonard Feather as an author of liner notes. Now if there is any single axiom that commands universal assent among such "critics," it is that one never turns down a chance to earn a ready $100 or $200 by annotating an album—regardless of what the critic may actually think of the artist or the recording.[13] Inasmuch as the critic is being paid in good coin to sell records, it is most unlikely that his notes will be found acceptable by his employer if they do not praise the LP they are intended to accompany. Hence whatever the critic's original sentiments may have been, by a process of retroactive rationalization this worthy soon comes to believe that the paeans he has inscribed reflect convictions he held all along.

Can one imagine a greater travesty on the idea of disinterested and unbiased criticism? In the case of the eminent

Mr. Feather, the hapless jazz fancier is left totally in the dark as to which of his "critical" positions is the genuine one: was Feather sincere in his 1962 condemnation of "anti-jazz," or are we to accept his later panegyrics to members of the jazz avant garde as representing his true sentiments? But isn't it rather the case that both opinions are spurious, both the results of considerations that ought to be extraneous to any type of aesthetic criticism, properly understood?

It is just because critical venality like Leonard Feather's wildly contradictory views on John Coltrane and "anti-jazz" abounds that even Ira Gitler—certainly no slouch when it comes to defending the virtue of white jazz critics—is compelled by the evidence to admit that "jazz criticism *is* a very tangled, ingrown thing, and the position of the combination reviewer-liner [note] writer is not a healthy one."*[14]

Be that as it may, it will not do to place sole responsibility for such a sorry state of affairs on recording-company executives and the "critics" they control. These individuals are, in actuality, caught up in a complex web of social forces whose nature they only dimly perceive; the evils they unwittingly perpetuate have long since become part and parcel of the industry's modus operandi, far too deeply entrenched for any such small and relatively powerless group to alter them. It is not unreasonable to suppose that the majority of recording firms would prefer to produce art of a high caliber

---

* Gitler makes a point of adding at once: "But as in any field of endeavor, you get to know who is jiving. If the reader uses his intelligence, he won't be fooled too often by a man who is writing out of both sides of his typewriter." Of course, the whole question of why there should even *be* any critics who are "jiving" or "writing out of both sides of their typewriters" is so explosive and potentially revealing that, rather than explore it, Gitler lets it drop before it can burn his hands any further. See "Ira Gitler to Frank Kofsky," letter to the editor in *Jazz*, July 1965, p. 7.

rather than kitsch—but what if there is a greater market for kitsch? Similarly, no one can doubt that the publicist whose sensibilities have not already been dulled beyond the point of protest experiences a surge of revulsion when faced with the task of writing the umpteenth album jacket in the same month for yet another organ-and-tenor-saxophone group. The natural temptation is to chuck the record into the wastebasket and be on to something more uplifting. Alas! The god of economic necessity still demands his daily sacrifice, so that umpteenth set of notes ultimately gets written—but not without much gnashing of teeth en route.*

The real villain, in short, is not the individual producer or writer, but a social and economic system that insists that art, like birth, death, and marriage (see *Bride* magazine and Jessica Mitford's book, *The American Way of Death*),[15] be huckstered as a commodity, and that only those commodities, whether artistic or otherwise, that pass the test of profitability deserve to survive. The system of art (one should really say *life*) as a commodity demeans everyone and everything with which it comes into contact. In jazz, it means that the musicians are pushed—either by outright coercion or through their own internalization of the criteria of the market—to produce works that are commercially acceptable; that the recording company executives feel they have little choice but to restrict musicians to that path; that writers, instead of being encouraged to practice objective criticism, find themselves employed primarily in glorifying a "product" to which, as often as not, they can feel no commitment whatsoever.

A long-term solution to this state of affairs can take

---

* Robert Levin, who was writing such notes in 1965 when a version of this chapter first was published as an essay, subsequently told me that I have here described the situation exactly. Levin subsequently quit that job and found another position.

shape only as a basic structural change in society. For the short run, some amelioration, insofar as criticism alone is concerned, might lie in the direction of bringing pressure to bear on newspapers and magazines to create positions for writers that would emancipate them from the incubus of the recording industry. (Wouldn't it be astonishing to discover our leading drama critics lending their name to the sale of theater tickets by composing laudatory comments for the back cover of the program?)

Even with so modest a proposal as this, implementation probably would not be easy. It is hardly a secret that jazz has been a music of the dispossessed and disinherited. Among whites, it has had an appeal to the more recently arrived ethnic minorities, especially Italians and Jews, beyond their proportion in the population at large. These groups, however, are not the ones to whom the upper-middle-class-oriented carriers of what passes for culture in the United States— the *New York Times*, the *Saturday Review*, *Harper's*, *The Atlantic*, and so on—traditionally have catered; I suspect, moreover, that the periodicals read by the rank and file of the jazz audience are not about to commission outspoken disquisitions on jazz by iconoclastic authors of the LeRoi Jones stripe. This situation, too, has to be recognized as part of the historical price that the jazz world as a whole has had to pay (and continues to pay) as the result of the music's origins among the black working class. In any event, as Jones has repeatedly made clear, there are some compensating advantages to being excluded from the often-dubious benefits of the pallid Anglo-Saxon middle-class mode of existence.

In the last analysis, it is perhaps to the continuing Negro revolutionary movement that we must look for a curative to the ills that assail the jazz body politic. It is virtually impossible to be unaware that this incipient upheaval poses on the agenda the question of a root-and-branch overturn of U.S. society, the ramifications of which will—if the movement is successful—certainly extend to culture in general and jazz specifically. Is it too much to hope that such a revolution may bring in its wake the opportunity to enjoy America's only genuinely original art freed from the economic straitjacket in which until now it has been confined?

B. Jazz criticism as social control

1. Leonard Feather—chief attorney for the prosecution

Why the critics?

That is a question I am asked fairly frequently, by friends and associates who want to know why I expend so much energy on this particular aspect of the jazz Establishment.

The answer is really quite simple. My point of departure is to analyze how the jazz critic might go about serving the music—that is, the musicians and their audience. I then compare this ideal with the actual accomplishments of the critics. As the comparison is so wholly unfavorable to the major critical figures—Leonard Feather, Ira Gitler, Gene Lees, Dan Morgenstern, Martin Williams, Michael Zwerin, and the entire editorial staff of *down beat*—I conclude that it is my responsibility to the jazz community to illuminate their failings in order to prevent them from leading their readers even further astray.*

---

* Thanks in no small part to the efforts of a new generation of scholars, in the 1990s it is no longer necessary to have to justify writing about critics, for as these younger intellectuals have demonstrated, it is always legitimate and germane to ask just who defines the canon in any given field and what are the criteria for inclusion. Jazz critics, by giving or withholding their imprimatur, play a disproportionately large part in determining what the public for jazz ultimately will accept and what it will reject; they also exert (as I brought out in the preceding chapter) considerable influence over what kinds of music recording companies are willing to disseminate. Thus, John Coltrane in 1960, *good*; John Coltrane after 1965, *bad*. Or, to anticipate an example I discuss below, John

What, then, are the critics able to do? For one thing, they can muckrake—they can lay bare the sordid conditions under which most practicing jazz musicians are compelled to labor. Should they so choose, the critics could probably bring about a fairly substantial degree of integration in the recording, television, and movie studios, simply by a consistent vocal assault on the existing policy of whites-preferred. They might also use the same methods to remedy the ghastly situation in the nightclubs, where exorbitant charges to the clientele are coupled with hyperexploitation of the artists (even the major ones, though with them the exploitation is more subtle and indirect than with the lesser-known figures). A picket line in front of the Five Spot, say, initiated and led by Martin Williams, Dan Morgenstern, and Michael Zwerin would, you can be sure, produce the most salutary results in that club's pricing and employment practices in short order!

To object that this is the work of journalism rather than criticism is not very pertinent. Most self-styled jazz critics are at most little more than glorified journalists to begin with—and not very glorified either, if the truth be known. For that matter, what is wrong with journalism? A little less insipid "criticism" and a little more crusading journalism would, at this particular stage of the game, very definitely be a welcome development.

A second and related task the critics could undertake, were they so minded, is that of relating the current revolution in jazz to the changes in society that have helped shape it. In the long run, of course, the success of any radical movement in the arts depends on its reception by the community of

---

Tchicai ("A Calm Member of the Avant Garde"—*down beat*), virtuous; Archie Shepp, Marion Brown, Albert Ayler, Pharoah Sanders, lunatics and axe-murderers, the lot. Critics, in short, have a great deal of *real* power; it behooves us to keep them under the closest possible scrutiny in hopes of limiting the frequency with which they abuse it.

practicing artists, especially the younger ones (which is, incidentally, why the triumph of the jazz revolution probably is assured). Nonetheless, the critics have it in their hands to smooth the way for the innovators by mediating between them and their public. To do so, however, would require the critics to abandon their own preconceptions and biases in the attempt to comprehend what motivates the youthful iconoclasts and how their art has been molded by the social and aesthetic environment. It was precisely this service that the critics generally did not perform in the 1940s; as a result, the bebop revolution of that decade produced a number of acrimonious splits that haunted the music for years thereafter.

When we come to score the leading critics on their performances of these two tasks, what we find is a record of almost total negligence—or worse. I have yet to read a column by Leonard Feather, Martin Williams, Dan Morgenstern, Michael Zwerin, or any of that crowd, that makes the least attempt to decry the virtually total segregation of the studios and symphony orchestras, nor has there been any protest on their part regarding the abominable treatment of both artists and public by nightclub owners like the Termini brothers of New York's Five Spot cafe, Shelly Manne (of the Manne-Hole) in Los Angeles, and others of that mentality.[*]

---

[*] Leonard Feather, for instance, devoted exactly one very brief column in a dozen years to the topic of discrimination against qualified black musicians in Hollywood studios and nightclubs such as the Manne-Hole; by his own admission in 1967, it was some "12 years ago" (in 1955) that he had last "complained bitterly . . . about the whole Jim Crow setup" in the Los Angeles area; "Feather's Nest," *down beat*, February 9, 1967, p. 13. One would like to know, of course, why, if Feather had indeed "complained bitterly . . . about the whole Jim Crow setup" during the mid-1950s, it took him over a decade to return for a second look at the subject.

What is more, even this single article by Feather was in fact the by-

If their performance as journalists of the exposé is dismal, the way in which these men treat the social components of the jazz revolution is nothing short of criminal. There is, in fact, a certain logic here. The easiest way to summarize the status quo in jazz is with the two words *white supremacy*. Themselves being the beneficiaries of the existing order, the foremost critics, all white, are blind to its inequities; they accept them, that is, as natural and even inevitable. But the jazz revolution, in its social aspect, is an indictment of the very inequalities of class and race that have given these critics their privileged position. Hence it would be genuinely astonishing were they able to offer their readers an objec-

---

product of a debate I had initiated some weeks before. Writing in the *Los Angeles Free Press* (hereafter, *LAFP*), a self-styled "underground" newspaper, late in 1966, I had vigorously denounced the exclusion of black musicians from local employment in the studios and nightclubs; see "The Jazz Scene: Is Shelly Manne Secretly a Harpist? Does André Previn Cut Cecil Taylor?" *LAFP*, December 2, 1966, pp. 10–11. This essay created an enormous controversy in the local jazz community, as a consequence of which the newspaper was bombarded with letters of protest from white studio musicians (for example, those of Bud Shank and Shelly Manne, *LAFP*, December 16, 1966, pp. 3, 5, respectively), I lost my column in this same "free" publication, and Feather—finally—was forced to take a public position on the issue in *down beat*, if only to preserve his standing among black musicians. Nonetheless, the patent similarity between our two commentaries suggests that had mine not been published, Feather would have remained discreetly silent:

KOFSKY: "Doubling [the ability to perform on more than a single instrument] could apply at most to reed players; nobody ever heard of asking a guitarist to double on piano, a bassist to play violin, or a trombonist to work out on trumpet. (Or does Shelly Manne really get all those studio dates because secretly he's a harpist?)"; "Jazz Scene," p. 10.

FEATHER: "It is not clear to me on what instruments . . . Negro trombonists, pianists and guitarists [the same three instruments I had mentioned] are supposed to double in order to crash the studio gates. I haven't heard of too many white trombonists doubling on sackbut or guitarists on zither"; "Feather's Nest," p. 13.

tive account of the revolution and the conditions that fuel it. Need I add that the critics make no such attempt? It is easy enough to document these charges. Consider Michael Zwerin of the *Village Voice,* for one. While with the Earl Hines group on a State Department tour of the Soviet Union, Zwerin bombarded his readers with a baleful account of the unhappy plight of the citizens on *that* side of the Iron Curtain. But he has never penned a line on the exclusion of black musicians from the studios, never written a column on working conditions for musicians in the dingy toilets known as jazz clubs—and this despite the fact that he is one of the few authors who could describe these things from firsthand experience. Or take Martin Williams. Instead of trying to assist his white audience in understanding the integral role of black nationalism (and other forms of social radicalism) in the jazz revolution, he continues to prate away in *down beat* about alleged "black supremacists," thus encouraging the unthinking, gut-level white racism that he should be at great pains to extirpate.[16] More than that, he toils mightily to discredit those writers who attempt to point out the central relationship between radicalism and the new music, condemning them for espousing, in his words, "opportunistic Marxist clichés delivered with a slightly Peking-ese accent."[17]

But for the title of champion demagogue, no one can take a back seat to Leonard Feather. Not long ago he asserted in *down beat* that musicians weren't interested in discussing such things as black nationalism and the U.S. war in Vietnam—it was all a plot of certain white writers (three guesses which ones) who were striving to convince Negro musicians that they, too, were soul brothers. (He actually did say this; I have not taken it from a publicity release of the House Committee on Un-American Activities.)[18]

Subsequently, however, he had an eyeball-to-eyeball confrontation with Archie Shepp when the saxophonist played

Shelly's Manne-Hole in Los Angeles. Apparently, this was enough to persuade Feather that musicians themselves were involved with those questions that he felt should be placed off limits. But far from revising his opinions after discussing them with Shepp in his home in the lily-white Hollywood Hills, Feather took another tack: he sought to mislead his readers into concluding that Shepp and those who share his views are racists.

In the first of what unfortunately has not been a short-lived series in *Cavalier* magazine, Feather implies in rapid succession that (1) Shepp is a phony who plays and dresses one way in public, another in private; (2) that his poetry is part and parcel of an effort to "find more work and sell more records"; and (3) that he is anti-white.[19]

What is the truth? Need you ask? When I visited Shepp at his home recently, he was wearing the same "eccentric outfits and Benjamin Franklin shades" that Feather would have us believe are "a part of his stage shtick."[20] (Notice the Yiddish—it lets us know the author is truly hip. Too bad such "hipness" doesn't extend to familiarity with dress mores in New York's East Village.) Only Shepp can clarify the motives behind his verse, but somehow Feather leaves me unconvinced that poetic dedications to Malcolm X and the late black Marxist intellectual W.E.B. Du Bois[21] are the best way to go about securing increased employment at Joe Termini's Five Spot, and the like!

As for Shepp's alleged anti-white proclivities, here Feather's unscrupulousness surpasses the permissible. Shepp has always had at least one white member, trombonist Roswell Rudd, in his group since he started working semi-regularly (none of the new musicians work *regularly*). When he performed in Los Angeles, where Feather resides, he added another white musician, bassist Charlie Haden, and since then, Haden has flown to New York to continue working with Shepp.

None of which, however, is of the least importance so

far as Feather is concerned. Articulate and militant black radicals like Shepp threaten him and his ilk, psychologically and socially. For that reason, they must be destroyed. Or so Feather, on the evidence, seems to believe.

2. Michael Zwerin—assistant to the chief

> Mister X [an anonymous correspondent] is right about aesthetic and social theories being something apart from music. As a matter of fact, I think a number of avant-garde jazz musicians would be better suited in politics— it would be a more direct expression for them.
>
> —MICHAEL ZWERIN[22]

> Art without ideas is like a man without a soul: it is a corpse.
>
> —VISSARION BELINSKY[23]

The two quotations above illustrate diametrically opposed ideas about the relationship between art and society. The first of these, of course, is today's critical orthodoxy insofar as jazz is concerned; it is, with only a couple of exceptions, the one subscribed to by all the big-name critics like Leonard Feather. (That it is also endorsed by Michael Zwerin, jazz correspondent for the *Village Voice*, is ample comment on the degree of enlightenment of that journal.) Essentially counterrevolutionaries, these authors labor long and hard to convince the public that the best art is devoid of content, apolitical, divorced from all social realities. Perhaps the clearest statement of this position comes from Feather, who, writing in *down beat Music '67*, misreads the course of jazz history in such a way as to "prove" that it would be "a basic denial of freedom" were the music not "to remain art, pure and inviolate."[24] Which is only another way of saying that art should never contain anything that might cause

Leonard Feather even momentary discomfort.

Ideologues can spew forth their "theories" until blue in the face—but so much the worse for them if reality does not correspond to their constructions! Perhaps there was a time when the Zwerins and the Feathers might have appeared halfway persuasive, but those times are long past, probably for good. As Isaac Deutscher, the masterful Marxist biographer of Leon Trotsky and Josef Stalin, writes in *Ironies of History:*

> An attitude of non-commitment [in art] can crystallize and become accepted only in a stabilized society where the foundations of national existence are generally taken for granted and where social conflict runs at a tension so low that it fails to communicate itself with art.[25]

Any moderately perceptive observer of the jazz scene would have to agree that there is precious little "stabilized" about contemporary capitalist society in the United States, and it is precisely the "foundations of national existence" that cannot be taken for granted by the black artists who produce the new music. Hence to expect the vapid kind of "art" that would please Feather & Co. under the chaotic and irrational conditions of today is like trying to find a quiet spot for a picnic in the midst of a raging artillery battle.

Nothing demonstrates more clearly the intertwined nature of politics and the new music than a concert that I had the good fortune to be able to attend over the 1966 holidays. The event, at New York's Village Theatre (later renamed the Fillmore East), featured, besides the artistry of Jackie McLean, Marion Brown, Archie Shepp, and their respective groups, a short speech by none other than Stokely Carmichael, the head of the Student Nonviolent Coordinating Committee (SNCC).

What Carmichael had to say has already been reported

and would be stale now, so I need not go into that. And in one sense, the content of his brief remarks was of secondary importance to the mere fact of his presence on the program: a leading advocate of black nationalism publicly united with some of the leading figures in the new music. One could hardly ask for a more vivid instance of the relationship linking the two.

At least as fascinating as Carmichael's appearance in tandem with the new jazz, however, was the way in which the presentation came about. Poet A.B. Spellman, the master of ceremonies, made a point of announcing that the idea for a benefit for SNCC had originated with Jackie McLean, who wanted a way to put his music at the service of the black liberation movement—something that Michael Zwerin, who devoted half a column to reviewing McLean's performance, somehow managed to omit.[26]

McLean's decision to raise money for SNCC is of particular significance because heretofore, so far as anyone knew, he was simply another one of the Establishment's good niggers in jazz. Though his playing had been lightly tinged with some of the ideas of John Coltrane and Ornette Coleman, McLean's roots were still in bebop, and it did not appear that he had committed himself wholeheartedly to the jazz revolution. More important to the Establishment, he had never given any indication of "unreliability"—never, that is, taken to seasoning his discourse with talk of exploitation, nationalism, radicalism, the U.S. war in Vietnam, boycotting the jazz business, organizing musicians' cooperatives, or any other contemporary heresy. That makes his desire to aid SNCC, and the cause of Black Power it espouses, so much the more notable. After all, no one would have been particularly surprised had the benefit been planned by Archie Shepp, Cecil Taylor, Marion Brown, or Bill Dixon. But *Jackie McLean?*

That Michael Zwerin could review the concert without

mentioning any of these matters is, in its own way, a significant social act: it reveals Zwerin's unwillingness to put jazz—and I mean *all* jazz, not just the new music—in its correct social perspective. But Zwerin's sin is at least only one of omission. What can we possibly think of this distorted account of the bebop revolution, given us by Leonard Feather in the article I cited at the start of this subsection: "Neither in the sounds produced by Gillespie, Parker, Kenny Clarke, and their contemporaries, nor in the titles or the arrangements, is there a relation to the brutal conditions that persisted through the bebop years."[27]

One wonders. Jackie McLean was among the musicians to be in on the ground floor of developments in jazz during the bebop period. If the music were really as removed from social reality as Feather would like us to believe, is it likely that McLean would turn up in the Black Power camp today? Apparently Feather finds it easier to "forget" the plain social implications in the decision of Charlie Parker—McLean's earliest mentor—to entitle one of his compositions "Now's the Time," to "forget" that Parker himself said, "Music is your own experience, your thoughts, your wisdom. If you don't live it, it won't come out of your horn." (Ironically, this statement is quoted by Nat Hentoff, attacking the proposition that "jazz can somehow be insulated from life," on the page following Feather's warped version of bebop history!)

Feather and Zwerin or no, jazz (as I sought to demonstrate in chapter 1) has *always* flowed out of the circumstances of the musicians' existence. In this respect, the critics could well stand to absorb a few lessons from Charlie Parker, to say nothing of his latter-day descendants. It is neither tenable nor realistic to assume that the black men and women of this century who have given us the music called jazz were any more unaware of their oppressive environment than the slaves who in the last century produced the spirituals, work songs, and other protestations against their condition.

Nothing could be more vain than to hope to sunder jazz and politics; the two have continually been wedded, and the closeness of the union must grow rather than shrink. For that reason, Jackie McLean's concert for SNCC can be only the beginning.

3. down beat: *political censorship, divide and rule, and other fun and games*

In what follows I intend to go beyond mere individuals, to make clear the pivotal *institutional* role that *down beat* magazine plays in helping to perpetuate the reign of white supremacy in jazz.

As a handy rule of thumb, you can estimate the stature that any art enjoys in a modern nation by the caliber of the journals devoted to it. Such being the case, you would never have to hear a single note of the music to be made aware that members of the American Establishment are convinced of the inferiority of jazz; all you need do is glance at a few issues of *down beat*. If the art it purports to discuss were considered "serious"—that is, European—there would be no room for the existence of a periodical of this nature. That the magazine not only exists but has the largest circulation of any of those treating the music offers the most immediate evidence I know of for the continued second-class artistic citizenship of jazz.

If jazz were the movies, *down beat*'s name would be *Silver Screen*—that is the quickest way to convey the essence of the magazine. And yet for all its unmitigated triviality, it has a greater degree of influence than any rival periodical. Owing to its aggressive sales of advertising, it has been able to outlast and outstrip all its competitors. *Metronome, Jazz Review, Record Changer, Jazz Quarterly, Jazz*—all these and others whose names I have forgotten have come and gone, while *down beat* has hung on since the late 1930s, riding out each new development in the "music business."

Its very longevity in a field where failure and quick demise is the dismal rule has made *down beat* a force with which one must reckon. Musicians like to pretend (with good reason, I might add) that they are indifferent to what passes for jazz "criticism" and therefore don't read the magazine; but secretly they all do. Even Miles Davis, whose independence and outspokenness are bywords in jazz circles, has his awards from *down beat* mounted in his living room. (Davis's proffered explanation, which writer Nat Hentoff naively repeats at face value, is that the trumpeter "has a particular liking for 'good wood.' " He hasn't made enough money to buy a piece of teak or mahogany from a lumber yard?)[28] Hence the views that *down beat*'s conservative editorial staff and publisher disseminate are a subject of more than passing importance.

"There hasn't been one time where I have been prevented from saying what I wanted to say—or has anyone, for that matter, been prevented from expressing his opinion."

That pious sentiment came from the mouth of *down beat*'s New York editor (later, editor in chief), Dan Morgenstern.[29] Sadly enough, it is a prescription honored far more in the breach than in the observance. In point of fact, *down beat* is quite cavalier in its mishandling of the truth and is all too eager to suppress dissenting opinions. As these are basic aspects of its *modus operandi*, it is worth making the effort to document these accusations in detail.

Item: I first became aware of political censorship at *down beat* when Ralph Gleason, then still writing on jazz, told me that one of his columns for the magazine had drawn the ire of the editorial and business staffs. His transgression, it seems, had been a few sentences connecting the political "winds of change"—for instance, the Cuban revolution led by Fidel Castro, the "sit-ins" of black students in the South and the drive to abolish the House Committee on Un-American

Activities in the U.S., the Campaign for Nuclear Disarmament in Britain, and so forth—with the musical ones represented by John Coltrane, Ornette Coleman, Cecil Taylor, and others.[30] Although this column somehow managed to see the light of publication (it was probably set in type with only a cursory reading), the publisher and advertisers were aghast, and the word quickly came down to Gleason from On High: *Cut out that Commie crap!* Next, Gleason discovered that his bylined columns and record reviews were being censored, ultimately prompting him to resign.[31] Shortly thereafter, my own writing for *down beat* began to be subjected to a similar treatment—the *San Francisco Chronicle* reported that my "reviews were not only cut, but the emphasis [was] altered"[32]—leaving me little choice but to resign as well. This development, however, did not bring the issue to a close. When the *San Francisco Chronicle* published an account of the entire sequence of events, the editor of *down beat*, Don DeMicheal, had the effrontery to deny all charges and accuse the *Chronicle* of "scrambling . . . facts and truths"![33]

 Item: Ordinarily, jazz magazines are only too pleased to have musicians contribute articles, columns, and reviews, for these enhance the publication's image of authenticity and also serve to attract readers, subscribers and, therefore, advertisers. The unspoken rule, of course, that any musician who wishes to write for such a periodical must operate within the narrow limits of what the publisher and editors consider politically acceptable, thereby excluding at the outset some of the most articulate candidates for the role of jazz-musician-cum-journalist. Composer-trumpeter Bill Dixon, the organizer of the Jazz Composers Guild in the mid-1960s, is a perfect case in point. He has stated with respect to jazz magazines that although he has "been a recipient of calls from *all* of them when it was information they were seeking," nonetheless, "both *down beat* and the old *Metronome* rejected articles that I'd written." "What makes it necessary," he would later demand to know,

> for you (and I mean the collective white American you) to tell me one thing, because you're seeking a certain kind of information and then later accept another man's view and discard mine. Is it because you look alike? And I'm not talking like LeRoi Jones!!! I'm reacting like Bill Dixon!!! Although I do agree with Jones about white America being totally unable to accept any kind of leadership from black Americans.[34]

One cannot fault Dixon's generalization, especially if one takes *down beat* as representative of "the collective white American you" whom he addressed. For not only has that periodical demonstrated itself to be "totally unable to accept *any* kind of leadership from black Americans," but it has not even been able to work up its institutional courage to the point of publishing so much as a single article from this seminal figure in the jazz avant garde.

Item: Robert Levin, a radical white author, has reported on his tribulations in having *down beat* print an article of his on the Jazz Composers Guild. After twice revising the original so as to dilute its tone and conclusions,

> a considerably milder version of the . . . article was accepted by *down beat,* in the form of an interview with the Guild's animator, Bill Dixon . . . but the following quote from Cecil Taylor . . . was deleted by [*down beat* editor] Don DeMicheal on the grounds that it "veered away from the subject of the Guild."

> "I don't know if the powers that be [Levin quotes Taylor] would want (musicians to work regularly) because you would be able to operate at maximum capacity on all levels. You could begin to think constructively in other

areas, too. You would be able to think in terms of what you would contribute to your community on all levels— not just the level of a musician. The artist . . . could become an engaged part of the community."[35]

The purposes of the Guild—one of whose founding members was this selfsame Cecil Taylor—certainly included the aims that the pianist enunciated in this passage. But leave it to *down beat* to rescue its readers from the threat of being contaminated by exposure to such dangerous thoughts by asserting that Taylor's remarks "veered away from the subject of the Guild."

Item: Ultimately, however, the pressure on *down beat* from committed black artists like Dixon and Taylor was so great that the editors were forced to make some gesture to defuse the potential confrontation. In this way, they finally decided—not without the greatest reluctance, one supposes— to publish a token article by one of the younger black musicians, an "honor" they eventually bestowed on saxophonist Archie Shepp. Of course, *claiming* you will print an article by Shepp is one thing; actually doing so is something else again. Shortly after the *down beat* editorial staff had received and read Shepp's article, the saxophonist relates, he had a telephone call from editor Don DeMicheal, who moaned:

"This article frightens me. Are you sure you want to say these [favorable] things about Ho Chi Minh and Fidel, because you know what people will say about you." And I said, "All right, man, let them say that, because the FBI has already been to my house." And they have.

So, owing to the earlier efforts of Bill Dixon, Cecil Taylor, and other radical black musicians, his own perseverance and the fact that *down beat* was totally lacking in any black presence, Shepp in the end was able to have some of his views appear in the magazine late in 1965. But one swallow does not a summer make; one short essay by Archie Shepp, however excellent, is not anywhere near sufficient to compensate for *down beat*'s prolonged and intrepid career of political censorship.[36]

Item: In its December 16, 1966, issue, *down beat* carried a simultaneously scurrilous and sanctimonious "Plea for Less Critical Infighting" by Leonard Feather, in which the critic denounced "two or three white critics" for "trying desperately to prove . . . to Negro musicians . . . that they think just like soul brothers" by "rail[ing] and rant[ing] about the white power structure" and "shedding crocodile tears for Malcolm X." Though Feather's condescending and insulting polemic was evidently aimed at me—he mentioned my name twice in this article—*down beat* refused to print even a single line of the letter I wrote in reply.* So much, I trust, for Morgenstern's contention that "there hasn't been one time" when "anyone" has "been prevented from expressing his opinion."[37]

---

* His self-serving "plea" notwithstanding, Feather has instigated more than his share of "critical infighting." In a column that appeared in a different publication the very same month as his hypocritical "plea," for instance, he took *New Yorker* columnist Whitney Balliett to task for voicing two conflicting opinions on Archie Shepp—the second one, as you might guess, was favorable—within the space of a few months; see Feather, "Music," *Cavalier,* December 1966, p. 16. A year earlier, moreover, Feather's colleague Stanley Dance had observed that "there have been plentiful examples of internecine critical warfare in the last year or so. *Show* for October, 1964, carried Leonard Feather's attack on a group of writers he called the Disestablishment. . . . Among those Feather called to account were Martin Williams and LeRoi Jones." Dance rightly noted that "what was ironic about Feather's stand was that he and Barry Ulanov, 20 years before, had been similarly attacked for their championship of bebop, then also a music cordially disliked by most older musicians and critics"; see Dance, "Please Take It Seriously," in *down beat Music '65,* ed. Don DeMicheal (Chicago: Maher Publications, 1965), p. 40.

It is my contention that the editorial and publishing staffs of *down beat* are thoroughly ingrained with the precepts of white supremacy—to such a degree, in fact, that these precepts form an integral part of the magazine's intellectual frame of reference, something that can be taken for granted without the need for continual reiteration. That is why black nationalism, as well as other forms of radicalism that threaten to disrupt the status quo, are anathema to its editors, why the magazine is at such pains to discredit all radical ideologies. Witness on this point the reaction of *down beat* editor Don DeMicheal to Archie Shepp's essay expressing solidarity with Fidel Castro and Ho Chi Minh: "This article frightens me." One can be certain of it.

To put *down beat*'s systematic attack on black nationalism and radicalism in its proper perspective, however, it will be helpful if I at least touch on its pervasive anti-black animus. A couple of representative incidents will serve the purpose.

Item: In the summer of 1966, *down beat* carried an article by one of our previous acquaintances, Michael Zwerin, about the contemporary painter Larry Rivers, who also happens to be an amateur saxophonist and has on occasion played with groups led by drummer Elvin Jones, a friend of long standing.[38] Following the publication of this article, Dan Morgenstern, the successor to Don DeMicheal as *down beat*'s editor in chief, wrote an essay on the paintings of clarinetist Pee Wee Russell, who at that time had been working in oils for about one year.[39] But the magazine has never printed a solitary word about the fact that Bill Dixon has had no fewer than *four* one-man shows in New York City. Why the discrepancy? One can be excused for suspecting it might just have something to do with Russell and Rivers being white and Dixon black. Similarly, *down beat* has yet to acknowledge that Archie Shepp has had many of his plays produced in Manhattan. Work by jazz musicians in other arts seemingly is news to the editors at *down beat* only when it is

CRITIQUING THE CRITICS / 189

their white brethren who are involved.

Item: In the same 1966 discussion from which I have already quoted editor Dan Morgenstern's sanctimonious disclaimer of censorship at *down beat,* Cecil Taylor made a quite explicit—and verifiable—accusation of racist practices on the part of Morgenstern and the publication for which he writes:

> I refer to you, Dan Morgenstern, in your selection of artists representing the new music in the Museum of Modern Art garden series just last summer, when you knew very well the [black] creators were ready, at whatever terms you suggested, to play. And what did you do? You ignored us and hired a former [white] sideman of mine, a man named Roswell Rudd, who was never heard of in the modern musical context until the record I made for Impulse in 1961."[40]

How did Morgenstern deal with this accusation? Did he attempt to clear himself of the charge of racism by concrete deeds? Not at all. First, as permanent consultant to the Jazz in the Garden series—which is, according to his employer, "co-sponsored by *down beat*"[41]—he once more refused to extend an invitation to Cecil Taylor or any of the other seminal black artists involved in originating the new music; second, he reinforced this sin of omission by one of commission, rubbing salt in Taylor's wounds with the following bit of hypocrisy, incorporated in a review of the pianist's 1966 Town Hall concert:

> This is music that, for lack of a better venue, belongs in the concert hall. Yet, while academic hacks and fashionable modernists reap the necessary grants and fellowships without which no 'serious' musician can sustain himself in our time, Taylor, regarded by the establishment [!] as

a "jazz" musician, is left to shift for himself.

Given his rightful opportunity to create and perform with that minimum of security that our society now grants talents much lesser than his, there is no telling what Taylor might accomplish, considering what he already has achieved in spite of the unfair odds against him.[42]

What garbage! While Morgenstern throws around all this "radical" language about "the establishment," "our society," and "unfair odds," he fails to do the one thing within his power to aid Taylor—provide him with a job. Actions still speak louder than words. Morgenstern's actions in excluding radical black artists like Taylor from the Jazz in the Garden series drown out his devout protestations about the pianist's talents and make manifest the white-supremacist preconceptions on which he—as well as the journal he edits—operates.

In the good old days when niggers supposedly knew their place and whites expected they would keep to it, social discipline in the jazz world was fairly easy. If you were a conservative white concerned about black nationalism, all you had to do was unleash a tirade in *down beat* about the evils of "reverse racism"—meaning, black musicians hiring other blacks instead of whites, and other highly significant manifestations of black oppression directed against hapless and helpless whites—and the situation would soon be set right. To a degree, as we have seen in chapter 2 especially, this sort of thing still can be found, particularly among the older Establishment critics.

But this tactic is crude and, worse yet, even ineffectual. For that reason it has given way among the more astute white conservatives to a new policy: divide and rule. Actually, there is nothing very novel in this approach; the British used it early in the last century to retain their hold on India, and the American ruling class has depended on it ever since it first came into existence in the seventeenth century.[43] In essence, the technique is simplicity itself: you merely find members of an oppressed group who, for one reason or another—venality, stupidity, naiveté—are willing to work with the masters against the slaves; you then appoint these "cooperative" and "responsible" slaves to be the "leaders" of the others, and control those others through the "leaders." (Another variant of the technique—one that reaches its zenith in American social and political life, of course—is to play all of these groups off against the others: Jews against blacks, blacks against immigrants, ethnic minorities against white women, heterosexuals against gay men and lesbian women, workers against environmentalists—the possibilities are endless, limited only by the power of human ingenuity to devise potent means of fomenting baseless fear and hatred.)

Thus, the newest *down beat* response to black nationalism. At first, during the early 1960s, its editors sought to wipe out black nationalism and other unhealthy attitudes among jazz musicians through a campaign based on direct attack. Recently, however, the magazine has taken to using the more-sophisticated methods of divide and rule to achieve its goal. These methods deserve our attention, as they demonstrate the cleverness of conservative white liberalism (or liberal conservatism, there being no appreciable difference) in maintaining the status quo of privilege and inequality.

If, for example, you wish to scuttle the radicalism of the jazz revolution while it's still aborning, you needn't stoop to dirtying your own hands. Instead, you can get a safe, domesticated neo-bebopper, like trumpeter Kenny Dorham, who feels economically imperiled by the new developments—"If this thing isn't quarantined, we'll all be in the garment center pushing wagons," was Dorham's response in *down beat* to an Albert Ayler recording[44]—and he can do the job for you.

That way, no one can accuse *you*, a white editor and/or critic, of hostility toward the young black radicals: "What the hell. The musicians themselves don't dig it, right?"

Or again, if your aim is to counteract the increasingly leftist sentiments that prevail among the new artists, you can best accomplish it by finding some atypical musicians to interview and extol, palming off their statements as wholly representative. A good place at which to begin might be with, say, John Tchicai, who, although partially of African descent, was born and has lived almost all of his life in the comparative racial utopia of Denmark. And, sure enough, what do we discover but *down beat*'s ubiquitous Dan Morgenstern lauding the virtues of "John Tchicai: A Calm Member of the Avant-Garde"—the obvious implication being that the *other* avant-gardists are raving lunatics.

As if that title weren't sufficient, Morgenstern goes out of his way to beat the point into the ground, telling readers, for example, that Tchicai "seems more relaxed and more at peace with himself, less aggressive [a favorite pejorative!] and aggrieved, than the self-appointed spokesmen and standard-bearers [read: uppity niggers] of the new music." Later, Morgenstern reports Tchicai as saying: "I think there is also a tendency among a lot of Negro musicians to only look at this—that they are Negroes and that there will always be more opportunities for white musicians. But I think that is wrong."[45] (Hear that, Archie Shepp, Bill Dixon, Cecil Taylor?) And still later, in an effort to deny the primacy of black artists in the creation of all the major stylistic innovations in jazz: "I've heard Negro musicians talk about 'black music.' The music doesn't have any color. You can't see music, so how can you give it a color."[46] That bit of profundity certainly ought to tell these other niggers where to get off!

That this use of isolated black artists to create disunity among the new musicians and prevent the spread of radical ideas is standard *down beat* policy is clear from the fact that like-minded articles pervade the magazine's pages. Another illustration, from which I shall not quote this time, is Morgenstern's interview with Freddie Hubbard (December 1, 1966). Hubbard, you must understand, is not at all a full-fledged participant in the jazz revolution; his position is closer to that of an ambivalent observer located somewhere on the periphery. As you can readily learn from a few minutes conversation with him, he is a very amiable young man who is as yet uncommitted to any hard and fast doctrines, political or aesthetic, and certainly doesn't want to be considered *too* unconventional by his mates. More than that, by virtue of his temperamental caution and his reluctance to align himself fully with the jazz revolution, he has open to him a variety of employment opportunities that are closed to many of his more *engagé* peers, so the grinding poverty that bears down on and shapes the views of artists like Marion Brown and Archie Shepp is absent in Hubbard's case. To ask this man to evaluate the contributions of the jazz revolution is therefore somewhat akin to asking Kerensky what he thinks of the Bolsheviks. Yet it is precisely because of this equivocal stance that Hubbard's views are so highly prized by Morgenstern and *down beat* magazine.

So far as that goes, Dan Morgenstern appears to have been the principal architect and chief executioner of *down beat*'s Grand Design for pitting black musicians against each other and thereby continuing to rule in jazz. His efforts at manipulating the statements of certain favored black artists in order to discredit those radicals *down beat* regards as beyond the pale, however, have not been entirely successful. Indeed, on at least one occasion such an attempt blew up directly in its author's face.

The incident in question revolved around an article by Morgenstern on the then-expatriate composer, theoretician, and pianist, George Russell. As was true in the cases of John Tchicai and Freddie Hubbard, Morgenstern's interest in Russell per se was obviously secondary to his desire to twist the musician's comments into a weapon fit for bludgeoning the likes of Archie Shepp, Cecil Taylor, Bill Dixon, *et alia*. This crude aim was unmistakable from, among other things, the remark of Russell's that Morgenstern wrenched out of context to employ as a caption under a picture of the artist: "Avant-garde is the last refuge of the untalented."[47]

But in Russell, Morgenstern misjudged his subject rather badly. Seeking to turn the composer's comments to his own base purpose of waging war against the new black music—and Archie Shepp, for one, clearly considered himself to be among the intended targets[48]—the journalist found himself on the receiving end instead. In response to Morgenstern's deliberately misleading account of his opinions, George Russell lodged a series of charges against the writer and *down beat* that, in sum, bear out everything I have said above:

> The game was played on me when I naively expressed my views to one of your staff editors, Dan Morgenstern, last May. He proceeded to orchestrate them (*db*, July 29, 1965) into a cantata of conservatism, which, I suspect, is a result of his having listened to me with a biased ear. To serve his reactionaryism, he lifted a phrase out of the little qualifying context he had allowed it in the article and used it as an eye-catching banner under a picture.
>
> The phrase "the avant-garde is the last refuge of the untalented" is not a new concept. . . . However, lifted out of context, it can be interpreted to mean that I am making the absurd assertion that all musicians who consider themselves to be avant-garde are untalented.

Russell continued by condemning this "attempt to use me to exploit the popular delusions of people who are hostile to, or suspicious of, avant-garde jazz." But, Russell emphasized, he had no desire to be "anybody's darling"; he "especially"

did "not want to be the darling of a group of men who, after all these years" of neglect "have suddenly found a use
for me . . . to batter a segment of the avant-garde they don't
like over the head."[49]

Yet if the editors of *down beat* learned anything from this
experience, the lesson, as we shall witness, seems to have
been nothing more than the necessity of choosing their good
niggers with greater care in the future.

So far, the examples of *down beat*'s anti-radicalism that
I have cited have been of a "mixed" nature, both social and
aesthetic. This mixed nature reflects the fact that in jazz especially it is near-impossible to discuss the music in isolation
from the social context (although this doesn't seem to have
stopped the majority of white critics from trying), and vice
versa. Nonetheless, there are cases, particularly frequent
after 1965, in which the magazine has unleashed social or
political proclamations pure and simple, without even seeking to give them the fig leaf of a musical "cover." That these
pronouncements have been blatantly hostile to any kind of
radicalism goes almost without saying; but that *down beat*
has been able to utilize the pen of a black writer to compose
them is something of a novel twist. (Until about 1959, *down
beat* was as lily-white as the Ku Klux Klan, notwithstanding the overwhelming preponderance of black musicians in
jazz and the sizable black readership that the magazine has
always enjoyed.)

The writer in question is one Brooks Johnson, whose
perspective on black nationalism in particular and radicalism in general one can perhaps infer from the fact that his
employer is, according to *down beat*, the Governmental Affairs Institute in Washington, D.C. At any rate, his debut
in the magazine consists of an onslaught against something
he has dubbed "neo-neo-Uncle-Tomming," whose prime
practitioner seems to be the orchestra leader and composer
Sun Ra. Sun Ra's nationalist militance and refusal to be a

pawn for the white-owned recording industry is translated in Johnson's hands into irrational paranoia "about his relationships with white people and the white race." (After all, what would happen if *every* black musician were to follow Sun Ra's example?) For the dull-witted, Johnson spells out the moral in blunt and unmistakable terms: "Success is not based upon alienation, but accommodation." Following this pontification, he informs the reader that the artists involved in the new black music deserve to be dismissed as "jive punks" who "have to be more way out" on social and racial questions "to compensate for their lack of talent." Far from creating an art that is "representative" of black people, the work of the jazz revolutionaries is "based in ignorance and a talent void. Further, I have heard these same men"—it is a reasonable surmise that Johnson has in mind musicians like Archie Shepp—"rant about how they have been taken advantage of, and yet they have been up on the stand faking it, taking advantage of the listeners."[50]

It would be easy to go on quoting from Johnson ad nauseam. He descends even lower in the rhetorical scale, for example, by describing the new musicians as an "unattractive, negative element . . . in contemporary music" and characterizing poet-playwright LeRoi Jones as "their pimp"—certainly a tasteful way of putting the matter. But I have said enough already to convey the flavor—*odor* might be more exact—of Johnson's opinions. A subsequent disquisition on "Racism in Jazz"—pianist Andrew Hill acutely observes that "the system is such that when the black man speaks his mind, then it's time to call it 'racism'"—while adding nothing new, continues fulminating in a similar vein, rehearsing the same threadbare complaints about an alleged "perversion of black pride in jazz," condemning nationalists as musical incompetents ("it is easier to be a racist than it is to be a good trumpeter"), and painting the radicals as "black phonies and musical panderers in jazz."[51]

To what end?

It ought to be evident that this outpouring of vitriol can have no other intent than to undermine the appeal of those blacks who, like Shepp, Taylor, Brown, and Dixon, are uncompromising in their protests against all forms of exploitation. Ironically, if anyone is engaged in "neo-neo-Tomming," "neo-Tomming," or just plain old-fashioned Tomming, it is Johnson himself, who has allowed his talents to be used by *down beat* for such ignoble ends. The artists he maligns so intemperately are, as he might learn if he were to take the trouble to search them out, inveterate enemies of all distinctions based on class *or* race *or* sex—they seek, as David Izenson, the bassist with Ornette Coleman, told me, to construct a "classless society."[52]

Yet even so, the blame is not so much on Johnson as on *down beat*, for attempting to indoctrinate its readers into accepting the perverse notion that radical opposition to an evil status quo is somehow to be equated with racism and charlatanism.

Happily, however, it seems as if the school of thought that *down beat* distills so pungently no longer reigns unchallenged in jazz. During the last few years there has emerged a group of young writers whose primary orientation is that of the social critic, rather than the jazz critic. Doubtless you will know who I mean—figures like poets LeRoi Jones, A.B. Spellman, and John Sinclair, playwright-essayist Robert Levin, and (it pleases me to believe) myself. In its short existence, this loose grouping has already produced two of the finest and most important books on jazz ever written, Jones's *Blues People* and Spellman's *Four Lives in the Bebop Business*, as well as such stirring manifestos as Robert Levin's incomparable article in the first issue of the now-defunct *Sounds & Fury*.[53] Besides that, the new movement has left its permanent stamp on jazz journalism. That *Jazz* magazine sponsored a public forum on "Jazz and

Revolutionary Black Nationalism" with Archie Shepp and LeRoi Jones among the participants is in part attributable to the pressures generated by these young writers.[54] Paradoxically, the very fact that *down beat* now feels constrained to devote space to publishing diatribes against black nationalism is a measure of the influence that the group is capable of bringing to bear.

Meanwhile, behind the new authors there stand the new musicians, in whose furious discontent we writers dip our pens.

NOTES

1. From the transcript of a colloquy among Gitler (a jazz critic), Martin Williams (a critic), Dan Morgenstern (an editor of *down beat*), Don Schlitten (a record producer), and others, "The Jazz Avant Garde: Pro & Con—A Discussion" in *down beat Music '65*, ed. Don DeMicheal (Chicago: Maher Publications, 1965), p. 94; ellipsis in original.

2. In *ibid.*, p. 95; the editors identify Schlitten as someone whose "love and understanding of jazz are deep" (p. 87).

3. From the interview in chapter 13, below.

4. John Tynan, "Funk, Groove, Soul," *down beat*, November 24, 1960.

5. LeRoi Jones, *Blues People* (New York: William Morrow, 1963).

6. Several years ago, before he abandoned writing on jazz, the late Ralph Gleason told me of an incident that offers an excellent case in point. A correspondent (whom Gleason identified by name) reviewing the Monterey Jazz Festival for *down beat* early in the 1960s attempted to submit his liquor bill to the festival's management for reimbursement—this, on top of the fact that the festival's promoters had already agreed to pay for the gentleman's lodgings. When this absurd demand was refused, the correspondent retaliated by giving that year's festival an unmerciful panning, despite his absence from several of the concerts, his advanced state of inebriation

at many of the ones he did attend, and the all-around agreement of the audience and other critics on the excellence of the music. Our intrepid journalist resolutely refused to allow any of these considerations to interfere with his efforts at pouring balm on his badly wounded pride, not to mention pocketbook.

7. Stanley Dance, "Please Take It Seriously," in *down beat Music '65*, p. 40; *idem.*, "Liner Notes: An Apologia," *down beat*, January 12, 1967, p. 19.

8. The dominance of such "ins-and-outers" is skillfully dissected by Thomas J. McCormick, *America's Half-Century: United States Foreign Policy in the Cold War and After*, 2nd. ed. (Baltimore and London: Johns Hopkins University Press, 1995), pp. 12–16, 92, 97, 156.

9. As of 1965, according to Ira Gitler, who has probably written as many album notes in his career as anyone, $75.00 was "more like the average . . . check for services rendered [writing liner notes]. One company pays $35.00; another $50.00; several others, $75.00. The $200.00 [Kofsky] hints at is an *extremely* rare thing." "Ira Gitler to Frank Kofsky," letter to the editor in *Jazz*, July 1965, p. 7. In my own experiences with several recording companies in the late 1960s, $75 for a set of notes was essentially the standard fee for less famous writers. It must be added that, besides annotating albums, there is always the possibility that a writer favored by a company's executives can generate additional income by cranking out publicity releases, taking photographs, and the like, for the company in question.

10. See, for example, Leonard Feather, "Feather's Nest," *down beat*, February 15, 1962, p. 40. I treat this controversy, and Feather's leading role in it, more extensively in chapter 8.

11. See the notes by Feather to the following recordings: *The Eric Dolphy Memorial Album* (Vee Jay 2503); Elvin Jones, *And Then Again: Elvin Jones* (Atlantic 1443), *Poly-Currents* (Blue Note 84331) and *Coalition* (Blue Note 84361); McCoy Tyner, *Tender Moments* (Blue Note 84275); Alice Coltrane, *Ptah the El Daoud* (Impulse 9196); Ornette Coleman, *Love Call* (Blue Note 84356). Feather has also authored commentary for works by a number of other avant-garde artists; see as a case in point Andrew Hill, *Judgment* (Blue Note 84159) and *Lift Every Voice* (Blue Note 84330).

12. Leonard Feather, entry for Coltrane, John William, *The En-cyclopedia of Jazz in the Sixties* (New York: Horizon Press, 1966), pp. 99–100.

13. To call again on Stanley Dance, even for some of the "dozen persons throughout the world who exist solely by writing about jazz ... liner notes are a means of survival—or the difference between a jazz life and a return to the farm"; "Liner Notes," p. 19. By way of illustration, in 1968, when I was at my most impecunious, Bob Thiele, who produced all of the jazz and rock recordings for Impulse Records (a subsidiary of ABC Records), offered me the opportunity to write notes for *The Honeysuckle Breeze*, an album by studio saxophonist Tom Scott and the California Dreamers, so called; the latter were professional singers of advertising jingles, assembled strictly for the purposes of this recording. Although Tom Scott's playing was inoffensive, if somewhat vapid, the sound of the "California Dream-ers" was so full of treacle and so lacking in conviction and authority that despite my impoverished state, I could not bring myself to as-sociate my name with this particular concoction, and so informed a somewhat incredulous Bob Thiele. Not long afterward, however, I happened to see a copy of this album, whose cover boasted a glow-ingly enthusiastic set of notes by former jazz critic Ralph Gleason. Of such incidents is the fabric of jazz "criticism" woven.

14. "Ira Gitler to Frank Kofsky," p. 7.

15. Jessica Mitford, *The American Way of Death* (New York: Simon and Schuster, 1963).

16. See Martin Williams, "Bystander," *down beat*, June 30, 1966, p. 12.

17. *Idem.*, "Mostly Modernists: Coltrane Up to Date," *Saturday Review*, April 30, 1966, p. 67.

18. Leonard Feather, "Feather's Nest," *down beat*, December 16, 1965.

19. *Idem.*, "Music," *Cavalier*, December 1966, pp. 16–17; the quotation is on p. 16.

20. *Ibid.*, p. 16.

21. See Shepp's compositions "Malcolm, Malcolm—Semper Mal-colm," *Fire Music* (Impulse 86) and "On This Night (If That Great

Day Would Come)," *On This Night* (Impulse 97); the latter recording Shepp dedicates to Du Bois.

22. "Jazz Journal: Mister X," *The Village Voice*, December 15, 1966, p. 21.

23. Isaac Deutscher quotes this literary, critical, and political essayist in *Ironies of History: Essays on Contemporary Communism* (London: Oxford University Press, 1966), p. 240.

24. Leonard Feather, "Whatever Happened to Beauty—Or, Who Wants Pleasant Music?", in *down beat Music '67*, ed. Don DeMicheal (Chicago: Maher Publications, 1967), p. 19.

25. Deutscher, *Ironies of History*, p. 240.

26. Michael Zwerin, "Jazz Journal: One of My Heroes," *Village Voice*, December 29, 1966, pp. 10–11.

27. "Whatever Happened to Beauty?" p. 21. See also the discussion in chapter 1 of Feather's perverse misinterpretation of bebop's origins and history and of Parker's unbridled opposition to racism.

28. Nat Hentoff, "An Afternoon with Miles Davis," *The Jazz Review*, December 1958, p. 9.

29. In the partial transcript of a discussion among Morgenstern, Archie Shepp, Cecil Taylor, Rahsaan Roland Kirk and others, "Point of Contact," in Don DeMicheal, ed., *down beat Music '66* (Chicago: Maher Publications, 1966), p. 10.

30. Ralph J. Gleason, "Perspectives," *down beat*, April 27, 1961, p. 66.

31. Gleason wrote that *down beat* "lost this writer as a . . . reviewer when signed reviews were cut." "Lively Arts: Jazz Is Too Serious to Be Mishandled by Polls," *San Francisco Chronicle*, "Datebook" section, July 31, 1962, p. 31.

32. *Ibid.*

33. A copy of DeMicheal's unpublished letter of August 13, 1962, is in my possession; the quotation is from the second of its two pages.

34. Bill Dixon, "Bill Dixon," *Sounds and Fury*, July–August 1965, p. 39.

35. Robert Levin, "Some Observations on the State of the Scene," *Sounds and Fury*, July–August 1965, p. 6; see also Levin's article,

"The Jazz Composers Guild: An Assertion of Dignity," *down beat*, May 5, 1965, pp. 17–18.

36. Shepp's description of his telephone conversation with Don DeMicheal is in "Point of Contact," p. 110 (see note 29 to this chapter for a full citation); his article, "An Artist Speaks Bluntly," appeared in *down beat*, December 16, 1965, pp. 11, 42. Incidentally, *down beat* by no means has a monopoly on political censorship in jazz. In 1968, in order to have *Jazz* publish my editorial defending LeRoi Jones (Amiri Baraka) against charges of having incited an uprising in Newark, New Jersey, I had to threaten to resign my position as associate editor and sever all connections with the magazine. Although Pauline Rivelli, the editor and publisher, finally agreed to run such an editorial on Jones's trial in the April 1968 issue, it was printed over my name—the only signed editorial in the magazine's history—by way of a disclaimer. Extensive excerpts from my correspondence with Pauline Rivelli over this matter are in my 1973 doctoral dissertation in history at the University of Pittsburgh, "Black Nationalism and the Revolution in Music: Social Change and Stylistic Development in the Music of John Coltrane and Others, 1954–1967."

37. See Leonard Feather, "Feather's Nest: A Plea for Less Critical Infighting, More Attention to the Music Itself," *down beat*, December 16, 1965, p. 13, and Frank Kofsky to the editor of *down beat*, unpublished letter of December 6, 1965.

38. Michael Zwerin, "Larry Rivers: A Look into Two Camps of the Painter-Jazzman," *down beat*, August 11, 1966, pp. 21–22, 27.

39. Dan Morgenstern, "Pee Wee the Painter," *down beat*, December 1, 1966, p. 13.

40. In "Point of Contact," p. 31; the recording Taylor referred to is one devoted to his music and that of composer John Carisi, although it was confusingly issued as Gil Evans, *The Gil Evans Orchestra: Into the Hot* (Impulse 9), despite the fact that the work of Gil Evans nowhere appears on it.

41. See "News," *down beat*, July 28, 1966, p. 10, and October 10, 1966, p. 9.

42. Dan Morgenstern, review of Cecil Taylor concert, "Caught in the Act," *down beat*, July 28, 1966, p. 24.

43. Probably the best discussion of divide-and-rule as the decisive

technique by which the American ruling class manipulates elements of the non-ruling classes against each other to retain power for itself is in Howard Zinn, *A People's History of the United States: 1492–Present*, rev., updated ed. (New York: HarperCollins, 1995); for the origins of this system, see Edmund S. Morgan, *American Slavery American Freedom: The Ordeal of Colonial Virginia* (New York: Norton, 1975).

44. Kenny Dorham, review of Albert Ayler, *Spiritual Unity* (ESP 1002), Byron Allen, *Byron Allen Trio* (ESP 1005), Giuseppi Logan, *The Giuseppi Logan Quartet* (ESP 1007), in *down beat*, July 15, 1965, p. 29.

45. Dan Morgenstern, "John Tchicai: A Calm Member of the Avant-Garde," *down beat*, February 10, 1966, p. 20.

46. Tchicai quoted in *ibid.*, pp. 49–50.

47. Dan Morgenstern, "Random Thoughts from George Russell," *down beat*, July 19, 1965, p. 9.

48. "I address myself to George Russell," Shepp wrote to those he presumed his detractors in "An Artist Speaks Bluntly," p. 11.

49. George Russell, "Popular Delusions and the Madness of Crowds: A Letter from George Russell," *down beat*, April 7, 1966, p. 14. Revealingly, this same issue of the magazine contained another installment in its endless campaign against the thesis that jazz is a species of black music. An article by Gus Matzorkis (a pseudonym for Gene Lees?), "Down Where We All Live: Today's Avant-Garde Revolution as Seen in the Light of Jazz' Long History of Internal Strife," Part I, was graced with an inscription ("sidebar") at the top of p. 22 that blared, in type larger than that of the headline, "It is one thing to acknowledge the central role Negro musicians have played in jazz but quite another to conclude that jazz is Negro music." Need one say more?

50. Brooks Johnson, "[Uncle] Toms and Tomming: A Contemporary Report"—as if the magazine had ever before or since carried *any* kind of a "report" on "Toms or Tomming"!—*down beat*, June 16, 1966, pp. 24, 44. Brooks Johnson, I discovered, had served Dan Morgenstern in exactly the same capacity some four and one-half years earlier, when the latter was similarly inveighing against black nationalism from his position as editor of *Metronome*. See

"Forum for Three: Gene Ammons, Bennie Green and Dexter Gordon Interviewed by Brooks Johnson," *Metronome*, December 1961, pp. 12–14.

51. See *idem.*, "Racism in Jazz," *down beat*, October 6, 1966, p. 15; the quotation from Andrew Hill is in Don Heckman, "Roots, Culture & Economics: An Interview with Avant-Garde Pianist-Composer Andrew Hill," *down beat*, May 5, 1966, p. 20.

52. Interview with the late David Izenson, Manhattan, August 15, 1966.

53. Jones, *Blues People*, discussed at length in chapter 5; A.B. Spellman, *Four Lives in the Bebop Business* (New York: Pantheon, 1966); Robert Levin, "Some Observations on the State of the Scene" and "The Jazz Composers Guild" (see above, note 35, for the full citation to these two articles).

54. A transcript of this discussion among Shepp, Jones, Robert F. Thompson, myself, and others, was published in *Jazz* between April 1966 and July 1967, usually a page or two at a time. The idea for such a symposium was mine, but credit for trivializing it by chopping it into tiny parcels belongs strictly to the editor of Jazz, Pauline Rivelli; see her letter to me of November 19, 1965, quoted in Kofsky, "Black Nationalism and the Revolution in Music" (full citation in note 36). As usual when I attempted to work with Rivelli, my ideas were solicited—then subverted or ignored. Despite my best efforts, the panel that conducted this discussion ended up with fewer blacks than whites and fewer musicians than non-musicians. One does the best one can with the materials at hand.

4

The blues people of LeRoi Jones

*In due course, no doubt, emancipated American Ne-
groes will have their own "New Orleans revival," being
sufficiently distant from the old South to separate the
original cultural achievement of their people from the
conditions of oppression in which it took place.*
—FRANCIS NEWTON (E.J. HOBSBAWM)
The Jazz Scene[1]

From our current vantage point in the 1960s it has become
unmistakably apparent that the white American Left has
never adequately comprehended the nature of either Negro
music or Negro nationalism.

With the honorable exception of Sidney Finkelstein in
the United States[2] and E.J. Hobsbawm (writing under the
pseudonym Francis Newton) in Britain, white radicals have
been content to indulge in a nostalgic cult of "folk music,"
an art of dubious content drenched in yearning for days

gone by—but then, isn't this true of so much of the white Left today, whose primary public is comprised of alienated middle-aged intellectuals and perhaps momentarily rebellious white college youth? If ever there has been an art exhibiting beyond question all the properties of "bourgeois decadence," this—and not jazz—is it. Yet the single music that conceivably more than any other deserves the designation "folk" has never been any further away than a switch of the radio dial: on the rhythm-and-blues AM stations (one or more in every urban center with a sizable Negro ghetto) and, more recently, on the all-jazz FM stations as well. But while jazz has been evolving from the bebop and neo-bebop of the 1940s and 1950s into the contemporary extended improvisations of Miles Davis, John Coltrane, and Cecil Taylor, and as rhythm-and-blues underwent a tremendous revitalization at the hands of singers such as Ray Charles, the majority of white leftists were still to be found at the same shopworn stand, carrying that execrable hammer to the Cap'n!

The juxtaposition of jazz and black nationalism in the initial paragraph is more than fortuitous—indeed, it is their intimate connection that makes the cultural abdication of white radicals in reality so shameful. As poet, jazz critic, playwright, and belletrist LeRoi Jones makes abundantly clear, jazz, like revolutionary black-nationalist ideology, springs from the most oppressed stratum of United States society, the Negro working class, or "blues people," in the author's felicitous phrase.[3] And to the same degree that black nationalism implicitly poses on the agenda a thoroughgoing transformation of American society, the aesthetic values of jazz cry out for equally fundamental changes in this country's banal and tepid white middle-class cultural values.

But there is still another, more deep-seated sociological relationship linking jazz with black nationalism. Whereas Negro intellectuals and artists in other fields must for the most part appropriate the canons of European culture, there are no such canons on which the Negro jazz musician can draw. On the contrary, the source of such inspiration can stem *only* from his or her "racial" subculture. Thus, even though the recording companies, night clubs, festivals, and other means of jazz distribution are in white hands and much of the jazz audience itself is white, the Negro musician is of necessity *constrained* to reflect the collective mind of the ghetto in a way that painters or writers ordinarily are not.[4] That is why we find that (as I stated in previous chapters) long before the Nation of Islam (Black Muslims) gained notoriety—as far back as the late 1940s, in fact—"advanced" Negro musicians were renouncing Christianity and their Western "slave" names for Islam; the hard bop-funky-soul movement of the 1960s was also an early anticipation of the later mass-based black nationalism; and "Freedom Now," recently adopted as the name of an all-black political party, had its original debut in 1961 as the title of a jazz recording—generally misunderstood by white critics and ignored by white radicals—by nationalist-inspired drummer Max Roach and his wife at the time, singer Abbey Lincoln.[5]

For all of that, we should not make the mistake of thinking that this recasting of jazz in terms of an *explicitly* Afro-American aesthetic was either effortless or instantaneous. "The direction, the initial response, which led to hard bop," Jones tells us, was

> as much of a "move" within the black psyche as was the move North in the beginning of the [twentieth] century. The idea of the Negro's having "roots" and that they are a valuable possession, rather than the source of ineradicable shame, is perhaps the profoundest change within the Negro consciousness since the early part of the century. It is a re-evaluation that could only be made possible by the conclusions and redress of attitude that took place in the forties. . . . The form and content of Negro

music in the forties recreated, or reinforced, the social and historical alienation of the Negro in America, *but in the Negro's terms* [my emphasis]. . . . By the fifties this alienation was seen by many Negro musicians not only as valuable, in the face of whatever ugliness the emptiness of the "general" culture served to emphasize, but as necessary.[6]

It is this "profoundest change within the Negro consciousness" that LeRoi Jones has set himself to explore in *Blues People*—and far from the least delectable paradox of his immensely provocative book is that it is a product of the very forces it attempts to delineate. Yet if *Blues People* is impossible to imagine without a prior shift in black consciousness, at the same time Jones has accomplished that rare feat of raising himself (as the authors of the *Communist Manifesto* put it) "to the level of comprehending theoretically the historical movement as a whole." The work, in short, is considerably more than a reflection of the developments that have taken place during the last two decades. It is, rather, a reasoned and reflective account ("this book should be taken as a strictly theoretical endeavor") of the world-historical events leading up to and producing those changes. I can think of very few others capable of having written it.[7]

Those who approach this volume as simply another tome on jazz and its history should be forewarned that they are likely to be disappointed. For notwithstanding its author's repute as a jazz critic, *Blues People* is not concerned primarily with jazz per se: its province is more accurately conveyed in the subtitle: *Negro Music in White America*. What Jones has in actuality done—a thing so disarmingly obvious one wonders that no one has thought to carry it out before—is to use Negro music as a sociological tool to analyze the role and position of the Negro in United States society. In his own words:

> If the music of the Negro in America, in all its permuta-
> tions, is subjected to a socio-anthropological as well as
> musical scrutiny, something about the essential nature
> of the Negro's existence in this country ought to be re-
> vealed, as well as something about the essential nature
> of this country, i.e., society as a whole.[8]

And again:

> The most expressive Negro music of any given period will
> be an exact reflection of what the Negro himself is. It will
> be a portrait of the Negro in America at that particular
> time. Who he thinks he is, what he thinks America or
> the world to be, given the circumstances, prejudices and
> delights of that particular America.[9]

To recount Jones's conclusions in full is, of course, beyond
the scope of the most ambitious review. Instead, I will single
out some of his salient points.

One necessarily begins with an examination of one of the
consequences of the continued exclusion of the Negro from
contemporary American society—an early chapter of Jones's
book bears the heading "The Negro as Non-American"—except in his or her central role as superexploited subproletarian.
Here Jones reminds us that "adaptation or assimilation was
not much of a problem for most Negroes in the nineteenth
century," since there was always "a border beyond which
the Negro could not go, whether musically or socially. . . .
The Negro could not ever become white and that was his
strength; at some point, always, he could not participate in
the dominant tenor of the white man's culture."[10] But by a
rich dialectical contradiction, it was precisely the existence
of this "boundary," this "no-man's-land" beyond whose
confines Negroes were forbidden to pass, that provoked the
development of a distinctive music vastly more vital than

the thin "culture" whose ideologues were so unyielding in their rejection of black people.

But if the Negro masses turned their imprisonment in white America to good use by creating this most ambitious of the indigenous American arts, the achievement went largely uncelebrated by the black would-be bourgeoisie. Jones's emphasis on the schism along class lines in the Negro community is another aspect of his book that marks it unmistakably as an outgrowth of the black-nationalist ferment. With respect to the embryonic Negro middle class, Jones is on firm ground in asserting that it "represented (and represents) not only an economic condition," but a characteristic ideology and worldview; it has consistently operated on the assumption

> that it is better not to be black in a country where being black is a liability. All the main roads into America have always been fashioned by the members of the black middle class (not as products of a separate culture, but as vague, featureless Americans). . . .
> It was the growing black middle class who believed that the best way to survive in America would be to *disappear* completely, leaving no trace at all that there had ever been an Africa, or a slavery, or even, finally, a black man. This was the only way, they thought, to be citizens.[11]

The "middle-class black man" in this way came to develop "an emotional allegiance to the middle-class (middlebrow) culture of America," one that actually deemed hideous anything stemming from beyond this cramped area. In sum: "The black middle class wanted no subculture, nothing that could connect them with the slave."[12]

Jones's insight into the antagonisms between the essentially white-minded black bourgeoisie and the more

nationalist-oriented blues people yields an especially fruitful interpretation of contemporary jazz styles in his closing
chapter, "The Modern Scene." Although previous writers
have hinted at the nationalist impulse that animated many
of the bebop innovators, Jones adds another dimension to
the thesis: bebop was not only a rebellion against the white
commercialization of jazz that had taken place during the
swing era, but also a rejection of the stultifying "whitening"
tendencies of the Negro middle class that had to be overcome
if the music was to retain its vitality. (Moreover, the development of bebop, which was protest music at an avowedly
artistic, intellectual level, occurred simultaneously with a
rank-and-file revolt by the blues people against white middle-
class values in music, culminating in the post–World War
II renaissance of urban rhythm-and-blues. Jones is, to my
knowledge, the first to have called attention to the underlying connection between bebop and the rhythm-and-blues
revival.) Bebop was thus at one and the same time the only
thing "that could have restored any amount of excitement
and beauty to contemporary jazz" and "the idea that abruptly
lifted jazz completely out of the middle-class Negro's life."
Jazz, for the middle-class Negro, now became "as it was for
any average American, 'deep' or 'weird.'"[13]
    Besides its repudiation of the Negro petty bourgeoisie,
what Eric Hobsbawm (writing as Francis Newton) has accurately termed the "bebop revolution" also signified the
first stirrings in recent years of an overt Negro nationalist
consciousness.[14] Tinged though it may have been by cult-
ism and a predilection for the exotic—traits that may have
been due more to bebop's followers than to its creators—the
music nonetheless contained "a deep emotional recognition
. . . of the rudimentary sterility of the culture" that Negroes
had "all their lives been taught to covet." Bebop musicians
sought to compensate for this sterility by creating "a meta-
culture as isolated as their grandparents', but issuing from

the evolved sensibility of a modern urban black American who had by now achieved a fluency with the sociocultural symbols of Western thinking."[15]

In this world nothing remains unchanged for long—least of all, given the conditions of the Negro in America, jazz. Since the bebop revolution reached fruition now almost two decades ago, several notable developments have occurred. The chasm separating the jazz artist from the ordinary citizens of the ghetto has to some extent been bridged by the arrival in the last years of the 1950s of the hard bop-funky-soul genre, which had as its proclaimed goal the reaffirmation of black values in jazz. But the dominance of this genre (as I explained in chapter 1) turned out to be remarkably short-lived; within a few years the more adventurous figures—Miles Davis, Sonny Rollins, Charles Mingus, Max Roach and, above all, John Coltrane—were plunging into uncharted waters, having freed themselves from the rigid orthodoxies of the soul clichés. (As for Thelonious Monk, never having tried to hide the readily identifiable Negro roots in his playing, he seems to have felt no compulsion to exhibit them in public during the orgy of soul-baring, nor to retract them after that moment had passed.) These performers have more recently been joined by a crop of younger iconoclastics—predominantly saxophonists, but with the other instruments also represented—among whom the names of Ornette Coleman and the truly formidable pianist, Cecil Taylor, may be most familiar.

No revolutionary movement, as Trotsky was fond of observing, ever advances along an unbroken upward curve. Not all of the innovations of what Jones here and elsewhere calls the jazz avant-garde have resulted in overwhelming success, yet it seems reasonable to suppose that in the long run the new approach will be victorious. In this connection, Jones's intrepid defense of the avant-garde from the attacks of the jazz Establishment—those white writers who augment their income as record-company executives and publicists by composing jazz "criticism" as an avocation—is not the least valuable service his book performs, and performs well. He could not be more correct in writing, with respect to the latter-day critical reactionaries:

> The same kinds of comment and misguided protest have greeted the music of [Ornette] Coleman and other young musicians that greeted the music of [Charlie] Parker and [Dizzy] Gillespie and [Thelonious] Monk in the forties. Where the music of Parker, et al., was called in *Downbeat* magazine "ill-advised fanaticism," Coleman's music is called "antijazz."[16]

Another aspect of the bebop revolution that today looms large, albeit one that Jones does not explore to the fullest, was the tremendous appeal of the then-new music for disaffected and alienated white nonconformists ("merely by being a Negro in America one was a nonconformist," Jones wittily remarks[17])—with the prominent exception, sad to say, of the political Left. This rejection of "their own" culture by a relative handful of whites prefigured the much larger exposure to Negro music that the generation of white youth just now entering its adult years has enjoyed. Needless to say, such exposure can in no sense substitute for a politically awakened and working-class-based radical movement capable of offering meaningful support to the black revolution. But at a time when all classes of whites have drunk so heavily and long at the fount of white-supremacist ideology—a point that certain Marxists have yet to digest—one should not dismiss this experience out of hand. I, for one, am quite convinced that if push should come to shove, more than a few whites would find themselves on the "wrong" side of the barricades simply because a Ray Charles or a Miles Davis has changed their perception of the world in a way that, under existing circumstances, nothing else could have done. The traditional Left in this country may have fallen far short of its fundamental goal of heightening the class consciousness of white workers, but in some cases, at least, Negro culture has frayed the fabric of white supremacy by making a vivid impression on those young whites with an opportunity to have been exposed to it.

Moreover, although white radicals seem mostly unaware of it, spokesmen for the culture of the blues people like Le-Roi Jones are, through their critique of the barbaric mores and values of white America, making a profound contribution to the eventual reconstruction of society on humanist (or perhaps just human) lines. Of course, cultural "criticism" per se is hardly a novel phenomenon. Ever since the rise of widespread literacy in Western Europe and the accompanying mass reproduction of the objects of popular art, there has always been a certain stratum of the intelligentsia eager to inveigh against the degraded tastes of the swinish multitude. (Currently, it is Jacques Barzun who most clearly represents this point of view.) Now there is no denying that much of what we are exposed to in the mass media is genuinely abominable; as Walter Benjamin and others have demonstrated, the inevitable consequence of treating art, including "entertainment," as a commodity to be mass-produced for maximum profit is a rapid descent to the lowest common denominator, with the result that a sort of Gresham's Law soon prevails: bad art drives out good.

Thus far, the intellectual critique possesses a certain amount of justification. But with what do the intellectuals hope to replace the "mass culture"—over which, incidentally, the masses have precious little control—that they so vehemently denounce? It is the answer to this question that, more surely than any other, reveals the bankruptcy of elitist ideology. For by and large, members of the intelligentsia have nothing more substantial to offer than the desiccated works of the fashionable salons and academies over which they, as the self-anointed guardians of culture, reign. Isolated from the mainstream and hostile to it, these individuals come to glory in their status, thus neatly transforming necessity into virtue. Because of their contempt for all popular art, they have lost the ability (if ever they had it) to distinguish the commendable from the trashy. To them, popular art is uniformly worthless—otherwise, how could it be popular? The clearest evidence of this attitude can be observed in the intellectual treatment of jazz and Negro culture in general. Outside of an occasional nod here and there, the magazines of the liberal intelligentsia—*Harper's, Atlantic Monthly,* the *New Yorker,* the *New York Review of Books,* the *New York Times Magazine, Commentary,* and the like—either ignore jazz totally, or treat it as a manifestation of "nigger exotica" (the recent *Time* cover story on Thelonious Monk is symptomatic in this respect,[18] even if *Time's* politics are hardly liberal), or else relegate it to the same obscurity as the crossword-puzzle department and the astrology column. And in this the Left has apparently found nothing better to do than ape the liberals!

Fortunately, the whole issue is rapidly being taken out of the hands of white liberals and radicals alike. The most telling strictures against the insipidity of virtually every aspect of white culture are now advanced by black nationalist–influenced Negro writers; the names of Jones, Harold Cruse (who occasionally lacks clarity), Robert Vernon (in many ways keenest of the lot), and the staff of *Liberator* magazine come first to mind. Outspokenly hostile to the prevalent cultural sterility in the United States, these writers have posed the strongest challenge yet to the norms of white middle-class America—in sharp contrast to the tendency of all too many white radicals to acquiesce in the spiritual aridity that is the status quo (remember "Communism is twentieth-century Americanism"?).

What sets the nationalist (using the word in the broadest

sense) critique at opposite poles from the liberal-intellectual attack on "mass culture" is that the former is based not on narrow, elitist premises, but on the democratic idea that art, to be significant, must remain organically connected to everyday humanity, reflecting the joys and travails, the aspirations and frustrations of the common people. To illustrate that this is no idle fantasy, the nationalists can point to jazz and the other manifestations of the "Negro soul"; for here are vigorous and flourishing arts that have retained their roots in a flesh-and-blood community without having sacrificed anything in the way of aesthetic value. Armed with firsthand knowledge of a subculture that has produced such remarkable creations as jazz music, repelled by the hollowness and sickening amorality of American society, Jones and his fellow writers are defying the liberal shibboleth of "integration" by demanding to know: into *what?* By taking this step, they have brought down on their heads the undying enmity of liberals, white and black; all the more reason, then, for genuine white radicals to tender them appreciation and support.

At this point we have come full circle to this essay's opening lines. It says something important about the nature of the times that even a book whose ostensible main concern is music cannot avoid ending on a political note:

> The American Negro is being asked to defend the American system as energetically as the American white man. There is no doubt that the middle-class Negro is helping and will continue to help in that defense. But there is perhaps a question mark in the minds of many poor blacks (which is one explanation for the attraction of such groups as the Black Muslims) and also now in the minds of many young Negro intellectuals. What is it that they are being asked to save? It is a good question, and America had better come up with an answer.[19]

It is dangerous to assume—if history offers us any insight—that the ruling class will take much notice of even the best-intentioned warnings. Quite the contrary: in all probability, its members will attempt little or nothing until the opportune moment has already slipped by—and I am profoundly in error if yesterday was not already too late. But if the white power structure has shown itself to be blind to all the auguries of an impending conflict, one may venture at least a timid hope that the much-battered, fragmented, and disoriented American Left will not continue to persist in its long-standing insensitivity about where its real interests lie.

NOTES

1. Francis Newton [E.J. Hobsbawm], *The Jazz Scene* (Harmondsworth, Middlesex: Penguin Books, 1961), p. 269.

2. See Sidney Finkelstein, *Jazz: A People's Music* (New York: Citadel Press, 1948).

3. LeRoi Jones, *Blues People* (New York: William Morrow, 1963).

4. "The only Negroes who found themselves in a position to pursue some art, especially the art of literature, have been members of the Negro middle class. Only Negro music, because, perhaps, it drew its strength and beauty out of the depths of the black man's soul, and because to a large extent its traditions could be carried on by the 'lowest classes' of Negroes, has been able to survive the constant and willful dilutions of the black middle class and the persistent calls to oblivion made by the mainstream of the society." *Ibid.*, p. 31.

5. Max Roach, *We Insist!: The Freedom Now Suite* (Candid 8002).

6. *Blues People*, pp. 218–19. See also the discussion of the 1940s in chapter 1 of this work and chapters 6 and 7 of Frank Kofsky, *Black Music, White Business: Illuminating the History and Political Economy of Jazz* (New York: Pathfinder Press, 1997).

7. The quotation in parentheses occurs in *Blues People*, p. ix. I must regretfully add that Jones has been done a pronounced disservice by the publisher's unacceptably lax editing. Elementary errors of grammar abound, and there are some passages that suggest that they have not even been proofread. With little effort one can find puzzling parenthetical phrases which begin but, due to the absence of a closing parenthesis, never end, appositions lacking commas to set them off, and a whole series of other misconstructions that would be absolutely unacceptable in any freshman English class.

8. *Ibid.*, pp. ix–x.

9. *Ibid.*, p. 137.

10. *Ibid.*, pp. 79–80.

11. *Ibid.*, pp. 123–24.

12. *Ibid.*, pp. 131–32.

13. Jones relates this anecdote apropos the early days of bebop: "'You can't dance to it,' was the constant harassment [directed against the new music]—which is, no matter the irrelevancy, a lie. My friends and I as youths used only to emphasize the pronoun more, saying, 'You can't dance to it,' and whispered, 'or anything else, for that matter.'" *Ibid.*, pp. 199–200.

14. See Newton, *The Jazz Scene*, pp. 204–08, 212–13.

15. Jones, *Blues People*, p. 201.

16. *Ibid.*, pp. 234–35; in actuality, it was the playing of John Coltrane and Eric Dolphy that was first denigrated with the "anti-jazz" epithet. See chapter 8 especially for additional details.

17. *Ibid.*, p. 188.

18. See Barry Farrell, "Music: The Loneliest Monk," *Time*, February 28, 1961.

19. Jones, *Blues People*, p. 236.

5

Black music: Cold War 'secret weapon' *

It is no secret that the United States government has discovered jazz. For several years, Washington has employed jazz as a means of entry into nations that, if not openly hostile to this country, were not particularly interested in learning about the United States or its people. . . . [T]he government's use of jazz as an adjunct to diplomacy or, less politely, as a propaganda weapon . . . is common knowledge.

—down beat EDITOR DON DEMICHEAL, 1963[1]

---

* The title of this chapter derives in part from a front-page article in the *New York Times* of November 6, 1955, by Felix Belair, Jr. Datelined Geneva, Switzerland, Belair's story reported:

"America's secret weapon is a blue note in a minor key. Right now its most effective ambassador is Louis (Satchmo) Armstrong. A telling propaganda line is the hopped-up tempo of a Dixieland band heard on the Voice of America in far-off Tangier. . . .

"American jazz has now become a universal language. It knows no national boundaries, but everybody knows where it comes from and where to look for more. . . ."

Is black music—specifically, jazz—an instrument of United States Cold War diplomacy?

A controversy over just this question erupted in the pages of *Jazz* magazine during the mid-1960s, set off by the remark of Willis Conover, director of jazz programming for the Voice of America, that a European musician had reported to him, "the uncommitted people may very well indeed be attracted to the American position" in the Cold War "by your broadcasts of American music." "And meanwhile," Conover himself added, "our music helps maintain contact with people already inclined to sympathize with the United States. . . ."[2]

Even a cursory search reveals that similar comments abound in jazz magazines and journals. On the basis of the program that Willis Conover conducts for the Voice of America, for example, *down beat* editor Don DeMicheal was moved to gush over the disc-jockey as

> the most important man in international jazz. His world wide audience has been estimated at 30,000,000. . . . Following a trip to Communist satellite countries, jazz promoter . . . George Wein said "Eastern Europe's entire concept of jazz comes from Willis Conover."
>
> Even more important to the country, Conover represents, personifies, the United States to his listeners. As one letter writer told him, "You symbolize freedom."[3]

Conover's ostentatiously "modest" rejoinder to this lavish praise is instructive: "I'm only a lower-case voice identified with the music that symbolizes freedom to them."[4]

As Conover cited with such unconcealed relish the comment that his broadcasts were helping attract "the uncommitted people . . . to the American position" in 1965, at the height of the U.S. ground, air, and sea assault on the peoples of Southeast Asia, I considered it a moral obligation to protest against the policy of using jazz to offset the growing international revulsion against this genocidal war of counterrevolution. Conover's consummately disingenuous response was that the conversation he had repeated had occurred "some years ago, before we were in Vietnam."[5]

Leaving aside the fact that the U.S. effort to prevent Southeast Asia from falling into the hands of its own people goes back to 1948, when the Truman administration began assuming roughly 70 percent of the cost of France's campaign to exterminate the revolutionary Viet Minh,[6] Conover's denial is implausible on the face of it, as emerges quite clearly from an examination of the role of his employer, the Voice of America (VOA). The Voice, Don DeMicheal explained for the benefit of *down beat*'s readers, grew out of "an Office of War Information [that was] established in 1942 as a propaganda adjunct to the war effort. It became known as the Voice of America in 1945."[7] As the U.S. began to transform its policy vis-à-vis the Soviet Union from one of cooperation to one of military "containment," the VOA metamorphosed, in Conover's words, into "the radio arm of the United States Information Agency" (USIA),[8] which, as is well known, supervises the dissemination of pro-U.S. and antisocialist propaganda throughout the world.

Even employees of the USIA themselves make no bones about what it is they do. "Many agency officials see most of its output as evidence that USIA is in the propaganda rather than information business," journalist Stanley Karnow reported in the *Los Angeles Times*.

The view is confirmed by [Agency director Frank] Shakespeare's own affirmation that USIA is "a propaganda agency." . . . As one of his senior subordinates explains it, Shakespeare basically sees the world in terms of security and therefore holds that *USIA's function is to support America's international military posture* [with no exception for Southeast Asia; my emphasis]. . . .

In USIA jargon, consequently, "better balance" signifies displaying only the good side of the United States to offset the image of poverty, violence, racial tensions and other shabbiness in commercial American films and novels.

Accordingly, the Agency simply refused a request "to produce a movie on university life in America" on the grounds that, as one of Shakespeare's top aides put it, "we would have to show student dissent and that tarnishes our image."[9]

With respect specifically to USIA-VOA efforts at employing jazz "as a tool of the U.S. government" in the Cold War,[10] long before the dispute between Conover and myself the editor of *down beat* already had observed that

> if the State Department's cultural presentations program is the most dramatic use of jazz by the [federal] government . . . then the U.S. Information Agency's use is the most far-ranging and has gained more friends for this country—*the raison d'être of jazz in government* [my emphasis]. . . .[11]

More specifically yet, DeMicheal concluded that of all the jazz-related programs broadcast by the Voice, "the most important and influential . . . is Willis Conover's 'Music U.S.A.'"[12]

Indeed, the scope and significance of Conover's propaganda activities in behalf of U.S. imperialism have been acknowledged at the highest levels of government. During the administration of John F. Kennedy, for instance, White House press secretary Pierre Salinger was pleased to inform Don DeMicheal that the Soviet citizens he had met on a visit to the USSR "knew more about jazz than I did, knew more of the names. They listen to Willis Conover's Voice of America program—it's their point of contact." Even Kennedy himself, Salinger added, "was very much aware of jazz and what it is doing."[13]

To summarize, then, the USIA and its VOA offspring are strictly outgrowths of the Cold War, and were that war to end tomorrow, the USIA would soon vanish, taking with it the VOA, jazz and all.[14]

Notwithstanding all the evidence to the contrary, Conover still stubbornly maintains that his work at the Voice of America does not amount to Cold War propaganda: "my purpose in doing the Voice of America program is . . . to show us as we are." One may be permitted to express a modicum of doubt, however, especially in light of the USIA director's widely recognized proclivity for "displaying only the good side of the United States." Consider, for example, Conover's version of the United States "as we are": "What's changed," he insisted in 1965, "is the circumstances most of us live in, changed for the better, and continuing to change for the better," and that "in ten years at the most, there'll be nothing but a few illiterate old diehard racists left in a few backwoods Southern shanties" as the last vestiges of racism. Pressed to substantiate such a sweeping generalization, he fell back on the assertion that "Sarah Vaughn and I can dance at the White House," whereas twenty years ago, when "Washington *was* a segregated Southern town, we had to go to an illegal uptown after-hours club" [my emphasis].[15] Progress, indeed!

These methodical distortions of life in the United States are not in the least accidental; they are, rather, part of the USIA's openly admitted effort at picturing this country, and its black-white relations in particular, in the most flattering light. Before being deposed from the presidency of Ghana, Kwame Nkrumah criticized USIA-VOA broadcasts in Africa as "the chief executor of U.S. psychological warfare, [glorifying] the U.S. while attempting to discredit countries [like Ghana under Nkrumah] with an independent foreign policy."[16]

Nkrumah also accused the two agencies of "planning and coordinating [their] activities in close touch with the Pentagon, CIA [Central Intelligence Agency] and other Cold War agencies, including even armed forces intelligence centers." In this vein, Nkrumah pointed out that when governments in Togo and the Congo (Leopoldville) indicated they intended to permit information centers from the Soviet Union as well as the United States, "Washington threatened to stop all aid, thereby forcing these two countries to renounce their plan."[17]

There can be little doubt that Nkrumah's picture of the USIA is accurate. The deputy director of the agency during the Kennedy administration, Donald M. Wilson, for instance, told the House Foreign Affairs Subcommittee that his agency had "very close" relations with the CIA. "We have daily contact with them [CIA and other intelligence agencies] on a number of levels."[18] In their book, *The Invisible Government*, David Wise and Thomas B. Ross term the VOA "the official voice of the United States Government." "It should be obvious," they continue, that its broadcasts "across national boundaries to other nations, particularly behind the Iron Curtain, are among the mechanisms of United States foreign policy."[19]

All of which disturbs Willis Conover not in the least. "What is wrong," he wants to know, "with presenting a good music program?"[20] Here we have the parable of the Emperor's new clothes in reverse: something painfully obvious to everyone else has somehow managed to escape Mr. Conover's field of vision.

But the USIA and VOA are not the only official governmental agencies to take advantage of jazz as a means of attaining U.S. Cold War diplomatic goals. According to *down beat*, in fact, "the greatest use of jazz in government is by the State Department . . . in the form of tours by jazz groups." These tours are, in editor Don DeMicheal's words, part of "the State Department's cultural exchange program, or as it is formally titled, The President's Special Program for Cultural Presentations . . . this country's answer to the Soviet Union's use of artists as Cold War troops."[21]

A textbook illustration of how the State Department exploits the international popularity of jazz to score gains in the Cold War occurred in the spring of 1966; the headline over the story in the *New York Times* caught the gist in a nutshell:

SOVIET POETS FAIL

TO CAPTURE DAKAR

Duke Ellington the Winner

in Propaganda Skirmish

Ellington's "win," as the *Times* insisted on calling it, had taken place at Senegal's first World Festival of Negro Arts; and to underline the point that more was involved than merely art-for-art's-sake, Lloyd Garrison wrote that Soviet poet Yevgeni Yevtushenko "had been urgently summoned from Moscow to do for Soviet propaganda what Duke Ellington had done for the Americans. . . ."[22]

It is, of course, saddening that the works of artists of the stature of Ellington and Yevtushenko are debased into ideological counters in the Cold War. But what makes it even more disturbing, as far as the United States is concerned, is the degree of hypocrisy involved. For if the Soviet Union brings to bear its poets, its dancers, and its musicians in the propaganda battle, it at least pays them the elementary courtesy of giving them a decent livelihood and an honored position in Soviet life. Contrary to American practice, the Soviets do not send their artists and intellectuals abroad as roving ambassadors, only to consign them to second-class citizenship at home. Instead, there the artist is generally on a par with the scientist, the professional, the government bureaucrat, and even the Communist party member.[23] Would that this were true in the United States! If the *Times* had wanted to be more thorough, not to mention ironic, it could have followed up its account of Ellington's "triumph" in Dakar by pointing out that the same Ellington had been rejected for a Pulitzer Prize in music less than a year before.[24] This juxtaposition—not atypical, just more glaring than most—exemplifies the unwritten rule that jazz may be eminently serviceable for Cold War campaigns abroad, but when it comes to winning acceptance *at home*, there the prospects are considerably more grim. So far as the cultural-intellectual Establishment is concerned, jazz is the unwanted stepchild of the arts. It is utilized for Voice of America broadcasts, its performers are eagerly sought for State Department tours, yet should it be proposed to the representatives of the Establishment who are so concerned with the worsening U.S. "image" that a jazz musician deserves to receive a foundation grant, a visiting professorship, or a Pulitzer Prize, the response would be one of shock and dismay.[25]

Possibly the best way to understand just where jazz stands with respect to the Establishment is to look at the position it occupies—or rather, doesn't occupy—in the university. I say this because the university is in some ways a microcosm of the Establishment as a whole. As we now know from studies that appeared as the by-product of protest movements at campuses all over the country during the second half of the 1960s, universities are governed by boards of regents, trustees, et cetera, on which sit representatives of the dominant business groups in the community.[26] In a general way, the curriculum of the university is shaped to the demands of this corporate elite for an institution that will mass-produce mid-level technicians with all the approved social attitudes (an idea most frequently propounded by Clark Kerr in his concept of the "multiversity"). Consequently, if one wishes to see the value that this pinnacle of the Establishment places on jazz domestically—as opposed to its usefulness to the ruling class as a Cold War instrument—one could do worse than look at the university curriculum.

With this in mind, I carried out a short survey of fifty college and university catalogs chosen at random. Of the fifty institutions, only three offered courses in jazz (though no course title mentioned jazz by name, preferring instead the less risqué euphemism "stage band"). It bears emphasizing, moreover, that the dearth of jazz on the campus is not to be explained by its relative newness. As forms of art, photography and jazz are of roughly the same age; but photography—perhaps because its origins cannot be traced to "niggers"—has been able to breach the walls of the university, whereas jazz, aside from some very rare exceptions, has not. In these same fifty colleges and universities, there were eight with courses in photography, almost three times the number of those with classes in jazz. The University of California at Los Angeles (UCLA), for instance, has an entire graduate department in cinematic arts, while Yale now offers a course in the aesthetics of filmmaking—but neither one makes any mention of jazz in its catalog. At California State University at Los Angeles, where I taught in 1964–65 and again in 1968–1969, one may take up to seven courses in photography, including one in motion-picture photography. Of jazz courses, however, there is not a one. For that matter, the opportunities for music students to play jazz for academic credit are so limited on this campus that alto-saxophonist Jimmy Woods—who is sufficiently talented to have recorded at the head of a group that included Elvin Jones and pianist Andrew Hill[27]—preferred sociology to music as his major.

There are no grounds for believing that conditions elsewhere are any better, as the experiences of John Handy at San Francisco State University at the other end of the state attest. Despite the fact that he was regarded by his music professors as their outstanding student and a model for the others, Handy, an inventive saxophonist who worked with bassist Charles Mingus before forming his own group, found that his insistence in trying to obtain courses that offered credit for jazz playing resulted in nothing more than a head-on collision with the department.[28]

For each case of a university (North Texas State, for example) that offers a jazz-oriented education to the tyro musician, Handy's story could, I am sure, be repeated several times over. And the bias against jazz extends beyond the music department. Every four-year college and university presents a series of performances and lectures by visiting artists and writers—but almost never jazz. There is, for instance, a Committee on Arts and Lectures (CAL) that plans such programs at the University of California, and well do I remember the hour of fruitless wrangling I spent with one of the upper-echelon administrators of CAL on this subject. Why, I wanted to know, were jazz artists never included in the CAL programs? The answer was simple: jazz is "entertainment," not art. Against this arbitrary verdict I expostulated in vain, until, sensing the futility of that approach, I shifted ground. Perhaps there was something I had overlooked that would explain how the presence in the coming year's series of comedienne Anna Russell, who is noted for her operatic spoofs, could be justified under the heading of "art." If Anna Russell, why not, say, the singers Lambert, Hendricks, and Ross? At this juncture the conversation disintegrated completely. My opposite began spluttering about how "everyone" loved Anna Russell . . . one couldn't take these things too seriously . . . of course, you understand . . . perhaps next year . . . and so on, until finally, unable to bear any more, I excused myself. Thus, jazz had to wait for its introduction on the Berkeley campus until the spring of 1960, when the Students for Racial Equality sponsored a concert to benefit what was later to become the Student Nonviolent Coordinating Committee. Naturally, the administration of Clark Kerr then refused to let the group send the money off campus to aid black students in the South—but that is another story, whose narration properly belongs in an introductory chapter of a history of the Berkeley Free Speech Movement.

For brevity's sake I have concentrated on the university, but I could have looked just as well at other cultural indicators and derived exactly the same results. Take, for example, the Establishment "intellectual" journals—periodicals like the *New York Review of Books*, the *New York Times Magazine*, *Commentary*, *Atlantic Monthly*, *Harper's*—and compare the amount of space they devote to jazz with that they lavish on European music, painting, books, or any other art that the Establishment deems of value. Very few of these publications discuss jazz at all, and fewer yet with any regularity.[29] Contrary to what one might expect, furthermore, the smaller-circulation journals of the liberal and radical left offer no dissent from the Establishment's view of jazz; if anything, there is less coverage of jazz in such journals as the liberal *Nation* and *New Republic*, or the radical *Monthly Review* and *National Guardian*, than one can read in *Harper's* or the *New York Review*. But the differences are in any case negligible in the face of the overwhelming lack of respect for jazz which all of the aforementioned periodicals exhibit.

The dispensation of fellowships for jazz artists, black ones especially, offers further evidence of the low esteem in which the Establishment's cultural elite holds jazz. It is "characteristic" of that Establishment's "attitude toward jazz," A.B. Spellman has observed, that the Rockefeller Report on the Performing Arts, which attempted to survey the entire situation of the performing artist in America and to propose concrete means of improving the situation, made no mention whatever of jazz. Nor does the recent Federal law to aid the arts [by establishing a National Endowment for the Arts] make specific provisions for jazz musicians.... There is actually a controversy, as this is being written, about whether jazz qualifies as "folk art" under the terms of the bill.[30]

Why this intransigent hostility to jazz on the part of Establishment educators, administrators and patrons of the arts? The answer, as I have maintained throughout, lies in the origins of jazz—particularly its black origins. Regardless of whether jazz came up the river from New Orleans or was born at Harlem rent parties, the popular stereotype of it is—bluntly— nigger music.* Attitudes of white intellectual supremacy and European ethnocentrism are so thoroughly ingrained that it is impossible for many whites, even those with good intentions, to conceive of a Negro art as equal in aesthetic value to a white one. To be sure, one may occasionally find a piece of African sculpture in the home of some white academicians; that is "quaint," or "primitive." Undeniably, it is now fashionable to own the recordings of Negro performers like Lightnin' Hopkins or Big Bill Broonzy; that is accept-

---

* When a group of Stanford students sought to produce a series of jazz concerts during the 1965–1966 academic year, they had to contend with the objections of the University's Public Exercises Committee—to wit: "the head of the committee was worried about allowing the rabble to invade the campus en masse—mightn't many of them be Negro, after all?" See Alan Heineman, "Stanford Jazz Year," *down beat,* September 22, 1966, p. 25. I suspect that the same thinking was at the root of the difficulties I encountered in attempting to persuade the University of California Committee on Arts and Lectures to schedule jazz concerts on the Berkeley campus.

ably "folksy." But what is seemingly too threatening for any number of whites to bear is the notion that Afro-American artists can produce a music that rivals European music in its complexity and demands on the listener's intellect. So even as the grants are handed out, the visiting professorships dispensed, and the awards announced for outstanding American artists, one can scan the list from beginning to end without encountering the name of a single jazz musician. I don't deny that there are occasional exceptions to this rule, but these are usually more apparent than real. Almost always the musicians so honored will be white, and therefore their triumphs comprise merely another slap in the face of African-American jazz musicians, nothing more. It is important to understand why rewards for white musicians are not a vindication of the music itself. It is not that whites are incapable of playing jazz. Clearly, such is not the case, although (as I discussed in chapter 1) nearly all whites of necessity choose black models. The point is, however, that whites are not now and have never been anything like the principal source of *innovation* in the music. A few white jazz musicians at most have been able to leave a permanent imprint on the jazz that came after them; the major new developments have always originated in the black ghetto. This generalization is as applicable today as it was in New Orleans in this century's first two decades, in Kansas City in the 1930s, in New York in the 1940s. A simple tabulation of the more than 200 instrumentalists listed by name in the 1965 *down beat* International Jazz Critics Poll, for example, shows that over 70 percent of the most distinguished jazz artists are black—and even that statistic probably understates the case.[31] Nonetheless, owing to the same causes that have prevented jazz from assuming its rightful place among the other arts, whenever the Establishment seeks to acknowledge the achievement of a jazz musician, almost invariably it is a white hand that reaches out to grasp the prize. Most black artists rightly view such occasions not as a victory *for* jazz, but *over* it.*

By way of further illustration, consider two jazz musicians whose versatility and schooling in the European tradition are roughly comparable. Pianist Cecil Taylor and trumpeter Don Ellis can both boast of an extensive "legitimate" education; insofar as they differ in this regard, it is because Ellis is white, Taylor black. Need I say which one received a visiting professorship at UCLA, a Rockefeller Foundation grant, and regular employment at Shelly's Manne-Hole in Los Angeles to boot? With all due appreciation for Ellis' talent, his good fortune must be held a monstrous injustice to Taylor and to jazz. The history of jazz in the 1960s and since cannot be written without pages devoted to the influence of Cecil Taylor; in that same history, Don Ellis would merit a footnote. Yet it is Ellis who obtains the academic appointment and who works steadily, while Taylor lacks all but sporadic employment and by the same token the opportunity—so necessary to the creative jazz musician—to experience the response of a flesh-and-blood audience to his music.[32]

Invitations to the White House for jazz musicians furnish a second index of the way in which the Establishment channels its rewards primarily to whites. To my knowledge, the jazz artists who have received such invitations during the 1960s are Sarah Vaughn, Duke Ellington, Gerry Mulligan,

---

* "At this point a couple of questions that are asked time and time again can be interjected. Why the almost systematic exclusion of qualified Negro jazzmen from collegiate and [music] clinic jazz programs? Why in a list of thirty clinicians listed for a summer jazz clinic are there only three Negro clinicians? Even more ridiculous is the low percentage of Negroes teaching jazz in the colleges and universities that offer or specialize in jazz courses." David Baker, "Jazz: The Academy's Neglected Stepchild," *down beat,* September 23, 1965, p. 29. The author, an Afro-American, played trombone with an avant-garde sextet led by George Russell and is currently a professor of music at Indiana University.

Paul Winter, and Dave Brubeck, the latter three being white. With all due respect for the attainments of these performers, it is simply a willful perversion of reality to argue that they represent a cross section of the best or most interesting, vital or relevant that the music has to offer. Why Gerry Mulligan or Dave Brubeck, when the jazz public holds the contributions of either Thelonious Monk or Miles Davis in much higher regard? Why Paul Winter, of whom nine out of ten jazz followers have probably never even heard (his outstanding accomplishment to date having been a State Department trip to Latin America), rather than the revolutionary innovations of John Coltrane? I don't have definitive answers to these questions, naturally, but a plausible guess is that whoever did the choosing judged the invited groups to be more acceptable on both musical *and* social grounds. One can sit chatting, after all, and appear to be enjoying Paul Winter's music without ever really paying much attention. But can you imagine responding that way to Coltrane or Miles Davis, who are so deep in the throes of creation as actually to *sweat* while they play? Really, my dear! *Black sweat* at the White House?

This pattern of whites obtaining a disproportionate share of whatever fitful recognition the Establishment is willing to bestow on jazz is anything but a new one. Regardless of the almost exclusive creation of the music by Negroes, they have never been the ones to reap the most lucrative returns. In the 1930s, as I related in chapter 1, it was Benny Goodman instead of Count Basie, Duke Ellington, or Fletcher Henderson who grew wealthiest on the craze for swing music; and two decades later it was Goodman and his sometime drummer Gene Krupa who had movies made out of their lives— not Ellington nor Basie, not Jo Jones nor Lester Young, not Henderson nor Don Redman, though all of these artists had infinitely more to do with the genesis of swing than Goodman or Krupa.[33] The situation has not changed appreciably in the interim. In the 1950s, Dave Brubeck preceded Thelonious Monk on the cover of *Time* by several years, despite the fact that Monk's music antedates Brubeck's by the better part of a decade and has exerted a much more powerful pull on the ultimate critics of the music, the performers themselves.

Furthermore, when *Time* finally did get around to doing a feature on Monk, there was a marked difference between its treatment of him and Dave Brubeck. The latter it portrayed as a respectable middle-class citizen with all the conventional bourgeois attributes and only one minor idiosyncrasy—that of being a jazz pianist. Monk, on the other hand, was presented to the magazine's readers as a combination of mad savage (he wears funny hats, he does ritualistic dances) and some sort of pharmacological eighth wonder of the world.

Witness, moreover, *Time*'s depiction of other leading black jazz luminaries in the same article, heaping ridicule on distinguished artists as if they were resident performers in a carnival sideshow. Sonny Rollins: "a Rosicrucian who contemplates the East River, letting his telephone ring in his ear for hours while he studies birds from his window." Charles Mingus (always a preferred target for white-critical abuse, as I noted in chapter 2): "so obsessed with goblins from the white world that person to person he is as perverse as a roulette wheel; his analyst wrote the notes for his last record jacket." John Coltrane: "a health addict—doing push-ups, scrubbing his teeth, grinding up cabbages"—clear evidence of lunacy, no doubt. Miles Davis: "broods in his beautiful town house, teaching his son to box so that he won't fear white men . . . a man who needs to shout, but his anger is trapped in a hoarse whisper caused by an injury to his vocal cords." And so on, ad nauseam.[34]

It is worth stressing that more than mere honorifics are involved in the differing receptions afforded whites and blacks by the Establishment: a performer's whole way of life can be altered, depending on the response his music obtains. Benny

Goodman has been able to retire from the ignoble occupation of jazz musician to the rarefied heights of Mozart clarinet concerti; but Duke Ellington and Count Basie are forced to continue presenting their artistry in dance halls and dingy nightclubs under a schedule of one-night engagements that no self-respecting "legitimate" artist of their stature would dream of accepting.

One can thus summarize a great deal of jazz's history with the observation that notwithstanding the sweeping changes in the music since the time of Goodman, the distribution of economic returns has not altered substantially. Regardless of how many times white jazz journalists reiterate that all artists (or all avant-garde artists, if they are the ones under discussion) "have the same problems," there is little basis for this inane bit of conventional wisdom. Bill Dixon, an avant-garde trumpeter, composer, and the principal organizer of a short-lived musicians' cooperative, the Jazz Composers Guild, states unequivocally that white avant-garde musicians are treated "significantly better . . . than are black musicians," adding, "white players have a leverage which Negro players do not. Many of them also play in symphony orchestras or work with other avant-garde white musicians in a non-jazz idiom and get grants and subsidies from that. Those [white] cats may be criticized a lot, but they are recognized as artists."[35]

Dixon's argument has particular relevance to the area of "studio work"—that is, semi-permanent employment by one of the large recording firms, radio or television studios, or motion-picture corporations in New York City or Hollywood. Jazz musicians value studio work highly because it provides a safety net of economic security against the possibility of hard times, and also because it enables the musician to avoid the hazardous and debilitating experience of "going on the road." But with some minor exceptions, employment in the studios for jazz musicians has in general been reserved for whites. Arthur Davis, a virtuoso New York bassist fluent in a wide variety of idioms, worked extensively with John Coltrane's groups when the saxophonist was using two basses to give his music a polyrhythmic texture. "Sickening" is the word he employs to describe the kind of discrimination that black musicians of his caliber routinely encounter:

> I am denied the opportunity to play in a symphony orchestra . . . to play in a staff orchestra or any other jobs that have dignity. I have more than ample qualifications. There are less than five non-whites in all the symphonies [in New York City]. We took a survey. There are NO Afro-Americans on any of the steamship lines or any . . . of the society orchestras. These people have been visited by us . . . without success.
>
> A top arranger and composer wanted me to do the television score; this was the large symphony orchestra and I was solo bass, plus [was to be] paid very handsomely. He told me the date and time and said he told the contractor [who actually hires the musicians] of this. The contractor was the musical director of this nationwide network. He never did call when he found out who I was. I happened to go in this studio that day to put my bass [there,] as I had a later session. I saw all concerned. The arranger later told me he had undue pressure, etc. Of course there is a law that any leader can get who he wants. The contractor must get whomever the leader tells if he is available.

Not surprisingly, Davis ends on a somber note: "I could write a book of incidents. They are definitely intent on keeping [black] people out of secure prestige work."[36]

At the other end of the country, alto saxophonist Sonny Criss had a similar tale to relate to a journalist: "[T]alk about Los Angeles, I lived here since I was twenty-five [some twenty years] and never saw the inside of a movie studio. In

France, within six months, I was on the Riviera playing in and for a high-budget film . . . with Tony Perkins—making $200 a day!" *37

Arthur Davis is surely guilty of no exaggeration in stating that he could "write a book" cataloging experiences similar to his own and those of Sonny Criss. George Russell, a talented and much-admired avant-garde composer and theoretician who became an expatriate to Europe toward the end of the 1960s, offers another illustration. In a letter to *down beat* in 1966, Russell spoke of "dreary subway trips to Macy's or scrubbing floors or washing dishes in a Harlem, Bronx, or Brooklyn luncheonette" to keep alive. "Until last year," he continued, "I held a membership card in Local 1199, Retail Drug Workers' Union of New York"—a statement that few white musicians of Russell's eminence could match.[38] Indeed, the situation for Afro-American avant-garde jazz artists has become so bleak that one of them, the imaginative pianist Andrew Hill, was in 1966 reduced to the expedient of calling on readers of *down beat* to send him one dollar each "so I can survive, and that will be appreciated in the true sense of brotherhood."[39]

One concludes from this chilling survey that the attempt of the Establishment to use jazz for winning Cold War propaganda "victories" like that of Duke Ellington at Dakar has not resulted in any noticeable improvement in the jazz musician's social status and/or economic well-being. On the contrary, this phenomenon is but the most recent in a series of expropriations by which black artists are denied

---

* It was not only the availability of studio work that explains the enthusiasm Criss felt for France: "People listen here. And racially . . . oh, man, racially, it is the greatest feeling over there. . . . I must admit, for the first time in my life—and that means from my childhood in Memphis right up to Los Angeles—I was completely relaxed. . . . Result? I played in a way that I never played before."

the fruits that by rights they should have reaped from their musical innovations.[40]

Yet if the status quo has not materially altered, the response of the black artists has. Consciousness of the exploitative conditions under which jazz musicians are forced to create has always been present, of course, but only recently has protest against those conditions become explicit and unremitting. In the early fifties an anonymous California musician bemoaned the plight of the black man in jazz to German critic Joachim Ernst Berendt in despairing tones:

> You see, as soon as we have a music, the white man comes and imitates it. We've now had jazz for fifty years, and in all those fifty years there has not been a single white man, perhaps leaving aside Bix [Beiderbecke], who has had an idea. Only the coloured men have ideas. But if you see who's got the famous names: they're all white.
>
> What can we do? We must go on inventing something new all the time. When we have it, the whites will take it from us, and we have to start all over again. It is as though we were being hunted.[41]

Now, however, the tone of despair is gone, replaced by one which mingles militant discontent—"We are not angry young men," tenor saxophonist Archie Shepp told one interviewer, "we are enraged"[42]—and political radicalism in equal proportions.

"The black people are becoming more and more dissatisfied. And if changes don't take place within ten years, there'll be a revolution." Those are the words not of some "aggressive"— a favorite term among white writers—upstart, but of trumpeter Dizzy Gillespie, one of the most popular and admired jazz musicians ever to put trumpet to lips—and, incidentally, one most often chosen by the State Department to go on tour.[43] As shocking as Gillespie's statement has seemed to some in the jazz world, it pales beside the sentiments heard from the younger generation of black avant-garde artists. It is widely rumored, for example, that prominent avant-garde musicians on the West Coast have joined the left-wing W.E.B. Du Bois Clubs, while in New York Archie Shepp voices his denunciation of "these United States, which, in my estimation, is one of the most vicious, racist social systems in the world—with the possible exceptions of [Southern] Rhodesia, South Africa, and South Viet Nam." Describing himself as "for the moment a helpless witness to the bloody massacre of my people on streets that run from Hayneville [South Africa] through Harlem," Shepp demands of his readers,

> Don't you ever wonder just what my collective rage will . . . be like, when it is—as it inevitably must be—unleashed? Our vindication will be black as the color of suffering is black, as Fidel is black, as Ho Chi Minh is black. It is thus that I offer my right hand across the worlds of suffering to black compatriots everywhere. When they fall victim to war, disease, poverty—all systematically enforced—I fall with them, and I am a yellow skin, and they are black like me or even white. For them and me I offer this prayer, that this twenty-eighth year of mine will never again find us all so poor, nor the rapine forces of the world in such sanguinary circumstances.[44]

Here speaks the new radicalism of the black jazz musician. Given this degree of political engagement and the willingness to express it, one suspects that as an Establishment weapon in the Cold War, jazz may yet turn out to be a double-edged sword.

Afterword

It is, of course, impossible to sum up in a handful of sentences all of the changes during the last quarter-century in the position jazz occupies in American social and intellectual life. At most, I can touch upon what I think are some of the most important developments.

With respect to *fellowships and university programs,* there have been some improvements—but not nearly enough. Due to the widespread demands of black students during the late 1960s and early 1970s, a number of prominent jazz musicians—bassist Richard Davis at Wisconsin, Archie Shepp at Massachusetts, saxophonists Jackie McLean at Connecticut and Nathan Davis at the University of Pittsburgh—are now tenured full professors in university music departments. As the Spaniards say, however, there are no roses without thorns. While I rejoice that these outstanding artists are steadily employed and conveying an understanding of jazz to legions of young people, I mourn the fact that their academic responsibilities have kept them from recording and touring as often as I, for one, would prefer.

Thus, as welcome as university appointments for jazz musicians are, they cannot substitute for fellowships. The difference, if I may oversimplify, is that a fellowship enables a jazz musician to remain in his or her community, interacting with other artists and the jazz-loving public. Too often, however, as I remarked just above, a position at a prestigious university ends up taking a jazz artist largely out of circulation. Although both Cecil Taylor and Ornette Coleman have been the recipient of sizable fellowships since the 1960s, one shouldn't allow oneself to be misled by isolated examples. So far as jazz as a whole is concerned, the level of fellowship support is woefully inadequate. Nor is it about to change for the better, so far as I can see, anytime soon.

A survey of jazz and the mass media presents a similarly mixed picture. Commercial all-jazz radio stations, relatively widespread in the 1960s and 1970s, are almost entirely defunct. In their place, however, have sprung up a number of jazz-oriented public-radio stations, usually in association with a college or university. Although the absence of commercials hectoring one to buy this or that unnecessary or useless commodity certainly comes as a welcome relief, I must say that the caliber of the programming on the two all-jazz public-radio stations to which I listen (KCSM in San Mateo, a San Francisco suburb, and KXJZ in Sacramento) leaves a great deal to be desired. Not only is there an excessive preoccupation with the latest releases, but the limited range of the music these stations broadcast is disheartening. Suffice it to say that in the last few years I cannot remember ever hearing a selection by Ornette Coleman or Cecil Taylor—surely two of the major innovators of the last thirty-five or forty years—and those few pieces by John Coltrane that manage to get on the air are almost without exception examples of his ballad style. I think I would faint dead away if either one of these stations ever worked up the courage to play, say, the version of "Chasin' the Trane" that he recorded at the Village Vanguard, or any of the on-location renditions of "Impressions."

When it comes to newspapers and magazines, there have also been few changes. The *New Yorker* still reports on jazz with some frequency; the *Atlantic Monthly* carries articles on jazz more rarely; and for the *New York Review of Books* and *Harper's*, the topic does not even exist. Over the past two decades, there has been an enormous profusion of books on jazz, many of them brought out by university presses at that. (By no means are all of them worth reading, but that's another matter.) Biographies of Charles Mingus, Miles Davis, John Coltrane, Charlie Parker, Billie Holiday, Count Basie, Lester Young; studies of jazz of the 1920s and the swing era; accounts of hard bop and the avant-garde of the 1960s—all these have made their debut between hard covers since 1970. No matter—the *New York Review* could not be more sublimely indifferent. I wouldn't want to stake my life on it, but I don't think I have seen a book on jazz treated in its pages for more than twenty years.

The newspapers, at least in the San Francisco Bay area, are no less remiss. The *San Francisco Chronicle* has the largest circulation of any daily newspaper in the region. Its coverage of jazz runs the gamut from mediocre at best to nonexistent at worst. The standard I like to use for evaluating a newspaper's approach to jazz is its treatment of European concert music. Suffice it that no symphony or opera, no performance in San Francisco by a midsize orchestra (such as the Orchestra of the Eighteenth Century, the Academy of St. Martin in the Fields, and the like) or halfway-prominent chamber group goes unnoted in the *Chronicle*'s pages. Indeed, its reviewers will even venture far afield to comment upon the San Jose, Marin County, and California Symphony orchestras (the last located in Contra Costa county, some thirty-five miles from San Francisco).

I have no quarrel with any of this; all I ask is that the same solicitude be extended to jazz artists of comparable significance. I am not holding my breath. For all one could read about them in the *Chronicle*, Cecil Taylor's last two engagements in the Bay area, for example, might have taken place on Mars (where, come to think of it, the novelty probably would have generated greater coverage). This omission is especially unforgivable in the case of his most recent appearance, in San Francisco's new Performing Arts Theatre in October 1995. On this occasion, Taylor led a fifty-piece ensemble through a truly unprecedented program of collective improvisation, the likes of which I have not only never heard before but which I doubt I will ever have the good fortune to experience again. (Taylor himself told me that for years he had wanted to stage a concert of this magnitude in New York, but that circumstances had made it impossible for him to do so.)

If the pianist-composer had been, Vladimir Ashkenazy, say, or Philip Glass, there is no question that the *Chronicle*'s account of this remarkable performance would have run on the first page of its entertainment section—maybe, even, on the first page of the news section, space permitting. As only a mere black jazz musician was involved, however, the newspaper evidently considered it beneath its dignity to take notice. The year was 1995—but for all the difference it made, the last two digits might as well have been reversed.[45]

NOTES

1. Don DeMicheal, "Jazz in Government," part 1, *down beat*, January 17, 1963, p. 15.

2. These quotations are from an adulatory article in *Jazz* magazine by its editor, Pauline Rivelli, "The Voice of Jazz: Willis Conover," September 1965, p. 14. For the ensuing controversy, see "Frank Kofsky to Willis Conover" and "Willis Conover to Frank Kofsky," letters to the editor in *Jazz*, November 1965, p. 6 and pp. 6–8, respectively, and Kofsky, "A Reply to My Critics," *Jazz*, December 1965, pp. 6–7, 30.

3. DeMicheal, "Jazz in Government," part 2, *down beat*, January 31, 1963, p. 20.

4. Quoted in *ibid.*

5. "Willis Conover to Frank Kofsky," p. 7.

6. On which see, among other works, William S. Borden, *The Pacific Alliance: United States Foreign Economic Trade Policy and Japanese Trade Recovery, 1947–1955* (Madison: University of Wisconsin Press, 1984); Frank Costigliola, *France and the United States: The Cold Alliance since World War II* (New York: Twayne Publishers, 1992); Lloyd C. Gardner, *Approaching Vietnam: From World War II through Dienbienphu* (New York: Norton, 1988); Andrew J. Rotter, *The Path to Vietnam: Origins of the American Commitment to Southeast Asia* (Ithaca, N.Y.: Cornell University Press, 1987).

7. "Jazz in Government," part 2, p. 19.

8. Quoted in Rivelli, "Voice of Jazz," p. 14.

9. Stanley Karnow, "Lots of Words but No Say: Era of Glam-

our Passes for USIA," *Los Angeles Times,* January 3, 1972, part 1, p. 17.

10. DeMicheal, "Jazz in Government," part 2, p. 20.

11. *Ibid.,* p. 19.

12. *Ibid.* The direct linkage between jazz and the United States in the title of Conover's program is quite revealing in the context of this discussion.

13. Quoted in De Michael, "Jazz in Government," part 1, p. 15.

14. Not a bad prediction, given the attempts in Congress to abolish or drastically curtail operations of both the USIA and the VOA following the collapse of the Soviet Union in 1991.

15. "Conover to Kofsky," p. 7.

16. Kwame Nkrumah, *Neo-Colonialism: The Last Stage of Imperialism* (New York: International Publishers, 1966), p. 249.

17. *Ibid.,* pp. 249–50.

18. Quoted in David Wise and Thomas B. Ross, *The Invisible Government* (New York: Bantam Books, 1965), p. 251, note.

19. *Ibid.,* p. 345.

20. "Conover to Kofsky," p. 7.

21. DeMicheal, "Jazz in Government," part 1, p. 15.

22. Lloyd Garrison, "Soviet Poets Fail to Capture Dakar," *New York Times,* April 30, 1966, p. 31. Such incidents led *down beat*'s Don DeMicheal to gloat that "the government's discovery of jazz has been advantageous . . . to Washington," and on that basis to assert that "[t]he music has proved itself." "Jazz in Government," part 2, p. 20. It is a sorry comment on the mentality of such individuals that jazz must "prove itself" by serving as a means of muting the international reaction against the policies of U.S. imperialism.

23. I would be the last to deny that Soviet artists are subject to censorship, harassment (as in the case of Shostakovich) and outright persecution (as in the case of Solzhenitsyn). My point is not that the Soviet Union is a paradise for artists, but that those artists—unlike U.S. cultural "ambassadors"—receive the best treatment *that particular society has to offer.* Note, too, that neither the U.S. nor the USSR bestows its favors on dissidents: it is, after all, Duke Ellington and not Cecil Taylor nor Archie Shepp whom the State Department

chooses to send into battle against Yevtushenko in Africa. Each side, in short, rewards artists who do not overtly challenge the status quo and punishes those who do; only the means differ.

24. It remained for France to make good where the U.S. had failed by awarding Ellington the Legion of Honor in 1973.

25. The situation has improved *somewhat* in the twenty-five years since I first wrote this statement, but it still leaves a great deal to be desired—as any working jazz musician will be only too happy to tell you.

26. See, for example, the following: staffs of the Africa Research Group and *The Old Mole,* and others, *How Harvard Rules* (Cambridge, MA: published by the authors; no date); staff of the North American Congress on Latin America (NACLA), *Who Rules Columbia?* (New York: NACLA, 1968); Marvin Garson, "The Regents" appendix in Hal Draper, *Berkeley: The New Student Revolt* (Grove Press, New York, 1965), pp. 215–21.

27. See *The Jimmy Woods Sextet: Conflict* (Contemporary 3612).

28. I owe these details to John Handy himself. In a case of truly poetic justice, student protest at the end of the 1960s forced San Francisco State to initiate a black studies curriculum and hire as part of that program none other than John Handy, who has remained a member of the music department on that campus ever since.

29. The *New York Review of Books,* by way of illustration, reviewed the grand total of *one* book—*Blues People* by LeRoi Jones (New York: William Morrow, 1963)—during the first decade of its existence. Although it has barely managed to sustain that average in subsequent decades, its editors would no doubt howl with outrage if anyone were to accuse them of a racist cultural bias. Yet the truth of the matter is that articles and reviews on the great European symphonists—some even by performers such as pianist Alfred Brendel and composers such as Virgil Thomson and Ned Rorem— regularly grace the pages of the *Review.* You may call it what you will; to me, it looks like racism.

30. A.B. Spellman, *Four Lives in the Bebop Business* (New York: Pantheon, 1966), p. 46. Both the amount of money and the number of grants allocated to jazz by the National Endowment for the Arts have consistently been minute in comparison to the money devoted

to music in the European symphonic tradition.

31. See "International Jazz Critics Poll Results," *down beat*, August 12, 1965, pp. 14–19.

32. In the 1980s, I am pleased to report, Cecil Taylor began to attain some of the long-overdue recognition he deserved.

33. As Abbey Lincoln put it with admirable succinctness: Hollywood "did Gene Krupa's life story, and Jo Jones [is eating] grits." See "Racial Prejudice in Jazz," part II, *down beat*, March 29, 1962, p. 24.

34. Barry Farrell, "Music: The Loneliest Monk," *Time*, February 28, 1961; alas, despite much effort, I have never been able to turn up a Charles Mingus recording for which "his analyst wrote the notes." If I didn't know better, I might think that here we have another typically slanderous white critic attempting to appear clever at Mingus's expense.

35. Quoted in Robert Levin, "The Jazz Composers Guild: An Assertion of Dignity," *down beat*, May 6, 1965, pp. 17–18. Along the same lines, Dixon also states: "You know . . . the sad thing, and it is indeed sad, about the entire situation is that most white musicians don't really dig the situation as it is. It's just that they don't *do* anything about the obvious inequities. I don't care what *anyone* says—it's obvious that black musicians are locked out of certain areas in the money making part of the music business. And reeling off the names of a half-dozen black musicians who haven't been excluded doesn't eliminate *that* fact!" Bill Dixon to Frank Kofsky, February 15, 1967.

36. Arthur Davis to Frank Kofsky, August 10, 1962.

37. Quoted in Harvey Siders, "Sonny Criss: One-Horn Man," *down beat*, May 19, 1966, p. 29.

38. George Russell, "Popular Delusions and the Madness of Crowds: A Letter from George Russell," *down beat*, April 7, 1966, p. 14; I discuss this letter and the circumstances surrounding it in more detail in chapter 3.

39. Quoted in Don Heckman, "Roots, Culture and Economics: An Interview with Avant-Garde Pianist-Composer Andrew Hill," *down beat*, May 5, 1966, p. 20.

40. Thus, USIA bureaucrat Willis Conover enjoys a comfortable living from his work as an apologist for U.S. imperialism, but the musical artists whose recordings he plays derive not a single cent in royalties when their work is broadcast over the Voice of America. If this state of affairs does not constitute exploitation, pray tell, what does?

41. Joachim Ernst Berendt quoted by Francis Newton [E.J. Hobsbawm] in *The Jazz Scene* (Harmondsworth, Middlesex: Penguin Books, 1961), p. 205.

42. Quoted in Leonard Feather, "Blindfold Test: Archie Shepp," part 2, *down beat*, May 19, 1966, p. 41.

43. Gillespie quoted in Theodore Sorenson and other respondents, "Is America a Dying Country?", *Fact*, September 1965, p. 59.

44. "An Artist Speaks Bluntly," *down beat*, December 16, 1965, pp. 11, 42. This column—celebrated or notorious, depending on your point of view—prompted *down beat* editor Don DeMicheal to telephone Archie Shepp and whimper, "This article frightens me." Shades of J. Alfred Prufrock! Shepp quotes DeMicheal in the partial transcript of a panel discussion among himself, Cecil Taylor, Rahsaan Roland Kirk, and others, "Point of Contact," in *down beat Music '66*, ed. DeMicheal (Chicago: Maher Publications, 1966), p. 110.

45. Not that the *Chronicle*'s policy of malign neglect of jazz is the least bit new, as witness the fact that I first began raising such complaints at least as far back as 1980; see, for instance, Frank Kofsky, "Indecent Coverage," *The Threepenny Review*, I :1 (1980).

Part 3

*Black nationalism and
the revolution in music*

6

The revolution in black music: origins and directions

In my music, I came up with a music that didn't require European laws applied to it. This was a revolutionary breakthrough. . . .

—ORNETTE COLEMAN[1]

Mostly, black musicians feel they can better relate to Africa . . . because a lot of musicians are realizing that this is where the roots of the music came from, as far as this music is concerned.

—MCCOY TYNER[2]

I think even Indian music has its origins in the African art form. You can see the influences. Whatever we do, it can be traced back to some of the African forms.

—ELVIN JONES[3]

At the climactic moment of LeRoi Jones's allegorical drama, *The Dutchman,* Jones has the enraged hero (representing

Black America) denounce his blonde would-be "seductress" (actually his enslaver) in a scathing passage that runs, in part, as follows:

> Old baldheaded four-eyed ofays [white people] popping their fingers . . . and don't know yet what they're doing. They say, "I love Bessie Smith." And don't even understand that Bessie Smith is saying, "Kiss my ass, kiss my black unruly ass." Before love, suffering, desire, anything you can explain, she's saying, and very plainly, "Kiss my black ass." And if you don't know that, it's you that's doing the kissing.
>
> Charlie Parker? Charlie Parker. All the hip white boys scream for Bird. And Bird saying, "Up your ass, feeble-minded ofays! Up your ass." And they sit there talking about the tortured genius of Charlie Parker.[4]

This speech has a reality that transcends the question of whether or not Jones is "factually" correct in a narrow sense (the truth is the whole, as Hegel long ago put it). Regardless of what Bessie Smith was actually singing, or even what she thought she was singing, or what Parker intended with his music, the view that Jones enunciates is becoming increasingly representative of the current crop of Young Turks in jazz—and of course not just in jazz: the avant-garde generation, if you will. Indeed, I am deliberately understating the case; my intuitive suspicion is that the alienation of thinking young Negro radicals—including many of the jazz avant-gardists—from the white-Protestant American Dream has gone much further than the public at large is aware.

As for the reasons behind this massive repudiation of the Dream, it suffices to note that the Negro was never meant to be anything in America but a slave. The "freeing" of Negroes in the Civil War was widely regarded by whites in the North as a regrettable but unavoidable consequence of the military struggle against the Confederacy. In his Emancipation Proclamation—which, recall, specifically exempted loyal slave states from its provisions—Lincoln three times justified this measure on the grounds of military necessity. He made no bones about the fact that saving the Union, rather than liberating blacks from bondage, was his supreme goal, and if he could accomplish the former without having to resort to the latter, so much the better.

In the decades before the Civil War, moreover, white people made the life of one-quarter of a million free Negroes in the *North* a hell; all the institutions of Jim Crow and second-class citizenship were, in fact, brought to perfection not in the magnolia-scented South, but in the more business-minded North. So inconceivable in the American social structure was the notion of a creature who was both free and Negro that either the freedom had to be destroyed or the Negro had to be harried out of the land. Under these conditions, it comes as no surprise to learn that Negro nationalism—black rejection of an oppressive white-dominated society—sprang up as early as the decade of the 1850s among northern free Negroes.[5]

Nor did the post–Civil War years bring about any marked improvement, for neither in the North nor the South did white majorities have any intention of allowing Negroes to experience genuine equality.[6] Thus, Leon Litwack recounts that the voters of New York State turned down a constitutional amendment to enfranchise Negroes in 1869—four years *after* the Civil War—and the New York electorate was in no wise atypical.[7]

The white consensus on excluding the Negro from both constitutional "rights" and American abundance, in short, has never been decisively shattered, for there is nothing in the American experience that would undermine it, no influential vested interests concerned with altering the status quo. On the contrary, the ruling powers all more or less aligned themselves with the policy of subordinating blacks.

In the political sphere this was most apparent. Woodrow Wilson was an ardent segregationist, and Theodore Roosevelt and Herbert Hoover both sought to build up a "lily-white" Republican party in the South.[8] Northern industrialists— the ruling-class group that, after the Civil War, converted the South into an economic appendage of the North—concurred: cheap labor meant high profits; and besides, Negro strikebreakers could always be put to good use in labor stoppages—eloquent testimony to the racist attitudes of the white workers. In these ways and countless others, racism maintained the position it had held at least since the end of the seventeenth century: a staple item in American life.[9]

The association of racist philosophies with the Axis foes during World War II brought about an epochal change in the United States: for the first time it became unfashionable to profess white-supremacist sentiments in public. Pressured by Negro militants and white radicals, anxious to avoid being embarrassed by such protests as A. Phillip Randolph's March on Washington movement, the same Roosevelt administration that had on several occasions allowed antilynching bills to be talked to death in Congress reluctantly moved to prohibit the most blatant manifestations of Jim Crow. For those old enough to remember the overtly racist character of the government's wartime anti-Japanese propaganda ("dirty Japs"), the sincerity of this belated conversion is open to question.[10] Indeed, Negro Seabees found the administration's anti-Japanese propaganda so repugnant that they engaged in a series of strikes to compel the federal government to withdraw the worst of it from circulation.

For all of that, it is clear that the combination of increased demand for industrial labor and the official U.S. ideology of a "victory over racism" did produce some tangible wartime benefits for black Americans;[11] moreover, it proved impossible to restore the full range of Jim Crow practices following the end of the war in 1945. To begin with, a minority of young and idealistic whites, perhaps touched by the social radicalism prevalent in the 1930s, took the slogan of a "victory over racism" seriously. Still more important, U.S. Cold War policies placed crucial significance on wooing the formerly colonized nations of Africa and Asia away from a possible rapprochement with the Soviet Union. To this end, it was imperative that the United States divest itself of the more obvious trappings of racism. Ultimately, just such logic prompted the 1954 Supreme Court decision on "desegregation" of the public schools: not a root-and-branch overturn of the pattern of second-class non-citizenship, but a propaganda gesture intended primarily for foreign consumption. Hence the U.S. Attorney General's supporting brief in this case quite openly proclaimed, "It is in the context of the present world struggle between freedom and tyranny that the problem of racial discrimination must be viewed. . . . Racial discrimination furnishes grist for the Communist propaganda mills."

"Within a few hours after the Supreme Court's decision was read in 1954," C. Vann Woodward relates, "the Voice of America had broadcast the news to foreign countries in thirty-five separate languages." The purpose of the decision, however, was to influence audiences in the Third World; implementation in the United States was something else again. The Court, according to the same author, made no secret of its

acknowledgment of the many difficulties that would be involved in doing away with segregation and its evident tolerance of a gradualistic approach toward a solution. It was quite evident that a long transitional period was inevitable. . . . The possibilities of delaying tactics were large, and it is well known that many things that have been declared unconstitutional have continued to exist for a long time.[12]

Nothing, then, has ever wrought a meaningful alteration in the "place" to which white America wishes to consign—and has more or less successfully until now consigned—"its" Negroes. This is as true today as it was a generation or more ago, especially inasmuch as comparative statistics indicate that the Negro's relative economic position has not improved in the last two decades or so, but has worsened. The myth of "Negro progress," as C.E. Wilson has astutely pointed out, is just that: a myth, and nothing more. The hard, brutal economic facts of life all contradict the comforting illusion that things are miraculously getting better of their own accord without the necessity for human intervention.[13] For that matter, white America is determined—and by a substantial majority—to keep things pretty much the way they have always been, with the Negro confined to the bottom. The most authoritative recent survey of white attitudes on this question demonstrates that "white people are . . . adamant that there should not be a strict 10 percent quota for Negroes in job hiring (rejected by over 40 to 1) or that Negroes should actually be given job preference over whites (turned down by a staggering 31 to 1 margin)."[14] The implication is that, for all white America cares, Negroes may continue to fester forever in pestilential urban slums—as they surely will unless provided with massive economic assistance of just the type that whites find so objectionable. So long as no white skin has to suffer for it, a tepid "Negro revolution" is permissible; beyond that point, however—nothing.

This is the framework within which black disaffection with the white-American consensus is reaching ever more vocal proportions. It is through the prism of this disaffection that we should view such developments as, for instance, the indisputable popularity of the late Malcolm X in the ghettos of the North. Like all radical agitators attuned to the needs and aspirations of their constituencies, Malcolm X articulated what others felt, but, for a variety of reasons, were unable to speak. He was unequaled at voicing the discontent of what LeRoi Jones has called the "blues people"—their lack of faith that the American Dream will ever enable them to attain a decent way of life, their fervent wish for an existence of their own without the suffocatingly painful foot of white supremacy crushing their chests.[15] The Black Muslim doctrine of a separate state for Negroes, so uniformly derided in the white press, is only another tacit recognition of the intense yearning in the ghetto for a social and political system in which the destinies of black people lies in the hands of blacks themselves.

But one should not make the mistake of thinking that the domestic aspects of the Afro-American freedom movement are the only ones, for politically aware young Negroes (including not a few musicians) increasingly are connecting their campaign for liberation with similar struggles of the former colonial nations to rid themselves of white-imperialist domination. Indeed, by now it has become a commonplace that the emergence of newly independent countries, particularly in Africa, has had a dramatic effect in altering the "self-image" of Negro Americans, imbuing them with a heretofore unprecedented sense of pride in their ancestral heritage and achievements.[16] The political implications of this trend, however, have yet to be fully appreciated. One corollary of the appearance of these new nations on the world stage is that Negroes in the United States now realize that there are other viable alternatives available to them besides that of transforming themselves into carbon copies of white people. The importance of this development can scarcely be overemphasized, because in effect it opens a door for a Negro movement of mass dimensions based on an explicit rejection of the American Dream.

What I have been saying, therefore, comes down to this: as the futility of relying on white largesse as a means of reaching genuine equality becomes ever more undeniable,

258 / part 3: the revolution in music

whites can anticipate that Negro estrangement from the American consensus will grow apace. Malcolm X's Organization of Afro-American Unity, which had taken on only rudimentary form at the time of his mysterious assassination, represents, in fact, an early attempt to crystallize this mood of alienation and rebellion in a political form. In jazz music this estrangement has already progressed quite some distance; here the vehicle through which it is expressing itself is, as you might imagine, the youthful avant-garde movement (coupled with the efforts of a few of its better established precursors). But in all cases the crucial point is that this deep discontent *does* exist among those imprisoned within the ghetto; it is not merely a product of Black Muslim rhetoric; it will not vanish with the corpse of Malcolm X; it is a stubborn fact that must be reckoned with in any more-than-superficial examination of contemporary Negro culture in general or jazz in particular.

There is a second thesis I want to explore before leaving this subject. To many white Americans, the idea that there can be any connection between anticolonial liberation struggles, such as those in Vietnam or Central America and the Caribbean, and the Negro freedom movement in the United States is nearly incomprehensible. Nonetheless, the parallel is there, and the spokesmen whom Negroes themselves regard as authentic are emphasizing it more strongly with each passing day. First of all, could there be anything more transparently absurd than the notion that the government of the United States is fighting for the freedom and democratic rights of people of color in Vietnam when it permits those same rights to be violated with impunity by any Ku Klux Klan racist who takes it into his head to raise his status among his peers by "getting him a nigger"? To Negroes, that is to say, the Marines are needed to intervene not in Santo Domingo, Saigon, or Phnom Penh but in—Alabama: democracy, like charity, ought best begin at home.

Second, the very fact that the U.S. military juggernaut is using the Vietnamese people as raw material for its military "experiments"—as virtually all the major news sources have admitted—serves at once to strip away the fig leaves in which Washington strives to clothe its policy of naked aggression and betrays more accurately than could anything else the very real contempt that white America harbors for all non-whites.[17] Thus, it is only logical that the United States now follows the path marked out by Nazi Germany, which also maintained an ideology of superior and inferior races and took full advantage of its undeclared participation in the Spanish civil war to test the most advanced means of destruction then known against another of the "inferior" peoples.[18]

To whites, this comparison of the United States with Germany may appear ludicrous, if not downright obscene, but not all Negroes view it that way. "There is a favorite joke among many black people," writes Ossie Sykes in *Liberator* magazine, "that states that Martin Luther King, Jr., is going to be the one to lead us to the gas chambers singing 'We Shall Overcome.' This writer fails to see the humor because it can happen here just like it happened in Germany. . . ." In the same issue, C.E. Wilson asserts that "[this] culture is fully prepared to isolate, incarcerate, and kill, if need be, those [Negroes] who are too proud and too daring to submit to the current level of dehumanization and destruction. . . ."[19] Clearly, then, while whites reject with horror the idea that their society could ever follow in the footsteps of Nazi Germany, shrewd and sophisticated black thinkers are already preparing themselves for the possibility of an American version of the "final solution."

But what relevance to *jazz* do the preceding remarks have? My answer is that today's avant-garde movement in jazz is a musical representation of the same vote of "no confidence" in Western civilization and the American Dream that we find in the words of black intellectuals like Ossie Sykes and C.E. Wilson—that Negro avant-garde intransigents, in other words, are saying through their instruments, in LeRoi Jones's phrase, "Up your ass, feeble-minded ofays!"

Before proceeding to defend this thesis, however, I need to note certain obvious qualifications to it. Despite what those who oppose my position are sure to allege, I am *not* contending that every member of the jazz avant-garde is necessarily brimming over with a desire to undermine and overthrow the status quo, hates whites, or is choking with the suppressed rage of the downtrodden. Such a mechanical formulation would really be untenable, although many of the avant-garde persuasion have left no doubt that to them the aesthetic revolution is closely linked with the social-political one. Beyond that, some of the avant-gardists, though probably a minute fraction, may be truly apolitical: they are involved in the movement for aesthetic reasons, and are, by and large, impervious or indifferent to what takes place outside the narrow sphere of their art.

What is more, my argument does not stand or fall on the question of white participation in the avant-garde movement. In every generation, a handful of white dissidents has chosen to reject America's racist institutions and values and gone over to "the other side." In the pre–Civil War years, such a person might seek to play the role of a John Brown; in the 1930s, he or she could, like Mezz Mezzrow, flee white society and become an "expatriate" to Harlem; similar figures today might be found in the ranks of the white field workers of the Student Nonviolent Coordinating Committee, or among the white partisans of Malcolm X. Regardless of the form the rebellion takes, the existence of these disaffected souls indicates that the Negro "cause" will always attract a scattering of white adherents. But—and this is the critical point—these adherents do not in and of themselves alter the character of the movement they have joined. The evolution of jazz, to which white contributions have been of strictly secondary significance (as I explained in chapter 1), demonstrates the validity of this assertion.

These qualifications noted, it is legitimate to ask what objective evidence exists to support the idea that the avant-garde movement in jazz is a manifestation of Negro repudiation of the American consensus. Here I shall be the first to admit that we are treading over tricky ground. I suspect that, given adequate time and patience, and blessed with the kind of research endowment that ruling-class foundations prefer to lavish on comparatively trivial and irrelevant questions, I could amass enough supporting data to send social scientists into paroxysms of delight. But revolutions have a nasty habit of unfolding at their own pace; they are not about to accommodate themselves to the requirements of the scholars and their elaborate behavioral methodologies, least of all in this supremely revolutionary epoch in all corners of the earth. The unwelcome but inescapable fact is that we are reduced to using, for want of anything more serviceable, what the distinguished Norwegian sociologist Svend Ranulf called (with some disdain) "the method of plausible guesses." [20] That the "plausible guess" can never be wholly satisfactory, that it can readily lead one astray, I will not deny; my rationale for employing it nonetheless is that the risk of error pales beside the penalties we must unavoidably pay if we do nothing but keep a discreet silence on social questions of immeasurable gravity.

Perhaps one must live with the avant-garde for a long while before it becomes fully intelligible. It was, at any rate, only after I had listened to Archie Shepp's recording, *Four for Trane*,[21] for what must have been the tenth time that the thought struck me: this is simply not European art; it has moved wholly away from the traditional canons of Western music. Once one begins to toy with that seemingly innocent notion, whole new vistas suddenly appear, and the superficially chaotic diversity of the avant-garde insurrection begins to display a kind of order.

Suppose, for example, that one continues thinking along the same line and asks, in what respects is this music non-Western? The answer lies not in any supposed "atonality," because, for one thing, the music of the avant-garde is generally tonal and, for another, atonality has been, since Arnold Schoenberg at least, a staple feature of the European musical landscape. Rather, the peculiarly non-Western character of the avant-garde seems to reside in what I take to be its deliberate abandonment of the equal-tempered tuning of the piano and the conventional chromatic (12-note) scale; for once one surrenders these, the entire harmonic foundation of European music—which evolved in synchrony with, and on the basis of, equal temperament and the chromatic scale—becomes vulnerable to the most radical rethinking.

I might note in passing that, even though it goes against the grain of the Western dogma that we should fall on our knees before the miracle of equal temperament, there is really nothing divinely ordained about the concept. Like everything else in the universe, it was born in a specific time and place, and if and when it should outlive its usefulness, it will perish. Even in the art music of Western Europe, where equal temperament reached its apex, it is a comparatively recent development, scarcely two hundred years old as a fully accepted convention. Furthermore, virtually all the indigenous non-European music of the world—that is, the music of an overwhelming majority of the planet's population—has somehow managed to be created without the marvels of equal temperament.

From the standpoint of the social history of music, the perfection of equal temperament and the piano keyboard in its present form signaled the waning or outright suppression of the rhythmically richer folk-dance music of the peasantry in favor of a new (and high-status) preoccupation with harmonic movement.[22] From the broader perspective of European history as a whole, equal temperament is inextricably bound up with the triumph of the bourgeoisie: in conjunction with the formalization of harmonic theory, the growth of the large symphony orchestra and the construction of the modern piano keyboard, it enabled the bourgeoisie to put its stamp on a unique music of its own, one that was as distinct from the folk music of the swinish multitude as it was different from the traditional music of Church and Court. Along with such other bourgeois innovations as Cartesian coordinates, double-entry bookkeeping, Newtonian celestial mechanics, the invention of movable type, new methods of navigation, the factory system of manufacturing, the streamlining and standardization of modern Western European vernacular languages, and countless other examples too numerous to recite, equal temperament and the 12-note scale reflect just that passion for order, systematization, simplification, rationalization, and control of all variables (an infinity of possible musical tones drastically reduced to a very finite eighty-eight) that has in every case characterized the bourgeois mentality.*

---

* With the development of equal temperament, the 12–note chromatic scale, conventions of written music, a definition of "good tone," and the symphonic ensemble, a nineteenth-century European composer could write confident in the knowledge that his or her work would receive essentially the same interpretation in London, Leipzig, Vienna, Berlin, or Budapest. Similarly, a violinist trained in, say, Prague could be certain that he or she could employ the same technique in Paris. The close parallel with simultaneous advances made by the bourgeoisie in business, industry, and science—two of the most obvious examples being the standardization of bookkeeping procedures and the replacement of individual craft-work by the uniform methods of the factory-and-machine system—is sufficiently unmistakable as to need no further discussion. One may indeed look at the constellation of inventions that includes equal temperament, the piano keyboard, an agreed-upon method of notation, and conventions governing musical tone as being

An immediate consequence of the departure from equal temperament in avant-garde groups, of course, is that the role of the piano must be rethought. For if improvisers are to be free to create what they hear in their mind's ear, they cannot be confined to the eighty-eight notes allowed by equal temperament. This consideration may explain why, amidst the profusion of avant-garde musicians, there are so relatively few pianists. To avoid being misunderstood, I want to make it explicit I am not arguing that the abolition of equal temperament requires the exclusion of the piano from avant-garde jazz, but merely to point out that it can no longer serve, as it has up to now, to delineate the basic structure of a composition. John Coltrane, to name one prominent example, has found it possible to retain the piano in his group and still go beyond the 12-note chromatic scale by having the piano fall silent when he wishes to depart from a European harmonic framework. Electing to travel a different path, pianist Cecil Taylor (and to a lesser extent, Andrew Hill) expands a precedent set by Thelonious Monk (and Henry Cowell) in using tonal clusters to give his playing an anti-diatonic cast. In any event, it seems reasonable to expect that should the avant-garde idiom become dominant in jazz, the importance of the equal-tempered, 12–note scale will decline substantially.

Aside from that, can we anticipate any other roads the avant-garde is likely to travel? To answer that question is no easy task. Although it requires scant effort to discern what the avant-gardists oppose, what they favor is not always wholly clear. Yet I do believe that two main tendencies are

---

the equivalent in the musical realm of the factory-machine system in the industrial. For a detailed and complementary account that is more deferential and less irreverent, see Sidney Finkelstein, *How Music Expresses Ideas* (2nd rev. ed.; New York: International Publishers, 1970), pp. 37–51 *passim*.

coming to the fore: one of these would diminish European influences in jazz and replace them with others from Africa and/or Asia; the other tendency also seeks to lessen European elements, but it points deeper into the urban Negro ghetto. The distinction between the two is actually somewhat arbitrary. Both tendencies, as I will discuss, symbolize the effort to escape from the confines of the West, and to that degree are obverse sides of the coin. Where they differ is over the question of what route to take; on the exodus itself, however, there is fundamental agreement.

Let me comment on the latter tendency first. It has been written so often as to be a cliché that the avant-gardists are striving to simulate the sound of human speech in their playing. Even a casual perusal of a few of their recordings will illustrate the correctness of this assertion, but what has yet to be fully appreciated is the *kind* of "speech" involved. Naturally, it would be difficult to prove the point, but if one listens with care and an open mind, what one will hear in the music of John Coltrane, Eric Dolphy, Ornette Coleman, Sam Rivers, Pharaoh Sanders, Albert Ayler and especially Archie Shepp is not speech "in general," but the voice of the Negro ghetto.

This statement, I realize, may seem like so much mysticism; certainly it defies any "objective" demonstration. Yet my intentions are anything but mystical, and in the absence of decisive evidence to the contrary, I maintain that Archie Shepp's growling, raspy tenor saxophone locutions, for example, distill the quintessence of Negro vocal patterns as they can be heard on the streets of Chicago, Detroit, Philadelphia, Harlem, or wherever you choose. Although the speech-like attributes are perhaps less obvious in their work, this is also the significance of Coltrane's eerie shrieks and *basso profundo* explosions, the jagged bass-clarinet squeals of Eric Dolphy,[23] even the more stately and oblique lamentations of Ornette Coleman: all invoke, to one degree or another, those cadences and rhythms that are unique to the lives of black people in the urban environment. (I have focused on saxophonists here because they appear to predominate in the new music.) Viewed in this light, the avant-garde stands as the logical artistic culmination of, and successor to, the self-conscious search for roots in the gospel and blues traditions—a movement known initially as "funk," later as "soul"—that (as I said in chapter 1) was so conspicuous in the jazz of the second half of the 1950s and early 1960s.

I fully expect to be told that the presence of sounds resembling Negro speech is nothing new in jazz; that it goes back to Louis Armstrong and Duke Ellington in the 1920s, if not before. Quite so—and quite immaterial. What happened in the 1920s cannot meaningfully be compared with what is taking place now because so many historical transformations have occurred in the intervening decades. It is not surprising that Armstrong and his peers found inspiration for their music in the sound of Negro song and speech; as self-taught and largely unlettered performers, excluded from white society since their early youth, it would have been truly astonishing if they had done otherwise. Much the same holds good for the bulk of the musicians in the early Ellington orchestras,[24] if not for Ellington himself.

But this is a far cry from what one finds at present, when the possession of a baccalaureate by a fledgling jazz musician is run-of-the-mill, and one takes for granted his or her ability to sight-read even the most complex scores. If today's innovating jazz radical faces toward the ghetto and away from the European tradition, rest assured that this stance springs not at all from any limitation of technique or educational deficiency. Whatever the seeming similarities between the speech-inflected music of the twenties and the current work of the avant-garde, it is the differences that are, in the final analysis, more significant.

The other trend in avant-garde jazz, toward the incorporation of Afro-Asian contributions, is also ubiquitous. And in reality, one should not make too much of the distinction between the two, for the difference in principle between the jazz artist who looks to the ghetto environment for inspiration and the one who chooses to call on African and Asian sources instead is not great. As we saw in chapter 1, jazz musicians began to experience a strong pull in both directions beginning in the 1950s, if not before. With respect to the second trend, one thinks of the African-influenced drum suites of Art Blakey, the Middle Eastern strains in the music of Yusef Lateef, the excursions of Miles Davis into Moorish-derived *cante hondo* (flamenco), and the like. But here, too, it remained for the black innovators of the 1960s to bring this movement to fruition.

The quotations that appear at the head of this chapter indicate that the application of Afro-Asian musical ideas to African-American jazz has been methodical and deliberate. As pianist Alice Coltrane puts it, "In order to trace your roots from anything"—a characteristic preoccupation of the new breed of jazz artists—"you have to go back to the source. . . . And I think it's when you go East, musically East, I think we can even trace the whole culture, the whole beginning of man." Similarly, Ornette Coleman proudly announces that he "came up with a music that didn't require European laws applied to it," which he termed "a revolutionary breakthrough." McCoy Tyner concurs: "black musicians feel they can better relate to Africa . . . because a lot of musicians are realizing that this is where the roots of the music really come from, as far as this music is concerned." For his part, Elvin Jones declares that "even Indian music has its origins in the African art form. You can see the influences. Whatever we do, it can be traced back to some of the African forms." Hence in playing on the John Coltrane recording, *Africa/Brass*, Jones, as he later explained, "was trying to think in terms of the African interpretation, as much as I was capable."[25]

Mention of John Coltrane, McCoy Tyner, and Elvin Jones is appropriate at this point, because it is probably through their closely attuned collaboration (together with the work of bassist Jimmy Garrison and his predecessors, Arthur Davis, Reginald Workman, and Steve Davis) that the dense cross-rhythmic textures so suggestive of African music have become a permanent part of the jazz tradition.[26] To begin with, Coltrane has consciously incorporated African themes and motifs in his compositions. Curious to see if I could learn more on this subject, I decided to do a bit of detective work in hopes of unearthing some of the African sources he used. In this way, I discovered recordings of two Dahomean drummers, Albéric and Frédéric Glélé, chanting what to my ears seem the identical rhythms that Coltrane assigned to bassists Arthur Davis and Reggie Workman on his compositions "Africa" (on the album *Africa/Brass*) and "Dahomey Dance" (on the album *Olé*).* [27]

Besides weaving African melodies into his compositions, in the last two years of his life Coltrane also often brought additional percussionists into his ensemble to enhance the African cross-rhythmic qualities of the music,[28] a topic I explore at much greater length in chapters 10 and 13. We also get insight into his intentions from the titles he bestowed on

---

* Nearly 30 years later, I was overjoyed to have my findings confirmed by the recollections of McCoy Tyner:

> [Coltrane] was into Indian music and into African music, and different social groups. On "Dahomey Dance" he had a record of these guys who were from Dahomey, which is why he used two bassists. He showed that rhythm to Art Davis and Reggie Workman. So the influence was there

Which is, of course, essentially what I have contended all along. Tyner's comment is in Peter Watrous, "John Coltrane: A Life Supreme," in *The Jazz Musician*, ed. Mark Rowland and Tony Scherman (New York: St. Martin's Press, 1993), pp. 177–78.

various of his compositions, names that reflected his interest in the Afro-Asian nations. Included under this heading are "Dial Africa," "Oomba," "Gold Coast" (then about to become Ghana) and "Tanganyika Strut," all recorded under Wilbur Harden's leadership for Savoy Records, and "India," as well as the aforementioned "Africa" and "Dahomey Dance," which Coltrane recorded at the head of his own group.[29]

At the same time he was incorporating African or African-like cross-rhythmic elements into his music, Coltrane also put other non-European traditions to good use. From Indian raga he took, among other things, the idea of constructing an improvisation with only a drone note (or tonic, in Western nomenclature) in the bass and a mode or scale (that is, a raga) from which to fashion his melodies. And so warm was his friendship with Ravi Shankar that one of Coltrane's sons bears the same first name as the Indian sitar master.

Coltrane's ability to synthesize African cross-rhythms with the practices of Indian raga was, of course, an artistic tour de force of the first order. But beyond that, these aesthetic divergences from the Western tradition—since emulated by innumerable other young black musicians—signal the inability of European musical thought to stimulate further developments in jazz and convey as well the non-Western, or even anti-Western, mentality of the musicians themselves. This is the *social* meaning of Ornette Coleman's proclamation that he "came up with a music that didn't require European laws applied to it." Here Coleman spoke not just for himself, but as the representative of an entire *generation* of black musicians. One cannot but agree with his assessment that the new music that he—in conjunction with John Coltrane, Cecil Taylor, Bill Dixon, Albert Ayler, Sun Ra, Archie Shepp, Pharoah Sanders, and countless others—created does in truth comprise "a revolutionary breakthrough."

But is this particular interpretation of the impulse away from the West the best? Isn't it possible that what we are witnessing is merely an artistic phenomenon and that it is mistaken to construe it as a social gesture? Although current knowledge does not allow me to refute this argument as decisively as one might like, I nonetheless find it wholly unsatisfactory.

At bottom, the proposition that the avant-garde movement is an aesthetic revolution only, not possessed of any broader social implications, is untenable because of the nature of both historical change and jazz. My fundamental premise is that major transformations in the improvisational styles of jazz do not "just happen"; that because of the intimate relationship between jazz and the urban Negro community, such profound changes in the jazz aesthetic occur primarily due to a simultaneous (or earlier) shift in the collective consciousness of the ghetto. This is not the usual approach to the study of jazz innovation, I readily acknowledge, but it is my contention (developed at greater length in chapters 1 and 10) that the conventional treatment—which tears jazz out of its social setting and "explains" the decline of one style and burgeoning of another as the result of a happy series of accidents that throw together an isolated coterie of individual geniuses—obscures more than it illuminates. When we are dealing with an art such as European concert music or avant-garde painting, where the potential audience is limited and the role of a handful of collectors, middlemen, academic authorities, lay patrons and the artist's own professional contemporaries is influential, then it *might* make sense to describe stylistic changes without relating them to contemporary social and historical developments. But surely this has not been the situation in jazz, nor is there much that suggests it is about to become so.

Here it may help to approach the matter from another direction by conducting a sort of contrary-to-fact "thought experiment." Suppose we ask what the outcome would have been, so far as jazz alone is concerned, had there by now occurred a substantial amount of racial integration—that is, had Negroes been incorporated into all levels of the economy in proportion to their number in the overall population (rather than, as historically has been the case, overwhelmingly relegated to the lowest levels of the pyramid). In these hypothetical circumstances, we would certainly anticipate that differences between Negro and white musics would become increasingly blurred, as the two ethnic groups took on more nearly identical ways of life. With respect to jazz, it seems a defensible conclusion that some kind of hybrid music would ultimately emerge from the process of integration and cultural exchanges: in short, a variant of that forced marriage between jazz and symphonic music that, under the name *third-stream music,* enjoyed a small and short-lived vogue in the late 1950s.

And yet, nothing could be more striking than the inability of third-stream music to survive. Not only has it utterly failed to generate a sizable audience, but more important, those young black musicians with the best preparation to perform it—artists of the caliber and background of Cecil Taylor, Eric Dolphy, Archie Shepp, Bill Dixon, Ken McIntyre, Arthur Davis, Richard Davis, Jaki Byard, and numerous others—have generally held themselves aloof from this attempt at artistic fusion. With the single possible (and very occasional) exception of Ornette Coleman, the musicians active in promoting the third stream have been either white composers such as Gunther Schuller, or else Negro performers like John Lewis whose ties, emotionally and aesthetically, are with the previous generation. If the leading avant-garde insurgents have had any significance in this attempt at creating a new "middle way" for jazz, it is only by their continued absence. One thus concludes that much of the abortive character of third-stream music has resulted from the futile effort (if you will forgive the pun) to swim against the prevailing currents.

What I have been urging in the preceding paragraphs is a two-pronged thesis: first, that the trend of the avant-garde has been to shun a wedding of European music with jazz, moving instead toward a more non-Western approach that draws inspiration from the black ghetto, from Africa and Asia, or from some combination of both. Second, this trend is fundamentally *political,* not just artistic, in nature, paralleling and mirroring the loss of faith of Negroes in a peaceful and gradualist American Dream. That loss of faith, in turn, has grown out of a recognition that the dream historically has been predicated on the permanent exclusion of Negroes from all but the dregs of what, in material terms, this society has to offer.

I am not so deluded as to think that this thesis will be welcomed with open arms; it challenges too many received dogmas for that. Still, if I may paraphrase Trotsky, you may ignore the forces of social change if you wish—but you have no guarantee that they will ignore you in return. Jazz has never existed hermetically sealed in a historical and political vacuum. For better or worse, it is created by flesh-and-blood human beings who lead specific lives in certain concrete conditions, usually within one of the country's larger Negro ghettos. To hold that what transpires in these ghettos will not shape and mold jazz—to maintain that the thoughts, feelings, emotions, aspirations, and frustrations of the musicians performing it will not somehow be incorporated into this music that, more than any other, puts a premium on expressiveness—is simply to display a kind of willful blindness that exacerbates predicaments by stubbornly refusing to acknowledge their existence. Yet surely the issues are too grave to permit such infantile attitudes to persist much longer. Surely the beauty that jazz has given us places us under a moral obligation to respond with all the rationality, realism, maturity, and wisdom of which we are capable. Or so, at any rate, one may hope.

NOTES

1. Quoted in Charlie L. Russell, "Ornette Coleman Sounds Off," *Liberator*, July 1965, p. 14.

2. From the interview with McCoy Tyner in chapter 12.

3. Quoted in Don DeMicheal, "The Sixth Man," *down beat*, March 1963, p. 17.

4. In *The New Theatre in America*, ed. Edward Parone (New York: Dell, 1965), p. 211; the first ellipsis is in the original.

5. Leon F. Litwack narrates the history of white-racist cruelty to *antebellum* "free" black people in his classic work, *North of Slavery: The Negro in the Free States, 1790–1860* (Chicago: University of Chicago Press, 1961); see also Eugene H. Berwanger, *The Frontier Against Slavery* (Urbana, IL: University of Illinois Press, 1967); V. Jacque Voegeli, *Free But not Equal: The Midwest and the Negro During the Civil War* (Berkeley: University of California Press, 1968); James A. Rawley, *Race and Politics: "Bleeding Kansas" and the Coming of the Civil War* (Philadelphia and New York: J. B. Lippincott, 1969); Eric Foner, *Free Soil, Free Labor, Free Men: The Ideology of the Republican Party before the Civil War* (New York: Oxford University Press, 1970). For the black-nationalist response to white persecution, see, among others, John H. Bracey, Jr., August Meier, and Elliott Rudwick, eds., *Black Nationalism in America* (Indianapolis and New York: Bobbs-Merrill, 1970), pp. 51–120 *passim*.

6. On Afro-Americans in the southern states, see, for example, C. Vann Woodward, *The Burden of Southern History* (New York: Vintage, 1960), especially chapter 4.

7. Litwack, *North of Slavery*, p. 91.

8. See, among others, Melvin Steinfield, ed., *Our Racist Presidents: From Washington to Nixon* (San Ramon, CA: Consensus Publishers, 1972).

9. One manifestation of racism's abiding presence is the fact that Negro children learn to view themselves with disdain at a remarkably early age, especially in an "integrated" setting, as Mary Ellen Goodman makes clear in her study, *Race Awareness in Young Children* (New York: Macmillan, 1964). This book has the not-

inconsiderable merit of demonstrating conclusively that it is white social institutions, rather than the Nation of Islam (Black Muslims) or other black-nationalist groups, that, as the phrase has it, "teach hate." Worst of all, the *kind* of hatred they teach is often directed at the self of the impressionable black child.

10. As John W. Dower brings out especially well: *War Without Mercy: Race and Power in the Pacific War* (New York: Pantheon, 1986).

11. A point I treat at much greater length in chapter 6 of *Black Music, White Business: Illuminating the History and Political Economy of Jazz* (New York: Pathfinder Press, 1997).

12. C. Vann Woodward, *The Strange Career of Jim Crow* (New York: Oxford University Press, 1967), pp. 120–121, 148–149. The Court's leisurely pace of enforcing desegregation should be compared with the urgency with which it insists on, say, legislative redistricting.

13. See C.E. Wilson's penetrating discussion, "The Myth of Negro Progress," *Liberator*, January 1964, pp. 3–6, 19. Wilson draws attention to the fact that median income for black families as a percentage of white stood at a higher level in 1955 than in 1961, 55.4 percent *versus* 53.4 percent, respectively. By 1972, median black-family income had risen less than six percent, to 59 percent that of white families. Similarly, black unemployment as a percentage of white increased from 219 percent in 1955 to 230 percent in 1963. In 1972, the situation was no more promising: "the unemployment ratio between the races [was] once again rising, with twice as many blacks as whites on the jobless rolls. Black unemployment was 10 percent, compared with 5 percent for whites. . . . The black teen-age unemployment continued its upward climb, going from 26.3 percent in 1967 to 33.5 percent [in 1972]." The number of black people below the federal government's "poverty line," moreover, in 1972 "stood at . . . 33 percent of the total black population, while the number of white poor was . . . 9 percent . . . representing declines in the number and the percentages [of white poor] since 1967. . . . However, the bureau [of the Census] reported there is some evidence of a small increase between 1971 and 1972 in the number of Negroes below the low-income level, whereas the number of low-income whites

declined." And so on. See "Blacks' Income Is Still Lagging," *San Francisco Chronicle*, July 23, 1973, p. 6. An analysis of the 1970 census by syndicated columnist Tom Wicker leads to a similar conclusion: young white men are 50 percent more likely to complete high school, four times as likely to complete college; "the percentage of housing with inadequate plumbing occupied by blacks remained at 30 percent during the 1960s"; black life expectancy at age twenty-five "is six years less than white"; and the black infant-mortality rate "far exceeds the white" ("News Behind the News," *Sacramento Bee*, July 26, 1973, p. B–7). More than one decade later, then, the title of C.E. Wilson's article is still very much apropos.

14. Louis Harris and William Brink, *The Negro Revolution in America* (New York: Simon and Schuster, 1964), p. 149. Given the obviously long-standing white antipathy to any measures that might remedy the effects of previous racist discrimination, from the vantage point of the 1990s one can say only, *plus ça change.* . . . As a somewhat more-bizarre indication of how refractory are some white beliefs about black people, Helen and Sue Bottel report that the third-largest number of letters written to their personal-advice column in the months immediately before July 1973 concerned an "'outlandish' letter about how the auctioned-off black slaves 'had it so good.' Would you believe," the authors ask rhetorically, "half the answers agreed with the letter? . . . Which is a pretty sad commentary on 'free' America!" "Generation Rap," *Sacramento Bee*, July 12, 1973, p. F–7; ellipsis in original.

15. See the moving account by Robert Vernon of a street meeting addressed by Malcolm X, "At a Black Muslim Rally," in *The Black Ghetto* (New York: Merit Publishers, 1964), pp. 9–11.

16. For an insightful discussion of this phenomenon, see Harold R. Isaacs, *The New World of Negro Americans* (New York: Viking Press, 1964), chapter 3.

17. Musicians have not been slow to grasp this point. Consider, for example, the comment of composer Bill Dixon: "what they *really* mean when they call the Chinese atom bomb 'primitive' is that yellow men created it"; quoted in Robert Levin, "The Jazz Composers Guild: An Assertion of Dignity," *down beat*, May 6, 1965, p. 12.

18. See the lengthy discussion of Nazi policies in Spain in Hugh

Thomas, *The Spanish Civil War* (New York: Harper & Row, 1963). *Newsweek* reports that "though U.S. officials are understandably sensitive to comparisons between Vietnam and the Spanish civil war as a 'laboratory for war,' the parallel nonetheless exists" (May 24, 1965, p. 47). This article then goes on to provide a detailed inventory of the countless death-dealing devices being "tested" on the hapless populace of Southeast Asia. For more on this topic, see Vietnam Veterans Against the War, *The Winter Soldier Investigation: An Inquiry into American War Crimes* (Boston: Beacon Press, 1972), a work whose title is self-explanatory.

19. See in *Liberator*, November 1964, Ossie Sykes, "A 'Final Solution' for the USA?", p. 6, and C.E. Wilson, "No 'Final Solution' Yet," pp. 7–8, 12. The factual basis underlying such fears as Sykes and Wilson express is set forth by Sidney W. Wilhelm, *Who Needs the Negro?* (Garden City, NY: Doubleday, 1971), and Samuel F. Yette, *The Choice: The Issue of Black Survival in America* (New York: Berkley Publishing, 1971).

20. See Svend Ranulf, *Moral Indignation and Middle Class Psychology* (2nd ed.; New York: Schocken Books, 1964), p. 4.

21. Archie Shepp, *Four for Trane* (Impulse 71).

22. The tendency to concentrate on harmony at the expense of melody and rhythm graphically illustrates one of the most persistent problems arising out of white criticism of an essentially black art—namely, that critics continually insist on imposing judgments based on European criteria, rather than letting the nature of the music itself suggest new and more appropriate standards. A pair of reviews of John Coltrane recordings by Bill Mathieu, a composer-arranger who worked with Stan Kenton, offers a classic (if one may use that word in this context) instance of such wrongheadedness. Because he was obsessed with harmonic development (and insensitive to rhythmic movement), Mathieu was unable to appreciate Coltrane's work: "There is one aspect of this music that leaves me dissatisfied," he wrote. "This is the alternation of [only] two chords, which . . . create [*sic*] hypnotic [harmonic] non-movement. . . . The alternative? More creative attention to harmonic thought." Mathieu's strictures also extended to the playing of pianist McCoy Tyner, whose "long and vivid solos . . . from the harmonic point of view, become

hysterically dull." Review of John Coltrane, *Coltrane Live at Birdland* (Impulse 50), in *down beat*, April 9, 1964, p. 26. Mathieu later reiterated this complaint in discussing two other Coltrane recordings: "There has been one musical problem that, over the years, has prevented me from becoming an all-out Coltrane fan"—the "narrow harmonic area," the "harmonic stasis," that "makes the music dull." Review of John Coltrane, *Coltrane's Sound* (Atlantic 1419) and *Crescent* (Impulse 66), in *down beat*, October 8, 1964, p. 27. Evidently, it never occurred to Mathieu to try to understand *why* Coltrane, whose compositions at the end of the 1950s were brimming with dense, rapidly shifting harmonies, had felt compelled to move to the opposite musical pole.

23. See, for an early and utterly incontrovertible example, the wonderful dialogue between Dolphy's bass clarinet and Charles Mingus's bass on "What Love," *Charles Mingus Presents: The Charles Mingus Quartet Featuring Eric Dolphy* (Barnaby Z 30561).

24. Taking as my source the *New Encyclopedia of Jazz* (2nd. rev. ed., New York: Horizon Press, 1960), Leonard Feather, comp., I estimate that as late as the 1930s, fewer than half the musicians in Ellington's group had had any formal musical instruction; some of the biographical entries in the *Encyclopedia* are very brief, however, and therefore may be incomplete.

25. The quotation from Alice Coltrane is in my unpublished interview with her, Berkeley, California, April 23–24, 1971; see also Frank Kofsky, "Views: A Conversation with Alice Coltrane," *Renaissance 2: A Journal of Afro-American Studies*, no. 3 (1973, Yale University). The quotations from Ornette Coleman, McCoy Tyner, and Elvin Jones are in the sources cited above in footnotes 1, 2, and 3, respectively; for Elvin Jones's simulation of African drumming, see his solo on "Africa," on John Coltrane, *Africa/Brass* (Impulse 6).

26. Musicologist Wilfrid Mellers, for example, believes that Coltrane's music "recall[s] not only field hollers and Asiatic music, but African ritual music itself"—a contention that, as I will demonstrate momentarily, rests on tangible musical evidence. Mellers also states that "Coltrane's pentatonic ululations are more obviously Asiatic or flamenco-like, and . . . the cross-rhythmed ostinati of piano . . . and of percussion are intermittently Latin-American and primitively

African." See *Music in a New Found Land: Themes and Developments in the History of American Music* (London: Barrie and Rockliff, 1964), pp. 348, 369.

27. The *Niegpadoudo* rhythm of Dahomey, chanted by the brothers Albéric and Frédéric Glélé is in the collection, "Music of the Princes of Dahomey," *Anthology of Music of Black Africa* (Everest 3254/3). "Dahomey Dance" and "Africa" are on John Coltrane, *Olé* (Atlantic 1373) and *Africa/Brass* (Impulse 9), respectively.

28. See, for example, John Coltrane, *Kulu Se Mama* (Impulse 9106) and *Om* (Impulse 9140).

29. See Wilbur Harden, *Jazz Way Out* (Savoy MG 12131) and *Tanganyika Strut* (Savoy MG 12136). "India" is on John Coltrane, *Impressions* (Impulse 42). My unsystematic impression is that Coltrane used more African-related titles for his compositions than any other jazz artist.

7

The new black radicalism

Jazz . . . is looked upon as something "primitive"—like what they really mean when they call the Chinese atom bomb "primitive" is that yellow men created it.

—BILL DIXON[1]

The system is such that when the black man speaks his mind, then it's time to call it racism.

—ANDREW HILL[2]

Is it simply the music some of these men are making or the turning social circumstances that still causes so much anxiety and resistance among many clubowners, record executives, and critics? "I'm getting tired of Negroes," remarked one critic after an Albert Ayler set.

—ROBERT LEVIN[3]

During the autumn of 1964, a series of avant-garde jazz concerts took place in New York's Cellar Cafe. Although the music itself was of great significance, of equal importance was the title chosen for the series: The October Revolution.

To be sure, most of the reporters present missed the implications in the reference to the triumph of Bolshevism in 1917—an interesting commentary on the political awareness of jazz journalists[4]—but this was not at all the case with the participating musicians. Subsequent events have shown the October Revolution to be only one of a number of signs of a thoroughly radical upheaval, musical and social, taking place among young Negro jazz artists.

In every respect the combined social-musical revolution in jazz (as I suggested in the preceding chapter) amounts to a repudiation of the values of white middle-class capitalist America. This is most obvious from the statements of the musicians themselves, but it is also apparent—to those who care to listen with an open mind—in the wild and exciting music the revolution is producing.

Among its leaders, three names top the list: John Coltrane, Ornette Coleman, Cecil Taylor.* To name the leaders, however, is simpler than to describe the movement they head. The substance of the music, for one thing, is too elusive; the range of styles, for another, is too great. Still, beneath the apparently endless variety there are common themes that unify the diverse aspects of the revolution.

On a strictly musical level, one of these themes is the attempt of the revolutionaries to replace the fixed rhythmic

---

* Which is not to say that others, such as Sun Ra and Bill Dixon, have not made major contributions to the jazz revolution, despite the limited recognition their work has received. In reality, it has been largely through the groups maintained by the latter two artists and Cecil Taylor that many of the younger musicians—including John Gilmore, Ronnie Boykins, Marshall Allen, and Pat Patrick with Sun Ra; Albert Ayler, Archie Shepp, Sonny Murray, Jimmy Lyons, Andrew Cyrille with Taylor; and Rashied Ali, David Izenson, Howard Johnson, Marc Levin with Dixon—have had their formative experiences in the new music.

pulse and unvarying cycle of chords that jazz artists have used as a framework for their improvisations since Charlie Parker and Dizzy Gillespie first pointed the way in the mid-1940s. The new musicians have been moving away from these now-threadbare guideposts toward a fresh concept of group, as opposed to individual, improvisation. The reasons for this shift are, as I have said, both musical and social. At the social level, let it suffice that collective improvisation symbolizes the recognition among musicians that their art is not an affair of individual "geniuses," but the musical expression of an entire people—the black people in America. In any event, that a recasting of the balance away from the individual and toward the collective has been an important element in the work of John Coltrane, Ornette Coleman, Cecil Taylor, and their numerous followers is no longer seriously disputable.

A second and related unity underlying the "new black music"—a name bestowed by poet-playwright-essayist LeRoi Jones, who himself functions as an unofficial advocate for the musicians[5]—is a rejection of Western musical conventions. Such a rejection, I argued in the preceding chapter, surely has clear social implications above and beyond the artistic ones. In point of fact, it reflects the larger decision of the Negro ghetto to turn its back on an exploitative and inhumane white American society. Thus saxophonist Coltrane draws on the non-white world, especially Africa and India, for inspiration (his compositions bear titles like "Africa," "Dahomey Dance," "India"), while alto saxophonist Coleman manifests his black pride by proclaiming that he "came up with a music that didn't require European laws applied to it," a "revolutionary breakthrough" for jazz.[6]

If the world of color abroad has been influential in shaping the new music, the same applies to the world of color at home—Harlem and Watts. "The greatness in jazz," Cecil

Taylor has remarked, "occurs because it includes all the *mores* and folkways of Negroes during the last fifty years."[7] Despite outraged denunciations from white writers who claim that statements such as Taylor's are "racist,"[8] there is not much question that the pianist is correct. His remarks, moreover, illustrate a growing trend for jazz artists to draw on the ghetto environment for their material. It has often been remarked, for example, that the new jazz closely resembles human speech. True enough; yet it is ghetto speech and not speech "in general" that (as I maintained in chapter 6) one hears in the work of the jazz avant garde.

Nowhere is the indebtedness of the jazz revolution to the vocal patterns of the ghetto more manifest than in the huge, raucous sounds that emerge from the tenor saxophone of Archie Shepp, who performed with Cecil Taylor before forming his own group. Shepp, who describes himself as "an antifascist artist,"[9] also exemplifies the social radicalism inherent in the new music. He has scandalized the conservative white jazz Establishment with eloquent manifestos (some of which I quote elsewhere in this volume) linking jazz, black nationalism of the Malcolm X persuasion, and revolutions of national liberation in the Third World. Jazz, he thus asserts, is

> one of the most meaningful social, esthetic contributions to America. . . . It is antiwar; it is opposed to Vietnam; it is for Cuba; it is for the liberation of all people. . . . Why is that so? Because jazz is a music itself born out of oppression, born out of the enslavement of my people.[10]

Another representative of this unprecedented radicalism in jazz is trumpeter-composer Bill Dixon, the chief organizer behind the 1964 October Revolution. Like Shepp, Dixon is eloquent in both poetry and prose.[11] Also like Shepp, Dixon is an uncompromising enemy of the racial and social status quo. The experience of the October Revolution led him to realize the need for an organization that could "protect the musicians and composers from the existing forces of exploitation." He was convinced that if radical black musicians were willing to reject "the crumbs that up to the present they have been forced to accept," they could drive out many of the absentee owners from what is accurately called the jazz *business*.[12] In the aftermath, Dixon was able to persuade Taylor, Shepp, and several other avant-garde musicians, black and white, to form a cooperative, the Jazz Composers Guild.

The Guild, it turned out, was a noble experiment that failed. Its quick demise was in part due to the unshakable position of the white businessman in jazz—a position that Archie Shepp conveys with his customary pith: "You own the music, and we make it." But this outcome was also the result of racial frictions that led to schisms in the group. Dixon told Robert Levin, one of the few white writers in sympathy with the aims of the jazz revolution, that there was "a subtle, but apparent, indignation on the part of the white members . . . that a black man . . . could conceive and execute an idea that would be intelligent and beneficial to all."[13]

Despite its failure, the Guild may be an omen of things to come. To understand why this is so, one need merely examine the circumstances under which these proud musicians are forced to create. Three representative incidents— out of the legion one might select[14]—serve to lay bare the inner workings of the jazz world as they impinge on black musicians.

Item: Robert Levin has related that

Anyone present at [Cecil] Taylor's March 17th concert at Town Hall [in 1965] will tell you that at least 500 people were in attendance. Norman Seaman, who runs the hall and is in charge of delivering the artists their percentage of the gate, claimed a count of only 247 ticket stubs. Would he have dared to do that to a white artist? To, say, Bill Evans?[15]

Item: To most devotees of jazz, John Coltrane possesses a stature comparable to that of, for example, Vladimir Horowitz, Artur Rubinstein, or Jascha Heifitz in European art music. As one token of Coltrane's achievement, consider his awards in the single year of 1965: named to the "Hall of Fame," his album *A Love Supreme* (Impulse 77) selected as Record of the Year, and elected to first place in the tenor-saxophone category by the readers of *down beat;* honored as Jazzman of the Year, for the Jazz Composition of the Year, for the Jazz Album of the Year, and with a first place among tenor saxophonists by the readers of *Jazz* magazine; *A Love Supreme* voted Record of the Year and Coltrane awarded one first prize (for tenor saxophone) and one second prize (for "miscellaneous instrument"—soprano saxophone) in the *down beat* International Jazz Critics Poll; *A Love Supreme* chosen as both Jazz Composition of the Year and Jazz Album of the Year by the writers responding to the Jazz Album of the Year Poll sponsored by *Jazz.* Small wonder that one jazz periodical dubbed 1965 "The Year of John Coltrane."[16]

Yet for all of these tributes, John Coltrane remains "just another nigger" to the jazz Establishment. Toward the end of March, 1965, Coltrane and his group appeared at what was ostensibly a benefit concert for LeRoi Jones's Black Arts Repertory Theatre/School. I say "ostensibly" because in retrospect it appeared as if the main purpose of the concert was to provide Impulse Records, which recorded the performances and later released some of them on an album titled *The New Wave in Jazz,*[17] with an opportunity to turn an easy profit from the jazz revolution. Thus, the Coltrane ensemble three times began to play, only to be interrupted each time by the recording engineer's insistence on readjusting his equipment and even repositioning the artists. Thanks to Cecil Taylor, we have an eye-witness account of these scandalous proceedings:

> [T]he engineer on that occasion was the celebrated Rudy Van Gelder, the man with the white gloves, and while Coltrane was playing at one point, Van Gelder went up with his white glove and said, "STOP! STOP! STOP!" because he wasn't ready. Everybody sat there and watched this, and allowed Van Gelder to go up to THAT guy [Coltrane] and shout . . ."STOP!" [18]

Finally, on the group's fourth attempt, the engineer allowed the musicians to proceed—the dictates of stereophonic sound and the profit system had been satisfied.

Here again, Robert Levin's rhetorical question is apropos: would any record company have *dreamed* of treating a "legitimate"—that is, white—artist in such a contemptuous manner? Can you imagine the reaction of Glenn Gould or Isaac Stern under these circumstances? But then, Gould and Stern are not black jazz musicians. For the latter, the blatant implication is that, as niggers, they will take whatever the Establishment sees fit to dish out and jolly well like it.

Item: Finally, the case of Archie Shepp. As late as 1965 Shepp could write, in an especially bitter moment:

> I've been in this music for fifteen years, and I've never worked [as a musician] for a solid week in this country. I've never made my living playing jazz. I work now as a merchandiser for Abraham & Straus.[19]

A break came early in 1966, however, when Shepp was offered a two-week engagement at a new San Francisco nightclub, the Both/And, followed by another two weeks at Shelly's Manne-Hole in Los Angeles. But notwithstanding the packed houses he drew in California, Shepp returned to New York to find himself once more without musical employment—and this time without a job at Abraham & Straus to cushion the fall. In desperation, he pawned his saxophone.

Now lacking both job and saxophone, Shepp came across an advertisement in which the Selmer Company, a manufacturer of musical instruments, had used his name.[20] Perhaps Selmer would provide him with a saxophone in exchange for the privilege of featuring him in its ads? "We never give our instruments to musicians," was the answer Shepp heard from Selmer. Once more, one wonders: would Steinway mention Van Cliburn in one of its ads without the pianist's permission? And then dare to refuse him a piano?

In any event, outraged at this high-handed treatment without even a hint of compensation, Shepp checked with Impulse Records, where he was under contract, to determine if he had any legal recourse. At this point it seemed for a moment as if fate were about to intervene in his behalf: an Impulse executive told Shepp that the company would buy a new saxophone for him from Selmer. Naturally, this was too good to be true. A few days later, he learned that the saxophone's cost was more than Impulse was willing to bear; only if he consented to write, say, half-a-dozen compositions and copyright them through Impulse's music-publishing subsidiary would the company follow through on its commitment to him.

When I left him in New York at the end of April 1966, Shepp was still slaving over these same compositions; owing to his lack of an instrument, his group, which had begun to hit its artistic peak during its stay on the West Coast, had already gone several weeks without rehearsing.[21] Yet the representatives of the jazz Establishment have the gall to protest when Shepp writes "with some authority about the crude stables (clubs) where black men are groomed and paced to run till they bleed, or else are hacked up outright for Lepage's glue." [22]

Painful to relate, the incidents I have recounted are all too typical of what the dedicated jazz artist must endure in order to find an audience. Taken en masse, they go far toward explaining the mood of bitter revolt sweeping through the ranks of the younger black musicians. Cecil Taylor, for one, has become so disgusted with the prevailing conditions that he has called for "a boycott by Negro musicians of all jazz clubs in the United States. I also propose that there should be a boycott by Negro jazz musicians of all the record companies . . . all trade papers dealing with music . . . and that all Negro musicians resign from every federated union in this country." "Let's take the music away from the people who control it," his manifesto concludes. [23]

None of which is meant to suggest that the artists caught up in the jazz revolution aim only at redressing their own grievances. At bottom, they recognize that the problems they face are different only in degree from those that beset the black ghettos whence they sprang. As Archie Shepp observes, the white entrepreneurs who dominate the music business "are only the lower echelon of a power structure which has never tolerated from Negroes the belief that we have in ourselves, that we are people, that we are men, that we are women, that we are human beings. That power structure would more readily dismiss me as an uppity nigger or a fresh nigger than to give me my rights." [24]

The hope of the avant-garde revolutionaries, then, is that their music will prove relevant to the plight of the ghetto. Indeed, Cecil Taylor is convinced that the jazz Establishment wishes to keep radical musicians from steady employment for just this reason. Were these artists to work regularly—which almost none does—he argues, "they would be able to operate at maximum capacity on all levels," thereby becoming "an engaged part of the community." In this case, because the jazz musician is "so close to reality, he would be able to spell out in language the community could understand exactly what his work is about and how it has relation to them—how it comes out of perhaps the same problems they're struggling with."[25] Saxophonist and critic Don Heckman, who speaks from the vantage point of a participant, sums up the situation succinctly: "Some of today's players conceive of jazz as a symbol of social change—even social revolution." Such is the state of mind that today prevails among the artists who play the new black music. No one save the fatuous expects that it will be dispelled before the prison walls of the ghetto are themselves shattered.

NOTES

1. Quoted in Robert Levin, "The Jazz Composers Guild: An Assertion of Dignity," *down beat*, May 6, 1965, p. 12.

2. Quoted in Don Heckman, "Roots, Culture and Economics: An Interview with Avant-Garde Pianist-Composer Andrew Hill," *down beat*, May 5, 1966, p. 20.

3. Robert Levin in "How They Voted," *down beat*, August 12, 1965, p. 42.

4. See, for example, Dan Morgenstern and Martin Williams, "The October Revolution—Two Views of the Avant Garde in Action," *down beat*, November 19, 1964, pp. 15, 33.

5. See, as a case in point, LeRoi Jones, notes to John Coltrane, Albert Ayler, Archie Shepp, and others, *The New Wave in Jazz* (Impulse 90).

6. "Dahomey Dance," "Africa" and "India" are on John Coltrane, *Olé* (Atlantic 1373), *Africa/Brass* (Impulse 9), and *Impressions* (Impulse 42) respectively. Ornette Coleman is quoted in Charlie L. Russell, "Ornette Coleman Sounds Off," *Liberator*, July 1965, p. 14.

7. Quoted in Bill Coss, "Cecil Taylor's Struggle for Existence: Portrait of the Artist as a Coiled Spring," *down beat*, October 26, 1961, p. 20.

8. See in particular the analysis of such critics in chapter 3.

9. Archie Shepp, "An Artist Speaks Bluntly," *down beat*, December 15, 1965, p. 42.

10. Quoted in the (partial) transcript of a panel discussion among Taylor, Archie Shepp, Rahsaan Roland Kirk, and others, "Point of Contact," in *down beat Music '66*, ed. Don DeMicheal (Chicago: Maher Publications, 1966), p. 111.

11. It is typical of this generation of jazz artists that their accomplishments extend in a multitude of directions. Shepp, besides his poetry and musicianship, is a professional actor—he appeared in the original production of Jack Gelber's *The Connection*—and has had a number of his own plays staged in New York City; see the article by the director of one of them, David Long, "Archie Shepp—Jazz Playwright," *Jazz*, January 1966, p. 26. Bill Dixon is a talented oil painter with several shows in New York to his credit. Cecil Taylor, who holds a degree from the New England Conservatory, is a knowledgeable balletomane as well as a poet; his poems "Scroll No. 1," "Soul Being's Gravity a Focal Point Touched Anoints the Darkened Heart" and "Rain" are in *Sounds and Fury*, July–August 1965, pp. 45, 46–47 and 48, respectively. And so forth.

12. Dixon is quoted in Levin, "The Jazz Composers Guild," p. 18.

13. Shepp, "An Artist Speaks Bluntly," p. 11; Dixon is quoted in Levin, "The Jazz Composers Guild," p. 17.

14. For a full-scale discussion of the subject of racist exploitation of black artists by white entrepreneurs and corporation executives, see chapters 2–4 in my study, *Black Music, White Business: Illuminating the History and Political Economy of Jazz* (New York: Pathfinder Press, 1997).

15. Robert Levin, "Some Observations on the State of the Scene," *Sounds and Fury*, July–August 1965, p. 6.

16. "Thirtieth Annual *down beat* Reader's Poll," *down beat*, December 30, 1965, pp. 19–20 (the "Year of John Coltrane" phrase is on p. 19); "First Annual *Jazz* Reader's Poll," *Jazz*, May 1966, pp. 10, 15; "*down beat*'s International Critics Poll Results," *down beat*, August 12, 1965, pp. 14–16 *passim;* "The JAY [Jazz Album of the Year] Winners," *Jazz*, February 1966, p. 8. A revealing, if not especially surprising, sidelight of Coltrane's triumph is the fact that

290 / PART 3: THE REVOLUTION IN MUSIC

his achievements have been appreciated more readily by European than by North American critics, as one can demonstrate by computations based on any of the various "polls" in which writers from both continents participate. In the 1965 International Critics Poll (*down beat*, August 12, 1965, pp. 14–19), for instance, only nine of the twenty-nine U.S. and Canadian writers, or 31 percent, voted for Coltrane in the tenor-saxophone category, whereas the proportion of Europeans voting for him, seven of eleven (64 percent), was twice as large. One also finds the same general 2-to-1 ratio between European and North American respondents in the voting for Jazz Album of the Year conducted by *Jazz* magazine (February 1966, pp. 8–11, 13–14).

17. According to LeRoi Jones, who annotated the album in question (Impulse 90), "the Impulse record called *The New Wave in Jazz* was supposed to be called *New Black Music*" (*down beat*, February 10, 1966, p. 48). Clearly, however, the latter title is much less salable to a "mixed" public—hence much less profitable—than the former.

18. Taylor quoted in Pat Griffith, "Reasoning of Cecil Taylor," *Changes*, December 15, 1971, p. 23. Note another of Taylor's observations: "So, you see, most of the musicians who appeared at [this event] . . . a million dollars worth of talent, recorded for Impulse— a billion-dollar business concern—for maybe five hundred dollars. Now from my point of view, this don't make no kind of political, economic or social kind of sense" (p. 23).

19. Shepp quoted in "Point of Contact," p. 29.

20. See, for instance, the Selmer advertisement that reads, in part: "You'll play better with a Selmer . . . and look at the company you'll keep!"; *Jazz*, February 1966, p. 32 (outside back cover). The same advertisement also appeared, in the identical position, in *Jazz* for May and June 1966 (p. 32 in each case). Owing to the fact that Shepp had taken a first prize in one division of the 1965 International Jazz Critics Poll, his name had suddenly become of value to Selmer. What irony! Good enough for the critics—at least the European ones (see note 16, above)—but not good enough for a two-week engagement in one of New York's many jazz establishments.

21. This account is based on a series of conversations I had with Shepp in the second half of April 1966.

22. "An Artist Speaks Bluntly," p. 11.

23. Taylor quoted in "Point of Contact," p. 19. Note also the similar statement of Bill Dixon: "By now it is quite obvious that those of us whose work is not acceptable to the Establishment are not going to be financially acknowledged. As a result, it is very clear that musicians, in order to survive—create their music and maintain some semblance of sanity—will have to 'do it themselves' in the future." Quoted in Levin, "The Jazz Composers Guild," p. 17.

24. Shepp quoted in "Point of Contact," p. 17.

25. Quoted in Levin, "Some Observations," p. 6.

8

John Coltrane and the
black music revolution

*It became apparent when [Thelonious] Monk and Col-
trane worked together . . . and later when John recorded
Hard Drivin' Jazz with Cecil [Taylor], that a whole new
area of sound had opened up beneath us and new directions were imminent.*

—ARCHIE SHEPP[1]

Thomas S. Kuhn's study, *The Structure of Scientific Revolutions,*[2] is a work that demands the attention of anyone
interested in a *theoretical* approach to the question of how
and why changes from one major jazz style to another take
place. Kuhn, to be sure, is concerned primarily with the
abrupt replacement of one scientific theory by another, an
event he terms a scientific revolution. But much of what he
has to say has immediate applicability to the arts as well.

Kuhn's thesis is that science does not—indeed, cannot—
develop in a smooth, continuous fashion, science textbooks
to the contrary notwithstanding. Scientists can carry out

their day-to-day activities—what Kuhn terms "normal science"—only so long as they have a model ("paradigm") of their particular portion of the universe that seems to explain the phenomena they consider of paramount importance (for no paradigm ever explains *all* the phenomena). Sooner or later, however, as scientific experiments produce new knowledge, there emerge certain crucial findings that disagree with what the paradigm predicts. When enough of these anomalies have accumulated, they begin to undermine the authority of the old paradigm and the science then enters a phase of crisis. Although Kuhn does point out that not all discrepancies are of equal significance, he does not attempt to explain what gives decisive weight to some and not to others. Nevertheless, it seems a straightforward conclusion that a scientific theory's defects are likely to appear acute when they begin to act as a substantial obstacle to further economic-technological advancement. Hence, for example, the long revolution in astronomy beginning with Copernicus and ending with Isaac Newton occurred in the seventeenth century—when a developing capitalism in Western Europe was eagerly seeking improved understanding of celestial navigation for purposes of trade and exploration, of the methods of warfare (especially the aiming of projectiles) for purposes of acquiring plunder and territory, and of clock-making for purposes of rationalizing business transactions— and not, say, in the tenth or the twentieth.[3]

The hallmark of a period of crisis in science arises from the fact that the current paradigm no longer provides an adequate account of the most important natural phenomena, while no single new one exists to replace it. In this fluid situation, scientists will advance all kinds of new hypotheses, and the adherents of each will compete for the support of the remainder of the scientific community. The crisis ends when one of the new paradigms obtains the approval of the majority of practicing scientists and "normal science" once again becomes the order of the day. The rapid and discontinuous shift in paradigm that has thus taken place is nothing more or less than a scientific revolution.

Yet the matter does not end here, for the physical universe—that is, the universe as the scientists view it—is never the same after the revolution as it was before. One result of discarding the old paradigm for the new is that some problems that were viewed as legitimate before the revolution are demoted to the status of pseudoproblems after it. Astrology becomes scientifically disreputable after Newton; likewise for alchemy following the chemical revolution that overthrew phlogiston theory in the eighteenth century.

Not every scientist is able to make the transition to the new paradigm, however. Specifically, those older scientists who have done the greater part of their lives' work using the old paradigm will ordinarily have an extremely strong emotional attachment to it, and therefore may be unable to sunder their ties to the now-outmoded way of thinking. They may, in consequence, be ostracized by their former colleagues and, perhaps, ultimately even hounded out of the scientific community. But in any event, the final outcome serves to ensure the triumph of the revolution and the concepts associated with it. Later, textbook writers will quietly efface the revolutionary origins of the new concepts in the interest of presenting to students beginning their education a rosy picture of uninterrupted and irreversible scientific progress. All subsequent "normal" scientific activity will—until the inescapable next revolution—take place within the boundaries implicitly set by the newly crowned paradigm. In the wake of Newton's achievement of accounting for planetary motion by countervailing gravitational and centrifugal forces, scientists devoted increasingly less attention to the question of what *caused* gravity—an issue that had preoccupied such of Newton's predecessors as William Gilbert and Johannes Kepler—and correspondingly more on the *effects* of gravitational attraction. It was only in the twentieth century, when the paradigm formulated by Einstein and others toppled that of Newton, that the former problem regained its pre-Newtonian scientific primacy.

Admittedly, all of this may *seem* far removed from the world of jazz—but the distance, as I will try to demonstrate, is more apparent than real. By way of illustration, take the concept of an aesthetic revolution as a shift in paradigm: surely there is no more succinct or precise way (once one has digested the terminology) of describing the momentous changes wrought by Charlie Parker, Dizzy Gillespie, Thelonious Monk, and their associates in the early 1940s in substituting for the swing paradigm of improvisation based on the melody of a composition and a quarter-note rhythmic feeling the bebop paradigm of improvisation based on the harmony of a composition and an eighth-note rhythmic feeling. Kuhn's thesis likewise illuminates what occurred after the bebop paradigm displaced swing. Younger musicians who themselves had no profound commitment to swing were able to abandon it and immerse themselves in the new style with relative ease; many members of the previous artistic generation were unable to sever their attachment to the older music and remained with it for the rest of their lives; the canons of orthodoxy were then redrawn so as to exclude the swing stylists. The fact that there was a subsequent reconciliation between revolutionaries and conservatives does not detract from the essential correctness of this (necessarily oversimplified) account of the bebop revolution, for such reconciliations are, in fact, invariably a feature of many (or possibly all) kinds of revolution.

There are, of course, obvious limits beyond which one ought not push the analogy between scientific and aesthetic revolutions. For one thing, inasmuch as scientific hypotheses succeed only on the basis of their ability to describe objective physical reality (a statement with which I gather

Kuhn does not agree), science possesses an established criterion for choosing among rival paradigms that jazz and every other art lacks. There is, in other words, no *absolute* frame of reference permitting one to assert unequivocally that this artistic idiom is "better" and that one "worse," any more than one can decide the ancient question of whether it is the landscape that is "really" moving by the train or the train moving by the landscape (or both).

Another notable difference between the two kinds of revolution, especially in the short run, stems from the substantial amount of independence that scientists, in comparison to artists, have come to enjoy in determining whether to accept a proposed paradigm. By virtue of a three-thousand-year history from which to learn, we have begun to understand that attempts to dictate the contents of scientific theories from without—whether as in the case of Platonic theological astronomy, American eugenics in the early twentieth century, or Lysenkoism in the Soviet Union more recently—have invariably been disastrous. The jazz musician, on the other hand, enjoys no such privilege. This is especially true in the event of a revolution. (One ought not overestimate the amount of scientific independence in any country, however, for ruling classes find ways—usually indirect—of making certain that scientific *research*, as distinct from scientific theory, advances their interests first and foremost.)

Granted that intellectual upheavals can be marked by acrimoniousness in the best of circumstances, the scientist is not additionally burdened by having mutually hostile groups of critics, recording company executives, concert and festival promoters, nightclub owners, and the like, enter the fray in order to defend their own particularistic economic interests. It is unlikely that these worthies alter the outcome of a jazz revolution much one way or another over the long haul, inasmuch as the fate of a new paradigm rests on its reception by musicians themselves; in this respect, the arts and the sciences are similar.* Nonetheless, by the very fact that these uninvited participants are all to one degree or another parasitic on the jazz musician's art, their eagerness to take sides in a revolutionary conflict only obscures the issues at stake, exacerbates antagonisms, and to that extent obstructs the efforts of the musicians themselves to heal the breach. To see these processes in action, we need look no further than the avant-garde revolution in jazz that is under way even as I write.

It is to that revolution that I wish to apply Kuhn's concepts, as I have outlined them above. If it was the bebop paradigm in all its multifaceted splendor that emerged from the successful jazz revolution of the forties, it should by now have become abundantly clear that this paradigm has been seriously impaired—probably beyond recovery. Does this mean, then, that a successor paradigm has already emerged? Although it may be tempting to give a "yes" answer, on balance a more judicious response has to be in the negative. The jazz avant-garde has firmed up its ranks and gained immeasurably in self-confidence, in my estimation, in recent years; still, any attempt to force its myriad and diverse styles to conform to a single pattern would do it more than a little violence. What we have to deal with instead is a situation which, were it to occur in one of the sciences, would fit nicely into Kuhn's model of a crisis: the old paradigm is rapidly breaking down, numerous new contenders compete to fill the vacuum, but as yet no single idiom dominates.

Supposing my appraisal is correct, it sheds some light

---

* It is also true that, in contrast to the case with the sciences, a dedicated lay public can sustain an older paradigm in the arts long after it has ceased to engage the attention of the most talented artists. As a result, artistic revolutions are more diffuse and less thoroughgoing than those in science, and therefore often more difficult to delineate as well.

on recent trends in jazz. Leonard Feather has called attention to the ambivalence of musicians and critics alike when faced with the task of pronouncing judgment on one of the leading revolutionaries, Ornette Coleman. But Feather is deeply mistaken in choosing to dismiss these responses to Coleman as mere "fence-sitting," for they are entirely predictable reactions, considering that the "normal" standards have become obsolete and there are no universally agreed-upon substitutes in sight. Lacking firm criteria for deciding one way or another, the majority of both musicians and critics, not surprisingly, equivocate, vacillate, and contradict themselves repeatedly. Feather's confident assertion that "the musician is less likely to be fooled into believing a bad performance is good" might be a useful assumption—if only the musicians themselves could arrive at a consensus as to what constitutes "good" or "bad" in jazz. Far from demonstrating the superiority of musician-critics over their amateur counterparts as Feather intends, his farrago of quotations on the subject of Ornette Coleman reveals that musicians and the critics alike are wandering over uncharted terrain, desperately searching for landmarks to guide them. Such landmarks will not appear, however, until a new paradigm has won the approval of the jazz artists themselves.[4]

Although the avant-garde is not defined by any single dominant style, it by no means follows that we can say nothing at all useful about it. Even if it is still too soon to have a definitive understanding of what the avant-garde is, we need not be so hesitant in proclaiming what it is not. And one of the things that it very definitely is not is: atonal. Quite often avant-garde improvisations are *untempered*— that is, they are not confined to the eighty-eight notes found on the modern equal-tempered piano—but one should not confuse this quality with atonality, the absence of a tonal center (or centers). Incidentally, the writer most responsible for muddying the difference between the two, Martin Wil-

liams, appears finally to have been able to distinguish between the atonal and the untempered. Apropos of Ornette
Coleman, whose playing Williams has been in the habit of
describing as atonal, he remarks, "Sometimes he isn't free
enough, you know, because *he always plays modally*. People say he's too free—no he's not, *he's always right in that
key*" (my emphasis).[5]

I will return to Williams and some of his more idiosyncratic views momentarily. Meanwhile, though, as long as I
am dispelling misconceptions about Ornette Coleman, it is
worth mentioning that, despite the sheer mass of verbiage
devoted to him in the jazz press (and not only there), the
single most influential figure on and in the avant-garde is
not he, but John Coltrane. Inasmuch as this idea may come
as a revelation to some, the evidence for it—which is more
than ample—merits examination in some detail. (One item
of that evidence is the fact that the initial diatribe against
"anti-jazz" had Coltrane's group, at the time including Eric
Dolphy, rather than Coleman as its principal target.) Before
undertaking that examination, however, I want to focus
on certain aspects of Coltrane's career prior to 1961, a date
that marks a rough watershed in his relationship with the
avant-garde.

One could hardly find a better example than the contrast
between Coltrane's development before and after 1961 to
buttress the thesis (inspired by Kuhn) that art *of necessity*
proceeds by revolution. Although it was not widely realized
at the time, what Coltrane was in actuality attempting until that time was to carry jazz improvisation forward by a
non-revolutionary extension of the basic bebop conventions.
Consider: Coltrane served his musical apprenticeship under
bebop masters—Dizzy Gillespie, Thelonious Monk, Miles
Davis.[6] And if, as André Hodeir contends in *Jazz: Its Evolution and Essence*,[7] we may schematically describe bebop as
differing from swing in the former's use of (1) the eighth

note rather than the quarter note as the basic rhythmic unit, (2) harmonic rather than melodic improvisation, and (3) more complicated chord sequences, then the inescapable inference is that Coltrane was as late as the end of the 1950s seeking to push the approach introduced by the bebop revolutionaries to its logical, evolutionary conclusion; he was not striving to subvert this approach—even though that was the ultimate outcome of his search for a way to break out of the stagnation that by then had overtaken bebop-style improvisation.

Thus, the Coltrane "sheets of sound" technique—cascades of notes played so rapidly as to become a glissando—that seemed to puzzle so many critics in the late 1950s appears in this perspective as the direct successor to the improvisations of Charlie Parker (possibly this is what one writer intended in adverting to the "general essences of Charlie Parker" in Coltrane's style).[8] First of all, Coltrane heightened the rhythmic complexity by inserting three chords where Parker and the early beboppers had put only one (the "three on one" approach); second and consequently, Coltrane then had to subdivide his improvised melodies into sixteenth (and shorter) notes in order to be able to touch on the scales he associated with each chord. Of this stage in his artistic maturation—the analysis of which by pianist Zita Carno remains unsurpassed[9]—Coltrane later recalled, "When I was with Miles [Davis], I didn't have anything to think about but myself, so I stayed at the piano and chords! chords! chords! chords! I ended up playing them on my horn!"[10]

These two fresh departures—the sixteenth notes and the thicker harmonic textures—quite naturally interacted to produce the sheets of sound as the only way of referring to each chord in the allotted number of beats (or even parts of beats); they also led to an original kind of rhythmic attack and phraseology that was as intricately demanding as anything played by the first generation of bebop musicians. "I found," Coltrane wrote as he was about to emerge from this period, "that there were a certain number of chord progressions to play in a given time, and sometimes what I played didn't work out in eighth notes, sixteenth notes, or triplets. I had to put the notes in uneven groups like fives and sevens in order to get them all in."[11] If for no other reason than the immense advance in rhythmic-harmonic sophistication and technique they required of a performer, Coltrane's sheets of sound belong in the front rank of contributions to the literature of jazz improvisation. For all of that, however, they went largely unsung among the critical fraternity—when, indeed, they were not the object of outright abuse.

Most jazz musicians—or most scientists—would be more than content to be able to lay claim to a single major innovation in their lifetime; Coltrane's name is rightly associated with several. Having brought the sheets of sound to perfection in the latter 1950s, he was forced to let them drop shortly thereafter. To believe that this outcome was due merely to capriciousness would be to misunderstand it sorely. In reality, Coltrane's decision reflected his perhaps-reluctant recognition that although thickening the harmonic framework of bebop had posed a challenge to him initially, once he had surmounted that challenge, he was right back where he began: confronting the problem of how to infuse improvisation built on a foundation of chord sequences with new vitality. Merely increasing the harmonic complexity of bebop by replacing one chord with several—a procedure Coltrane sometimes described as the "three on one" approach—bought time, but in the final analysis only compounded the problem; it did not, and could not, provide a solution.

Thus, having brought the sheets of sound to their zenith, Coltrane changed directions and began experimenting with two other musical ideas. Both of these, however, like the sheets of sound before them, made the bebop improvising structure more arduous and constricting, hence in the end the saxophonist would move beyond them as well.

From the spring of 1959 to the autumn of 1960, Coltrane recorded one series of compositions in which he improvised while the piano, bass and drums played an ostinato, or short rhythmic-melodic figure, that continued throughout his solo (the earliest examples include "Spiral," "Syeeda's Song Flute," "Fifth House," and "Like Sonny"). During the same months, he also recorded a second group of pieces characterized by new, faster-moving harmonies—the underlying chord changed every other beat, on the average, even at the most blistering tempo—rather than on superimposing three chords where one had stood before. For this second approach—the best-known and certainly most powerful examples of which are Coltrane's various performances of his composition "Giant Steps"—the sheets of sound were neither necessary nor suitable; instead, Coltrane worked out in advance a set of melodic patterns that he could deploy and manipulate at every speed, no matter how rapid. (The following two chapters analyze the evolution of Coltrane's style during this period in considerably more detail.)

Even after formation of his own group with McCoy Tyner, Elvin Jones, and Steve Davis in the summer of 1960, moreover, Coltrane for some time persisted with both of these improvisational strategies, that based on ostinatos and that built on the "Giant Steps" harmonies and melodic patterns. His readings of "Summertime" and "Body and Soul" (as well as his own compositions "Equinox," "Mr. Day," and "Mr. Knight") show Coltrane's abiding interest in ostinatos, while the "Giant Steps" chords and patterns serve as the underpinnings of both his composition "Central Park West" and his version of the Gershwins' song, "But Not for Me." For that matter, even in the case of "My Favorite Things," Coltrane's most open-ended vehicle from this period, he initially improvised with an ostinato constantly sounding in the background.[12]

From one standpoint, we may view the history of jazz as the continuing emancipation of the soloist from the underlying rhythmic and harmonic architecture. The net result of the bebop revolution, on this analysis, was (as I discuss in greater depth in chapter 10) twofold: first, it made the rhythmic pulse more subtle by doing away with the steady beat from the bass drum and the pianist's left hand; second, it widened harmonic horizons through use of the upper intervals of a chord. Both of these developments gave the soloist new freedom. Yet Coltrane's various extensions of accepted bebop practice, paradoxically enough, had just the opposite effect: during his sheets-of-sound phase in the late 1950s, the dense ("three on one") harmonic matrix he favored and the tremendously rapid speeds of execution needed to refer to all of the chords threatened to smother any ordinary soloist beneath their combined weight. Subsequently, at the start of the 1960s, Coltrane's use of ostinatos and/or the "Giant Steps" chords and patterns merely imposed a different, but ultimately no less inhospitable, group of restrictions. Only a supremely gifted creator—only a Coltrane, in short—had the ability to maneuver within each of these straitjackets and still produce something of value.

And in the end, even he found the game not worth the candle. Implicit in Coltrane's decision to abandon the sheets of sound, the ostinatos, and the "Giant Steps" harmonies was the conclusion that the daring improvisational procedures introduced by the bebop revolutionaries of the preceding decade had by the end of the 1950s turned into an artistic cul-de-sac. In that respect, bebop was no different from its predecessors: beyond a certain point, further artistic progress was possible only by demolishing the dominant paradigm—not by relatively minor tinkering with this or that aspect of it. (The parallel with the bebop revolution is even more striking when one bears in mind that Coltrane, like Parker and Gillespie before him, was thoroughly schooled in the music that he subsequently did so much to undermine.) Nothing offers us a more direct demonstration of the applicability of Thomas Kuhn's thinking to aesthetic revolutions than the sudden and wholly unexpected changes in Coltrane's style after he reached what then appeared to be the pinnacle of his career.

I realize that the foregoing account still does not resolve all the questions about the historical causes of aesthetic revolutions, especially that of *timing*. Even if bebop sooner or later had to yield to newer forms that allowed the soloist greater freedom, that fact does not in itself explain why the transition began to occur in the late 1950s instead of, say, half a dozen years before or after. But as I have stated at numerous points heretofore, we can best understand the avant-garde revolution in jazz as a response to a massive constellation of social and economic forces impinging on the urban Negro ghettos during the late 1950s and early 1960s: increased technological unemployment of unskilled Negro laborers; the consolidation of Afro-American determination to remove, and white insistence on maintaining, the chains of second-class citizenship; the movement for African independence; and not least, the growth of explicit black-nationalist sentiment.

Although, as we have seen throughout, the great majority of white writers do not agree with this interpretation, their objections do not strike me as especially convincing. There is ample evidence that long-term, deeply rooted historical developments affecting the ghetto—the Great Depression, the rise of industrial unionism, migration from the rural South to urban centers, the integration of Negroes into the industrial economy during World War II and the experiences abroad of Afro-Americans in the armed services—were reflected in the drastic changes in jazz and other Afro-American musics in the 1940s.[13] Why should this principle be any more outlandish when applied to the postwar era? Surely, the fact that any broad movement, artistic or otherwise, is formed and molded—pulled in this direction, tugged in that—by the most powerful contemporaneous social forces does not diminish the importance of either the movement itself or its leadership. To state that avant-garde jazz is an expression of certain concrete historical events, therefore, should neither interfere with one's enjoyment of the music nor reduce it to a "purely sociological" phenomenon. On the contrary, it is more likely that some firm scientific knowledge of the circumstances out of which it has sprung will enhance one's appreciation and comprehension of any art. This principle is so well established in the field of art history, to mention only one example, as to be a commonplace: no one would think of discussing the paintings of the Renaissance and early modern period in Europe without reference to the vast social and economic changes sweeping over the continent. Why is it somehow illegitimate to apply the same logic to African-American jazz?

This interpretation of the origins of the avant-garde finds particularly striking confirmation, moreover, in the career of John Coltrane. Throughout the late 1950s, as we have witnessed, he sought to revitalize jazz by thickening its harmonic texture, first with the "three on one" approach, then with the "Giant Steps" chord sequence. Had this attempt succeeded, it would have, by increasing the emphasis put on harmonic movement, taken the music in a more European direction. Instead, however, in mid-1960 Coltrane abruptly changed course; from that point on (as the following two chapters also discuss), his preoccupation with European harmony would fade, to be replaced with new ideas drawn from African concepts of polyrhythm and Indian improvisatory practice.

In turning next to a detailed examination of the question of Coltrane's relationship to the avant-garde, we are fortunate that he was well known prior to identifying himself with the jazz revolution so that we can document reasonably well through recordings his earliest steps beyond bebop. The first of them, dating from the second half of 1958, consists of his appearance as a soloist with a jazz orchestra playing the works of composer-theorist George Russell, followed by a more prominent role in a quintet assembled by Cecil Taylor for the pianist's recording, *Hard Driving Jazz*. Already Coltrane's avant-garde credentials were substantial, at least so far as Cecil Taylor was concerned, for the pianist subsequently would remark, "See what happens when Coltrane and I play together. He and [Eric] Dolphy can hear me."[14]

Taylor's linking of Coltrane and Dolphy was more than fortuitous, for by 1962 Coltrane had on many occasions incorporated this gifted flute, bass-clarinet, and saxophone virtuoso into his ensemble—the first, as it turned out, of a series of young iconoclasts whom Coltrane would thus befriend and promote.[15] Coltrane explained at the time how he happened to invite Dolphy to perform with his group:

> Eric and I have been talking music for quite a few years, since about 1954. We've been close for quite a while. . . . We always talked about it, discussed what was being done through the years, because we love music. What we're doing now was started a few years ago.
>
> A few months ago Eric was in New York, where the group was working, and he felt like playing, wanted to come down and sit in. So I told him to come on down and play, and he did—and turned us all around. . . . It was like having another member of the family. He'd found another way to express the same thing we had found one way to do.[16]

Coltrane's connections with the avant-garde went beyond his friendship with Eric Dolphy, however. Even before Dolphy entered his group, Coltrane and trumpeter Don Cherry,

Ornette Coleman's most frequent collaborator, in 1960 recorded an album of compositions by (or associated with) Coleman, who was then regarded as the epitome of the jazz revolution.[17] After Dolphy's departure to become a leader in his own right, Coltrane next took under his wing another saxophonist, Archie Shepp, interceding with Impulse Records to obtain a contract for the younger artist—a debt that Shepp acknowledged in titling his initial recording for Impulse *Four for Trane*. For a brief period, Coltrane brought Shepp into his group, as he had Dolphy earlier. Apparently, there are no recordings of Shepp performing with Coltrane before an audience, but the two did record together in the studio on at least a pair of occasions.[18]

By this point, around the beginning of 1965, Coltrane's group was becoming a haven for young and mostly obscure black musicians who, attracted both by his charisma, his openness, and by the tumultuous collective improvisations of Coltrane, McCoy Tyner, Elvin Jones, and bassist Jimmy Garrison, often queued up three- and four-deep around the bandstand hoping for a chance to "sit in." Coltrane, for his part, was increasingly turning to some of these young artists to share ideas about where jazz was heading.[19] Out of this immersion in the new music came Coltrane's decision to assemble an imposing collection of the leading young black innovators—tenor saxophonists Archie Shepp and Pharoah Sanders, alto saxophonists Marion Brown and John Tchicai, trumpeters Freddie Hubbard and Dewey Johnson, bassist Arthur Davis, in addition to Tyner, Jones and Garrison—to record an indescribably powerful 40-minute collective improvisation, *Ascension*.[20]

Had there been any doubt about Coltrane's true sentiments, *Ascension* made it unmistakable that his identification with the avant-garde was complete. Thereafter, neither his music nor his group would ever be the same. Just as his debut with the soprano saxophone on his *My Favorite Things* recording signaled a new course (as I demonstrate in greater detail in the next chapter), so did *Ascension* betoken another radical shift in the direction of Coltrane's art. To an even greater degree than with Eric Dolphy or Archie Shepp earlier, Pharoah Sanders now became a permanent, and pivotal, member of the post-*Ascension* Coltrane ensemble; he would appear on all but one of the "on location" recordings Coltrane made between *Ascension* and his death in July 1967,[21] and several of the studio recordings as well. Coltrane's incorporation of Sanders into his group also initiated a period of rapid and drastic changes in its personnel, culminating when Jones and Tyner left in 1966, to be replaced by Rashied Ali and Alice McLeod Coltrane (the saxophonist's wife), respectively. By the time of his demise the following year, then, Coltrane's central position within the avant-garde was beyond dispute. He was, moreover, the only established artist of the first rank who had seen fit to throw in his lot wholeheartedly with the new movement.

Beyond his association with such rising avant-garde luminaries as Eric Dolphy, Archie Shepp, Pharoah Sanders, and Albert Ayler, there are other, equally fundamental manifestations of Coltrane's influence on the jazz revolution. Naturally enough, this influence is most apparent in the case of saxophonists, although by no means confined to them. As long ago as 1961, LeRoi Jones already could remark—accurately—that "most of the avant-garde reed men are beholden to John [Coltrane]";[22] the passing of time has done nothing to lessen the validity of Jones's observation. Gary Bartz, Wayne Shorter, Sam Rivers, Dewey Redman, Joe Henderson, Nathan Davis, John Handy, Charles Lloyd, Joe Farrell, Carlos Garnett, Benny Maupin, Jimmy Woods, Prince Lasha, Huey (Sonny) Simmons, Ken McIntyre, Paul Plummer—these are a few of the musicians whom one could cite as paying open deference to Coltrane on their instruments. Archie Shepp and Eric Dolphy, whose careers, as we have seen, Coltrane vigorously fostered, are also indebted to him for certain elements of their styles, but in a fashion more subtle and diffuse than with the other artists.[23] The number of saxophonists under the sway of Ornette Coleman to a comparable degree is, to put it charitably, enormously smaller.

Coltrane's influence on the avant-garde extends beyond the ranks of the saxophonists, however. Years ago, André Hodeir astutely noted that Charlie Parker's genius was illustrated not only in his playing, but in his choice of accompanists who shared his revolutionary approach to the rhythmic and harmonic foundation of jazz.[24] The same applies equally well to Coltrane. His inventions in rhythm—worked out, according to him, in conjunction with his entire group—have been particularly fertile; even where musicians have not adopted them whole, these ideas have been of overriding importance (as I argue in chapter 10) in accelerating the emancipation of bass and drums from the role to which bebop confined them. I am at a loss as to why the critics have so generally tended to neglect Coltrane's contributions in the field of rhythm, when it should be obvious that they have been of great significance. Nonetheless, I have still to read the analysis which gives proper weight to Coltrane's use of two basses, for example, as an initial step toward shattering the approach to timekeeping that, prior to Coltrane, was all-prevalent.[25] It is impossible to digest the work of such drummers as Jack DeJohnette, J.C. Moses, Beaver Harris, and Sonny Murray except as offshoots of Elvin Jones,[26] or that of some of the "free" bassists—say, the irrepressibly inventive Richard Davis or Cecil McBee—without the previous explorations of McCoy Tyner, Elvin Jones, and Arthur Davis (and later, Reginald Workman and Jimmy Garrison). For that matter, isn't it significant that Elvin Jones himself turns up with increasing frequency on avant-garde recordings these days?[27]

FRANK KOFSKY

John Coltrane

McCoy Tyner

Elvin Jones

FRANK KOFSKY

Albert Ayler

FRANK KOFSKY

Jimmy Garrison

FRANK KOFSKY

Pharoah Sanders

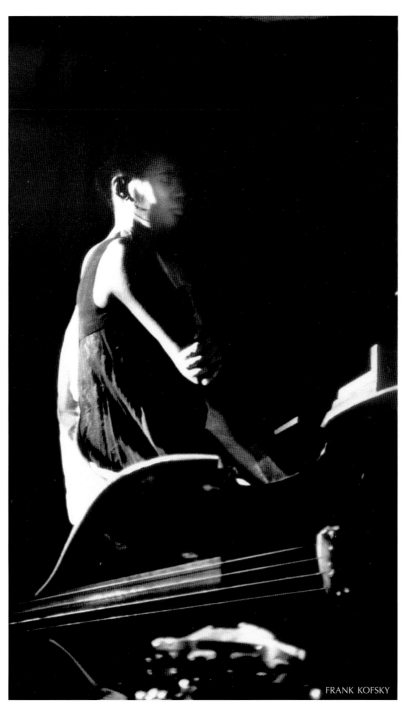

FRANK KOFSKY

Alice Coltrane

Ray Appleton, Jimmy Garrison, Pharoah Sanders,
Rashied Ali, John Coltrane

FRANK KOFSKY

Archie Shepp

VAL WILMER

Cecil Taylor

Max Roach

Sonny Rollins

VAL WILMER

Thelonious Monk

Miles Davis

Ornette Coleman, David Izenson

FRANK KOFSKY

John Coltrane

In retrospect, it should not be especially surprising that Coltrane's breakthrough to a new concept of jazz rhythm came in the second half of 1960. For one thing, as I emphasize in tracing the evolution of jazz rhythmic practices in chapter 10, it was at this moment that he finally succeeded in bringing together a group of musicians—Tyner, Jones, and bassist Steve Davis—with whom he could begin exploring certain concepts he had been pondering for some time. For recording purposes, of course, Coltrane had been a "leader" on numerous earlier occasions. But "leading" for a few hours in a recording studio is one thing—playing night after night for weeks or months at a time with the same musicians is quite a different proposition. Having a regularly working group of his own—especially one so superbly attuned to his own thinking—gave Coltrane his first opportunity to integrate theory and practice; it allowed him to try out a new idea, retain or modify it if it appeared promising, or let it fall by the wayside if it did not. Coltrane did not hesitate for an instant in taking advantage of this favorable environment; as a result, his progress toward a new style went at a torrid pace.

But not only was Coltrane setting off in a fresh direction with his own group; simultaneously, he was also making his initial forays with the soprano saxophone. It is reasonable to infer (as I explain further in the following chapter) that the problems involved in creating a style on an instrument so different from the tenor saxophone—and one for which there was no immediately relevant modern jazz tradition in the bargain—ultimately led him to reassess and then revise his overall approach. Heretofore, to take one example, the length of Coltrane's solos had always been based on the number of measures in the composition on which he was improvising. In a 12-measure blues, for instance, Coltrane's solo would extend over an integer multiple of 12 measures; in a typical 32-measure American popular song such as "I

Got Rhythm" or "Body and Soul," he would improvise for some multiple of 32 measures. Surely it is significant, therefore, that the first time Coltrane ventured to create a solo whose length was *not* determined by the number of measures in the composition itself, he was playing the soprano saxophone; the composition, of course, was "My Favorite Things." [28] Coltrane himself would later confirm the importance of the soprano saxophone in altering his approach to improvisation:

> KOFSKY: Do you think that learning how to play the soprano saxophone changed your style?
> COLTRANE: Definitely, definitely. It certainly did. . . .
> It caused the change or the willingness to change and just try to play as much of the instrument as possible.
> KOFSKY: Did it give you new rhythmic ideas, too?
> COLTRANE: I think so, I think so. A new shape came out of this thing and patterns—the way the patterns would fall.[29]

It seems quite clear, therefore, that the combination of adopting the soprano saxophone at the same time his new group was taking shape reinforced Coltrane's determination to pursue hitherto untrodden paths. "I've got to keep experimenting," he stated around this time. "I have part of what I'm looking for in my grasp, but not all." [30] The same theme recurs in many of his conversations from this period. "I don't know what I'm looking for," he said on another occasion, "something that hasn't been played before. I don't know what it is. I know I'll have that feeling when I get it and I'll just keep on searching." [31]

At this point, it is appropriate to pause for a moment's reflection. Those who have stood so ready to condemn Coltrane for his relentless probing of the music's furthest reaches might do better to ponder the alternatives. An artistic style that once was pulsating with vitality may, through nothing more than its unconditional acceptance over time, seem lifeless and banal to a later artistic generation. By the end of the 1950s, when Coltrane and many others were embarking on a root-and-branch restructuring of the improvisatory tradition, such was the case in jazz. It would have been more convenient, perhaps, if there were a new paradigm to hand as soon as the old one showed itself obsolete—but the universe is seldom that beneficent. Hence the only realistic options were, on the one hand, an interval of open-ended searching in a multitude of directions—itself the certain indicator of breakdown and crisis—or, on the other, stagnation. The most creative musicians (including, to a degree, Max Roach, Miles Davis, and Charles Mingus in addition to Coltrane), naturally, preferred the former. Rather than indulging in endless acerbic complaints, the jazz public and critics alike ought more properly to be grateful that they have some of the invaluable progress reports from that period preserved on recordings (which is more than we possess for the early days of bebop).

It goes practically without saying that not everyone concurs with this conclusion. The top dogs in the critical Establishment, for one, would have us believe that the procedures that have served jazz for the past two decades will suffice equally well for the next two—or, perhaps, forever. Such a static outlook is ahistorical in the extreme. It is contradicted by the entire evolution of jazz to the present, and for that reason is, as a philosophy of artistic development, really beneath refutation. As an aspect of the social history of black music, however, the virulent criticism leveled at Coltrane particularly (but not exclusively) at the outset of his turn toward the avant-garde at the start of the 1960s clamors for more attention.

I have already presented a wealth of evidence (especially in the first three chapters) demonstrating the hostility of the majority of the better-known jazz critics to anything smacking of a social interpretation of the music. As part of their attempt at preserving the status quo—and, one imagines, their own perquisites from it—these gentlemen have been unswerving in their efforts to discredit the propositions that, among other things, (1) jazz is fundamentally a black music in terms of its origins and most vital innovations; (2) that almost all white musicians are therefore necessarily obliged to "borrow" the leading elements of their styles from black innovators; (3) that black musicians historically have received, and continue to receive, a disproportionately small share of the financial rewards from an art of their creation; and (4) that jazz, a music born and nurtured within the black community, reflects the dreams, hopes, fears, anger, ambitions, aspirations, resentments, and desires of that community. All this Establishment critics have resolutely denied, simultaneously insisting with utmost intransigence that jazz has always been and must always remain totally divorced from anything so mundane as the social forces that shape the lives of the flesh-and-blood human beings who daily re-create it.

Yet precisely their own adamant animosity toward the black avant-garde of the 1960s—a movement exemplified in the music of John Coltrane and his various collaborators—gives the lie to the critics' ideological dogma of an impassable gulf separating art and life. For when we examine more closely the roster of those white writers who have taken it as their mission to stifle the voices of Coltrane and his fellow iconoclasts, we discover just those same names that are already familiar to us from their leading role in the campaign to extinguish all social interpretations, all black-nationalist thinking, all radical ideas, from jazz: Leonard Feather, Ira Gitler, and their colleagues among the editors of *down beat* magazine.

Surely, this fact reflects no mere coincidence. Having attained a certain expertise in the jazz styles of the 1940s and 1950s, these critics are loath to see their entrenched position undermined by a new wave of black innovations—especially when those innovations are accompanied by equally revolutionary social and political ideas. Hence given that the chief beneficiaries of the *social and racial status quo* in jazz are likewise among those with most to lose from an overturning of the *musical status quo*, it is only logical and natural that the foremost figures in the battle to suppress black nationalism and radicalism in general would also spearhead the crusade seeking to crush the avant-garde musical revolution. In this way has the indissoluble bond between social forces and stylistic change once more been reaffirmed.[32]

The critics began their counter-revolutionary thrust against the avant-garde in conjunction with their related assault on black nationalism in jazz (described in chapters 2 and 3). The opening salvo, aimed at John Coltrane while he was still a member of Miles Davis's group, came from the pen of *down beat* associate editor John Tynan in 1960. In the course of reviewing a concert by the Davis group, Tynan offered this appalling description of the saxophonist's playing:

> Slashing at the canvas of his own creation, Coltrane erupted in a fantastic onrush of surrealism and disconnected musical thought best appreciated within the dark corridors of his personal psyche. The philosophical implications of his performance, with its overtones of neurotic compulsion and contempt for an audience, belong in another area of journalistic examination.[33]

Not content to deliver only a single blow, Tynan returned to the offensive the following year, shortly after Coltrane began touring at the head of his own group. In a column devoted entirely to a strident condemnation of the "musical nonsense currently being peddled in the name of jazz by John Coltrane and his acolyte, Eric Dolphy," Tynan heaped unrestrained abuse and invective on the heads of these hapless artists:

> Recently I listened to a horrifying demonstration of
> what appears to be a growing anti-jazz trend exempli-
> fied by these foremost proponents of what is termed
> avant-garde music.
>
> I heard a good rhythm section . . . go to waste behind
> the nihilistic exercises of the two horns. . . . [Coltrane and
> Dolphy] seem bent on pursuing an anarchistic course in
> their music that can but be termed anti-jazz.
>
> Melodically and harmonically their improvisations
> struck my ear as gobbledygook. . . . [T]o these ears, the
> sum of the sounds remains musical nonsense.[34]

Notwithstanding its scurrility, this choleric outburst
gradually might have faded from memory—its author, after
all, was a critic of minor standing—had Leonard Feather not
quickly rushed to endorse it. A few months earlier, Feather—
always eager to play the role of prosecuting attorney—had
aligned himself with *down beat* editor Gene Lees in the latter's equally churlish diatribes against the black-nationalist
views and actions of Charles Mingus; a few months later,
he would take part in the inquisition that the same magazine mounted against Max Roach and Abbey Lincoln (see
chapter 2 for a full recounting of this latter effort). In the
interim, Feather put his time and energies to good use by
dashing to the aid of his comrade John Tynan, whose "comments on the 'anti-jazz' jazz trend," were, according to the
former, "as acute as they were timely" (an appraisal with
which I could not be more in agreement). Feather next proceeded to assert—with his usual cavalier disregard for historical truth—that

> the generally negative attitude toward anti-jazz held by
> most musicians . . . contrasts sharply with the almost
> immediate enthusiasm shown by many leading jazzmen
> during the last real jazz revolution, the arrival of bop.

It is significant that the most vocal adherents of anti-jazz include a high proportion of nonplaying experts, some of whom, at the time of the arrival of Dizzy Gillespie and Charlie Parker, the true jazz radicals of the last 20 years, opposed them violently. Could it be that they are now afraid . . . of missing another boat . . . ? It could be and very probably is.[35]

Even though he had couched his censorious remarks on Coltrane and Dolphy in less vituperative tones than John Tynan, Feather's greater reputation ensured that they would not be ignored or dismissed. Accordingly, the two culprits, Coltrane and Dolphy, were almost immediately summoned before the *down beat* High Tribunal and instructed by editor Don DeMicheal to "answer [to] the jazz critics" for their crimes—essentially the same procedure, the reader may recall from chapter 2, that this august journal also employed in its witch-hunting trial of Max Roach and Abbey Lincoln for voicing their black-nationalist heresies.

In the case of *down beat* versus Coltrane and Dolphy, the indictment included such *non sequiturs* as: "Coltrane and Dolphy play on and on, past inspiration into monotony"; "in his playing . . . Dolphy at times sounded as if he were imitating birds [something entirely unprecedented in the history of music, no doubt]"; "sometimes, it is said [by *whom?*], the striving for excitement *per se* within the [Coltrane] group leads to nonmusical effects . . . [allegedly justifying] the 'anti-jazz' term"; and "one of the charges is that what Coltrane and Dolphy play doesn't swing."[36] These accusations were as palpably preposterous as they were unanswerable. How, after all, are musicians supposed to prove *with words* that their improvisations are inspired rather than monotonous, infused with genuine passion rather than a sinkhole of "anti-jazz" or a collection of gratuitous "nonmusical effects"? Nevertheless, Coltrane demonstrated his abiding good will at the close of this miniature star-chamber session by volunteering to participate in another dialogue with his detractors. If he could "meet them and discuss what has been said so that he could see just what they mean," *down beat* paraphrased his words, then he could "answer his critics adequately."[37] It was, significantly, an offer that failed to elicit a response.

Meanwhile, as if to underscore the point that the powers that be at *down beat* had no intention of halting their prosecution of Coltrane and Dolphy, the very next issue of the magazine carried a review by Ira Gitler that continued in the same vein already well mined by Messrs. Tynan and Feather.[38] Hurling the term "anti-jazz" at Coltrane once again—and, incidentally, following the lead of writer Nat Hentoff's notes on the album jacket in mistaking the tenor saxophone for the soprano[39]—Gitler mercilessly excoriated Coltrane's improvisation on the selection "Chasin' the Trane":

"Chasin' the Trane" . . . is more like waitin' for a train—a 100-car freight train—to pass. . . . If you were to take away [Elvin Jones's] backing and leave Coltrane's solo standing naked, the latter would become more insignificant than it seems. Shakespeare's "sound and fury" [signifying nothing] is musically illustrated here.

Coltrane may be searching for new avenues of expression, but if it is going to take this form of yawps, squawks, and countless repetitive runs, then it should be confined to the woodshed [that is, to practicing in private]. . . . Whatever it is, it is monotonous, a treadmill to the Kingdom of Boredom.

Nor was Gitler appreciably more fond of Eric Dolphy, whose

one appearance in the album . . . contains several repetitions of his pet cliché run. He periodically falls back on it, and his solo has no definite direction. In fact, he seems to be playing the same solo, from record to record, these days.[40]

Lest one think that this deluge of critical billingsgate is too ludicrous or trivial to merit such scrutiny, consider Coltrane's own view of his antagonists. "Oh, man," he told me,

> I never could figure it out! I couldn't even venture to [explain] it now. Because as I told them [at *down beat*] then, I just felt that they didn't understand. . . . I did offer them, in an article in *down beat*, that if any of you men were interested in trying to understand, let's get together and let's talk about it, you know?[41] I thought if they were really genuinely interested or felt there was something here, that instead of just condemning what you don't know about, if you want to discuss it, let's talk about it. But no one ever came forth, so I don't think they wanted to know what I had to say about it.

Because of such shabby treatment, Coltrane recalled, he "kind of froze up on those people at *down beat*. I felt that there was something there that wasn't—I felt that they were letting their weakness direct their actions, which I didn't feel they should have." Nor could the timing of these critical onslaughts been more inopportune:

> That was a funny period in my life, because I went through quite a few changes, you know, like home life—everything, man, I just went through so many . . . Everything I was doing was like that, it was a hell of a test for me. . . .

Later in the same conversation, Coltrane was moved to speculate about the degree to which such critical broadsides had contributed to the premature death of Eric Dolphy, by creating an atmosphere in which it became nearly impossible for him to find work for his own group in the United States:

> COLTRANE: Eric, man, as sweet as this cat was and the musician that he was—it hurt me to see him get hurt in this thing.
> KOFSKY: Do you think that this possibly contributed to the fact that he died so young? . . . [Not] that it was directly the cause, but—
> COLTRANE: Indirectly?
> KOFSKY: Yes.
> COLTRANE: Yes. The whole scene, man. He couldn't work. . . .
> KOFSKY: That's what I meant, really.[42]

McCoy Tyner—who, of course, worked with Dolphy frequently in John Coltrane's group during the early 1960s—also fixed partial responsibility for Dolphy's predicament on the critical response to his music during these years:

> TYNER: Yeah, that's the thing. See, that's what I'm talking about. That's something—I can't accept that. And I mean, after the man [Dolphy] dies, put him in the [*down beat*] Hall of Fame—that's ridiculous!
> KOFSKY: The same people who put him in poverty—
> TYNER: That's what I mean, see, he couldn't work, he couldn't work in this country.[43]

Clearly, as inane as was the barrage of "anti-jazz" rhetoric deployed against Coltrane and Dolphy, at the time its effects were hardly conducive to levity and laughter.

I would not, however, like to leave the reader with the erroneous impression that all of the journalistic harassment of John Coltrane came from the likes of Leonard Feather, Ira Gitler, and their associates at *down beat.* On the contrary, even as the Feather-Gitler-*down beat* faction was so cruelly berating Coltrane from the right for his alleged excesses, at the same time he was absorbing additional verbal punishment from Martin Williams for his ostensible failure to be sufficiently revolutionary! Inasmuch as Williams is the author or editor of numerous books on jazz *and* the director of the prestigious Smithsonian Institution's jazz program, it would not do to close the curtain on the critical response to the innovations of John Coltrane without some attempt to put his writings on Coltrane in their proper perspective.

Like Feather, Gitler, and John Tynan, Williams has shown himself to be a doggedly persistent opponent of John Coltrane's music at every stage of its development. With his critical colleagues, too, Williams shares a dread of black nationalism and other radical doctrines.[44] Where he parts company with them is in his support for Ornette Coleman and some (but certainly not all) other artists involved in the jazz avant-garde.

This seeming paradox—brickbats for John Coltrane coupled with applause for his fellow revolutionaries—is in fact quite easy to resolve. Williams's contradictory critical stance derives directly from his attempt to reconcile a long and uninterrupted history of denigrating Coltrane on the one hand with his aspiration to become the recognized advocate-in-chief for "the new thing," as he terms the jazz revolution.

Let us take these points in order. Evidence of Williams's great disdain for Coltrane's increasingly iconoclastic style is abundant. As early as 1959, for example, Williams published an article touting the virtues of Ornette Coleman—as an antidote to the ideas of John Coltrane. The latter artist he dismissed with a backhand slap: "Like a harassed man in a harmonic maze," Coltrane "invite[s] the melodic disorder of running up and down scales."[45] And that was that.

Three years later, the substance of Williams's complaint had changed slightly, but the pejorative tone remained: Coltrane, he charged, "makes everything into a handful of chords." (In reality, the compositions that Williams attempted to discuss were based on modes or scales, not chords—a characteristic bit of Williams confusion, as we shall witness). His overall response to this particular Coltrane recording was to

> question whether . . . this exposition of skills adds up to anything more than a dazzling . . . array of scales and arpeggios. If one looks for melodic development or even for some sort of technical order or logic, he may find none here.[46]

That was in 1962. Another four years elapsed, with Williams still purveying the same merchandise: "Some of [Coltrane's] music seems to me repetitious and some of it banal"[47]—seemingly a case of what psychologists refer to as "projection." By 1967, however, Williams finally was ready to let the full truth emerge:

> To be entirely subjective about [Coltrane's] work, I was and am repeatedly disengaged. After three or four minutes my attention wanders, and giving the records try after try does not seem to help.[48]

The question that naturally springs to mind is whether the music of John Coltrane deserves to be lambasted time and again merely because of the insufficiency of Martin Williams's abbreviated attention span. Give the man credit for consistency, though: he hated John Coltrane's music when Coltrane improvised on bebop chord sequences; he hated it when Coltrane improvised on modes and scales; and he hated it when Coltrane improvised on nothing more than a tonic note and pulse. What, one wonders, could Coltrane have done to please Williams? Commit suicide?

In any event, the eruption of a teapot-tempest about "anti-jazz" in 1961–1962 turned out to be something of a godsend for Williams, who took the opportunity the controversy afforded to attempt to have John Coltrane banished from the ranks of the avant-garde once and for all. Emphasizing that "my opinion of John Coltrane's current work in no way reflects my opinion of Ornette Coleman," Williams sought to establish the existence of a vast and unbridgeable chasm between Coltrane's music and that of such other prominent jazz revolutionists as Coleman and Eric Dolphy:

> Basically, Coltrane's playing is conventional and traditional in its point of departure. Coltrane plays improvisations based on chord changes. So does Eric Dolphy, although Dolphy's fleeting departures from harmonic-orientation seem to come more often than Coltrane's. . . . Coleman's playing, on the other hand, is predominantly modal, occasionally atonal.[49]

What a mass of confusion! What a thicket of mumbo jumbo! Williams's attempt to distinguish between the improvisations of Coltrane and Dolphy show only too vividly how little one has to know—and how poorly one can write—in order to be admitted to the critical guild. To begin with, the notion that "Coltrane plays improvisations based on chord changes" was at best a half-truth: by the spring of 1962, when Williams's screed appeared, Coltrane had been improvising on scales or modes for nearly two years; "Impressions," "My Favorite Things," "Naima," "Spiritual"—these are just a few of the compositions whose framework consists of nothing more than a scale or two (or, in the case of "Naima," a pedal point or two). Next, if Coltrane's playing is truly "predominantly modal," his improvisations *cannot* be "based on chord changes"—the two approaches are simply antithetical.* And from the standpoint of history, even so benighted a soul as Martin Williams should have known that Coltrane (as we saw earlier in this chapter) moved toward modal improvisation precisely to escape being restricted by fixed sequences of chords. As for the notion of "departures from harmonic-orientation" and music that is "occasionally atonal," one doesn't know whether to laugh or cry. Suffice it to say that so long as the soloist's improvisation is accompanied by a bassist (or two) plucking notes chosen either from a mode or an agreed-upon series of chords, it is absurd to refer to atonality, the dictionary definition of which reads: "The absence of a tonal center and of harmonies derived from a diatonic scale corresponding to such a center; lack of tonality." [50] Regardless of whether the bassist's notes derive from a mode or a chord progression, they establish just such a tonal center; the only "atonality" possible under this circumstance is that existing in the imagination of certain muddleheaded would-be guardians of the canons of jazz.

That Williams had to resort to such linguistic contortions was anything but accidental, however. Given his continued record of hostility to Coltrane's music, such a tactic was, in fact, the only means by which he could hope to salvage his reputation as an Authority-with-a-capital-A on the avant-garde. But as we have seen, for Williams to espouse this position—whatever he may have meant by it—unavoidably embroiled him in a welter of self-contradictions that

---

* It is possible to derive chords from the notes in a mode or scale—after all, sounding any two notes simultaneously creates a chord—but that is not what jazz musicians mean by a "chord progression." Such a progression consists of an *ordered set* of chords; the customary practice is to play this harmonic sequence from start to finish during the statement of the melody of the piece, during the ensuing improvisations (with the progression continuously repeated until all the soloists have had their say), and during the final restatement of the melody.

did violence to matters of fact, logic and, not least, his own previous writings.

Consider, for instance, Williams's claim that Eric Dolphy's work was qualitatively different from that of John Coltrane. At the same time Williams was engaging in this ploy, Coltrane was leaving no doubt that he and Dolphy thought along very similar lines. The two artists, Coltrane explained in 1962,

> have been talking about music for quite a few years, since about 1954. We've been close for quite a while. . . . We always talked about it, discussed what was being done down through the years, because we love music. What we're doing now [in Coltrane's group] was started a few years ago.

Coltrane's reaction when Dolphy joined his group again emphasized that the two shared a common musical philosophy: "it was like having another member of the family." [51] This was hardly a statement that would lead a reasonable person to infer that immense differences separated Coltrane's approach from that of Dolphy. Ironically, even Williams himself had earlier turned up evidence that such a separation was entirely his own creation. "When I asked Eric Dolphy whom he listened to," Williams wrote in 1960, "the first two names that came to him were Art Tatum and John Coltrane." [52]

Williams's characteristically opaque notion that Eric Dolphy's "fleeting departures from harmonic-orientation seem to come more often than Coltrane's" stands up no better to close scrutiny. In the same article in which Williams reported Dolphy's admiration for John Coltrane, he also quoted Dolphy's remarks on precisely this question, the harmonic foundation of his improvisations: "Yes," Dolphy answered Williams,

I think of my playing as tonal. . . . *I don't think I "leave the changes"* [chord progression], *as the expression goes; every note I play has some reference to the chords of the piece* [my emphases].[53]

Nor had Williams forgotten this comment by Dolphy in the interval between 1960 and the "anti-jazz" critics' war of 1961–1962. In the notes to a recording by Ornette Coleman that appeared as the conflict was waxing hot and heavy, Williams repeated what he had written two years prior: Dolphy "has said that he thinks of everything he does as tonal and harmonic," and "ordinarily he will use the harmonic framework of a piece and its choruses [?]" as a basis for his improvisation.[54] This, mind you, is the selfsame Eric Dolphy whose supposed "departures from harmonic-orientation" while working in John Coltrane's group Martin Williams claimed to be able to detect—and "more often than Coltrane's" at that![55]

If for nothing else, one has to be impressed—in a perverse sort of way—with the mental agility that Martin Williams displayed in seeking to define the jazz revolution in such a way as to exclude Coltrane from its ranks. In his 1962 essay on Coltrane, Dolphy, and Coleman, however, Williams adopted one other strategy that, alas, also requires our attention before we can bid him farewell. In order to refute the idea that Coltrane was a member in good standing of the jazz avant-garde, Williams declared that "basically, Coltrane's playing is conventional and traditional in its point of departure."[56] The unstated implication, of course, is that a musician whose style is "basically . . . conventional and traditional" can hardly be considered a stalwart of the jazz revolution. But in a subsequent paragraph of *the same article*—ah, consistency—Williams dashed to the defense of Ornette Coleman (against the slings and arrows of John Tynan and Leonard Feather) by contending that "a legitimate part of the jazz tradition is involved" in Coleman's playing.[57] So, just as was the case with Williams's treatment of the "harmonic-orientation" of John Coltrane and Eric Dolphy, it appears that beneath all this bandying about of "tradition," the real question is: whose ox is gored.[58]

To thicken even further the semantic haze surrounding Williams's antithetical use of "tradition"—a word with favorable connotations when applied to Ornette Coleman, but negative ones when applied to John Coltrane—meditate, if you will, on some of his choices in the 1961 International Jazz Critics Poll, the results of which appeared not long before his 1962 article: Louis Armstrong, Roy Eldridge, trumpet; Jack Teagarden, Benny Morton, trombone; Johnny Hodges, Benny Carter, alto saxophone; Coleman Hawkins, Ben Webster, tenor saxophone; Pee Wee Russell, Edmond Hall, clarinet; Elmer Snowden, banjo—all musicians whose major accomplishments date from the pre-1940 era.[59] Such is the self-proclaimed apostle of "the new thing in jazz"! Well might one marvel at an elastic concept of tradition that can serve to damn John Coltrane and apotheosize Ornette Coleman at one and the same time. How is it that a writer who is so ready to disparage Coltrane's music as "basically . . . conventional and traditional" can experience no qualms in selecting Jack Teagarden, Edmond Hall, Lonnie Johnson, and Elmer Snowden as the outstanding musicians in jazz during 1961. It is hard to resist the conclusion that the gross logical contradictions that permeate the writings of Martin Williams disqualify his work from any serious consideration.

By this point, I trust the reader needs no further convincing of Coltrane's central position within the jazz revolution; if they serve no other useful purpose, the innumerable oxymoronic fallacies in which Martin Williams repeatedly embroils himself show the consequences of asserting the reverse. Are we therefore entitled to conclude that Coltrane's style will become the model for the avant-garde revolution?

Will we, after a few years have elapsed, be able to refer to the jazz revolution of the early sixties by his name in the same way that we think of the seventeenth-century revolution in astronomy as "Newtonian" or the twentieth-century one in physics as "Einsteinian"? The situation, as I have already said, is still too fluid, the trends too mixed and uncertain, to allow one to answer this question with finality. It may not be totally amiss, however, to probe the subject a bit more deeply.

It is in no way inconsistent with the tremendously exhilarating and liberating effect that Coltrane has had on contemporary jazz to observe that the young insurgents have set forth in a multitude of directions. What we need here is a certain amount of insight into the psychology of artistic upheavals. The avant-garde revolution is at the moment still in its infancy: the old restraints are being summarily tossed aside, the new conventions that will eventually replace them are only partially developed. In this "glorious dawn," we can hardly be surprised if all kinds of ideas—some of which would have been thought bizarre, unworkable, or anarchic not too long ago—are now brought forward in the name of art. Doubtless something very similar has occurred in every artistic revolution of the past—and surely in every social-political one. Revolutions, after all, are famous for releasing enormous amounts of previously untapped energy. Having just smashed the "dead hand of tradition," the youthful black radicals are intent on savoring their musical freedom—too often, the only kind they enjoy—to the fullest. And indeed, who (other than the Philistines) can blame them for that? The fact that this artistic revolution coincides with and partially reflects an in-progress *social* rebellion, as I have tried to establish in previous chapters, only lends heightened urgency to the work of these jazz insurrectionaries.

When such symptoms of a crisis par excellence exist, one cannot seriously expect that any aesthetic revolution will settle at once into a single new style, no matter how dramatically different or radical or compelling it may be. That the avant-gardists appreciate Coltrane's immense achievement in overcoming the stultification that afflicted bebop in the late 1950s and early 1960s is indisputable (evidence in the afterword to the next chapter will support this point more fully); but that they intend to confine themselves to the trail he has blazed is, for the time being at any rate, not a necessary corollary.

For my part, I continue to believe much of Coltrane's work is as "advanced"—and surely as powerful and majestic—as anything the avant-garde has produced. Yet I can also understand that some of the conventions the artistically mature Coltrane has deliberately retained (the use of modes as a basis for improvisation, for example, or the presence of a piano in his groups) may rankle those among the avant-garde who find even these few holdovers from the past too constricting. Still, it is by no means precluded that the jazz revolution will ultimately go in the direction that Coltrane's most profound and lasting innovations already have taken. Be that as it may, for any individual, whether an artist or an observer on the sidelines, to maintain that there is one single course the avant-garde revolution *must* follow strikes me as being the height of folly and presumption. As the world already has a surfeit of both, I see no necessity for me to increase the supply.

NOTES

1. "A View from the Inside," in *down beat Music '66* (Chicago: Maher Publications, 1966), ed. Don DeMicheal, p. 40. Note that Shepp, perhaps unconsciously, here renders the title of the Cecil Taylor recording with John Coltrane, *Hard Driving Jazz* (United Artists 4014), in black argot.

2. Thomas S. Kuhn, *The Structure of Scientific Revolutions* (Chicago: University of Chicago Press, 1964). If it is now a commonplace that Kuhn's insights extend beyond the boundaries of science, that was certainly not the case when I wrote the first version of this essay in 1965.

3. For a more thorough discussion of this point, see Herbert Butterfield, *The Origins of Modern Science: 1300–1800,* rev. ed. (New York: Collier Books, 1962).

4. See Leonard Feather, "The Jazzman as Critic," in *down beat Music '65,* ed. Don DeMicheal (Chicago: Maher Publications, 1965), p. 38.

5. Williams's comments appear in a partial transcript of a panel discussion, "The Jazz Avant-garde: Pro and Con—A Discussion," in *down beat Music '65,* p. 89.

6. Coltrane himself left the matter in no doubt. "Miles and Monk are my two musicians," he told a journalist in 1958. "Miles is the number-one influence over most of the modern musicians now. There isn't much harmonic ground he hasn't broken. . . . By the time I run up on something, I find Miles or Monk has done it already. Some things I learn directly from them. Miles has shown me possibilities in choosing substitutions within a chord and also new progressions [chord sequences]." Quoted in Ira Gitler, "Trane on the Track," *down beat,* October 16, 1958, pp. 16–17; the table of contents lists this article under the title, "John Coltrane: A Happy Young Man." Two years later, Coltrane himself wrote that "working with Monk brought me close to a musical architect of the highest order. I felt I learned from him in every way—through the senses, theoretically, technically. I would talk to Monk about musical problems, and he would sit at the piano and show me the answers just by playing them. I could watch him play and find out the things I wanted to know. Also, I could see a lot of things that I didn't know about at all. . . . I think Monk is one of the true greats of all time. He's a real musical thinker—they're not many like him. I feel myself fortunate to have had the opportunity to work with him." John Coltrane with Don DeMicheal, "Coltrane on Coltrane," *down beat,* September 29, 1960, p. 27; the table of contents lists this article as "Coltrane Writes about Coltrane." Although many of the critical

opponents of the new music have charged its leading figures with insufficient musical knowledge or instrumental technique to play bebop, such baseless accusations, as his remarks establish, are completely absurd when it comes to John Coltrane.

7. André Hodeir, *Jazz: Its Evolution and Essence,* trans. David Noakes (New York: Grove Press, 1956), pp. 107–11, 217–23, *passim.*

8. Gitler, "Trane on the Track," p. 17.

9. Zita Carno, "The Style of John Coltrane," part 1, *The Jazz Review,* October 1959, pp. 16–21; part 2, November 1959, pp. 13–17.

10. Coltrane quoted in Ralph Gleason, notes to John Coltrane, *Coltrane's Sound* (Atlantic 1419).

11. Coltrane with DeMicheal, "Coltrane on Coltrane," p. 27.

12. "Spiral," "Syeeda's Song Flute" and "Giant Steps" are on John Coltrane, *Giant Steps* (Atlantic 1311); "Fifth House" and "Like Sonny" are on *Coltrane Jazz* (Atlantic 1354); "But Not for Me," "Summertime" and "My Favorite Things" are on John Coltrane, *My Favorite Things* (Atlantic 1361); "Body and Soul" is on *Coltrane's Sound* (Atlantic 1419); "Mr. Day" and "Mr. Knight" are on *Coltrane Plays the Blues* (Atlantic 1382). All of Coltrane's recordings as a leader or coleader for Atlantic Records during the period from January 15, 1959, to May 25, 1961, have been reissued as a single compilation, John Coltrane, *The Heavyweight Champion: The Complete Atlantic Recordings* (Rhino Atlantic Jazz Gallery R2 71984).

13. See the extended discussion of this subject above in chapter 1, and also in Frank Kofsky, *Black Music, White Business: Illuminating the History and Political Economy of Jazz* (New York: Pathfinder Press, 1997), chapter 6.

14. George Russell, *New York, New York* (Decca DL 9216); Cecil Taylor, *Hard Driving Jazz* (United Artists 4014); the latter was later reissued—misleadingly—under Coltrane's name as *Coltrane Time* (Solid State 18025). Cecil Taylor is quoted in Bill Coss, "Cecil Taylor's Struggle for Existence: Portrait of the Artist as a Coiled Spring," *down beat,* October 26, 1961, p. 21.

15. A broad selection of Dolphy's performances with Coltrane, both in the recording studio and before audiences, are available on the Impulse, Atlantic, and Pablo labels.

16. Coltrane continued: "After [Dolphy] sat in, we decided to see what it would grow into. We began to play some of the things we had only talked about before. Since he's been in the band, he's had a broadening effect on us. There are a lot of things we try now that we never tried before." Quoted in Don DeMicheal, "John Coltrane and Eric Dolphy Answer the Jazz Critics"—a revealing title—*down beat,* April 12, 1952, p. 21.

17. John Coltrane and Don Cherry, *The Avant-Garde* (Atlantic 1451).

18. Archie Shepp, *Four for Trane* (Impulse 71). Shepp plays on John Coltrane, *Ascension* (Impulse 95). In the notes that he wrote for his recording *A Love Supreme* (Impulse 77), Coltrane expressed his "deepest appreciation" to Archie Shepp and bassist Arthur Davis, "who both recorded on a track that regrettably will not be released at this time." As of 1996—three decades later—this selection remains unreleased.

19. On December 31, 1972–January 1, 1973, KPFA, the Berkeley FM radio station, broadcast a thirty-hour program on the music of John Coltrane that Larry Bensky, Warren Van Orden, and I produced and narrated. During the course of the program, we played the tape of my interview with John Coltrane that appears in chapter 13, which prompted several artists who had known Coltrane in New York to telephone the station and relate conversations they had held with him; they also described his friendliness to the younger musicians, his willingness to let them play with his group, et cetera. I have at various times heard similar accounts from Pharoah Sanders and Albert Ayler; see in this connection, Frank Kofsky, "An Interview with Albert and Donald Ayler," *Jazz,* September 1968, pp. 22–24, *passim.*

20. *Ascension* takes up all of the recording of the same name (Impulse 95). I discuss this performance in more detail and comment on its significance in the next chapter.

21. The exception was John Coltrane and Archie Shepp, *The New Thing at Newport* (Impulse 94). Contrary to what one might expect from the title, Coltrane and Shepp do not perform together on this album; instead, each leads his own group on a number of selections.

22. LeRoi Jones, "A Coltrane Trilogy," a review of John Coltrane, *Giant Steps, Coltrane Jazz,* and *My Favorite Things* (all cited fully in previous notes to this chapter), *Metronome,* December 1961, p. 34. This review is reprinted in Jones's anthology, *Black Music* (New York: William Morrow, 1968), but the date of publication given there, 1963, is incorrect.

23. For Coltrane's influence on Archie Shepp at an early stage of the latter's development, see Cecil Taylor, *The World of Cecil Taylor* (Candid 8006), and Cecil Taylor and Buell Neidlinger, *New York City R & B* (Barnaby KZ31035).

24. Hodeir, *Jazz,* pp. 113–14.

25. For examples of Coltrane's use of two basses, see John Coltrane, *Olé* (Atlantic 1373), *Africa/Brass* (Impulse 9), *The John Coltrane Quartet Plays* (Impulse 85).

26. "The turning point came for [Sunny] Murray when he heard Elvin Jones for the first time and realized that he and Jones 'were the only people playing out of a completely new bag.' He immediately determined to be different from Jones"—powerful testimony, in a backhanded way, about Jones's effect on other drummers. See Valerie Wilmer, "Controlled Freedom Is the Thing This Year," *down beat,* March 23, 1967, p. 16.

27. Including the following: Ornette Coleman, *New York Is Now* (Blue Note 84287) and *Love Call* (Blue Note 84356); Mugo Eddie Gale, *Black Rhythm Happening* (Blue Note 84320); Joe Henderson, *Inner Urge* (Blue Note 84189); *The Elvin Jones–Jimmy Garrison Sextet,* with Prince Lasha and Huey (Sonny) Simmons (Impulse 49); Wayne Shorter, *Night Dreamer* (Blue Note 84173), *Juju* (Blue Note 84182) and *Speak No Evil* (Blue Note 84194); McCoy Tyner, *The Real McCoy* (Blue Note 84264) and *Extensions* (Blue Note LA006–F); Jimmy Woods, *The Jimmy Woods Sextet: Conflict* (Contemporary 3612); Larry Young, *Into Somethin'* (Blue Note 84187).

28. The first recorded version of which occurs on John Coltrane, *My Favorite Things* (Atlantic 1361), dating from October 1, 1960.

29. Excerpted from the interview with Coltrane in chapter 13. Even earlier, Coltrane had dropped hints about the role of the soprano saxophone in catalyzing changes in his playing: "It lets me take another look at improvisation. It's like having another hand,"

he enthused. Coltrane is quoted in Bill Coss, notes to John Coltrane, *My Favorite Things.*

30. Coltrane quoted in Coss, notes to Coltrane, *My Favorite Things.*

31. Coltrane is quoted in Ralph J. Gleason, notes to John Coltrane, *Coltrane's Sound* (Atlantic 1419). Zita Carno vividly brings out the endlessly questing character of Coltrane's work in "The Style of John Coltrane," part 1, pp. 17–18; see also the interview in chapter 13.

32. The connection between opposition to social and musical change within jazz emerges perhaps most clearly illustrated by an article written pseudonymously by Gene Lees, but attributed to him (in conversation with the author) by his colleague and frequent confidant, Ralph J. Gleason. Recall that Lees, as editor of *down beat,* had in 1960 and 1961 assumed direction of the critical blitzkrieg against bassist Charles Mingus and black nationalism (see chapter 2 for details). In the article in question, Lees combined his antagonism to black nationalism with a no less passionate abhorrence for the music of John Coltrane, Eric Dolphy, Ornette Coleman, and the jazz avant-garde in general. Both the curiously apt name under which Lees wrote, Jean P. LeBlanc—literally, John the White—as well as the title of his essay, "Jazz: The Happy Sound Is Dying" (*Esquire,* April 1962), gave the reader an accurate foretaste of what lay in store. "Ornette Coleman, John Coltrane and Sonny Rollins," according to Lees-LeBlanc, have "an utter lack of concern for beauty of sound" (p. 75); later, this author denigrated what he termed "the cacophony of an Ornette Coleman, who rejects tone, chords, harmony and melody, [and] whose champions equate anarchy with progress," and "the rankling racket of John Coltrane" (p. 144). Lees next proceeded to link these musical currents explicitly with the spread of black-nationalist sentiments in jazz, in passages highly reminiscent of his previous wild-eyed denunciations of Charles Mingus & Company: "Malice, hostility, and hate denude much of today's music of the beauty that once was jazz. The anti-white attitude of the Muslim black Nationalists [*sic*], has spilled over jazz, in the form of the reverse prejudice known as Crow Jim. . . . Today Muslim-inspired Negroes [none of whom are named] are refusing to take jobs in white bands, advise their colleagues not to hire white

sidemen" (p. 144). These sentences, together with the fulsome and recurring praise bestowed on his friend Ralph Gleason, convince me that Lees is indeed their author. In any event, the peroration is matchless: "The uncomplicated, happy spirit that produced the most treasured moments of the Dixieland and swing eras is dying of ill will, malnutrition and critical attrition" (p. 144). The best rejoinder to all such unintentionally hilarious statements came some years later from Archie Shepp: "I address myself to those 'in' white hipsters who think niggers never had it so good (Crow Jim) and that it's time something was done about restoring the traditional privileges that have always accrued to the whites exclusively (Jim Crow). Some of you are becoming a little frightened that we—niggers—ain't keepin' this thing simple enough. 'The sound of surprise'? Man, you don't want no surprises from me." "An Artist Speaks Bluntly," *down beat*, December 16, 1965, p. 11.

33. John Tynan, "Caught in the Act," *down beat*, April 14, 1960, p. 42. The notion of Coltrane having "contempt" for an audience would be laughable—witness his words on this score in the interview in chapter 13—were it not so vile and slanderous.

34. John Tynan, "Take Five," *down beat*, November 23, 1961, p. 40. Judged by the number of times Tynan made him the butt of his attacks, Coltrane seems to have been the critic's target of choice, although Tynan was not at all averse to maligning Ornette Coleman in language every bit as violent and inflamed, as witness his review of one of Coleman's recordings: "Where does neurosis end and psychosis begin? The answer must lie somewhere within this maelstrom. . . . If nothing else, this witch's brew is the logical end product of a bankrupt philosophy . . . in music. 'Collective improvisation'? Nonsense. The only semblance of collectivity lies in the fact that these eight nihilists [evidently a favorite Tynan term of endearment] were collected together in one studio at one time and with one common cause: to destroy the music that gave them birth. Give them top marks for the attempt." From a review of Ornette Coleman, *Free Jazz: A Collective Improvisation by the Ornette Coleman Double Quartet* (Atlantic 1364), in *down beat*, January 18, 1962, p. 28.

35. Leonard Feather, "Feather's Nest," *down beat*, February 15,

1962, p. 40. Feather's harangue, which lumped Ornette Coleman with John Coltrane and Eric Dolphy as the foremost exponents of "anti-jazz," drew a heated response from Coleman's chief propagandist, Martin Williams. In his reply to Feather, Williams pointed out some of the more blatantly self-serving aspects of the former's misrepresentation of the history of jazz and his own role in it. "As long as you brought up the subject," Williams wrote, "may I ask you . . . to reconsider before again proclaiming in print your own early recognition of Dizzy Gillespie or Charlie Parker. In late 1944, by which time the originality of their work might have been clear to a really involved observer, you were not voting for them in the 1945 *Esquire* critics' poll, whereas [five other critics] did vote for Gillespie. (Your 'new star' choice on trumpet was Jesse Miller. . . .) And I think your comments on Thelonious Monk in 1949 in *Inside Bebop* indicate that you considered him a relatively minor contributor to modern jazz. . . ." "The Bystander," *down beat*, May 10, 1962, p. 39. Note, by the way, that Feather's loathing for the artists of the avant-garde, which he never subsequently disavowed, was not so strong as to prevent him from accepting paying assignments to write notes for albums by Ornette Coleman, Alice Coltrane, and former Coltrane associates Elvin Jones and McCoy Tyner; the details are in chapter 3, note 11.

36. Don DeMicheal, "John Coltrane and Eric Dolphy Answer the Jazz Critics," *down beat*, April 12, 1962, pp. 21–22.

37. *Ibid.*, p. 23.

38. Feather repaid the favor shortly thereafter, riding to the side of Gitler in the latter's persecution of Max Roach and Abbey Lincoln; see chapter 2 for the details.

39. Gitler wrote, "He [Coltrane] plays soprano [on "Spiritual"], but in his opening solo the soprano's timbre sounds much like his tenor"; review of John Coltrane, *"Live" at the Village Vanguard* (Impulse 10), *down beat*, April 26, 1962, p. 29. This first solo was, of course, actually played on the tenor saxophone, as the following exchange (from the interview with Coltrane in chapter 13) establishes:

KOFSKY: Did you ever use the two saxophones on the same piece, as you did on "Spiritual"?

COLTRANE: I think that's the only time I've done that. . . .
I think that's the only one on record.

Does it come as any surprise, given this representative incident, that jazz musicians do not hold the critical "profession" in higher esteem?

40. Gitler, review of Coltrane, *"Live" at the Village Vanguard.* The test Gitler proposed—stripping away the accompaniment to "leave Coltrane's solo standing naked," is doubly unfair. To begin with, if this is going to be the criterion for judging jazz recordings, it should be applied to every artist—not reserved for Coltrane alone. Second, given that Coltrane was deliberately moving in the direction of group improvisation, it does violence to his work to evaluate it as though he were playing unaccompanied. The first-violinist's part in a Beethoven or Bartok string quartet would not sound so glorious either, if heard apart from the melodic lines of the other three instruments.

41. See DeMicheal, "John Coltrane and Eric Dolphy," p. 23 (full citation in note 36).

42. All of these exchanges are from the interview in chapter 13. Ken McIntyre, a good friend of Dolphy as well as a musician who plays the same instruments, makes much the same point with a pair of rhetorical questions: "Had Eric been accepted realistically in America, would he have stayed in Europe? . . . Had Eric not remained in Europe, would he be dead now?" See Ken McIntyre, notes to Eric Dolphy, *Eric Dolphy* (Prestige 24008).

43. See the interview with Tyner in chapter 12.

44. On one occasion, for instance, Williams sought—with typical lack of clarity—to bring the minute band of radical jazz writers into disrepute, red-baiting them with the assertion that their work consisted of "opportunistic Marxist clichés delivered with a slightly Peking-ese accent"; see "Mostly Modernists: Coltrane Up to Date," *Saturday Review,* April 30, 1955, p. 67. A few weeks after that, he unleashed a sensationalistic denunciation of the "black suprema-cists" who had, according to him, "pursued" and "annoyed" Or-nette Coleman—the implication being that this alleged harassment had contributed to Coleman's reluctance at that time to perform in

public. See Martin Williams, "The Bystander," *down beat*, June 30, 1966, p. 12. In the same vein, he informed author and scholar Krin Gabbard, who had had the audacity to assert that merely writing about the music of an oppressed group like black Americans was a political act, "That is a basic Marxist-Leninist idea, as you may be aware. . . . I do say explicitly . . . that I reject Marxism." Martin Williams to Krin Gabbard, June 12, 1991; a copy of this letter is in the author's possession.

45. Martin Williams, "Letter from Lennox," *The Jazz Review*, October 1959, p. 32.

46. Or then again, "he" may; the secret, such as it is, lies in knowing how to listen, as I bring out in greater depth below. See Martin Williams, review of John Coltrane, *Africa/Brass* (Impulse A-6), *down beat*, January 18, 1962, p. 32.

47. "Mostly Modernists," p. 67.

48. Martin Williams, "John Coltrane: Man in the Middle," *down beat*, December 14, 1967, p. 17. See also chapter 6 in Frank Kofsky, *Black Music, White Business: Illuminating the History and Political Economy of Jazz* (New York: Pathfinder Press, 1997) for a painstaking analysis of Williams's musical and anti-Marxist social views.

49. Martin Williams, "The Bystander," *down beat*, May 10, 1962, p. 39.

50. *The American Heritage Talking Dictionary* on CD-ROM (Cambridge, MA: Softkey International, 1994).

51. Coltrane quoted in DeMicheal, "John Coltrane and Eric Dolphy," p. 21.

52. Martin Williams, "Introducing Eric Dolphy," *The Jazz Review*, June 1960, p. 16.

53. Dolphy quoted in *ibid.*

54. Martin Williams, notes to Ornette Coleman, *Free Jazz: A Collective Improvisation by the Ornette Coleman Double Quartet* (Atlantic 1364).

55. The hallmark of Williams's writing is its thoroughly murky and logically slovenly nature. By way of illustration, in addition to placing Eric Dolphy simultaneously on both sides of the "harmonic-orientation" boundary simultaneously, Williams, as I suggested

earlier, has also generated an equally remarkable amount of confusion over the question of "atonality" in the jazz revolution of the 1960s, especially as it does or does not occur in the music of Ornette Coleman. In a 1961 article on "'The New Thing' in Jazz" (*Harper's Magazine,* October 1961, pp. 59–75), for example, he made no fewer than a half-dozen references to atonality, such as: "with some accuracy [the new music] has been called 'atonal jazz'" (p. 69); "in the past three years, several . . . players have appeared who improvise atonally almost as a matter of course" (p. 71); "Bassist Charlie Mingus saw the coming deadlock [and] reached for atonality" (p. 72); "free and atonal music may invite faking at this stage" (p. 72); "Ornette Coleman came to atonal jazz by a very different route" (p. 72); and so on. Yet in a 1962 column on Coltrane, Dolphy, and Coleman—which appeared only a few short weeks after his article in *Harper's*—Williams in essence repudiated these reiterated invocations of "atonality" with his straightforward remark that "[Ornette] Coleman's playing . . . is predominantly modal, *occasionally* atonal" ("The Bystander," *down beat,* May 10, 1962, p. 39; my emphasis). If that is so, then why Williams's undisguised eagerness to throw around phrases about "atonal jazz" (not to mention other equally misleading concepts) with such great frequency? Finally, to render the confusion complete, Williams in a 1962 panel discussion off-handedly dropped the comment that Coleman "isn't free enough, you know, because he *always* plays modally. People say he's too free [that is, "atonal"]—no, he's not, *he's always right in that key*" (quoted in "The Jazz Avant-garde," p. 89; both emphases mine). "Atonal jazz," "predominantly modal, occasionally atonal," but "always in the key"—a graphic example of the ubiquitously self-contradicting intellect of Martin Williams at work.

56. "The Bystander," *down beat,* May 10, 1962, p. 39.

57. *Ibid.*

58. Especially so as it was no secret that two years earlier the "basically . . . conventional and traditional" John Coltrane had recorded an album with Ornette Coleman's closest associate, trumpeter Don Cherry, playing a repertoire consisting of three compositions by Coleman, one by Cherry, and one by Thelonious Monk. See John Coltrane and Don Cherry, *The Avant-Garde* (Atlantic 1451).

59. For Williams's choices, see "The Critics—How They Voted," *down beat*, August 3, 1961, pp. 51–52. In the "established talent" categories, Williams mentioned only a very few individuals or groups identified with the music of the post-1940 period; his single selection in the "miscellaneous instrument" classification, for instance, was Elmer Snowden, banjo—not exactly a prominent instrument in contemporary jazz.

9

John Coltrane and
Albert Ayler

*In 1960 and '61 . . . when I first started playing, I had
a thing that was free, you know? But when he [John
Coltrane] started playing, I had to listen just to his
tone, you understand? To listen to him play was just
like he was talking to me, saying, "Brother, get yourself together spiritually." Just one sound—that's how
profound this man was.*

—ALBERT AYLER[1]

In the previous chapter I suggested that the innovations of
John Coltrane—despite being condemned by white writers
from Leonard Feather and Ira Gitler to Martin Williams—
have been decisive for the thinking of younger jazz revolutionaries. My purpose here is to document that claim for
one particular jazz artist, Albert Ayler. Before taking up that
task, however, I want to dispel some misconceptions.

First of all, the matter of "influences." If we say that one
artist—or one scientist, or one writer—has been influenced

by another, I do not see that this detracts in the least from the reputation of the former. It is all very well to state, as one commentator has, that the new jazz musicians are influenced "by their own individuality."[2] But so far as that goes, who is not? More germane is the point that the artist's individuality is never the only root out of which his or her art grows. Every artist lives at a certain time, in a certain place; absorbs certain social and intellectual conventions, some implicit, some explicit; undergoes certain formative experiences, artistic and otherwise; and so on. All of these things, to a greater or lesser degree, are the "influences" that shape the artist's work.[3] It should be clear from this fact that there is nothing to be ashamed of in admitting to these influences; indeed, they could be avoided only if one were to be reared, Crusoe-like, in total isolation from the rest of humanity.

The question to ask about "influences," therefore, is not whether an artist has them; any artist who has learned enough from his or her predecessors to merit the title most assuredly does. The question is, rather, what *use* the artist makes of these influences. The artist of genius transmutes such raw materials into aesthetic gold.* The second-rater, in

---

* From time to time I have seen it written that Coltrane was "not a genius." Granted that genius, like beauty, may lie in the eye of the beholder, I nonetheless think that this judgment is based on at least two misconceptions. Because Coltrane was notorious for driving himself relentlessly—it was commonplace for him to return to his hotel room to practice for several hours *after* a performance, for example, stuffing a cloth into the bell of his saxophone so as not to disturb others— some have concluded that he was therefore lacking in genius. Such an assertion, however, confuses genius with apparent ease of creation: the only true measure of genius is the finished work of art itself—not the amount of effort it cost its author. A masterpiece, in other words, is a masterpiece, whether it was fashioned in a day or a decade.

This first misconception is reinforced by a second, which arises out of a comparison of Coltrane's career with that of Charlie Parker—a figure who, for many in the jazz world, defines the meaning of the word

contrast, remains rigidly bound by his or her "influences" and is unable to rise above the stature of imitator. Both Paul Quinechette and Sonny Rollins have drawn on the ideas of Lester Young—but what a world of difference in the way the two have employed them!

There are innumerable instances in jazz of a creative artist reworking ideas absorbed from others and presenting them to us in a brilliant and dramatically unexpected form. Charlie Parker may have been far from the first jazz performer to base his solos on the chord sequence of a song rather than its melody, but for all of that, no musician before him could come close to matching his unflagging inventiveness and musical imagination.

Similarly for John Coltrane. Many of the practices that we associate with him were in fact initially introduced by other musicians: in the case of drawing upon Mideastern sonorities and melodic ideas, Yusef Lateef; in the case of playing two or three notes on the saxophone simultaneously, the

---

"genius." Unlike Parker, who burst upon the scene with his style seemingly perfected, Coltrane's artistic evolution took place in full view of the public and his fellow musicians. But to conclude from this historical accident that the greatness of the former somehow exceeds that of the latter is to succumb to an illusion. Parker, as it happens, served his apprenticeship at a time when, for a variety of reasons, jazz recordings were not being produced for commercial release. Consequently, we are unable to trace his development and he *appears* to have arrived fully formed, like Athena from the brow of Zeus. We can, in contrast, document in almost microscopic detail Coltrane's progress from one artistic phase to the next. Thus, with Parker the only thing we see is the smooth and polished surface of the final product, whereas with Coltrane we witness all the false starts, dead ends, approaches tried and rejected, and so on, that went into his music. To deny Coltrane's genius on that basis, though, is not only woefully shortsighted, but also ignores the evidence that Parker, too, was (according to his biographers) striving to push his style in new directions when death overtook him. Had he lived longer, then, we might have observed him exploring as many varied paths as Coltrane traversed.

Philadelphia saxophonist John Glenn;[4] in the case of basing improvisation on a drone-note and a mode or scale, as opposed to a series of chords, Miles Davis and the Indian raga virtuoso Ravi Shankar.* (See chapter 13 for further comments on how Coltrane integrated these disparate elements into a form of musical expression that was unmistakably his own.) From this we conclude that there is much more to originality and creativity than mere artistic priority: what Coltrane does with harmonics is of vastly greater interest than whether he was the first saxophonist to play them. Similarly, it is due to Coltrane's use of the soprano saxophone that the instrument has become ubiquitous in contemporary jazz, notwithstanding the fact that Steve Lacy was playing it well before Coltrane ever thought of doing so. Hence it is profoundly mistaken to assume that creativity is simply a matter of being "the first" to do this or that; still less can it be equated with the absence of external "influences."

A second point concerns the relative importance of John Coltrane in the jazz avant-garde. There are those who have argued (with less than compelling logic, in my opinion) that in calling attention to Coltrane's role in the jazz revolution, I have slighted the contributions of other innovators.[5] In defense of my position I will say only that I have been guided by the aural evidence. I have always felt that the practicing

---

* Coltrane seems to have been a reluctant radical at first; evidently he needed something of a push before he would introduce into the repertoire of his own group compositions based on modes and scales, for as he acknowledged in 1959, it was Miles Davis who "made me go further into trying different modes in my writing" (the quotation is in the notes to John Coltrane, *Giant Steps*, Atlantic 1311). Even with Davis's urging, however, it was, as I discuss below, most likely the combination of his interest in raga and his taking up the soprano saxophone (which can be made to sound similar to the Indian *shenai*, a reed instrument) that led him to break with exclusive reliance on chord sequences as a basis for improvisation.

artists are the final arbiter of what is valuable and what is not in their art. The function of the critic, accordingly, is not to lecture artists, but to explain to the public what they are doing. Consequently, when I say that Coltrane's impact on the jazz revolution, particularly saxophonists, has been greater than that of, say, Ornette Coleman, I am merely committing to print what my ears detect in the playing of the young insurgents, not attempting to foist my own ideas on anyone else.

Nor does calling attention to Coltrane's significance in the jazz revolution mean that other artists have not helped shape the course of that revolution. Such a disclaimer is especially necessary with regard to Ornette Coleman. I must confess that, with the exception of Coleman's seminal *Free Jazz* album (Atlantic 1364), I do not hear in any of his recordings developments so earthshaking as to justify some of the hyperbolic titles (*The Shape of Jazz to Come, Change of the Century, Tomorrow Is the Question*) bestowed on his recordings.[6] Indeed, if one compares the rhythmic freedom of Coleman's groups with that of Coltrane's, it is hard to escape the conclusion that the latter's approach liberates the soloist to a much greater degree. That fact reflects the more-flexible rhythmic foundation of Coltrane's music, something that results not from the absence of a fixed pulse—only a few drummers of the jazz revolution, notably Milford Graves and Sonny Murray, have gone so far as to dispense with that—but from subdividing the beat into shorter notes, shifting the rhythmic emphasis to and from that beat, and juxtaposing various cross-rhythms (such as three against two, six against four, and four against three) against each other. (I analyze these aspects of the Coltrane quartet's handling of rhythm in the next chapter.)

Still, simply by proposing that the harmony, the bass line and the pulse of a piece can be varied at will by the musicians, Coleman has had a momentous effect on young musicians—

as well as on Coltrane himself, for that matter—and this would be true if he had never recorded so much as a note of music. Hence it is impossible to estimate Coleman's importance in the jazz revolution down to the last decimal place. Even if we don't hear his phrases popping up in the work of the new saxophonists anywhere nearly as often as those of Coltrane, we can nonetheless be certain that the thinking of these artists has benefited from his groundbreaking efforts. Indeed, it is quite possible that Coleman's ultimate significance for the jazz revolution will be primarily in the realm of theory rather than that of performance.[7]

In the preceding chapter, I presented some of the evidence for John Coltrane's central position in the leadership of the jazz revolution. To complete the argument, I intend to demonstrate that what one might call the revolution's second-generation saxophonists—including, besides Albert Ayler, such musicians as Byron Allen, Marion Brown, Giuseppi Logan, Pharoah Sanders, John Tchicai and Charles Tyler—also give signs of having fallen heavily under Coltrane's sway. Without attempting to go into great detail, I think it quite clear that there are echoes of Coltrane's innovations in the playing of all of these artists, with the single exception of John Tchicai, and that I will explain presently. Thus, even in a composition titled "Decision for the Cole-man," Byron Allen reproduces phrases that we recognize from Coltrane's lexicon, and Allen's genuflection in this direction is even more pronounced on the succeeding selection, "Today's Blues Tomorrow."[8] For Giuseppi Logan, the imprint of Coltrane's Mideastern-flavored soprano saxophone is plain in such compositions as "Tabla Suite" and "Dance of Satan."[9] Pharoah Sanders's descent from the Coltrane family tree is so obvious on his first recording that further comment would be superfluous.[10] Following Coltrane's untimely death in 1967, moreover, as I will bring out in the afterword to this chapter, Sanders's work again has begun to reflect the ideas of his original mentor.

Marion Brown's initial recordings, especially but not only "Capricorn Moon" from his earliest album on the ESP label, likewise indicate that he has incorporated Coltrane's concepts into his music.[11] From his work with Albert Ayler on the latter's *Bells* recording, it is easy to discern that Charles Tyler has translated onto the alto saxophone the style devised by Ayler on the tenor, so that my analysis of Ayler will stand as well for him. It is also worth noting, however, that Tyler's own recordings—in particular, the composition "Lacy's Out East" on his first album on the ESP label—contain ample references to the Coltrane idiom.[12]

One finds the single apparent exception to the universality of Coltrane's appeal to the new wave of saxophonists in the playing of John Tchicai. I say *apparent* exception, however, because Tchicai's geographical origins are European rather than American—his father is African, his mother is a Dane, and he spent his youth in Denmark—and his ideas have been shaped by forces different from those that have inspired black musicians in the United States. These considerations explain, for instance, the otherwise surprising fact that Tchicai's style shows the stamp of alto saxophonist Lee Konitz, who, like numerous other white musicians of the cool period, enjoyed much more sustained popularity in the Scandinavian countries than here. Tchicai has certainly made no secret of his indebtedness to Konitz, telling one reporter: "I decided what I wanted to be—a musician—when I heard Lee [Konitz] on a record with Miles Davis, 'Ezzthetic.' . . . Lee and Bird [Charlie Parker] were my main influences."[13] These remarks only go to underscore two points I have sought to make above: first, that the black-ghetto environment plays a leading role in the stylistic development of jazz's African-American innovators; second, that, willy-nilly, "influences" are as inescapable for the artist as are eating, drinking, and breathing for the remainder of humanity.

Given the paucity of his recordings and what must be the

relatively minute number of people who have ever seen him perform, the quantity of sheer nonsense that has been written about Albert Ayler is genuinely awe inspiring. White critics have been eager to read into his music all sorts of metaphysical implications: a manifesto of total freedom—whatever that may be—a philosophy of anarchic nihilism, and so on. I certainly have no objections to the interpretation of music; if anything, my constant lament, in the foregoing pages and elsewhere,[14] has been that Establishment critics are indecently eager to bury social interpretations of jazz. And for all I know, the writers who have reviewed—or reviled—Ayler with such virulence really do hear the unpleasant things in his playing that they claim. But at the very least our suspicions should be aroused by the fact that the anti-Ayler polemics have been devoid of any *musical* analysis. If, after all, Ayler is such an utter fraud, shouldn't there be some more persuasive way of demonstrating the strength of that contention than mere name-calling?

My own belief is that the absence of any musical analysis on the part of the saxophonist's foes is not simply accidental; that, in actuality, an examination of his music leads to conclusions just the opposite of those propounded by the anti-Ayler zealots. Ayler's music, as I hope the following discussion will establish, is not structureless, anarchic, or anything of that nature. It is, on the contrary, highly organized and gives every evidence of having been carefully thought out. But to appreciate this fact, one needs to have kept abreast of recent developments in jazz—which is just where the white critics have failed us. Similar situations in the other arts spring readily to mind. James Joyce's *Ulysses* was condemned by the literary critics of his day for the same alleged shortcomings of which Ayler is accused, even though, in retrospect, it is embarrassingly obvious that form and structure are the two properties that *Ulysses* has in abundance. What occurred with Joyce is the same thing that is happening today with Albert Ayler and the other exponents of the jazz revolution: the reigning critics, who have cut their teeth on other styles, are being outpaced by developments in the arts that are supposedly their province.

In contrast to the nay sayers of the Establishment, there are some critics who, though few in number, have refused to toe the line in denouncing Albert Ayler; two writers whom I have found particularly helpful in appreciating his music are LeRoi Jones and Frank Smith; their remarks form the jumping-off point for my own. To begin with, consider Jones's observation that "Albert Ayler has heard Trane and Ornette Coleman and has still taken the music another way."[15] If Jones is correct—and I have no doubts on this score—it follows that without coming to grips with Ornette Coleman and John Coltrane, it is impossible to grasp the mercurial essence of Albert Ayler.

Let us, however, rephrase Jones's statement about Albert Ayler, Coltrane, and Ornette Coleman in a different way. Suppose that one were to try and devise a symbolic "equation," or metaphor, to express the fundamentals of Ayler's style, I think it might look something like this:

$$\text{AYLER} = 50\% \text{ COLTRANE} + 20\% \text{ COLEMAN} + 30\% \text{ X}$$

where X represents Ayler's own unique additions to the earlier contributions of Coltrane and Coleman. Although these additions have been the source of much controversy, I will have relatively little to say about them here. My reasoning here is straightforward: as many followers of jazz—and in any event, most critics—have yet to comprehend the foundations on which Ayler's music rests, there surely is no point in attempting to go further until they attain at least that elementary degree of understanding. Hence my primary focus will be on Ayler as he relates to the music that preceded him, particularly that of Coltrane and Coleman. In electing this approach, it should be apparent that I intend no denigration of Ayler's "originality." I have already tried to explain why I believe that all artists possess roots in the tradition of their art. If I concentrate on these roots in the case of Ayler, I do so not to belittle his own stature as an innovator—the howls of outrage arising from critical circles should furnish ample testimony of that—but to provide a bridge to the new music.

Of the saxophonists Ornette Coleman and John Coltrane, the effect of the former on Ayler's thinking is the more obvious, but, in my opinion, the less profound. One hears echoes of Coleman chiefly in Ayler's writing, much less in his playing. Ayler's composition "Ghosts" (ESP 1002), for example, is reminiscent of such Coleman songs as "Ramblin' ": both evoke a perennial Southwestern blues-folk vein in jazz.[16] Similarly, the intricate tenor-saxophone-trumpet contours of Ayler's "Holy Ghost," performed in tandem with his trumpeter-brother Donald, is a direct offshoot from any number of the early works that Coleman recorded with trumpeter Don Cherry.

To anyone who has had more than incidental encounters with the music of Coleman, his impact on Ayler probably will be apparent at once. This ought equally to be so in the case of Coltrane, especially if, as I hold, Coltrane's artistry looms larger in Ayler's playing than that of Coleman. Be that as it may, Coltrane's significance in this connection has gone largely unperceived, aside from the writings of LeRoi Jones. There are reasons for this, of course, just as there are for everything else under the sun. The aspects of Coltrane's work most relevant to Ayler are displayed with greatest force and clarity on such of the former's performances as "Chasin' The Trane" (on the album *Coltrane "Live" at the Village Vanguard*, recorded in 1961 and released the following year), as well as on a variety of other selections that he recorded during the early 1960s.[17] Indeed, it is no exaggeration to assert that the breathtaking devices Ayler employs in such compositions as "Ghosts"—the anguished screams, the ferocious lower-register eruptions, the electrifying shrieks, the rasping harmonics—all have their roots in countless incomparable Coltrane works dating from this time. Nonetheless, "Chasin' the Trane" stands first and foremost in this regard. It was here that Coltrane gave us some notion of the extraordinary range of human passions that the tenor saxophone could convey; seen in proper perspective, therefore, it comprises a landmark in the history of the jazz revolution—or in the history of jazz itself, so far as that goes.*

Be that as it may, "Chasin' the Trane," like virtually all of Coltrane's most uncompromising work from this period, was unambiguously damned by Establishment critics when it appeared. As we saw in last chapter's survey of the disgraceful critical commentary of these years, Ira Gitler, one of the two writers to whom *down beat* assigned the record for review, dismissed this inspired statement as a collection of "yawps, squeaks, and countless repetitive runs. . . . It is monotonous, a treadmill to the Kingdom of Boredom." [18] Pete Welding, ordinarily somewhat better disposed toward Coltrane, was more eloquent but almost equally obtuse in

---

* When I attempted to argue the case for the immense importance of "Chasin' the Trane" for the jazz revolution, Coltrane, with his usual modesty, demurred: "It's a big reservoir, that we all dip out of. . . . I listened to John Gilmore [a saxophonist in Sun Ra's Arkestra] kind of closely before I made 'Chasin' the Trane,' too. So some of those things on there are really direct influences of listening to this cat, you see" (from the interview with Coltrane in chapter 13). The conclusion I draw, however, is a different one: what matters in artistic innovation, as I have said more than once, is not who does a certain thing *first*, but rather who does it *best* and most memorably. With all due respect to the talents of John Gilmore—and anyone else to whom Coltrane may have been paying particular attention in 1960 and 1961—we do not err in attributing the achievements of "Chasin' the Trane" to the person after whom it is named.

his appraisal. "In the final analysis," he declared, Coltrane's improvisation, with its "sputtering inconclusiveness," was "more properly a piece of musical exorcism than anything else, a frenzied sort of soul-baring." [19] Such verdicts—which were repeated in every key and at every tempo during the six years prior to Coltrane's death—came, mind you, in response to a performance that will certainly rank among the most magnificent and inspired this music has to offer.

The barrage of invective unleashed at "Chasin' the Trane" and similar Coltrane recordings from the early 1960s largely explains the neglect in which this phase of Coltrane's development has languished, so far as the most-prominent white critics are concerned. His self-confidence evidently shaken as a result of this assault (a point the interview in chapter 13 bears out), Coltrane, as I related in chapter 2, acceded to the wishes of Bob Thiele and Impulse Records by making three recordings that featured him in more restrained, even sedate, contexts: first sharing honors with Duke Ellington, then in an album entitled *Ballads,* and finally in a collaboration with baritone Johnny Hartman.[20] Without casting the slightest aspersion on these performances, it is nevertheless clear that they represent a substantial artistic retreat from the pinnacle that "Chasin' the Trane" represented.[21]

But while "Chasin' the Trane" and like-minded efforts were being roundly damned by the critics, this was not at all their fate with the jazz revolutionaries, who, as their music attests, were eager to benefit from the lessons Coltrane was teaching. Be that as it may, although the jazz revolution has gained something of a niche for itself, the artistic sources for this musical upheaval are still less than fully understood. One of my aims here, therefore, is to redress the historical balance by emphasizing the formative role that Coltrane's music—especially, but not exclusively, "Chasin' the Trane"—has played. And, inasmuch as Albert Ayler is among the most adventurous of the revolutionaries, I take it that if the argument regarding Coltrane's influence is applicable to him, it certainly will be equally valid for his less-iconoclastic peers.[22]

In a perceptive and enlightening essay on Ayler, Frank Smith notes that, "All of Albert's playing . . . follows the same simple straightforward format: a very lyrical tune with an old-timey feeling is set forth and then the playing gradually gets into something more and more intense and ferocious until the listener is practically overwhelmed."[23] Smith is absolutely correct in this discussion, and it is a continual source of amazement to me that no one before him has been able to discern this gradual heightening of complexity and intensity as the basis of Ayler's improvisations.

But there is still another facet of Ayler's approach, one not mentioned by Smith, which complements this technique. Here I am thinking of *thematic improvisation*—the construction of spontaneous variations based on the melodic contours of the theme, or on some other recurring motif, as well as on the underlying harmony.[24] This component of his music deserves at least as much stress as Smith has laid on the techniques of increasing complexity, provided we bear in mind that an enormous gulf separates thematic improvisation as practiced by Albert Ayler from thematic improvisation as it occurs in the music of, say, Thelonious Monk or some of Sonny Rollins's performances from the late 1950s. As for the missing link between Monk and Rollins on the one hand, and Ayler on the other—that is supplied by none other than John Coltrane.*

---

* Thanks to the second of the two essays by Gunther Schuller that I cite in note 24, it is almost a conditioned response in jazz circles to associate the phrase "thematic improvisation" with Sonny Rollins. Ironically enough, however, this approach to improvisation would never again play as prominent a part in Rollins's style as it had before Schuller's article appeared. To compound the irony, thematic or motivic improvisation took on much greater importance in John Coltrane's work during the 1960s—but in all the contrived furor over "anti-jazz," it went completely

The most direct way to apprehend the relationship between Coltrane and Ayler is by comparing one of Ayler's recordings for the ESP label with Coltrane's "Chasin' the Trane"; I have chosen for this purpose the second version of "Ghosts" from Ayler's recording, *Spiritual Unity*.[25] The former is, of course, a 12-measure blues, whereas the latter is a 16-measure piece with a Midwestern, or perhaps Southwestern, folksong lilt to it, yet in view of the fundamental similarities between the two, the differences are ephemeral.

Beginning with the Coltrane selection and following it with the Ayler, the first thing that may strike the listener are the parallels between the two: the same tonal devices that Coltrane employs as a means of creating tension and conveying emotion are those that Ayler also invokes (and in some respects extends). This is not to say that Ayler is a carbon copy of Coltrane, for such a statement would be totally false. Rather, my purpose in emphasizing Ayler's use of certain devices associated with Coltrane is to make it clear that the supposedly alien sounds emanating from the former's saxophone are in reality an integral part of the jazz vocab-

---

unnoticed at the time. Perhaps my remarks here will to some small degree repair the omission. Incidentally, Coltrane's interest in thematic improvisation may have been stimulated by the five months he spent as a member of Monk's quartet; hear in this connection Coltrane's solos on Thelonious Monk, *The Thelonious Monk Quartet: Live at the Five Spot: Discovery!* (Blue Note CDP 0777 7 99786 2 5), especially his reading of Monk's composition, "Epistrophy." (Contrary to what the notes to this compact disk state, however, I believe the drummer to be Roy Haynes rather than Shadow Wilson.)

A note on usage. In discussions of European music, it is conventional to distinguish between the adjectives "thematic," which refers to the initial melody of composition or a movement, and "motivic," which refers to a strain that is introduced after the main melody has been stated. In what follows, however, I follow the customary practice in jazz musicology by using the two terms interchangeably; I also treat "pattern" and "motif" as synonyms.

ulary—unless, that is, one is prepared to banish Coltrane as well as Ayler from the pantheon of jazz improvisers.

Once one hears the selections by Coltrane and Ayler in immediate succession, the similarities in timbre, in the use of the upper and lower register, multiple repetitions, harmonics, shrieks, cries, screams, and so on, should require no further commentary. But beneath the resemblances of tone and timbre there is an even more profound link between the two: each artist fashions the bulk of his improvisation from the theme, or on a set of short melodic fragments related to it. The point is a crucial one. Both Coltrane and Ayler possess a well-developed sense of structure (though Coltrane, as the more mature artist, has perfected it to a greater extent than Ayler). Contrary to what the critics have claimed, it is anything but true that their music is sprawling, formless, chaotic. Quite the contrary: the performances at hand show that the two saxophonists are capable of spinning out lengthy solos on the basis of at most a handful of underlying themes, an approach that imbues their inventions with a high degree of continuity.

Conceivably, that continuity may be easier to detect in "Chasin' the Trane" because the structure of this 12-measure blues is familiar to most jazz listeners. But even for a blues, "Chasin' the Trane" is exceptionally simple and straightforward. In it, there is none of the dense harmonic textures or intricate chord sequences characteristic of Coltrane's sheets-of-sound and "Giant Steps" periods (both of which I treat in chapters 8 and 10). Indeed, a close examination of this selection suggests that its creator chose, probably consciously, to eliminate any hint of unnecessary complexity in order to keep both himself and the listener focused on the emotional content of this near–sixteen-minute tour de force. Thus, for instance, several of Coltrane's choruses consist of little more than *a single note*, played in a variety of timbres by varying the fingering and/or the embouchure (see choruses 20 and 21, beginning around 4:02; chorus 30, beginning around 5:50; choruses 63 and 64, beginning around 12:11; and especially choruses 54 and 58, beginning around 10:29 and 11:14, respectively). It is as if the saxophonist has made a tacit compact with his audience: in exchange for being allowed to employ the unorthodox sounds and rhythms he needs to convey passion (such as the "glossolalia" that, beginning at about 11:55, occupies the last part of chorus 61 and all of chorus 62), he has stripped the harmonic and melodic structure of this piece down to the bone.

I will have more to say below on the subject of the relationship between Coltrane's innovations and the style of Albert Ayler. For the moment, however, with the foregoing paragraph in mind, let us plunge more deeply into "Chasin' the Trane." A close scrutiny reveals that Coltrane develops his improvisation, especially its first half (forty-one out of a total of eighty-one choruses),[*] around two main motifs: (1) a five-note pattern in eighth-notes, initially announced at 45 seconds and 48 seconds (in the fourth chorus), then repeated with variations at 51, 56 and 59 seconds (fifth chorus) and again at 1:01, 1:04 and 1:11 (sixth chorus); and (2) a subordinate four-note phrase, also in eighth notes, that makes its debut in the tenth chorus (1:50, 1:58) and extends through the eleventh (2:02, 2:05) and twelfth (2:20) choruses. Of the two, the five-note phrase whose rhythmic values are

is of much greater importance; it recurs several more times during the first half of the solo—for example, in choruses

---

[*] The actual improvisation starts with the third chorus and ends with the seventy-ninth; Coltrane states the melody of "Chasin' the Trane" in the first chorus, repeats and embellishes it in the second, and recapitulates it in the eightieth and eighty-first.

16 (3:02 to 3:13), 22 to 25 (4:14 to 5:01), 27 to 29 (5:14 to 5:50), 36 and 37 (7:00 to 7:02), 41 (7:56 to 8:07), 52 and 53 (10:07 to 10:28). Having used this pattern to establish a frame of reference in the first half of "Chasin' the Trane," Coltrane gradually leaves it behind in the second (although he does restate it in choruses 52 and 53). Evidently he had an abiding fondness for this pattern, as he returned to it in 1965 in constructing the melody of his composition, "One Down, One Up." [26] The second theme of "Chasin' the Trane," in contrast, is of substantially less significance. After putting in an appearance in the tenth through twelfth choruses, it does not occur again. Instead, Coltrane introduces a new two-note phrase in choruses 49 through 51 (9:38 to 9:57) and reverts to that third motif in choruses 72 and 73 (14:01 to 14:10).

If Coltrane began the process of paring down the framework of jazz improvisation to the bare essentials, Albert Ayler took it one step further still. The nature of his approach is readily apparent on "Ghosts," where *each one of his improvised choruses is shaped as a variation on the theme of the composition.* To appreciate this fact, it is not even necessary to count out the measures; all one need do is hum the theme while listening to the solo. As the recognition dawns that Ayler is ascending where the theme ascends, descending where it descends, breaking off his phrases where the melody shifts from one sequence to the next, and so on, whatever "mystery" one may have found in his playing should be dispelled.

Above and beyond their shared reliance on motivic or thematic improvisation, there is another aspect of the relationship between the music of Albert Ayler and that of John Coltrane that also demands mention, and that is the evolution of Ayler's style in the few years between Coltrane's death and his own. To an objective listener, I do not think there can be any question but that Ayler's music was moving, and with some rapidity at that, in the same direction that Coltrane's had been taking during the last year and one half of his life. The growing similarity between the two is especially striking in Ayler's slow pieces, which make up a large portion of his final works. Parts of his solos on such compositions as "Dancing Flowers" and "Love Flowers" on his *Love Call* recording—the last save two he would make—are eerily reminiscent of Coltrane's rendition of "Psalm," the fourth movement of his suite, *A Love Supreme*.[27] It is, however, in *The Last Album* that the resemblance between Ayler and Coltrane emerges with truly stunning force. Suffice it to say that I have witnessed even people very familiar with the music of John Coltrane guess that it was he rather than Albert Ayler to whom they were listening during the latter's performance of "Water Music," "All Love" and "Birth of Mirth."[28]

But to return to the subject of thematic and motivic improvisation, it is clear that Coltrane's involvement with this approach was no mere passing fancy, hence Ayler would have had ample opportunity to study Coltrane's handling of this type of improvisation. As a case in point from a few years later, in one of his best-known compositions, the "Acknowledgment" first movement of his 1964 suite, *A Love Supreme*, Coltrane develops almost all of his improvisation from a six-note motif made up of a pair of three-note phrases.[29] In each of these phrases, the second note is a flatted third (three half-steps) above the first, and the third is a whole step above the second. In the key of C minor, for example, these notes would be C, E-flat, and F (1, 3, 4, or *do*, *mi*, *fa*). The second three-note pattern is built on the same two intervals of a minor third and major second, but begins with the note on which the first motif ended, thus: F, A-flat, B-flat (4, flat-6, 7; *fa*, *la*, *ti*).

Interestingly enough, however, although this six-note motif is not the theme of the first movement of *A Love Supreme*, it *is* the theme of the third movement, "Pursuance";[30] Coltrane enunciates it at the conclusion of a long drum solo by Elvin Jones (at 1:32 from the movement's start) and reprises it at the end of the piece, where it prefaces a second Jones solo. To study the underlying motif in "Acknowledgment," therefore, it may be useful to begin by listening to the "Pursuance" theme. Coltrane states the motif in measures one and two, repeats it in the next two measures, and repeats it again in measures seven and eight of what is in form a 12-measure blues. By using the theme of the third movement of *A Love Supreme* as the basis of his improvisation in the first, Coltrane establishes an intimate connection between these two sections of the suite, as if to say that the whole is greater than the sum of a collection of unrelated parts.

After we have heard the six-note theme of "Pursuance" theme, we can trace its occurrence throughout "Acknowledgment." Coltrane introduces it at about one minute and five seconds (1:05) into the composition, and proceeds to create variations on it for the next 35 seconds. He repeats this procedure several more times: from 2:07 to 2:32, from 2:45 to 3:11, from 3:39 to 3:54, and from 4:14 to 4:51. Overall, therefore, roughly 60 percent of the improvisation between 1:05 and 4:51 consists of the "Pursuance" theme and its variants. At 4:57, Coltrane starts a seemingly new four-note motif, which he develops for over one minute, until, at 6:06, he begins to sing the words "a love supreme" to these same four notes (6:08 to 6:44). But if we examine this second motif a little more closely, we may notice that it uses the identical three notes as the first three-note pattern, the only difference being that it repeats the first note between the second and third notes. If, in other words, the three-note pattern in the key of C minor is C, E-flat, F, the four-note motif—representing the words "a love supreme"—is C, E-flat, C, F. Hence Coltrane has woven almost the entirety of his improvisation from the most elementary materials—a mere three notes (1, 3, 4) distributed over three intervals (a minor third, a major second and a major fourth).*

Here, by applying his inexhaustible creativity to the challenge of thematic improvisation, Coltrane truly has elaborated a pearl from the tiniest grain of sand. Granted that much of the popularity of *A Love Supreme* stems from the fact that one can actually hear him singing those words at the conclusion of the "Acknowledgment" movement, surely another source of its enduring appeal is the high degree of continuity this composition possesses by virtue of being built on a foundation of closely related variations on a simple motif. Without having to know a note of music, even the most uninitiated listener can intuitively sense that there is an underlying unity to this movement. If in his 1959 composition, "Giant Steps," Coltrane illustrated how one could use patterns (and their variations) to subdue even the most formidable chord sequences, as I will explain immediately below, in "Acknowledgment" he furnished a textbook illustration of how to employ patterns for an entirely different purpose: as a means of imposing a tight overall structure on a jazz performance in the absence of any chord sequences whatsoever.

Although trying to plumb the motives of an artist is always a risky endeavor, it is nonetheless worth speculating about what led John Coltrane and Albert Ayler to have recourse to improvisations built on variations on a theme or motif. In Coltrane's case, I believe this approach grew out of at least three separate but related developments during 1959 and 1960. The first of these, as I indicated directly above, was connected to his composition, "Giant Steps": in order to be able to improvise at all over the dense and swiftly moving

---

* After laboriously working out these relationships (with the assistance of pianist Matthew Goodheart of San Francisco), I discovered Jerry Coker's insightful analysis of *A Love Supreme* in his excellent book, *Listening to Jazz* (Englewood Cliffs, N.J.: Prentice-Hall, 1978), pp. 127–32.

harmonies of this piece and others built on the same foundation—a kind of bebop to the second power, in which the underlying chords change nearly every other beat—Coltrane devised a set of patterns that he could vary, recombine and permute during the course of a solo. Improvising on the basis of previously worked-out patterns was a novel departure for him, but it is hard to see how even he could have steered his way through the intimidating fast-paced chord sequence of "Giant Steps" had he not resorted to some such method. (Tommy Flanagan and Cedar Walton, the two pianists with whom Coltrane recorded more than one dozen versions of "Giant Steps," did not have the opportunity to prepare such patterns, and for the most part were therefore unable to cope with the intricacies of this ultra-demanding piece.)[31]

Of all the versions of "Giant Steps" that Coltrane recorded, none illustrates more unmistakably his reliance on patterns and motifs in improvising over this framework than that issued on the album of the same name (*Giant Steps*, Atlantic 1311), especially the second of his two solos, beginning approximately three minutes and forty-four seconds (3:44) into the performance. In the first measure of the first chorus of this two-chorus solo, in which each chorus is sixteen measures long, Coltrane plays a four-note ascending phrase (1, 2, 3, 5; *do, re, mi, so*) in eighth notes, then repeats it three half-steps (a flatted third) higher; later in the first chorus, he offers variations on the four-note phrase in measures five and six, as he does again in the following chorus at the end of the fourth and beginning of the fifth measures and at the end of the sixth measure.

Once we have become familiar with the four-note pattern from Coltrane's shorter second solo, we can then turn to the longer first solo and detect its presence in (among other places) measures five and six of the first, second, fifth, sixth, eighth, ninth and eleventh choruses (Coltrane most often employs the four-note motif at this point in the chorus), as well as in measures eleven and sixteen of the second chorus, measures one, five, and thirteen of the third chorus, measure five of the fourth chorus, measures one, eleven, and twelve of the seventh chorus, measures one and eight of the ninth chorus, measure one of the tenth chorus, and so on. (The listener also may find it helpful to follow this improvisation with the transcription of it in Frank Tirro, *Jazz: A History*, 2nd. ed. (New York: W. W. Norton, 1993), pp. 78*–83*).

Second, although Coltrane would soon abandon the thick harmonic textures associated with "Giant Steps," his interest in pattern-based improvisation intensified after he began using modes, scales, and drone-notes as a springboard for his melodic ideas. It isn't difficult, if my reasoning is correct, to understand why Coltrane would find patterns and motifs useful in this new musical environment. Chord cycles serve several purposes in bebop improvisation. They furnish both a structural framework and a sense of motion, as an improviser traverses the cycle from the beginning to the end and then starts over at the beginning. Chord sequences also offer an improviser the opportunity to create (and later, of course, to relax) tension by anticipating a harmonic change before it occurs, by not acknowledging it until it has come and gone, or by simply ignoring it altogether. For a musician like John Coltrane—who had spent his entire professional life inventing melodies in relation to underlying harmonies and had pushed this type of improvisation to its furthest limit—a substitute for chord sequences may have been both a musical and a psychological necessity.

At some point, therefore, I suspect it must have occurred to Coltrane that patterns in modal or scalar compositions could to a certain extent perform some of the same functions as chord sequences do in pieces with conventional harmonic architecture. To begin with, patterns, as we have seen in analyzing the "Acknowledgment" movement of *A Love Supreme*, can provide a degree of structure and unity that would otherwise be absent in modal compositions. (This consideration assumed greater importance as Coltrane's solos grew ever longer: without some means of maintaining continuity, it would be easy for a fifteen- or twenty-minute solo to degenerate into an amorphous mishmash, just as Coltrane's, and Albert Ayler's, detractors charged.) Accordingly, it is significant that motivic variations crop up with greatest frequency in Coltrane's performances of "My Favorite Things," "Impressions," parts of *A Love Supreme* (as I have just explained), and a variety of other modal or scalar pieces. The second portion of Coltrane's solo on the original recording of "My Favorite Things," as a case in point, is a veritable compendium of variations on a few short phrases.* Such passages tend to occur much less often in pieces that, like "Summertime," "Bye, Bye, Blackbird," and "I Want to Talk about You," have typical bebop harmonic underpinnings and therefore do not permit the improviser the same freedom to manipulate motifs at will.[32]

What is more, the use of patterns and motifs gave Coltrane an effective way of building and dissipating tension in the absence of fixed harmonic turning points. Rather than departing from and coming back to a composition's harmony, Coltrane could now unveil a motif, proceed to develop (vary) it—by transposing it, by changing one or more of its notes, by accelerating or retarding it, by inverting it, and so on—then alternately veer away from and return to it. In this way, he could achieve much the same effect as he had by adhering to and then diverging from the chords of

---

* The second (major-key) portion of this solo starts almost exactly ten minutes from the opening of "My Favorite Things" (John Coltrane, *My Favorite Things*, Atlantic 1361), and at once Coltrane embarks on a series of four-note patterns comprised of eighth-notes, of five-note patterns comprised of eighth-note triplets, and a variety of other patterns based on glissandi. Especially vivid examples are at eleven minutes, five seconds (11:05–11:13) and also at eleven minutes, forty-five seconds (11:45–11:59).

a piece, but by different means.

Third and last, the single decisive development in Coltrane's quest for a new style appears to have been his adoption of the soprano saxophone around the middle of 1960. Because each instrument makes its own unique demands on a performer, Coltrane's taking up of the soprano (as I mentioned in the previous chapter and will discuss further in chapters 10 and 13) led him to rethink his approach to improvisation from the ground up. Thus, it is surely no coincidence that once he had formed his own group, the very first piece in his repertoire to be based on scales rather than chord sequences was not only one in which he employed variation on patterns to give his solos an additional degree of coherence—that much we would have expected—but was *also* the piece on which he made his recorded debut with the soprano saxophone: "My Favorite Things." An excerpt from the interview in chapter 13 establishes the importance of this second instrument in shaping Coltrane's fresh approach to improvisation:

> KOFSKY: Do you think that learning how to play the soprano saxophone changed your style?
> COLTRANE: Definitely, definitely. It certainly did. . . .
> KOFSKY: Did it give you new rhythmic ideas, too?
> COLTRANE: I think so, I think so. A new shape came out of this thing and patterns—the way the patterns would fall.
> . . . In fact, the patterns started—the patterns were one of the things I started getting dissatisfied with on the tenor mouthpiece, because the sound of the soprano was actually so much closer to me in my ear. There's something about the presence of that sound, that to me—I didn't want to admit it, but to me it would seem like it was better than the tenor; I liked it more. I didn't want to admit this damn thing, because I said the tenor's my horn, it is my favorite. But this soprano, maybe it's just

the fact that it's a higher instrument, it started pulling my conception [style].

These remarks are especially noteworthy in this context because they underline the connection between Coltrane's use of the new instrument and the equally new emphasis he would place on patterns—and by implication, on modes and scales—as a foundation for improvisation. The soprano, with its somewhat nasal sonority, must have reinforced Coltrane's interest in making use of musical ideas from West Asia and Africa, for much of the improvised music of these regions is not only grounded on drone-notes and scales (as is certainly true of Indian raga), but permeated by variations on short patterns as well. Now, by incorporating these same characteristics into his own work, Coltrane might yet find a way out of the obsession with harmonic cycles that threatened to mire jazz—and the artist himself—in permanent stagnation. His own words leave us in little doubt that in the course of mastering the soprano saxophone, Coltrane found the path for which he had been searching so assiduously.

What, then, of pattern and motif in the playing of Albert Ayler? From the quotation at the top of this chapter, it is clear that Coltrane's music had a transforming effect on the younger artist. Although he states that already "in 1960 and '61," when he "first started playing," he "had a thing [style] that was free," Ayler adds that when Coltrane

started playing, I had to listen just to his tone, you understand? To listen to him play was just like he was talking to me, saying, "Brother, get yourself together spiritually." Just one sound—that's how profound this man was.

Given that Ayler was at this point still something of a beginner, and given further that Coltrane's impact on him, by his own admission, was extremely powerful, I don't think it untoward to propose that this impact extended well beyond "just . . . his tone." Particularly so as Coltrane was at this time in the midst of working out his ideas of how to create compelling improvisations outside the customary bebop matrix of chord sequences—confronting, in other words, the same musical questions with which Ayler necessarily was wrestling as he sought to develop his "thing that was free." Furthermore, although we don't have a great deal of information about his background, it isn't unreasonable to suspect that Ayler, like many of the avant-garde saxophonists, might not have served much of an apprenticeship playing bebop. If this supposition is correct, Ayler may well have found overwhelmingly daunting the prospect of mastering the kind of harmonic challenges that so preoccupied Coltrane during his sheets-of-sound and "Giant Steps" phases. In that case, such Coltrane performances as "Chasin' the Trane" and "My Favorite Things"—but especially the former, because it is much more relevant to improvisation on the tenor saxophone—would have come as a revelation: here, finally, Ayler could see a way to express himself in jazz without having to spend years immersed in the study of harmony on the one hand while still avoiding the possibility of chaos that totally unfettered improvisation threatened to unleash on the other.

And it was just that possibility that both Coltrane and Ayler had to confront. The most formidable problem that all musicians who hope to succeed at "free" improvisation must meet head-on can be put in a variety of ways, but is at bottom essentially the same: how to create some points of reference, some signposts that will prevent the listener from becoming dragged out to sea and submerged by what at first may seem nothing more than a huge, amorphous tidal wave of sound. The solution invariably involves introducing (or retaining) some restrictions. In practice, then, the best "free" improvisation is never completely devoid

of one or another kind of prearranged (or at least precon-
ceived) structure. This structure can be imposed by a written score—as it is in the work of Cecil Taylor and in John
Coltrane's composition, *Ascension*—supplemented, to the
extent that circumstances permit, by rehearsals.* It can
emerge semi-spontaneously from rehearsals alone, if they
are numerous and long enough to allow each musician to
see how to integrate his or her contributions with those of
the others. It can be the result of prior agreement on key
signature, meter, tempo, or any combination of the three.
But in one form or another, I believe, some structural elements within the music must exist.

Another means of achieving structure within a "free"
improvisation is by repetition and variation of a theme or
motif. (Indeed, a piece of music absolutely devoid of any
repetition would be as difficult to grasp as a piece comprised
of endless repetition would be boring.) In light of that fact,
it appears probable that both Coltrane and Ayler hit upon
the use of thematic or motivic improvisation as a key (or
perhaps *the* key) means of introducing a sense of structure
in the absence of bebop's harmonic architecture. Coltrane's
preference, growing out of the experiments of his "Giant
Steps" period of 1959–1960, was for pattern-based, or motivic

---

* Such a score, of course, will not be anything like that for a bebop
composition; rather, it may contain a set of general directions—play
in a certain register, at a certain volume, in a certain key—together
with some cues about when to move from one part of the piece to the
next. In Coltrane's composition, *Ascension*, for example, according to
Archie Shepp, "the ensemble passages were based on chords, but these
chords were optional. What Trane did was to relate or juxtapose tonally
centered ideas, along with melodic and non-melodic elements. In those
descending chords there is a definite tonal center, like a B-flat minor, but
there are different roads to that center. In the solo-plus-quartet parts,
there are no specified chords. These sections were to be dialogues between the soloists and the rhythm section." (Quoted in A.B. Spellman,
notes to John Coltrane, *Ascension*, Impulse 95.)

improvisation, whereas Ayler's was for improvisation built, as I illustrated above, on the overall contours of a composition's theme. In light of the great similarity between these two approaches, however, the differences are not significant. Nor is it likely that this similarity derives from mere coincidence: the compelling effect of Coltrane's music on Ayler was simply too great for that.

But not all innovations are created equal. To expand upon the last paragraph (and to introduce a thesis I will explore in much greater depth in the next chapter), there seems to be a principle of balance in artistic revolutions such that the most fruitful innovations are those that compensate for the discarding of established styles and procedures by making use of familiar elements from the more-distant past. In other words, those innovations that reject all connections with the past are also those likely to culminate in a dead end. Such a principle of balance makes perfect artistic and psychological sense. If, to go from the abstract to the concrete by way of reiterating a point I implied in dissecting "Chasin' the Trane," one strips away from jazz its conventional harmonic structure; if one replaces conventional instrumental techniques and melodies with a variety of shrieks, screams, growls, bellows, moans, cries, hisses, and other distended sonorities; if one composes music containing many passages of dense, blaring collective improvisation—if one does all of these things, then, by Jove, one had better be prepared to offer listeners (and less-radical colleagues) *something* tangible to prevent them from being overpowered by this onslaught of the new. Improvisation built upon a theme and/or a motif offers one way of doing just that.

Hence my intuition is that Albert Ayler employs the technique of elaborating a solo based on a simple theme because it allows him to create a series of *sounds* (as opposed to notes) of extraordinary force and efficacy while keeping the overall improvisation relatively direct and comprehensible. Thus, Ayler's approach (as well as that of Coltrane, especially in his post-modal period after 1965) in effect stands bebop on its head. In the latter style, musicians improvise over intricate chord sequences, but pay the price for such harmonic sophistication by being restricted in their choices of melody-notes and timbres. Ayler (and Coltrane before him) instead elected to sacrifice harmonic complexity in exchange for the freedom to evoke certain feelings and emotions with maximum immediacy. In any event, regardless of whether Ayler's reasoning has actually proceeded along these lines, if one listens to any of his compositions in the way I have suggested, it should be evident that there is a guiding logic to them. Indeed, the claim of some writers to discover nothing but raging chaos in his work would be merely ludicrous, were it not for the fact that each one of these misjudgments places new barriers between him and his potentially large audience.

To be sure, if I may refer one last time to Frank Smith, with Ayler "there is even less heed paid to the tempered pitch of the piano keyboard than in Ornette Coleman's playing." Well, and what of it? Let us not forget that we are no longer in, say, 1956. Coltrane and Ornette Coleman have, each in his own way, shown us that jazz need not be forever chained to the keyboard of a piano. For that matter—to restate what I have remarked in earlier chapters—one hallmark of the jazz revolution lies in the attempt to dispense with the framework of equal-tempered pitch, which several of the new black musicians now regard as an unnecessary restriction. It is only a question of time until this viewpoint becomes generally accepted, although it may never be the only one in jazz. Already one can hardly listen to Albert Ayler on *The New Wave in Jazz* recording and then immediately turn, as this record does, to the accepted neo-bebop style of improvisation without feeling that there is something terribly constricting, even banal, about these repetitive chords and invariant rhythms of the 1950s.[33]

Perhaps we can find an analogy to the present situation in jazz in the bebop revolution of the 1940s. Many musicians who served abroad during World War II were completely disoriented by the startling transformation that the music had undergone in their absence. Much the same sense of dismay and non-comprehension now prevails even within the ranks of those critics convinced of the necessity for aesthetic, to say nothing of social, change. Although they may harbor good intentions, their preparations seem sadly remiss—and this time there is no World War II on which to blame such deficiencies. Good will, if and when it exists, is fine as far as it goes—but it does not go far enough. Above all, the music emanating from the jazz revolution must be *heard,* and heard attentively—not only as it manifests itself now, but also as it evolved in its transitional stages since the late 1950s. Only in this way can we hope to remain in touch with those recent developments of greatest significance.

Faced with a schism between the aspirations of the most adventurous musicians on the one hand and the critical response to them on the other, I do not think we can escape the conclusion that it is the critics who have fallen behind the times, rather than the innovative musicians who have "gotten ahead" of theirs. When all of the white critical bluster and rant has long been buried and forgotten, the musicians and their music will still be here, and it will be their consciousness alone that determines what those who deem themselves lovers of jazz will in future years be privileged to hear.

Afterword: John Coltrane and the jazz revolution thirty years later

In my preoccupation with demonstrating John Coltrane's central significance for the jazz revolution of the 1960s, I quite failed to see what is in hindsight a fairly obvious corollary: if Coltrane was indeed the dominant figure in this revolution, clearly his untimely death in 1967 was likely to deal it a blow from which it well might never recover. Thus, the conclusive piece of evidence for the thesis that Coltrane's leadership was decisive for the jazz revolution was furnished—with bitter irony—by his demise. Only shortly after that unforeseen event, the revolution began to lose its momentum; before much more time had elapsed, what had once seemed a coherent movement collapsed into a handful of isolated fragments.*

What are we to make of this sudden and unexpected disintegration of the jazz revolution? And why did it, unlike its bebop predecessor of the 1940s, fail to supplant earlier styles? Much of the answer to these questions, I maintain, stems from Coltrane's premature death at age forty. Had he lived another ten or perhaps even five more years, the jazz revolution might have had enough time to arrive at a new synthesis (or paradigm, to use the language of previous chapters) sufficiently broad and persuasive to enlist the allegiance of the majority of jazz revolutionaries *and* of the jazz audience as well. In that case, it would have become the dominant style of the day, just as had bebop a generation earlier.

Is it an exaggeration to attribute such great significance to a single person? Doesn't it, indeed, even suggest that this may be a case of hero worship run rampant? I think not. To succeed, revolutionary movements, in art as in society, require not just a militant rank and file, but insightful and consistent leadership as well. The Spanish revolution of the 1930s, for instance, was aborted when Stalin used his secret-police agents to assassinate or imprison its radical leadership. For

---

* The collapse was, of course, accelerated by the death of Albert Ayler in 1970, although by then Ayler had begun incorporating elements of rock and soul music into his work and his commitment to the jazz revolution had become questionable.

an example closer to home, consider the fate of the African-American campaign for human rights that paralleled the jazz revolution of the 1960s. With the murders of Malcolm X and Martin Luther King, that movement, too, lost its chief tribunes and thereafter, for all intents and purposes, fell apart, succumbing to a variety of hostile forces from without and centrifugal forces from within. At no time within the last one-third of a century would it ever again enjoy its former size, power or visibility. (Hence another similarity between Coltrane and Malcolm X is what became of the movements they led after their deaths.)

Here, the utmost clarity is in order: I already have made enough enemies for one lifetime; I hardly wish to incur new ones through slipshod writing. First of all, then, what I am most emphatically *not* claiming is that the entire jazz revolution shut down the moment John Coltrane breathed his last. Obviously, such artists and groups as Cecil Taylor, Ornette Coleman, Bill Dixon, Sun Ra, the Art Ensemble of Chicago, and others, continued developing and refining their music, just as they had been doing all along. The truth of the matter is, however, that all too few jazz artists saw fit to emulate these models; were this not so, there would be no need to mourn the passing of the jazz revolution. This is a point I will return to below.

Second, I like to flatter myself that I am a trained historian with at least a modicum of competence at research and interpretation and a certain degree of intellectual integrity. If, therefore, evidence exists that causes other than the death of John Coltrane also played a role in taking the wind out of the sails of the jazz revolution, far be it from me to deny it. And, in reality, I can discern a number of developments that, above and beyond Coltrane's passing, contributed to the breakdown of the jazz revolution.

To begin with, after the U.S. withdrawal from Southeast Asia, the national mood—as nebulous as that concept may be—changed markedly, turning strongly hostile to the kind of free-wheeling iconoclasm and audacity that characterized both the black campaign for human rights and the jazz revolution. The consequence was to slow the progress of each. But because the jazz revolution drew much of its inspiration from the African-American human-rights movement, the collapse of the latter had a redoubled effect on the former.

What is more, the jazz revolution lost its geographical center—almost as important an asset as its top leadership—when academic positions for many of the foremost jazz revolutionaries (and semirevolutionaries) began to become available. Thus, Bill Dixon left New York for Bennington College in Vermont; Archie Shepp went to the University of Massachusetts; bassist Richard Davis joined the music faculty at the University of Wisconsin; Jackie McLean accepted a position at the University of Connecticut; and so on, many times over. What is more, others from the revolution's less radical wing, some of whom I will mention presently, in part or whole abandoned jazz for rock and/or funk; still others—like Joe Henderson, Andrew Hill, Bobby Hutcherson—quietly packed their bags and set out for more hospitable climes, often in California. Finally, in the wake of these departures—and conceivably demoralized by them— many of the jazz revolution's second echelon—performers such as Byron Allen, Mugo Eddy Gale, Steve Grossman, Noah Howard, Prince Lasha, Dave Liebman, Giuseppi Logan, Steve Marcus, Alan Shorter, Sonny Simmons, and Tyrone Washington—simply vanished from sight altogether. Some hung on longer than others, of course, but within a decade of Coltrane's death, not one of these individuals appeared to be actively involved in carrying on the jazz revolution.

Revolutions of any variety simply cannot come to fruition if their foremost exponents are not in constant communion; this is why visual artists flock to Paris—and why jazz musicians (and writers and painters) from the 1920s on always have gone to New York. No revolution in jazz has ever been fully consummated until it arrived in Manhattan; perhaps none ever will. In any case, the kind of heady collaborative ethos that permeated the jazz revolution in New York in the 1960s—an ethos I *know* existed, because I experienced it firsthand—could not long survive once many of the most talented musicians in the movement began decamping for less forbidding locales. Given the hand-to-mouth circumstances almost all endured in New York, their decision to leave is nothing if not understandable. Still, it is immeasurably sad that merely in order to practice their craft under halfway decent conditions, these artists had to forgo most opportunities to work in close and continuous contact with like-minded friends and associates. There is no telling what might have emerged from the jazz revolution had this mass exodus not occurred. Alas, the course of human history is strewn with such tantalizing might-have-beens.

If Coltrane had lived longer, could his presence have reversed these deleterious trends, or at any rate minimized their effects? Although that question necessarily defies any categorical answer, what is incontestable is that of all the artists active in the jazz revolution, only he had any chance of turning the tide. I emphasize, again, that this conclusion rests on eminently practical considerations. In the most general sense, at the psychological level, Coltrane served as a beacon to others in the movement, bolstering their confidence in their ability to navigate previously uncharted waters: "If Trane can do it, so can I." In this indirect fashion, he pushed several of the younger revolutionaries further than they might have gone without him, because to define a style of their own, they had to progress beyond mere imitation of what he was playing to find some fresh area of their own to explore.

Conversely, once Coltrane had died, those who had derived inspiration from the force of his ideas began to drift into stagnation. This is certainly the case with two of his best-known and most-celebrated disciples, Pharoah Sanders and Albert Ayler. Sanders's work in Coltrane's groups in 1966 and 1967 shot off more than a few sparks of sheer brilliance.[34] For all of that, however, the recordings he made once Coltrane was no longer around to challenge and stimulate him rather quickly degenerated into a morass of devices rehashed from Coltrane's most popular recordings, notably "My Favorite Things" and the "Acknowledgment" movement of *A Love Supreme* Sanders is especially partial to the "and-one, two-and" bass-and-drums ostinato in the latter:

Albert Ayler, whose artistic relationship to John Coltrane is the focus of this chapter, fell off the path in a different fashion. Besides developing a sound that, especially on slow pieces, was increasingly difficult to distinguish from that of his mentor—an aspect of Coltrane's influence on him that I noted earlier—Ayler surrendered to the siren-song of rock and soul music in the last two recordings before his death.[36] Perhaps I am naive, but it is hard for me to believe that Pharoah Sanders and Albert Ayler would have taken the directions they did if they knew they would be forced to confront John Coltrane face to face at some not-too-distant time.

That same observation can stand as well for those musicians in the "moderate" wing of the jazz revolution—including, most prominently, Wayne Shorter, Freddie Hubbard, Anthony Williams, Chick Corea, and John Handy—who, during the 1970s and thereafter, attempted to capitalize on the short-lived vogue for jazz-rock, jazz funk, and the like. Of these, trumpeter Hubbard is an especially interesting case, for he is the only musician to perform on both of a pair of landmark recordings of the jazz revolution, Ornette Coleman's *Free Jazz* and John Coltrane's *Ascension*.[37] Would he, one wonders, have been so quick to embrace rock if he thought he would have to justify his decision to the artist who called upon him for the making of *Ascension*?

Implicit here is a point relevant to the ultimate fate of the jazz revolution: no single figure in the history of jazz—regardless of style—ever possessed greater moral authority than John Coltrane. Even those who detested his music were compelled to concede his unequaled dedication, his unimpeachable artistic integrity. Hence so long as Coltrane threw the considerable weight of his reputation behind the jazz revolution, it was impossible to dismiss that movement—the efforts of some critics, members of the public and even musicians notwithstanding—as nothing more than the ravings of charlatans and lunatics.

What was especially crucial in this regard is that Coltrane, unlike Ornette Coleman and Cecil Taylor, had come up through the ranks of bebop musicians—had "paid his dues," as the phrase goes. The mere fact that Coltrane, easily the most formidable bebop improviser of his generation, tossed in his lot with the jazz revolution dispelled much of the suspicion regarding it that many conventional artists harbored ("the only reason those cats play that way is because they can't play right"). Hence just as the fact of their long apprenticeships in swing big bands enabled performers like Dizzy Gillespie and Charlie Parker to establish the artistic legitimacy of bebop, only someone like Coltrane, who had spent a good fifteen years prior to 1960 playing bebop, could win even a grudging acceptance of the jazz revolution from the community of "mainstream" musicians. That is one of the reasons why I contend that Coltrane's death in 1967, before the jazz revolution had been able to consolidate its gains and develop a firm footing, meant that the new music would not be able to supplant bebop as bebop had supplanted swing before it. With Coltrane's demise, the one person who in time might have been able to bring about such a transformation

passed from the scene—and there was no one remotely able
to take his place. We see once more that revolutionary leadership is a matter of the most profound significance. Deprived
of it, a revolution inevitably falls short of its goals.

Aside from the intangible issue of moral authority, Coltrane's leadership was essential, if the jazz revolution were to
prevail, for certain down-to-earth, dollars-and-cents reasons
as well. The very fact that such uncompromising, even ferocious Coltrane recordings as *Ascension, Meditations, Expression* and *Coltrane Live at the Village Vanguard Again!*
could sell in respectable numbers encouraged recording company executives, concert promoters, and booking agents to
take a chance with some of the more-prominent artists of
the jazz revolution.[38] But beyond that, Coltrane's intercession with these business figures was critical in advancing
the careers of a number of movement musicians. He brought
Archie Shepp and Pharoah Sanders to Impulse Records, and
after them, Marion Brown and Albert Ayler.[39] He arranged
for the groups of Shepp and Ayler to appear with his own
on festival and concert stages. He used Shepp in recording
A Love Supreme (although the selection on which Shepp
performs has never been released),[40] and Shepp, Pharoah
Sanders, and Marion Brown, among others, in recording
Ascension. In 1961, he incorporated Eric Dolphy into his
own group on an open-ended basis; four years later, he did
the same with Sanders. After 1965 especially, he allowed
almost any halfway-competent purveyor of the new music
to "sit in" with his ensemble (much to the dismay of Elvin
Jones—see the interview in chapter 11 on this score). He
did, in short, everything within his power—and far more
than anyone had a right to expect—to make sure that the
most thoroughgoing artistic rebels in jazz received a hearing.
His actions, moreover, were completely unprecedented: no
one else in jazz had ever sought out and fostered younger
iconoclasts the way Coltrane did. Coleman Hawkins did

not provide a platform for Lester Young; Lester Young did not provide one for Charlie Parker. But John Coltrane did exactly that—and not just for a single musician, but for a bevy of them at that.*

In sum, then, Coltrane was the one indispensable person for the viability of the jazz revolution. He—or rather, his sales figures—commanded respect among the hard-nosed business executives of jazz, who—albeit sometimes reluctantly—heeded his counsel and employed several of the artists he recommended. He commanded respect in bebop circles: if anyone could have won over musicians of that persuasion to the side of the jazz revolution, it was he. Finally, he commanded respect, perhaps even reverence, among the younger musicians, who were touched—as well they should have been—by the fact that an established performer of his distinction should have taken their fledgling efforts so seriously and gone so far out of his way to open doors for them.

All of this changed, however, once Coltrane died. Whatever interest the recording companies, booking agencies, festivals, and nightclubs had in the jazz revolution soon evaporated. Those bebop musicians who had conducted a mild flirtation with it—I have already supplied some of their names—by and large spurned the revolution after Coltrane was no longer a living participant; some, indeed, even went so far as to flee jazz entirely in pursuit of the supposedly greener fields of

---

* Bob Thiele, who was John Coltrane's producer at Impulse Records from 1961 to 1967, has acknowledged that it was only because of Coltrane's constant urging that he "became aware of Archie Shepp and many of the younger players. When John heard any good player, he would call me and ask that I please give him some consideration. I think that if we had signed everyone that John recommended, we'd have four hundred musicians on that label." (Thiele is quoted in Frank Kofsky, "The New Wave: Bob Thiele Talks to Frank Kofsky about John Coltrane," *Coda*, May–June 1968, p. 6.)

popular music. Last, and possibly most disheartening of all, Coltrane's protégés—the very artists who had drawn their sustenance (in more respects than one) from him—failed to keep his legacy alive in the only way that he would have wanted: by continuing his unending quest for a newer and more fully expressive style. In many cases they even beat a retreat—an artistic Thermidor, if you will—by relinquishing a certain amount of the ground that the jazz revolution, under Coltrane's leadership, had at one point appeared to have made its own.

Thus, with the passage of three decades, the arguments for Coltrane's preeminence in the jazz revolution have only gained in force and cogency. From the standpoint of the health and well-being of that revolution, it might have been better had its reception been less dependent on a single individual. Be that as it may, however, what is done is done; it cannot be undone. Had John Coltrane not provided inspiration and leadership, it is doubtful that the jazz revolution would have gone as far as it did as rapidly as it did, nor is it likely that its trajectory would have been so fully documented on recordings. Perhaps these thoughts can afford us some consolation for the fact that, in the final analysis, the jazz revolution was demonstrably unable to sustain its early momentum once Coltrane was no longer present to stand at its head.

NOTES

1. Quoted in Frank Kofsky, "An Interview with Albert and Donald Ayler," *Jazz*, September 1968, p. 22.

2. Frank Smith, "Frank Smith to Frank Kofsky," letter to the editor in *Jazz*, November 1965, p. 9.

3. Leon Trotsky has written: "They tell us that a writer begins where individuality begins and that therefore the source of his creativeness is his unique soul and not his class. It is true, without indi-

viduality there can be no writer. But if the poet's individuality and only his individuality is disclosed in his work, then to what purpose is the interpretation of art? To what purpose, let us ask, is literary criticism? In any case, the artist, if he is a true artist, will tell us about his unique individuality better than his babbling critic. But the truth is that even if individuality is unique, it does not mean that it cannot be analyzed. Individuality is a welding together of tribal, national, class, temporary and institutional elements and, in fact, it is in the uniqueness of this welding together, in the proportions of this psychochemical mixture, that individuality is expressed. One of the most important tasks of criticism is to analyze the individuality of the artist (that is, his art) into its component elements, and to show their correlations. In this way, criticism brings the artist closer to the reader, who also has more or less of a 'unique soul,' 'artistically' unexpressed, 'unchosen,' but nonetheless representing a union of the same elements as does the soul of a poet. So it can be seen that what serves as a bridge from soul to soul is not the unique, but the common. Only through the common is the unique known; the common is determined in man by the deepest and most persistent conditions which make up his 'soul,' by the social conditions of education, of existence, of work, and of associations. The social conditions in historic human society are, first of all, the conditions of class affiliation. That is why a class standard is so fruitful in all fields of ideology, including art, and especially in art, because the latter often expresses the deepest and most hidden social aspirations. Moreover, a social standard not only does not exclude, but goes hand in hand with formal criticism, that is, with the standard of technical workmanship. This, as a matter of fact, also tests the particular by a common measure, because if one did not reduce the particular to the general there would be no contacts among people, no thoughts, and no poetry." *Literature and Revolution*, trans. Rose Strunsky (Ann Arbor: University of Michigan Press, 1960), pp. 59–60.

4. On this point Coltrane himself stated: "[Thelonious] Monk was one of the first to show me how to make two or three notes at one time on tenor [saxophone]. (John Glenn, a tenor man in Philly, also showed me how to do this. He can play a triad [three-note chord] and move notes inside it—like passing tones!) It's done by false

fingering and adjusting your lip. If everything goes right, you can get triads. Monk just looked at my horn and 'felt' the mechanics of what had to be done to get this effect." John Coltrane and Don De-Micheal, "Coltrane on Coltrane," *down beat*, September 29, 1960, p. 27 (this article appears in the table of contents as "Coltrane Writes about Coltrane").

5. See, for example, "Frank Smith to Frank Kofsky," pp. 9–10.

6. Ornette Coleman, *Free Jazz: A Collective Improvisation by the Ornette Coleman Double Quartet* (Atlantic 1364); *The Shape of Jazz to Come* (Atlantic 1317); *Change of the Century* (Atlantic 1327); *Tomorrow Is the Question* (Contemporary 3569).

7. Inasmuch as my focus in this essay is primarily on saxophonists, I have made no effort to deal with the music of Cecil Taylor, Sun Ra, and Bill Dixon. Doubtless, however, their ideas, especially those of Taylor, have been nearly as crucial as those of Ornette Coleman for the development of the jazz revolution; the interview with Coltrane in chapter 13, for instance, reveals that the saxophonist gave the work of Sun Ra's Arkestra much more than passing attention.

8. Both of these compositions are on Byron Allen, *The Byron Allen Trio* (ESP 1005).

9. On Giuseppi Logan, *The Giuseppi Logan Quartet* (ESP 1007).

10. See Pharoah Sanders, *The Pharoah Sanders Quintet* (ESP 1003).

11. "Capricorn Moon" is on Marion Brown, *The Marion Brown Quartet* (ESP 1022), which, the name notwithstanding, actually contains selections performed by a quintet as well; see also Marion Brown, *Three for Shepp* (Impulse 9139).

12. "Lacy's Out East" is on Charles Tyler, *The Charles Tyler Ensemble* (ESP 1029); see also his work with Albert Ayler on the latter's recording, *Bells* (ESP 1010). Overall, the influence of Coltrane on Tyler is both direct and indirect, with the larger indirect component coming by way of Albert Ayler.

13. Quoted in Dan Morgenstern, "John Tchicai: A Calm Member of the Avant-Garde," *down beat*, February 10, 1966, pp. 20–21; I discuss this article, including its title's deliberately pejorative implications with respect to the black avant garde in jazz, in chapter 3.

14. See in particular Frank Kofsky, *Black Music, White Business: Illuminating the History and Political Economy of Jazz* (New York: Pathfinder Press, 1997), the last three chapters especially.

15. LeRoi Jones, notes to *The New Wave in Jazz* (Impulse 90), an anthology of selections by John Coltrane, Albert Ayler, Archie Shepp and others. See also the words of Albert Ayler on John Coltrane at the head of this chapter.

16. "Ghosts" is on Albert Ayler, *Spiritual Unity* (ESP 1002); "Ramblin' " is on Ornette Coleman, *Change of the Century* (Atlantic 1327).

17. John Coltrane, *Coltrane "Live" at the Village Vanguard* (Impulse 10). The name "Chasin' the Trane," incidentally, came not from Coltrane, but from engineer Rudy Van Gelder, at whose studio the master tape for this recording was mixed; see Frank Kofsky, "The New Wave: Bob Thiele Talks to Frank Kofsky about John Coltrane," *Coda*, May–June 1968, p. 3.

18. Ira Gitler, review of *Coltrane "Live" at the Village Vanguard* (Impulse 10), *down beat*, April 26, 1962, p. 29.

19. Pete Welding, review of *Coltrane "Live" at the Village Vanguard*, ibid.

20. For Bob Thiele's explanation of how *down beat*'s negative reviews impelled him to suggest that Coltrane record less controversial material, see chapter 2 and Kofsky, "The New Wave," p. 4. The recordings in question are *Duke Ellington and John Coltrane* (Impulse 30); John Coltrane, *Ballads* (Impulse 32); *John Coltrane and Johnny Hartman* (Impulse 40).

21. The fact that no such retreat took place in Coltrane's nightclub and concert appearances lends further support to the thesis that the idea for it originated with the recording company rather than the artist.

22. Actually, there is already a wealth of evidence that the saxophonists from the more conventional and conservative wing of the jazz avant-garde are greatly obliged to Coltrane—sometimes so much so as to verge on plagiarism. For evidence, compare, among others, Charles Lloyd's performance of "How Can I Tell You?" on *Discovery* (Columbia 9067) with Coltrane's rendition of the Billy Eckstine song, "I Want to Talk About You" on his albums *Soultrane* (Prestige 7142),

Coltrane Live at Birdland (Impulse 50) and *Selflessness* (Impulse 9161); Lloyd's reading of "Song of Her" on *Forest Flower* (Atlantic 1473) with Coltrane's composition, "Naima," on his album *Giant Steps* (Atlantic 1311); John Handy's piece, "If Only We Knew," on *John Handy Recorded Live at the Monterey Jazz Festival* (Columbia 9262), with its model, John Coltrane's composition, "Spiritual," on *Coltrane "Live" at the Village Vanguard* (Impulse 10). For another illustration, note the overall resemblance between the series of recordings by Wayne Shorter with McCoy Tyner and/or Elvin Jones—*Night Dreamer* (Blue Note 84173), *Juju* (Blue Note 84182), *Speak No Evil* (Blue Note 84194)—and Coltrane's work during the first half of the 1960s.

23. Frank Smith, "His Name Is Albert Ayler," *Jazz*, December 1965, p. 12.

24. On thematic improvisation in bebop, see Gunther Schuller's essays, "Thelonious Monk" and "Sonny Rollins and Thematic Improvisation," in *Jazz Panorama: From the Pages of the Jazz Review* (New York: Collier Books, 1964), ed. Martin Williams, pp. 216–38 and 239–52, respectively. It is, incidentally, indicative of Martin Williams's abiding distaste for anything associated with the music of John Coltrane—a disdainful attitude I documented in the previous chapter—that he has seen fit to omit from the anthology he edited pianist Zita Carno's masterly treatment of "The Style of John Coltrane," *The Jazz Review*, October 1959, pp. 16–21, and November 1959, pp. 13–17. This study ranks among the most lucid and insightful analyses of Coltrane's music ever published; its importance far exceeds that of most of the material that filled the pages of this periodical during its brief existence.

25. Albert Ayler, "Ghosts," *Spiritual Unity* (ESP 1002).

26. "One Down, One Up" is on John Coltrane and Archie Shepp, *New Thing at Newport* (Impulse 94); its melody derives directly from the five-note theme.

27. See Albert Ayler, *Love Cry* (Impulse 9165), and John Coltrane, *A Love Supreme* (Impulse 77).

28. See Albert Ayler, *The Last Album* (Impulse 9208).

29. John Coltrane, *A Love Supreme* (Impulse 77).

30. Just as the five-note pattern in "Chasin' the Trane" is the

theme of "One Down, One Up."

31. The best-known version of "Giant Steps," recorded with Tommy Flanagan, is on John Coltrane, *Giant Steps* (Atlantic 1311); an alternate version, with Cedar Walton replacing Flanagan, is on *Alternate Takes* (Atlantic 1668); there are still other versions, heretofore unreleased, on the reissue compilation, *The Heavyweight Champion: The Complete Atlantic Recordings* (Rhino Atlantic Jazz Gallery R2 71984). Coltrane employed a chord sequence similar to that of "Giant Steps" as a foundation for improvisation on several other pieces recorded in 1959 and 1960, including "Countdown" on the *Giant Steps* album, "Fifth House" on *Coltrane Jazz* (Atlantic 1354), "But Not for Me"—in many ways the most satisfying of the lot—on *My Favorite Things* (Atlantic 1361), "Central Park West" and "Satellite" (the latter a recasting of "How High the Moon" that barely conceals the original) on *Coltrane's Sound* (Atlantic 1419), and "26-2" on *The Coltrane Legacy* (Atlantic 1553).

32. There are performances of "Impressions" on the John Coltrane recordings *Impressions* (Impulse 42) and *Afro Blue Impressions* (Pablo Live 2620 101); both date from the early 1960s. Among the Coltrane albums with performances of "My Favorite Things" are *My Favorite Things* (Atlantic 1361), recorded in 1960; *Afro Blue Impressions* (Pablo Live 2620 101), recorded in 1961 or 1962; *Selflessness* (Impulse 9161), recorded in 1963; *Coltrane Live at the Village Vanguard Again!* (Impulse 9124), recorded in 1966; and *John Coltrane Live in Japan* (MCA Records and GRP Records, GRD–4–102), recorded—on *alto* saxophone for Coltrane's first solo and on soprano for his second—in 1966; the latter is especially rich in patterns and variations on them. "Summertime," recorded in 1960, is on *My Favorite Things*, cited directly above. "Bye, Bye, Blackbird" is on *"Bye Bye Blackbird": John Coltrane* (Pablo Live 2308–227), recorded in 1963. "I Want to Talk About You" is on *Afro Blue Impressions* (Pablo Live 2620–101), *The European Tour* (Pablo Live 2308–222), *Live at Birdland* (Impulse 50), and *Selflessness* (Impulse AS–9161); the former pair were recorded in 1962, the latter in 1963.

33. See John Coltrane, Albert Ayler, Archie Shepp, and others, *The New Wave in Jazz* (Impulse 90).

34. See in particular Sanders's solos on the following John Col-

trane recordings: *John Coltrane Live in Seattle: Featuring Pharoah Sanders* (Impulse 9202), *Kulu Sé Mama* (Impulse 9106), *Meditations* (Impulse 9110), *Expression* (Impulse 9120), *Coltrane Live at the Village Vanguard Again!* (Impulse 9124), *John Coltrane Live in Japan* (MCA Records and GRP Records, GRD–4–102), *Om* (Impulse 9140).

35. Using the abbreviations "MFT" and "A" to refer to "My Favorite Things" and the "Acknowledgment" movement of *A Love Supreme*, respectively, we can analyze Sanders's immediate post-Coltrane recordings as follows: "The Creator Has a Master Plan" ("A" ostinato) takes up 80 percent of *Karma* (Impulse 9181). "Sun in Aquarius" ("MFT") and "Hum-Allah-Hum-Allah-Hum-Allah" ("A") together make up all of *Jewels of Thought* (Impulse 9190). "Let Us Go into the House of the Lord" ("A") occupies one whole side of *Summun Bukmun Umyn: Deaf Dumb Blind* (Impulse 9199); "Thembi" and "Morning Prayer" (both reworkings of "A") account for more than one-third of *Thembi* (Impulse 9206); "Black Unity," comprising the entirety of the album of the same name (Impulse 9219), is in large part essentially a verbatim restatement of "A." And so on.

36. See *Albert Ayler: New Grass* (Impulse 9175); *Albert Ayler: The Last Album* (Impulse 9208).

37. Ornette Coleman, *Free Jazz: A Collective Improvisation by the Ornette Coleman Double Quartet* (Atlantic 1364); John Coltrane, *Ascension* (Impulse 95).

38. Full information on these recordings appears in the notes above.

39. Frank Kofsky, "The New Wave: Bob Thiele Talks to Frank Kofsky about John Coltrane," *Coda*, May 1968, pp. 6, 8.

40. "[T]o Archie Shepp (tenor saxist) and Art Davis (bassist) who both recorded on a track that regrettably will not be released at this time; my deepest appreciation for your work in music past and present. In the near future, I hope that we will be able to further the work that was started here." John Coltrane, notes to *A Love Supreme* (Impulse 77).

Part 4

The anatomy of the John Coltrane quartet

10

Elvin Jones, John Coltrane, and the evolution of jazz rhythm in the Coltrane Quartet*

A. The historical background

1. Artist in context—or 'star'?

Writing that purports to deal with the jazz musician as a creative or innovative artist has too often suffered from a conspicuous tendency to treat the musician in question in isolation as some sort of god-like genius—or, what is the other side of the same coin, freak—standing apart from the rest of the human race. Even though I have tried to keep this mentality from infecting my own writing, I do not delude myself that I have been entirely successful. In point of fact

---

* I use the phrases "the Coltrane quartet" and "the quartet" to mean the group comprised of John Coltrane, McCoy Tyner, and Elvin Jones, and Steve Davis, Arthur Davis, Reggie Workman, or Jimmy Garrison as the bassist. On occasion, Coltrane employed Arthur Davis as a second bassist in addition to Workman or Garrison, but in such cases I have allowed convenience to outweigh linguistic precision in referring to the group as a quartet nonetheless.

there is, as I will bring out, a pervasive body of myth and innumerable precedents that together lead us to depict the artist in this light.

Jazz may be African with respect to the antecedents of its leading musical conventions and procedures, but in terms of geographical origins, it is, for better or worse, strictly a child of the West. Owing to those features of early modern capitalism that led to the enslavement of Africans in the New World, the music we call jazz was born into a social and political setting whose dominant ideologies, folk beliefs, habits of thought, and so on, are almost entirely European in nature; and it has been impossible to prevent such attitudes from affecting the way that writers and scholars, as well as the public at large, perceive the jazz musician. The concept of "the creative artist" stems directly from the Renaissance period in European history, beginning, very approximately, in the fourteenth and fifteenth centuries. It took on enormously wider currency, of course, in nineteenth-century Europe, when it became standard practice to portray painters, writers, composers, and artists in general, as solitary, ascetic souls alienated from the unthinking masses, the latter in any event indifferent to the sublime considerations of art. Thus, "true" artists, according to this view, were doomed to a tortured existence of poverty and suffering, compelled to toil in cold, poorly lit garrets, producing works that would not be appreciated until long after they have been interred in the cruel earth. Such is the stereotypical portrait that the previous century has bequeathed us, and one need only conjure with the names of Baudelaire, Elizabeth Barrett Browning, Emily Dickinson, Gauguin, Poe, Van Gogh, Walt Whitman, *et* countless *alia,* to be reminded of it.[1]

As the biographies of such disparate twentieth-century figures as Marcel Proust, James Joyce, Ezra Pound, Ernest Hemingway, Virginia Woolf, F. Scott Fitzgerald, George Orwell, Dylan Thomas, Allen Ginsberg, and Jack Kerouac, among others, variously illustrate, such stereotypes, and their evident appeal to artists of all persuasions, have persisted virtually undiminished to the present. Regrettably, but understandably, this was the model that an earlier generation of black jazz revolutionaries, those who led the bebop revolt of the 1940s against swing, also appropriated as their own. Not that they could (or should) be blamed for that. To their way of thinking, there was a clear-cut distinction between the treatment afforded a musical *artist*—for example, a white orchestral musician who performed on the concert stage works composed in the European symphonic tradition—and an *entertainer*. The black bebop innovators had already witnessed the creative achievements of their predecessors go doubly unrecognized: for while upper-class white cultural arbiters during the 1920s and 1930s were dismissing jazz as vulgar musical trash, white popularizers, from Paul Whiteman to Benny Goodman, were simultaneously busy accruing sizable bank accounts and correspondingly large reputations by aping the black artists who pioneered the New Orleans and swing styles. Adamantly determined not to let this happen again, resolved to receive the full measure of respect due them and their creations in a black musical idiom, these bebop revolutionaries, as I have already remarked in chapter 1 and elsewhere, went out of their way to assert all of the characteristics and mannerisms that they associated with a somewhat idealized version of "the artist."

And with a vengeance! The result—which, as I will discuss shortly, had a number of other contributory causes as well—disrupted the delicate dialectical equilibrium that in the past had maintained a relative balance in jazz between the forces of collectivity and those of individualism. From the bebop revolution in the 1940s on, it is a safe generalization that the idea of artistic individualism has been firmly in the saddle, with a corresponding neglect of the elements of collective endeavor necessary to sustain the music. (That some of the avant-garde groups of the 1960s sought to break with this tendency does not make the tendency any less real or pervasive.)

But we can hardly attribute sole responsibility for this state of affairs to the artists themselves; in particular, it would be a grievous mistake to underestimate the significance of the jazz press in consolidating the dominance of this ideology of artistic individualism—that is to say, the ideology of artistic "stars." The truth is that the "star" system—the system of promoting ostensibly beautiful, talented, exciting, glamorous, alluring, and so on, individuals as suitable subjects for public adulation—sells newspapers, magazines and books. This generalization is as valid for the popular music press (including both jazz- and rock-oriented periodicals) as it is for the "celebrity" magazines of the *Silver Screen* and *People* type. Just as, week after week, month after month, one can observe on any magazine rack an endless profusion of articles in such periodicals on Elizabeth Taylor, the British royal family, Elvis Presley, Jacqueline Onassis, ad infinitum, so, too, has the "star" system been a great boon for popular-music publications. Not only will a cover picturing the currently fashionable individual or group, be it Miles Davis or Mick Jagger, Alice Coltrane or Alice Cooper, probably sell more copies of any given issue, but a superficially researched and hastily written piece on one of the in-vogue "stars" is easier for a usually underpaid and overworked music journalist to crank out than a penetrating and reflective essay on some less sensational but more important aspect of the popular-music field. All of which, I suppose I hardly need emphasize, contributes still further to the misleading idea of the artist, musical or otherwise, as a kind of superhuman creature who draws inspiration out of thin air as effortlessly as an infant imbibes milk from the mother's breast.

What is more, the anti-Communist neurosis that has been a permanent part of the national psychology of the

United States from the close of the Second World War (if not before) to the present has further contributed to an excessive focus on the individual artist and a corresponding neglect of the underlying forces that have nurtured that art. Precisely because it is a principle of Marxist theory that art, like all products of the human brain and hand, has its ultimate origins in a concrete and historically specific set of material conditions—a proposition light-years removed from such Soviet dogmas as "socialist realism," "proletarian art," and the like—just for that reason did it become obligatory in the United States to assert the opposite: that art has no roots whatsoever in the real world; that we must instead consent to be bound by a doctrine of "art for art's sake";[2] and that, in general, it is no more possible to shed light on the sources that have culminated in a work of art through a social analysis than it is possible to turn to the *Bhagavad-Gita* for a succinct account of the Trinity. Naturally, such benighted attitudes make it just that much the harder to see in the artist anything but an Olympian being who, while remaining wholly aloof from the remainder of humanity, has managed, by some miracle whose nature we are not permitted to probe, to suck a work of art out of his or her thumb the way a magician pulls a rabbit out of a hat. As applied to the history of the arts, I find it hard to conceive of a more threadbare and obscurantist set of assumptions.

Nor is it difficult to deduce the consequences of postulating that an artist's work in no way reflects this individual's numerous, multifaceted interactions with the people and events in the social and political environment. When we exclude from consideration everything beyond the boundaries of the work of art itself, we necessarily lose sight of those connections that bind the artist to his or her tradition. In so doing, we virtually guarantee our inability to develop a fully rounded understanding of the circumstances that have caused the work to come into being or the significance of what it represents.

To understand the importance of the connections I referred to in the previous paragraph, it may help to visualize them separately as the *vertical* and the *horizontal,* though in actuality the distinction between the two is not so absolute as this terminology may suggest. In any case, by vertical connections I mean those ties that the artist, in the course of developing a mature style, establishes with his or her predecessors in the field. In this book I offer several studies of such vertical connections, including the discussion in chapter 9 of the line of descent linking the music of John Coltrane with that of one of his outstanding disciples, Albert Ayler. Significantly, while Ayler himself was quite candid about his indebtedness to Coltrane—

> when [Coltrane] started playing [Ayler said], I had to listen just to his tone, you understand. To listen to him play was just like he was talking to me, saying, "Brother, get yourself together *spiritually.*" Just one sound—that's how profound the man was . . .

—at least one writer missed this point altogether because of his insistence that the artists who perform the new black music are influenced only "by their own individuality." [3]

Elvin Jones, in the interview in the next chapter, also furnishes some comments that allow us a glimpse into the nature of vertical connections and how they take shape:

> KOFSKY: When you yourself were developing as a drummer, were there any other drummers . . . on whom you might at one point or another have modeled yourself?
>
> JONES: There were a lot of them. Just about every drummer that was playing anywhere or played with anybody, I had a great deal of deep respect for and a burning desire

to listen to, just to find out what they were doing. That was my way—I've always felt like that and still do.[4]

Based on what others have told me, I can add that the state of mind that Jones has described was in no way unique to him, but is characteristic of any aspiring jazz musician: there is an insatiable thirst, in particular during the musician's formative period, to hear every possible performance, especially one by a major artist who plays one's own instrument. Such occasions provide an invaluable opportunity to further one's practical education, perhaps by observing precisely how to execute such-and-such a phrase—Jones, for example, wanted to watch Buddy Rich to learn whether the latter played a particular snare-drum figure "with one hand or two"[5]—or perhaps by appropriating some hip new "lick." Dedication of this sort is the mark of the serious novitiate.

Where vertical connections are those that aid the jazz musician (and by extension, all artists) in evolving a fully developed style through exposure to the work of earlier generations, horizontal connections are those interactions among musicians who perform together that contribute to the artistic growth of some or all of the participants. Of the two kinds of linkages, vertical and horizontal, it is the latter whose effects are immensely more difficult to detect. There are innumerable places where one can read that the trumpet playing of Dizzy Gillespie derives from Louis Armstrong by way of Roy Eldridge, or that Sonny Rollins initially modeled his style on the work of Lester Young and Coleman Hawkins, as modified and updated during the bebop revolution by Charlie Parker, Wardell Gray, and Dexter Gordon. Such considerations are not especially esoteric, and in some instances may even be downright obvious. What one almost never sees treated in any study of jazz, however, is the reciprocal and dialectical influence of, say, saxophonist Charlie Parker's method of improvisation on the style of drumming devised by Max Roach, and vice versa (although, to be fair, some writers have noted that pianists Earl Hines and Bud Powell were influenced by Louis Armstrong and Charlie Parker, respectively).

The almost total absence of such analyses is, I believe, largely a product of the artistic-individualism, or "star," approach to jazz, which treats each artist as a self-contained unit who, apart from the study of the works of his or her direct predecessors on the same instrument, might as well have burst into the world fully formed, like Athena from the brow of Zeus. The consequences of this "star" ideology, moreover, are as baneful as its supremacy is unchallenged. The least evil it has perpetrated is that the listening public is largely oblivious of the elusive and complex interactions among musicians that go into the creation of works of jazz of lasting value. On the contrary, the members of that public—acting on the dubious assumption that more means better—first look to see what artists are listed on a particular album jacket; if the names of enough of the modish "stars" of the day appear, then, ipso facto, the recording must be a good one. Hence the plethora of "all-star" recording sessions, more than a few of which even bear those words in their titles.

But, of course, if the premise is defective, the conclusion need not follow—and in this case, it certainly does not. There are innumerable albums that have been made by throwing together in a recording studio for three or six hours a collection of such "stars," turning on the tape machines and, some months thereafter, issuing the "product," as it is called in industry jargon. The lackluster qualities of the great bulk of these artifacts is undeniable. But so long as the public is willing to play the game of counting "stars," you can be sure that record companies will be more than delighted to meet the demand.

This fact, however, merely begins to itemize the damage

inflicted by the widespread acceptance of the "star" ideology and the type of reasoning it promotes. If you are able to persuade them to be candid on the subject, most working jazz musicians can tell some pretty tales indeed about what it is like to be a "sideman" * in the pay of some more famous— or at any rate, more frequently employed—"star."

For in reality, so all-pervasive has the "star" ideology become that even many musician themselves—or at least the leaders of groups—subscribe to it. The assumption that usually governs relations between the "star" who heads a group and its less prestigious members is that the latter will perform within the limits defined by the former; that is why, for instance, whether the tenor saxophonist be Johnny Griffin or Charlie Rouse, whether the drum chair be occupied by Roy Haynes, Frankie Dunlop, or Ben Riley, the group of Thelonious Monk always sounds like just that—the group of Thelonious Monk, as supported by a more or less interchangeable set of accompanists. Likewise for the ensembles of Horace Silver, Art Blakey, Cannonball Adderley, Bill Evans, and nearly every other prominent leader one might care to name (the small groups of Miles Davis and John Coltrane during the 1960s were among the very few exceptions). In some instances, this situation exists because the leader has evolved an identifiable group "sound" that, in his or her opinion, helps maintain a faithful following; other times, it is merely evidence of artistic stagnation. In either case, the result is the same: although jazz is preeminently a music of collective creation, the hierarchical arrangement of "star"-accompanist, employer-employee, in the end almost always prevails. An

---

* "Sideman," of course, is jazz vernacular for a musician whose status is that of accompanist-cum-employee in a group led by another. Because of its misleading implications, I have instead chosen to use the admittedly less-colorful and -precise term "accompanist" in its place.

accompanist can develop his or her talents, extend his or her musical concepts—but only to the degree that it does not ruffle the feathers of the boss. One very well-known and popular trumpeter-leader, I am told, habitually discharges his musical associates, saxophonists in particular, when audiences begin bestowing more applause on their solos than on his own.[6] Need one say more?

Indeed, to such a degree does the "star" ideology exert its sway that even the engineers and the executives of recording companies—though you might imagine they would know better—operate on assumptions derived from it. Elvin Jones's remarks on this topic are instructive. "Most of the time the engineers don't cater to sidemen, at least while recording in the studio," he answered when I inquired about the generally muddy quality of his drums on the John Coltrane recording, *My Favorite Things*.[7] Subsequently, he expanded on this point:

> Talking about engineers recording jazz groups, I think more attention should be paid to the sidemen there, because, after all, it should be realized that it is the *group* that is playing and it is the *group* that the people who are going to buy the album are interested in, and not just the leader. This is one of the problems in the recording industry that I think is very easy to correct, what with all the very expensive and very elaborate equipment. There can very easily be an improvement and that obstacle very easily overcome.

The only flaw in this reasoning is that the obstacle of which Elvin Jones speaks is *political*, rather than technical, in nature. So long as the "star" ideology reigns unchecked, there will be little recognition by the Powers That Be that such a problem even exists, much less any willingness to "overcome" it.

2. The dialectics of artistic development: Elvin Jones

The relevance of the preceding comments to Elvin Jones is simply this: if he had been confined to one of the established but musically less ambitious groups, rather than working for John Coltrane, who was constantly in search of new peaks to scale and conquer, my guess is that his artistry would not have developed either as rapidly or as extensively as it did. To state such a conjecture is only to reaffirm the idea I have been attempting to convey above—namely, that the plane of achievement to which a jazz performer is able to push his or her art depends, in part, on the nature of the musical environment. If that environment is conducive to artistic growth—if, that is, the leader is not possessed of an overweening ego or an overbearing personality, and if the other group members are similarly devoted to the fullest possible development of their talents—then all of the musicians, as well as the works they jointly produce, will be the better for it.

It bears emphasis, furthermore, that such growth is mutual, reciprocal, and dialectical: the leader benefits as much from the strides made by the other musicians as do the latter themselves; and, conversely, as the leader's playing continues to evolve, he or she naturally tends to pull the others in the same direction. Thus, while it is undeniable that the artistry of Elvin Jones was enhanced through his long association with John Coltrane, it is also true that Coltrane, in turn, was to some degree able to reach the heights he did because of Jones's remarkable drumming (a point I have alluded to throughout and will develop directly). For that matter, as I discuss more thoroughly later in this section, the Coltrane-Jones collaboration probably would not have flourished as fruitfully (or quickly) as it did had pianist McCoy Tyner not been available at the outset to take over certain of the time-keeping responsibilities from the drummer.

We are, as it happens, in the fortunate position of being

able to document, at least roughly, some of the effect that John Coltrane and Elvin Jones had on each other. Jones was not, as he makes clear in the interview in the following chapter, the first drummer that Coltrane engaged once he began assembling his own group, but was in fact preceded by Pete La Roca and Billy Higgins (in that order). Although La Roca did not record with Coltrane's group, Higgins did, playing on at least two pieces that Coltrane later re-recorded with Elvin Jones in the drummer's chair. Even if we make every conceivable allowance for the relative newness of the Coltrane quartet (then including McCoy Tyner and bassist Steve Davis, in addition to Coltrane and Higgins) when it first recorded these selections, the difference in the reading given them once Elvin Jones had replaced Higgins is, it must be said, little short of phenomenal—and immediately evident as well. With Jones at the drums, the entire quartet plays with vastly improved spirit and attack. Tempos increase just sufficiently and the articulation of rhythm has just the additional bite necessary to give the feeling of a constantly accelerating forward motion, or "swing," that was to become a hallmark of the Coltrane group. Conceivably most important of all, the playing of both Coltrane and McCoy Tyner demonstrated that the new percussionist was able to inspire them immeasurably more than had his predecessor.[8] Jones's arrival, it is now apparent, ended a period in Coltrane's career during which the saxophonist had been seeking, with only uneven success, a fresh path along which to continue his artistic growth. With Jones and Tyner to support him, and with the additional impetus that his recent adoption of the soprano saxophone provided,[9] Coltrane was able to crystallize a new style whose potentialities it would take him several years to exhaust, during which time he would create some of the most majestic works ever performed in jazz.

Our understanding of the immediately preceding phase of Coltrane's career—roughly, from the time between his

final break with Miles Davis in April 1960 to the formation
of his own group with Tyner and Jones later that year—has
benefited immensely from the fact that we can at last hear,
in chronological order (and sometimes in multiple versions),
almost every selection Coltrane recorded as a leader (or co-
leader) between January 1959 and October 1960,* thereby
enabling us to follow the course of his musical thought with
utmost clarity. As a result of being able to view this period as
a whole, we can discern that for much of the time Coltrane
was experimenting with two related approaches to stimu-
lating his muse, both of which made the bebop improvising
framework more restrictive: on the one hand (as I discussed
in the preceding chapter), he composed and recorded a set of
pieces (such as "Giant Steps," "Countdown," and a heavily
altered version of "How High the Moon" entitled "Satellite")
with indescribably dense and difficult chord sequences; on
the other, he wrote a second group of works that made use
of ostinatos or rhythmic patterns repeated throughout (for
example, "Syeeda's Song Flute," "Naima" and "Like Sonny").
(Toward the end of this period, Coltrane also made a recording with Ornette Coleman's principal associate, trumpeter
Don Cherry, but this venture had no lasting consequences
and therefore need not detain us further.) [10]
　　Seen in its totality, moreover, Coltrane's work during this
transitional year and one-half suggests that he was attempting nothing less than the resuscitation, or even reinvention,
of bebop by transforming its harmonic foundation on the
basis of the chord sequence he first unveiled in "Giant Steps."
Surely that is the meaning of the fact that during this brief
interval he chose to record re-harmonized versions of such

---

* Thanks to the release on compact disk by Rhino Records of John Coltrane, *The Heavyweight Champion: The Complete Atlantic Recordings* (Rhino Atlantic Jazz Gallery R2 71984), a model of how a project
of this type should be conceived and executed.

bebop anthems as Tadd Dameron's "Hot House" (itself derived from "What Is This Thing Called Love?") as "Fifth House," Dizzy Gillespie's "Night in Tunisia" as "Liberia," Charlie Parker's "Confirmation" as "26-2" and "How High the Moon" as "Satellite" (note the pun in the title).[11] Neither before nor after would Coltrane ever show as much interest in performing compositions so thoroughly associated with bebop's early years. But he did not do things on a whim or by happenstance; as methodical as he was, there had to have been a reason behind his decision to perform these particular selections at this particular time. Given their association with the first generation of bebop revolutionaries, the most plausible interpretation is that he was making one final effort at reinvigorating a musical style that, with the passage of time, had become uninspiring, predictable, banal, and clichéd. That he abandoned the effort shortly thereafter suggests that not even his ever-fertile imagination was equal to such a Herculean task. Bebop, in short, had been squeezed dry; there was no further juice to be obtained from this particular fruit.

Although the "Giant Steps" chord progression and repeated ostinatos were, in the final analysis, a pair of blind alleys, even after formation of his quartet Coltrane for a time continued working with them: the "Giant Steps" chords underlie such 1960 compositions as "Central Park West," "Satellite," and "26-2," as well as his reading of "But Not for Me"; Coltrane's versions of "Summertime" and "Body and Soul," like his own compositions "Equinox," "Mr. Day," and "Mr. Knight," reflect a persistent preoccupation with ostinato figures. By the next year, though, as I discussed in the last chapter, he had for the most part turned from complex structures of this sort toward less-intricate but more-hospitable modal or scalar frameworks ("My Favorite Things," "Impressions"), although even with some of these, Coltrane initially chose to improvise over a continuous rhythmic pattern in the background (as he did on the first recording of "My Favorite Things").[12]

One indication of how overjoyed Coltrane must have been with his new group is the fact that in three sessions between October 21 and October 26 of 1960, he, Tyner, Jones, and bassist Steve Davis put on record no fewer than nineteen complete selections—a prodigious output, especially in light of the classic status almost all of these performances quickly attained. Yet as perceptible as were the changes in the work of John Coltrane and McCoy Tyner following the arrival of Elvin Jones, they were no more striking than the enormous leaps made by Jones himself in this fresh and clearly felicitous setting. In his pre-Coltrane recordings, one can, with the advantages that retrospection confers, catch glimpses in embryo of what was to burst forth so impressively later in the 1960s. But these were, I reiterate, glimpses only: the full breathtaking power of Jones's developed style did not unfold completely until the drummer had spent several months playing in the company of Coltrane and McCoy Tyner.

Jones himself is not particularly enlightening on this subject, however, and in the interview in the next chapter, he tends to deny that any marked change in his playing resulted from his the time he spent working with Coltrane:

> [A]s far as I am concerned, I've always had a definite feeling about the way that drums should sound with different instruments, depending on their instrumentation. And I've always had that idea in my mind as to the way I would play if given the opportunity, and so on.

Be that as it may, I am more inclined to accept the observations of John Coltrane, who, with his usual diplomatic and compassionate way of putting things, had this to say regarding Jones's artistic growth after the drummer had joined the Coltrane group:

> He was there, Elvin was there for a couple of years—
> although Elvin was ready from the first time I heard him,
> you know, I could hear the genius there—but he had to
> start playing steadily, steadily, every night. . . .[13]

That genius, as I have already asserted, also required a
favorable musical environment—one that would nurture it,
stimulate it, and permit it to reach its zenith. Fortunately
for all concerned, John Coltrane was the sort of person who
knew how to aid his collaborators in developing their artistic
resources, how to build their self-confidence so they could
realize their capabilities to the fullest. He was not so insecure
or obsessed with his own importance, in other words, that
he felt it necessary to keep a tight rein on his accompanists
for fear of being eclipsed or overpowered in his own group.
It was during this same period, during the early 1960s, that
McCoy Tyner testified with palpable enthusiasm about his
pride in being

> part of an organization where each one is dedicated to
> the whole. And I really enjoy it.
> . . . There are no barriers in our rhythm section. Ev-
> eryone plays his personal concept, and nobody tells any-
> one else what to do. It is surprisingly spontaneous, and
> there's a lot of give and take, for we all listen carefully
> to one another. From playing together, you get to know
> one another so well musically that you can anticipate.
> We have an over-all [sic] different approach, and that is
> responsible for our original style. As compared with a lot
> of other groups, we feel differently about music. With
> us, whatever comes out—that's *it,* at that moment. We
> definitely believe in the value of the spontaneous.[14]

The degree of spontaneity that Tyner describes was possible only because of the phenomenal collective empathy that

existed within the group. Of course, every jazz ensemble that lasts any time at all generates a certain amount of rapport. But it is clear both from what Tyner says and the ardent tone in which he says it that the Coltrane quartet, by virtue of the mutual esteem and shared dedication that united its members, was different in kind rather than degree from other small jazz groups. The type and the amount of interaction fostered by Coltrane paid off magnificently both for the group as a whole and for each individual musician. Exactly how much of each artist's development came as a response to the contributions of the others is a mystery we probably never will be able to unravel. All the same, the close-knit, symbiotic relationship among the performers may well be a major reason why the music created by the Coltrane quartet during the years it remained together, from 1960 to 1966, is unsurpassed by anything in the entire tradition of jazz improvisation up to that time or since.[15]

3. Jazz rhythmic concepts to 1960

Thus far, I have been working from the general to the particular. I began by discussing the nature of the musical interactions that are a prerequisite for creating jazz of outstanding quality, then attempted to indicate in a broad way how we can witness those interactions in the art of the John Coltrane groups that included Elvin Jones and McCoy Tyner. Continuing along the same line, I want to set the stage for an examination of some of the innovative rhythmic devices that Jones, in his role of accompanist, introduced to such striking effect in the Coltrane quartet.

Note that I emphasize Jones's work as an accompanist, rather than as a soloist, despite the fact the great majority of the technical analyses of jazz drumming to date deal with it as a solo art. It is—or at any rate, should be—self-evident that solo performance cannot be the primary raison d'être for the inclusion of the drums in a jazz ensemble. A drummer whose solo playing is consistently outstanding but who is unwilling or unable to provide the proper rhythmic foundation for the group as a whole has the same useful-ness in a jazz context as a fifth wheel. *A fortiori* in the case of Elvin Jones, whose renown—notwithstanding the thun-derous ferocity and unsurpassed technique that go into his solos—deservedly rests on the sensitivity that he displays as an accompanist.[16]

To appreciate Elvin Jones's achievements, however, we need to put them in their proper historical perspective as part of the development of jazz rhythmic concepts. Here, a word of clarification is in order. In describing events in the world of jazz during the 1960s as a musical revolution, I in no way wish to imply that this, or *any*, upheaval has ever succeeded in sweeping everything from its path and beginning entirely afresh. On the contrary, the outcome of a revolution, whether in the political, aesthetic, or any other sphere, is a dialectical synthesis of both new and traditional elements. Granted, a revolution does introduce radically new ideas, procedures, and methods, and these comprise its discontinuous aspects—they are what make a revolution revolutionary. But at the same time, certain traditional elements survive by being reworked, reshaped, placed in new relationships with respect to each other, and so on. Preservation of these aspects of tradition ensures that hard-won human wisdom is not lost; that is to say, it allows the retention of those lessons distilled from previous expe-rience that promise to be useful in the post-revolutionary situation. In summary, then, a successful revolution will always contain both features that are wholly new as well as those carried over from the past (even if the traditional character of the latter is not immediately recognized as such). And so it is, as we will see presently, with the revolu-tionary innovations brought forward by the John Coltrane quartet: motifs, devices, and practices that are traditional in

Afro-American music—some of which, in fact, appear to extend as far back into black history as the African past—appear side-by-side with radically new approaches to jazz improvisation.

There is striking agreement among virtually all researchers that one of the leading attributes of every form of African-American music is its polyrhythmic character (provided we understand the word *polyrhythmic* in an Afro-American, rather than a purely African, sense).[17] Indeed, it is precisely this character that causes jazz to manifest the property of "swing," of seeming to accelerate rhythmically while the underlying pulse (the "time") in reality remains steady. In his monograph on *Early Jazz*, Gunther Schuller has provided very persuasive examples to illustrate how the small-group New Orleans jazz style can best be understood as a translation (with some marked simplifications) onto Western instruments of the rhythms and/or melodies performed by the members of a representative African musical ensemble (cantor, chorus and handclappers, bell players, drummers).[18]

As jazz styles evolved and the instrumental technique of jazz musicians—many of whom initially pursued music only as an avocation, until they discovered that it was possible to make it a vocation—improved correspondingly, the irregular shifting of rhythmic accents that is the basis of swing was retained, but its mode of expression was altered—a clear-cut instance of the way in which an aesthetic revolution combines new practices with traditional older ones. The simultaneous cross-rhythmic improvisation by several musicians that was feasible within the setting of a New Orleans–style quartet, quintet, or sextet was obviously beyond the bounds of possibility once jazz ensembles enlarged—as they were essentially forced to do in order to comply with the demands of a dance-oriented public—beginning in the late 1920s and continuing throughout the "big band" or "swing" era of the 1930s. To meet the new challenge, jazz musicians invented the "riff"—or, to be more exact, greatly enlarged its usage and significance.

Schuller defines the riff as "a relatively short [melodic] phrase that is repeated over a changing chord pattern, originally as a background device. . . ."[19] With the division of musical labor resulting from the size of the typical swing band—from ten to fifteen instruments, and in some cases more—it became possible to create tension during the course of an improvisation by having the brass section (trumpets, trombones) or the reed section (saxophones, clarinets) inject a phrase behind the soloist; a variation on the practice was to have both sections play the riff in call-and-response fashion. (The call-and-response phenomenon is, of course, another central and durable facet of African and Afro-American music.) Such riffs, examples of which I will supply shortly, were brief, highly syncopated motifs whose cross-rhythmic accents moved around in an unpredictable (but characteristically African or Afro-American) manner, some accents falling on the beats and some between them. By themselves, these often impromptu melodic fragments, with their shifting distribution of accents, could well have caused dancers and musicians to become disoriented, were it not for the fact that, underneath the riffing brass and reed sections, the swing "rhythm section"—piano, bass, drums and, frequently, guitar—maintained continuity. The rhythm section geared its playing to what musicologist André Hodeir has called "the notion of four equal beats"[20]—that is, a series of four relatively unaccented quarter notes in each measure, as shown in Example 1. The opening (on the odd beat) and closing (on the even beat) of the drummer's hi-hat cymbals—which make a softly sizzling *tzsss* sound when struck slightly parted, and a relatively high pitched and moderately penetrating *tchik* sound when closed with the foot pedal—served to establish a subtle demarcation between the odd and even beats, while the "comping" (accompaniment) of the pianist added a final

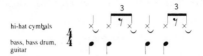

Example 1: Swing rhythm pattern (rhythmic values only)

Key: ✗ = hi-hat struck closed
     ⌣ = hi-hat struck open

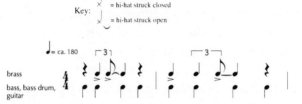

Example 2-a: Brass riff from *One O'Clock Jump* (rhythmic values only)

Example 2-b: Reed riff from *One O'Clock Jump* (rhythmic values only)

Example 2-c: Brass riff from *One O'Clock Jump* (rhythmic values only)

Example 2-d: Reed riff from *One O'Clock Jump* (rhythmic values only)

Example 3: Bebop rhythm pattern (rhythmic values only)

touch of cross-rhythmic orchestral complexity. Together, the combination of a fluid rhythm section supporting aggressively riffing brass and/or reed sections furnished dancers with a beat that was constant without being monotonous and simultaneously created a rhythmic-harmonic backdrop that challenged without overwhelming the ingenuity of an improvising soloist.

To conclude the discussion of the handling of cross-accentuated rhythmic patterns by the large swing orchestras, in Example 2 I supply four such two-measure patterns, whose rhythmic (but not melodic or harmonic) values I have transcribed from an archetypical source, the initial Count Basie recording of "One O'Clock Jump" (each riff is repeated six times through an entire 12-measure blues chorus). To grasp the full impact of these figures, the reader must not only strive to keep in mind the steady pulse of "four equal beats" from the rhythm section and the supplementary chords played by Basie's piano, but must also try to imagine the unfolding of an instrumental solo against this background.[21]

The bebop revolution demolished the type of cross-rhythmic accentuation perfected during the swing years in the same way that swing had earlier undermined the rhythmic ideas of the first generation of New Orleans musicians. Hodeir, in comparing the bebop rhythmic framework with that of swing, finds in the former a "decomposition of the beat, disintegration of the rhythm section, and non-continuity" as the principal new elements.[22] In actuality, these are three aspects of the same phenomenon. By 1940, when the bebop revolution was getting under way, the rhythmic sensibilities of jazz players and listeners were both already so sophisticated that to have three different instruments—bass drum, bass and guitar—all relentlessly underlining the same quarter-note pulse was coming to seem rather pointless, if not downright redundant. As the bebop revolution would shortly demonstrate, the bass alone was able to serve this purpose, allowing the guitar to be dropped from the bop ensemble, thereby beginning the "disintegration" of the rhythm section.

Changes in how drummers kept time accelerated the process. Instead of enunciating the beat primarily with the snare drum, bass drum, and hi-hat cymbals, as swing drummers had, bebop percussionists preferred the lighter, shimmering sound of the "ride" cymbal (a medium or medium-heavy cymbal, usually from seventeen to twenty-two inches in diameter).[23] Having reassigned the hi-hat to marking the second and fourth beats—a continuation of the African/ Afro-American rebellion against the tyranny of the European emphasis on the odd beats—the bebop drummer then employed a triplet eighth-note-based ride-cymbal pattern as a more subtle means of indicating accents within the basic 4/4 pulse "walked" by the bass player. In its most skeletal form, the bop rhythmic framework is that shown in Example 3 (although infinite variations on this rudimentary pattern are, of course, possible in practice).

Meanwhile, what of the piano? The pianist, like the drummer, was freed by the bebop revolution from a strictly time-keeping role. Accordingly, both could take advantage of their newly won liberation to inject accents wherever they felt them appropriate. Given that the bass was already providing a 4/4 pulse, further underscored by the closing of the drummer's hi-hat cymbals on the even beats, it was only natural that most such accents would fall between beats.[24] From the standpoint of swing, therefore, the four-to-the-measure beat had, to use Hodeir's terminology, been "decomposed" by bebop; the new rhythmic conventions that replaced it were ones marked by much greater unpredictability, that is, "discontinuity."

Between the inauguration of the bebop concept of playing "time" in the 1940s and the formation of the John Coltrane quartet in 1960, no fundamental changes occurred. During the height of the funk-soul movement late in the 1950s, some drummers, led by Art Blakey, had begun the practice of underlining the "backbeats" (second and fourth beats) very heavily, either with a snare-drum accent (or rim shot) or else, in the case of Blakey, with a deafening *choonk!* expelled from the hi-hat cymbals by playing them "stomp" style (raising the entire left leg in the air, then slamming the foot down on the hi-hat pedal). In reaction against this conversion of the backbeat into a new pseudo-downbeat, other drummers—principally Roy Haynes, followed by Philly Joe Jones and his successor in a series of Miles Davis ensembles, Jimmy Cobb—started to inflect the ride-cymbal rhythm with a very light emphasis both on the odd beats and a triplet eighth-note before them:

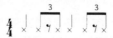

Aside from these relatively minor modifications, and some ventures into 3/4, 5/4 and other previously unexplored time signatures, however, the elementary conventions for projecting a jazz beat remained essentially unchanged from what they had become during the first half of the 1940s.

If we may telescope several generations of the history of jazz into a very few sentences, then, it is a fair statement that between the turn of the century and the culmination of the hard bop-funky-soul rebellion against the ennui of the cool style early in the 1960s, jazz musicians attempted to recapture the rhythmic complexity of African polyrhythms by two interrelated means. First, the process that Schuller denotes as the "democratization of the pulse" heightened the rhythmic stress on the even beats while simultaneously lowering that on the odd ones, thus smoothing out a 4/4 measure into Hodeir's "four even beats." Second, what Hodeir refers to as the "decomposition of the beat" allowed the interpolation of sequences of cross-rhythmic drum (and also piano) accents whose effect was to shift the rhythmic emphasis in an unpredictable manner. As I will argue immediately below, these tendencies reached their highest point of development in the jazz revolution chiefly associated with the music of the John Coltrane quartet. To establish this contention on a solid base of musical evidence, I devote the remaining pages of this chapter to a relatively detailed technical analysis of the style of Elvin Jones and its function within the context of the Coltrane group.

B. Rhythmic displacement and the artistry of Elvin Jones

In the course of achieving its apex of rhythmic sophistication and complexity, the John Coltrane quartet synthesized the leading facets of all previous epochs in the history of jazz—the collective improvisation practiced during the New Orleans period (recall the remarks of McCoy Tyner several pages earlier on this score), the riff figures of the large swing orchestras of the 1930s, the startling and dramatic rhythmic punctuations of bebop—into a single musical fabric (again illustrating that beside annihilating tradition, revolutions also recast and reorder its most valuable elements in ways that revitalize the tradition itself). But after reaching this point, it was not possible, within the confines of existing jazz conventions, to move further in the direction of the kind of polyrhythmic textures that characterize African music. Inasmuch as I shall have more to say on this topic momentarily, I will defer further discussion of it for now.

In preceding chapters I have sought to demonstrate the pivotal position of John Coltrane in bringing to fruition during the 1960s a set of innovations that, taken as a whole, revolutionized jazz; now it is time to call attention to the contributions of Elvin Jones in developing those innovations. Before launching into an examination of his work, however, both accuracy and fairness require that we acknowledge the immense importance of pianist McCoy Tyner in helping devise and consolidate the approach taken by the Coltrane group. At each turning point in the evolution of jazz, the responsibilities of the drummer have become more broadly defined, extensive in scope, and artistically demanding. The earliest jazz drummers were only a comparatively short distance removed from the performing style of the marching bands; the drummers of the swing years, although still primarily restricted to timekeeping, were capable of far more delicate shadings and nuances than their predecessors; and during the bop period, the drummer's ability to spur on the soloist with an array of left-hand (snare drum) and right-foot (bass drum) accents assumed increasing significance. It should be apparent that each successive redefinition of the drummer's duties, in a music in which the performers are as interdependent as they are in jazz, inevitably brought about concomitant changes in the roles of the other members of the "rhythm section." When, for example, bebop drummers stopped playing each quarter note on the bass drum, and when the guitar was dropped from the streamlined bebop ensemble, of necessity the relative responsibility of the bass player for maintaining an unwavering yet flexible 4/4 beat became greater.

Similarly, the fact that Elvin Jones, while in the Coltrane quartet, was able to discharge a continuous stream of figures and kaleidoscopically shifting pattern of accents at his own discretion is to some extent attributable to McCoy Tyner's assumption of a larger portion of the timekeeping than had been the lot of the jazz pianist in the immediate past. In retrospect, it is easy enough to see that if the post-bebop drummer was to devise a contrapuntal, cross-rhythmic accompaniment for the soloist, and if the pulse was to remain constant, some other member (or members) of the group might have to take over certain of the drummer's obligation to maintain the beat. But inventions are always obvious once someone else has already perfected them. The point is that McCoy Tyner's rhythmic sense as an accompanist and wide-ranging harmonic imagination established a musical framework for

Coltrane's improvisations that aided Elvin Jones in making the advances in jazz drumming that we credit to his name. Carrying the same line of reasoning one step further, it is at least open to question whether even John Coltrane could have driven his art to quite the commanding heights he attained without the inspiring rhythmic-harmonic foundation provided by the superbly attuned team of McCoy Tyner and Elvin Jones. All of which reaffirms still another time how mistaken it is, particularly with respect to jazz, to insist on abstracting the accomplishments of an artist from their social and aesthetic context and treating them as if they were solely the product of the genius of a single isolated and supposedly self-created individual.

Even though it has become commonplace to see the style of drumming pioneered by Elvin Jones described as "polyrhythmic"—an error of which I have probably been as guilty as anyone—the truth is that, as I remarked earlier, the kind of polyrhythmic drumming characteristic of African music simply does not exist in jazz.[25] The approach of which Jones is a proven master—one that very likely comes as close to African polyrhythmic concepts as is possible within a more-or-less conventional jazz setting—we can with greater accuracy refer to as that of *rhythmic displacement*. Regardless of whether Jones is the most impressive drummer in jazz from a purely technical standpoint or whether his solos are always the most compelling the music offers, in his ability to generate musical tension and interest through a never-ending manipulation of accents, he has no peer. Indeed, given that he has pushed this style of drumming to its furthest limits, I very much doubt that any rival to him in this department will soon—or maybe ever—be forthcoming.

Although neither of them use the phrase per se, both Hodeir and Schuller—undeniably among the foremost musicological students of jazz—agree that rhythmic displacement is essential to swing, and that the latter is, in turn, an integral aspect of Afro-American jazz.[26] Bebop drummers, as I noted above, introduced such rhythmic displacements by injecting sharp and unexpected accents, usually on the snare drum or the bass drum or some combination of the two. Beginning with this legacy from bebop as his initial point of departure, Jones has gone on to evolve a means of creating an additional dimension in the art of jazz drumming, particularly with respect to rhythmic displacement. Put in simplest terms, Jones's style involves the superimposition of one or more additional meters, usually involving some threefold division of the beat (into either quarter-note, eighth-note, or sixteenth-note triplets) alongside of the basic pulse. In and of itself, this feat would not be all that noteworthy. What gives it such exceptional effectiveness in Jones's hands is his ability to utilize this second meter to deploy a series of accents that generate musical tension by suggesting that the beat has been dislodged from its true position.

Inasmuch as it is extremely difficult to describe what Jones accomplishes in words alone, I will here have recourse to some musical examples. The bebop ride-cymbal rhythm I discussed earlier is, as Example 3 illustrates, a figure based on triplet eighth-notes.[27] In medium-tempo pieces, this fact encourages the drummer to play triplet eighth-note "fills" (probably so called because they fill in the empty spaces, or rests) on the snare drum and/or tom-toms, a rhythmic device that has been standard practice since the onset of the bebop revolution. If the drummer gives the triplet falling just before the beat a heavier accent than its predecessor, as shown in Example 4-a, the result is a certain amount of rhythmic displacement. What Jones often does instead of playing the figure as it appears in Example 4-a, however, is to move the two left-hand triplets forward by an eighth-note triplet, and then intensify the before-the-beat accent by delivering it not with the snare drum, but with either the bass drum (as in Example 4-b) or the hi-hat cymbals (Example 4-c).

Each of these latter figures, which Jones often employs in alternation, is more effective than the conventional triplet fill that by 1960 had become something of a cliché. The bass drum, for instance, is not merely capable of producing one of the loudest sounds of any component of the drummer's kit, but, as a vestige of jazz's marching-band origins, frequently announces the "strong" first beat in a measure; in other words, a forceful stroke on the bass drum often serves to help listeners (and even some musicians!) find their place in the music. By thus inserting it *before* the beat, as in Example 4-b, Jones takes advantage both of the instrument's volume and the listener's expectation of hearing the bass drum on the strong beat to create maximum rhythm dislocation. Analogously, one can bring together the hi-hat cymbals in such a way that the sound they make is almost indistinguishable from that of a light snare-drum tap. In closing the hi-hat cymbals an eighth-note triplet prior to

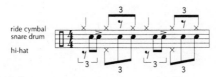

Example 4-a: Conventional eighth-note triplet "fills"

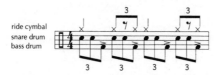

Example 4-b: Triplets with bass drum "displacement"

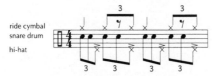

Example 4-c: Triplets with hi-hat "displacement"

the beat (Example 4-c), Jones first of all creates a continuous barrage of triplets with the accent off the beat, and further defies the listener's expectation by omitting the hi-hat where it is usually played, as another musical landmark, on beats two and four. Granted, other drummers—Max Roach, Roy Haynes—have used the patterns diagrammed in Examples 4-b and 4-c before Jones, but only in an isolated, episodic manner; whereas Jones, by extending these figures over several beats (sometimes over several *measures*), employs them to generate the feeling of two side-by-side pulses pulling away from each other. Finally, if he has continued the figure for some time, Jones will many times resolve the accrued tension by an emphatic and unmistakable reassertion of the actual beat, as in Example 5, where a snare-drum rim shot combines with a cymbal crash on the first beat of the first measure of a new chorus.

Examples 5 and 6 suggest how Jones puts into effect the ideas schematically depicted in Example 4. Example 5 is

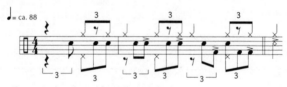

Example 5: *Blues to Bechet,* close of first Coltrane solo chorus

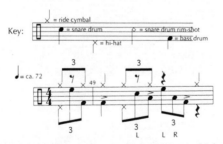

Example 6: *Blues to Elvin,* measure 49 of second Coltrane solo chorus

from the concluding measures of the first chorus of John Coltrane's solo on "Blues to Bechet," [28] a 12-measure composition dedicated to the first major soprano-saxophone soloist in jazz, Sidney Bechet. Notice that the figure starts with a snare-drum anticipation of the final beat in measure 11. Jones not infrequently plays a snare-drum accent in front of the hi-hat's closing on the second and fourth beats. Doing so has a double effect: first, it produces a kind of symmetry, or "democratization," between even and odd beats, as the drummer conventionally plays a similar pair of triplets on the ride cymbal on every odd beat (see Example 3, above); second, it attracts attention away from the imminent closing of the hi-hat cymbals, an effect that drummers during the funk-soul vogue of late 1950s so exaggerated that it became almost as trite as a bass-drum stroke on the first beat of every measure. Following this anticipation of the beat, Jones continues for three beats with the conventional triplet fill, then, just before the fourth beat of measure 12, he switches to the bass-drum-displacement variant of this figure, following that with a *double* bass-drum stroke on the weakest portions of the weakest beat, causing a momentary near-total rhythmic disorientation. Finally, Jones rescues the listener from this disorientation by announcing the start of the next solo chorus with a characteristically penetrating rim shot and cymbal crash in unison.

Another selection from the same recording—entitled, appropriately enough, "Blues to Elvin"—furnishes a fine demonstration of how Jones will use a variety of methods to suggest competing ideas of where the beat lies. The instance transcribed in Example 6 occurs in the first measure of the fourth (12-measure) chorus of Coltrane's second solo (a piano improvisation by McCoy Tyner separates the two saxophone solos). Jones starts the measure with a solid bass-drum-and-cymbal accent on the first beat, thus completing a tom-tom fill that originated in the previous measure. On the next beat, however, he begins another figure with his hi-hat cymbals, snare drum, bass drum, and tom-toms, the effect of which is to promote rhythmic movement away from the beat in several ways: (1) the six-note figure never reaches a full climax. The logical point of stasis would be on the fourth beat, where Jones does indeed produce a medium-loud cymbal crash; but the strongest accent, that of the last stroke of the bass drum, occurs just an eighth-note triplet before the fourth beat, leaving the resolution of the figure hanging in the air ambiguously. The net result is that no sooner is the measure's first and strongest beat accented than Jones pulls the rhythmic center of gravity away from it and towards *an anticipation* of the measure's weakest beat—a twofold displacement of emphasis. (2) The tuning of Jones's drums is such that it is difficult to distinguish among them—I would blush to admit how much time it took me to transcribe this "simple" phrase[29]—perhaps in order to shroud the exact nature of what is taking place at any given instant in even greater mystery. The listener can thus perfectly well *feel* the rhythmic activity occurring in opposition to the beat, but Jones does not project these subliminal cross- and counter-rhythms so forcefully that they overwhelm the beat and subvert the actual pulse of the piece entirely.*

Of course, as I have tried to make clear throughout this

---

* Jones's own comments in the interview in chapter 11 indicate that his tendency to play such fills at a volume where they can be sensed but not distinctly heard is a conscious one: "My brother Hank [a noted jazz pianist] told me to make my sound more definite, make it louder. You see, he made a few remarks about what I was doing in my left hand and wanted to know what it was that I was playing before, so I just played a little louder and made it come out more. That's an over-all feeling that I like to have when I am playing, to make the rhythmic sound blend with the harmonic."

section, it was not just Jones alone who was responsible for the style of rhythmic displacement in which the Coltrane quartet specialized. Rather, the entire ensemble was involved in this development. There is a most instructive case in point in the group's performance of "Equinox," from the album, *Coltrane's Sound*.[30] As Example 7 reveals, this composition is elaborated around a two-measure syncopated ground phrase,

that is reiterated by the piano and bass. The strong accent on the fourth beat of the first measure of the phrase gives the unwary listener the impression that it marks the downbeat of measure two, which arouses an expectation that the next "down beat" will occur after four more beats have elapsed. It

Example 7: *Equinox* rhythmic framework (rhythmic values only for piano and bass)

Example 8: Three variants of standard jazz 3/4 rhythm

just so happens, however, that four more beats takes us to the unaccented fourth beat of the phrase's second measure. The *real* downbeat—much to the consternation of the by-now thoroughly confused listener, unless he or she has been counting the time—is played one beat later, momentarily drawing all and sundry back into the actual rhythmic orbit. This pattern of throwing the listener on and off of the beat is maintained through eight measures (four repetitions), followed by two measures of standard jazz 4/4 time before the figure returns again for the remaining two measures of the chorus.

One of Elvin Jones's inspired contributions to this mystifying process of alternately gaining and losing one's place in the rhythm of "Equinox" is his use of the ride cymbal to imply a meter of 3/4 against what is formally a 4/4 time signature. Note from Example 8 that in 3/4 time the accepted jazz ride cymbal rhythm is

which (referring once more to Example 7) is exactly what Jones plays during most of the recurrences of the basic two-measure ground phrase of Equinox. That is, after three beats have elapsed in measure one, Jones treats the heavy accent on the fourth beat as though it were the downbeat for a second measure of 3/4, as I have indicated by the dotted lines and primed measure numbers (2' and 3') in Example 7. And in reality, this is a perfectly logical—if boldly unorthodox—approach. When jazz musicians play in 3/4, they normally do not accent just the first beat alone—that would be very un-African and exceedingly corny by jazz standards—but instead counterpose other, competing accents to keep the rhythm flowing and lively. Often they will emphasize the triplet just prior to the third beat (as in the third variant of

Example 8), thereby producing what in essence is a juxtaposition of two beats against three:

But precisely this same pattern of accentuation—on the
first quarter note, on the triplet before the third quarter note,
and on the fourth quarter note—occurs in the first measure
of "Equinox," hence there is unassailable musical thought
behind Jones's decision to regard the fourth beat of its first
measure as equivalent to the first beat in a second measure
of 3/4 time. In so doing, he divides the eight quarter notes
of this two-measure figure either into two measures of 3/4
and one of 2/4, or a measure of 3/4 followed by one of 5/4,
depending on how one chooses to interpret it.

Although the foregoing paragraph gives us technical
comprehension of what Jones is doing with his ride cymbal, it does not yet supply a full explanation of his musical reasoning. For that, we must refer back to the concept
of rhythmic displacement. Jones's regrouping of the eight
quarter notes in the two-measure phrase from "Equinox"
is a kind of textbook example of rhythmic displacement; it
induces a definite sensation of rhythmic motion across the
4/4 measure line in a way that the usual 4/4 ride cymbal beat
could never match. Hence besides being more appropriate to
the rhythmic character of the piece than the conventional
ride-cymbal pattern, the one Jones substitutes for it implies,
as is his wont, the presence of a second and opposing meter running in tandem with the formal 4/4 time signature
of "Equinox." Here once more we observe his gravitation
toward an African polymetric mode of expression, to the

extent that a jazz context will permit it.

In a thoroughly analogous fashion, Jones will introduce the 4/4 ride-cymbal pattern ·

into a composition written in 3/4 time, again as a means of establishing a rhythmic momentum that flows across the measure line and thus unobtrusively undermines the European hierarchy of "strong" and "weak" beats (as well as the somewhat weaker tendency—found in the waltz and the march—to place accents on rather than off of the beat). Presumably, the heavy "backbeat" accents on the second and fourth beats during the heyday of hard bop-funky-soul styles had a similar goal—but, lacking the subtlety of Jones's multi-faceted approach, they soon became a vivid instance of the cure being nearly as bad as the disease.

Example 9, a transcription of the ride-cymbal pattern Jones employs intermittently on John Coltrane's composition "Spiritual,"[31] nicely illustrates how Jones will depart from the orthodox jazz 3/4 cymbal beat if he feels the situation calls for it. When jazz drummers initially began to play in 3/4 late in the 1950s, as Example 8 indicates, that time signature was still sufficiently unfamiliar so that their tendency was to stress the downbeat of each measure; subsequently, the reaction against an overemphasis on the first beat led to placing a strong accent on the second as well. Although this did to some extent weaken the tyranny of the downbeat, jazz in 3/4 time, in comparison to jazz in 4/4 time, displayed a certain lack of suppleness and swing. The cymbal-ride figure in Example 9 represents an attempt by Jones to replace rhythmic rigidity with flexibility. Not only does he play a 4/4 cymbal rhythm that avoids the monotony of underlining every third beat, but he also closes the hi-hat cymbals on the triplet before the second beat of the odd measures—the basic unit here being, like that of "Equinox" and a number of other Coltrane compositions, a two-measure ground phrase—to good effect. The 4/4 cymbal ride against the 3/4 meter, as I have said, blurs the measure line and reduces the weight assigned to the downbeat of the first measure of the two-measure figure. In other words, rather than countering the traditional European stress on the measure's first beat with an almost equally predictable and unimaginative accent on its second, Jones instead brings his hi-hat into play to draw attention away from the former without allowing it to become fixated on the latter. He therefore escapes from the despotism of *one* by merely hinting at— rather than hammering on—*two*, and in this way (as was also the case in Example 6, above), ensures that the pulse is not chained obtrusively to either. Even this technique, moreover, is employed only in alternate measures—the odd measures are, by European canons, the stronger, which is why it is these whose downbeat Jones is more determined to undermine—so that the device does not become stale from overuse.

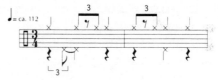

Example 9: Elvin Jones cymbal pattern on *Spiritual*

From "Spiritual" in 3/4 it is a natural step to investigate some of Jones's other performances in this time signature. One of his best-known—and one that puzzled me the most intensely when I originally encountered it at the start of the 1960s—is that on John Coltrane's first recorded version of "My Favorite Things."[32] Much as he did on "Equinox," Jones here depends to a great extent on the support he receives from McCoy Tyner and Steve Davis, especially the former. Example 10-a shows the basic two-measure piano ground phrase, or "vamp," over which the improvisations in "My Favorite Things" occur. The first measure, with accents on the downbeat and on the triplet ahead of the third beat, appears to contain little out of the ordinary. In the second measure, in contrast, the first beat receives scarcely any rhythmic recognition—Tyner occasionally marks it with a chord played *piano*—and instead there is a strong accent on the triplet before the second beat. Just as in "Equinox," where the rhythmic stress started on a "strong" beat, moved to an off-beat, and then to a "weak" beat, the piano vamp in "My Favorite Things" works first by both underscoring the beat then tugging the listener away from it.

From this performance, incidentally, we also can grasp why McCoy Tyner's presence in the Coltrane group was so essential. For all intents and purposes, Tyner—in addition to anchoring the rhythm and leaving Jones free to play cross-rhythms—also functions as would a reed or brass section in a large swing orchestra. That is to say, the rhythmic figures he executes throughout the piece are in fact updated and reinvigorated transformations of swing riffs. The extraordinary achievement of the Coltrane group—and I once more underscore its collective nature—was to recall the riff from its post-swing exile and combine it with the methods for introducing rhythmic discontinuity stemming from the bebop revolution, in the process raising each to a qualitatively higher aesthetic level. This radical recombination of traditional elements, this devising of new applications for well-worn procedures—features that, as I have already noted more than once in this essay, one can discern in every revolution—made possible an astounding feat: on the one hand, it gave Elvin Jones the latitude he needed to weave a web of rhythmic displacements that was more systematic, continuous, and profound than anything bebop permitted; on the other, it preserved the cohesion that kept the Coltrane quartet from being torn apart by the centrifugal force of antagonistic rhythms and meters. In this way, John Coltrane and his peerless associates devised a way of integrating and even enhancing the outstanding rhythmic characteristics of both swing (the riff) and bop (discontinuity)—characteristics that previously had been thought to be irreconcilably opposed—in a fresh and more advanced dialectical synthesis.

Turning now to the succession of rhythmic figures contained in Examples 10-a through 10-g, we can study not

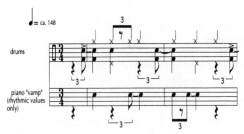

Example 10-a: First variant used on "vamp" of *My Favorite Things*

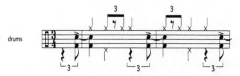

Example 10-b: Second variant on *My Favorite Things* (piano rhythm remains unchanged)

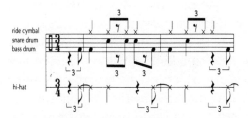

Example 10-c: First rhythm played behind McCoy Tyner's solo on *My Favorite Things*

Example 10-d: Second rhythm played behind McCoy Tyner's solo on *My Favorite Things*

only the rhythmic displacements elaborated by Elvin Jones, but also the manner in which he alters them according to the character of the improvisation he is accompanying (the rhythmic values of the piano vamp, aside from some occasional and very minor variations, remain essentially unchanged throughout). Due to the unsettling effect of the syncopated anticipation played by the piano in the second measure of this two-measure figure—an anticipation that induces precisely the kind of rhythmic disorientation as the piano-and-bass accent on the fourth beat of measure one in "Equinox" (Example 7)—this is a far cry from the run-of-the-mill 3/4 jazz performance; nonetheless, the rhythms Jones plays prior to the solos are in most respects conventional. The upper line in Example 10-a, for instance, closely resembles the second variant in Example 8 in making use of a double bass-drum stroke to announce the downbeat of each measure, a snare-drum tap on the second beat of the first measure, and so on. Example 10-b represents only a slight departure from Example 10-a: Jones drops the snare-drum accent on the second beat from measure one, and he switches over to the 4/4 ride-cymbal pattern.

Rhythmic dislocation takes on a more striking character once McCoy Tyner begins his solo. In Example 10-c, Jones still calls upon the bass drum at the start of each measure (compare this with the second and third variants in Example 8), but now he also uses the hi-hat cymbals as well to lead into the measure, a slight reduction of the rhythmic weight he gives the downbeat. (Note that juxtaposing the hi-hat pattern with the ride-cymbal figure yields a two-against-three rhythmic superimposition.) Jones breaks off this unusual hi-hat pattern as the solo progresses, however, and instead incorporates in measure two some of the snare-drum-triplet figures for which he is justly renowned (Example 10-d). Still, all things considered, Tyner's solo, notwithstanding its melodic charm and lyricism, is fairly restrained in comparison with his work of one or two years later, and Jones holds himself substantially in check during this portion of the piece.

An unmistakable change in Jones's playing, in terms of both content and intensity, emerges practically the moment Coltrane's solo begins (Example 10-e). Tyner greets Coltrane's entrance by stating the vamp with greater force, and Jones's reaction to this heightened emphasis, as we see from Example 10-e, is as radical as it is devastating: to counterbalance Tyner's stronger assertion of the initial downbeat—to "respond," as it were, to the "call" of the piano's chord on the opening beat of the first measure—Jones delays his bass drum accents until the *second* beat of the measure. A more striking instance of rhythmic displacement would be difficult to imagine. During all that has gone before, Jones has used the bass drum to announce the beginning of every measure. But following Coltrane's appearance, this statement of *one*

Example 10-e: First rhythm played behind John Coltrane's solo on *My Favorite Things*

Example 10-f: Second rhythm played behind John Coltrane's solo on *My Favorite Things*

Example 10-g: Third rhythm played behind John Coltrane's solo on *My Favorite Things*

is drastically relocated onto the second beat. It is as if the piece had suddenly developed a pair of downbeats—Tyner's resounding chord on the actual first beat, succeeded by Jones's powerful bass drum on the next—an effect whose capacity for producing rhythmic disorientation in the listener is all the greater for having been held in abeyance until midway through the piece. No wonder, then, that many years after my first encounter with this recording, I can still recall my confused efforts to discern, amidst this welter of accents, the time signature and, even more daunting, the location of the *real* downbeat during Coltrane's improvisations.

Note further in Example 10-e that Jones again draws on the hi-hat cymbals, this time in combination with his snare drum, to point to, and thereby additionally de-emphasize, the true down beat of measure one; as Coltrane's solo develops (Example 10-f), Jones also counterposes his snare drum and hi-hat cymbals on the second beat of the second measure as a "response" to the chordal "call" that Tyner placed a triplet before that beat.

It is solely in the final illustration from "My Favorite Things" (Example 10-g) that we are privileged to witness Jones exhibiting something like the full range of his uncanny skill as an accompanist. By now he has converted the double bass-drum stroke ending on the second beat of the first measure to the rhythmic focus of the entire two-measure phrase, as he leads up to it with a series of accented triplet eighth-notes extending over no fewer than four complete beats. In this way, the rolling triplet-based figure that he spins out on his snare drum builds up a cumulative rhythmic impetus that carries him over the measure line, by which time the rhythmic tension he has prolonged for four beats is virtually crying out for release. As a natural consequence, the resolution that Jones ultimately does provide, using his highly resonant bass drum (not as faithfully recorded as one would like, regrettably), becomes the center of rhythmic attention for the two-measure phrase as a whole. Not only does this augment the ambiguity about which beat, the first or the second, is the genuine down beat in measure one, but the fact that Jones's sequence of snare-drum triplets spans four rather than three beats serves to confer on the figure a sort of 4/4 overtone or flavor. Hence besides dislocating the primary rhythmic interest from the first beat of measure one to the second, Jones also manages to insinuate that this ersatz "downbeat" comes in reference to a time signature (4/4) that is not, in reality, the correct one! In sum, a musically creative tour de force—a superlative display of the genius for rhythmic displacement that the drummer was subsequently to reveal even more dramatically in his later work with this marvelously resourceful ensemble.

Example 11, recorded almost two years after "My Favorite Things" is a four-measure phrase played during the vamp that precedes the Coltrane quartet's rendition of "Out of This World," and it could reasonably be said to represent Jones's art at its pinnacle.[33] At any rate, it is difficult to see how one might improve upon this masterpiece of rhythmic displacement. Jones's figure begins with an anticipation by the bass drum of the initial downbeat; there is a sharp, piercing "Latin" rim shot[34] on the snare drum on the second beat of this measure. An even more dramatic rhythmic dislocation comes at the end of the measure, when Jones hits the small tom-tom with such force that the sound almost overshadows the conventional bass-drum stroke on the first beat of the next measure. Comparison with measure one in Example 10-g shows that the distribution of accents there—just before the down beat, on the beat that follows it, and on the final eighth-note triplet of the measure—is the same as that in the initial measure of Example 11, although Jones plays the accents on different parts of the drum-set in the two cases.

In measure two, a pair of driving bass-drum syncopations in immediate succession continue the off-beat accent pattern

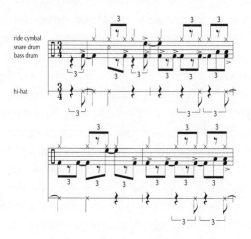

Example 11: Rhythm pattern during introductory "vamp" on *Out of this World*

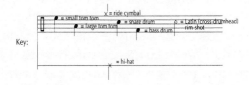

Key:

begun by the tom-tom in the preceding measure, and these in turn lead directly into a triplet-based figure whose notation can only be approximated. Jones accelerates the tempo a shade at this point—intentionally, in my opinion—not only in order to "get it all in," but also probably, and more importantly, to enhance the feeling of rhythmic acceleration and deceleration, tension and release, that is such an integral aspect of his style. Besides raising the emotional temperature, such brief but intense increases in tempo at the close of a measure also help Jones propel his phrases across the measure line, just as accumulated momentum helps catapult a pole-vaulter over the bar.

The third measure in Example 11 offers another instance of Jones's vast musical imagination—a displacement of a previous displacement. In measure three, Jones repeats the heavy tom-tom accent that heralded the downbeat of the second measure, but here he plays it an entire beat earlier— again no doubt throwing the inattentive listener momentarily off balance. The fourth measure in essence reiterates the second.

Out of a total of twelve beats in this four-measure figure, therefore, Jones has struck his drums only on four. In the three weaker measures, he does enunciate the downbeats; in the crucial first measure, however, one can at most infer the downbeat from its absence, as Jones instead puts the rhythmic emphasis both before and after it. The four on-the-beat drum strokes that he plays, one per measure, amount to Jones's sole concession to the agreed-upon time signature and meter. For the remainder of these four measures, he expends all his considerable energy on redirecting attention away from this framework. Each of the other eight beats that he does not state explicitly—beats one and three in the first measure, beats two and three in measures two through four—he in fact undermines by an anticipatory accent on the bass drum, tom-tom, hi-hat cymbals, or some combination of the three. This apportionment of accents is particularly effective at the close of measure four, where a dizzying cluster of notes (between triplet eighth-notes and sixteenth notes in value) surges forward toward a downbeat that never arrives! And as if all of this were not enough, the ride-cymbal pattern that Jones employs in measures two and four implies, as by now the reader may have come to expect, a 4/4 feeling superimposed on a 3/4 meter, further enhancing the impression of perpetual rhythmic motion that is the single most outstanding aspect of Jones's style.

It would seem that within the restrictions of measure line and fixed meter that then defined the outer limits of jazz improvisation, the amount of rhythmic displacement that Jones infuses into this performance, and innumerable others like it, is truly staggering—so much so, in fact, that the possibility of increasing it appears to be minute. Indeed, the degree of complexity of the figure in Example 11 is already so imposing that Jones does not attempt to play it in its entirety behind the soloists, instead dropping measures three and four and contenting himself with a series of variations[35] on the first two measures alone.

From which it is a safe conclusion that in order to move further along the path he was then traversing—one that led towards the re-creation of African-style polyrhythms—Jones would have to have abandoned certain fundamental conventions to which jazz had adhered throughout its history. Most likely, this development would have meant breaking with the principle that jazz improvisation, regardless of how rich in rhythmic displacement, must remain confined within a structure of clearly defined measure lines and time signatures. Even at that, it is likely that a single percussionist would be unable to create music of African-like rhythmic complexity; for that, a jazz ensemble might need additional percussionists, conceivably playing in different and/or variable meters.

There are substantial reasons to believe that just this kind of thoroughly polyrhythmic musical fabric was John Coltrane's ultimate artistic goal.[36] Ever since forming a group of his own in 1960, he appears to have been exploring different ways of attaining it. My hypothesis, as I have stated already, is that his early use of two basses was one manifestation of this desire for a more polyrhythmic foundation; an excerpt from the interview in chapter 13 likewise suggests that the same purpose led him to incorporate a second drummer, Rashied Ali, into his group in 1966:

KOFSKY: When I talked to you a couple of years ago . . . you said the thing you probably would do if you added anything [to the group], you would add drums. . . .

COLTRANE: I don't know, man. . . . I still feel so strongly about drums, I really do. I feel very strongly about these drums. I experimented in it [with Rashied Ali and Elvin Jones], but we didn't have too much success. I believe it would have worked, but Elvin and McCoy couldn't hold it; it was time for them to go.

I was trying to do something. . . . There was a thing I wanted to do in music, see, and I figured I could do two things: I could have a band that played like the way we used to play, and a band that was going in the direction that the one I have now is going in—I could combine these two, with these two concepts going. And it could have been done.*

But could it? The destination toward which Coltrane was traveling, to judge from the musical evidence as well as his own testimony, was that of a much more open concept of rhythm, without the limitations of a predetermined pulse and measure lines to restrict the possibilities of improvisation. So much we can conclude with some certainty on the basis of such of his late performances as the versions of "My Favorite Things" that he recorded during 1966 with Pharoah Sanders, Rashied Ali, and Alice Coltrane.[37] To begin with, in the six years between Coltrane's first and last recordings of this composition, its rhythmic structure has grown immea-

---

* Expressions of Coltrane's desire for a more complex rhythmic foundation appear in the notes to several of his recordings from the years 1965 to 1967: "I feel the need for more time, more rhythm all around me. And with more than one drummer, the rhythm can be more multidirectional. Someday I may add a conga drummer, or even a company of drummers" (*Meditations*, Impulse 9110). "I'd like . . . to be freer rhythmically. Also, I've got drum fever: I'd like to continue exploring the use of more than one drummer" (*Coltrane Live at the Village Vanguard Again!*, Impulse 9124). "I want more of the sense of the expansion of time. I want the time to be more plastic" (*Om*, Impulse 9140).

surably thicker, thanks to a continuous carpet of sound laid down by a variety of small percussion instruments (rattles, cowbells, tambourines, and so on). Of even greater significance, the role of the piano, bass, and drums has changed from that of maintaining fixed measure lines, meter and pulse to that of providing a broad backdrop of swirling instrumental textures and colors—the aural counterpart, as it were, of a 1960s "psychedelic" light show—over which the soloist invents freely, varying the tempo and meter essentially at will. It is difficult to see how this kind of everfluid rhythmic-harmonic framework could possibly have satisfied Elvin Jones and McCoy Tyner, given their obvious reluctance to improvise without the familiar guideposts of meter and measure line.*

The same verdict applies as well to what is unquestionably Coltrane's most ambitious work, as well as his most formidable challenge to conventional notions of jazz improvisation, *Ascension*, which also dates from this phase of his career. Performed by two trumpeters, five saxophonists, piano, two basses and drums, *Ascension* allows each musician an opportunity to solo with near-complete freedom. During these portions of the composition, according to Archie Shepp, who played on the recording, "there are no specified chords," nor fixed chorus length—nor for that matter, even time signature; in these "dialogues between the soloists and the rhythm section" (Shepp),

---

* Note in this regard Tyner's comments in the interview in chapter 12: "I can say this: that at times it's very hard to comprehend the structure of most of the newer attempts by some of the [avant-garde] groups. Of course, my way of doing it wouldn't be quite as . . . well, it would be sort of different from a lot of other groups. You know, I have a way of approaching a thing—free form, or whatever you want to call it—and it wouldn't be quite as 'free' as some of the other groups, if you want to use that term." Tyner made these remarks on August 16, 1966, at a time when memories of his experiences in the Coltrane quartet (which he had left less than one year before) were still quite fresh.

there is only an implied pulse and, perhaps, the hint of a tonality and scale (B-flat minor blues). It is in the ensemble sections, however, that Coltrane's yearning for polyrhythm finds its clearest expression, as all eleven instruments improvise simultaneously with only the loosest of restrictions. (The passages of collective improvisation "were based on chords," Shepp told A.B. Spellman, "but these chords were optional.")[38]

What were the implications of the kind of music *Ascension* represented for Elvin Jones, McCoy Tyner, and bassists Art Davis and Jimmy Garrison? To begin with, they would have to play much louder than usual during the ensemble sections merely to be heard over the massed fury of two brass and five reed instruments roaring at full volume. Second, they would have the additional responsibility—which might in time become a burden—of adapting to some seven (or eight, if one counts Tyner) different soloists. Third, for Tyner in particular, this arrangement was tantamount to an artistic demotion: from being the foil to Coltrane and the second-most-important melodic voice in a quartet, he has been reduced to the role of one improviser among nine, with a corresponding decrease in solo time. Tyner has never revealed his reaction to *Ascension* so far as I know, but it is hard to imagine that he would have been pleased by the diminished role to which it relegated him. As for Elvin Jones, there are good reasons for suspecting that although he might have enjoyed recording *Ascension* as a one-time adventure, such fare probably would not appeal to him on a steady basis.*

---

* As the following exchange from the interview in the next chapter suggests:

    KOFSKY: From time to time, John had other people in the group— Eric Dolphy before he died, and, I believe, Archie Shepp played with the group sometimes. And didn't Albert Ayler also sit in?
    JONES: Yes.
    KOFSKY: And of course Pharoah Sanders. I'm curious to know

Again, therefore, one must ask whether Coltrane's idea that he "could combine these two, with these two concepts going" was entirely well-founded. The sentiment is certainly understandable, but its realism is open to question.

Where, then, does this leave us? How do we reckon the balance? On the one hand, both John Coltrane and Elvin Jones rank among the foremost innovators in the evolution of jazz. On the other, there is a point beyond which Jones—in contrast to Coltrane, who repeatedly showed himself willing, even eager, to push each of his ideas to its logical culmination—had no wish to go. Supremely gifted in being able, with the support of his associates in the Coltrane quartet, to carry jazz drumming an impressive distance toward a fully polyrhythmic style, Jones, when forced to choose, elected not to take the final step across the boundary separating improvisation governed by defined meter and measure from improvisation that knows no such constraints.

Yet in the same breath one must quickly add that there is nothing in this last fact that can in any way diminish Elvin Jones's deservedly celebrated achievements. Indeed, as long as there exist jazz recordings and people who care to hear them, the magnificent inventions that he devised and perfected during his years with John Coltrane will attest to his signal importance as an artist of the highest order. Other than to reiterate yet again my oft-stated admiration for the uniquely compelling style that is his artistic signature, I can conceive of no greater words of praise.

---

if you formed any impression of these younger saxophonists. . . .

JONES: Well, if anybody jumps on the bandstand and wants to play until he exhausts everything that he's got in his mind, in addition to what we're *already* doing, it is a hardship, I believe, and it's not very respectful of people you profess to admire.

NOTES

1. An encyclopedia entry for Charles Baudelaire, e.g., is a classic in this respect: "His neurotic, eccentric personality led him along a road of poverty, misunderstanding, excesses, and disease. A perfectionist, he labored for years on his one volume of verse. . . ." etc.; see "Baudelaire, Charles," *The Columbia-Viking Desk Encyclopedia* (New York: Dell, 1964), ed. William Bridgwater, p. 162.

2. Thus Leonard Feather, for example, as part of his campaign against "the more militant young artists," demands "the freedom of art to remain art, pure and inviolate." See "Whatever Happened to Beauty—Or, Who Wants Pleasant Music?" in *down beat Music '67*, Don DeMicheal, ed. (Chicago: Maher Publications, 1967), p. 19.

3. I quote Ayler in "An Interview with Albert and Donald Ayler," *Jazz*, September 1968, p. 22; the second quotation is from Frank Smith's letter to the editor of *Jazz*, November 1965, p. 9.

4. This and all other quotations of Jones are, unless explicitly stated otherwise, from the interview with him in the next chapter. In a similar vein, Jones told Whitney Balliett: "I listened to all the drummers I could, on records and in person. I'd hear Buddy Rich, say, do something on a record and I'd wonder if he was doing that snare-drum pattern with one hand or two, and finally I'd get a chance to *see* him, with Tommy Dorsey, and I discovered he was using two hands. I saw Jo Jones with Basie, and on records I heard Chick Webb. . . . I heard Sid Catlett on 'Salt Peanuts' with Dizzy Gillespie and Charlie Parker, and he was flowing and flawless. And I listened to Dave Tough and Max Roach and Kenny Clarke and Tiny Kahn." As an outgrowth of these formative experiences, Jones "began to develop [his] theories on drums." See Whitney Balliett, *American Musicians: 56 Portraits in Jazz* (New York: Oxford University Press, 1986), p. 370.

5. Jones quoted in Balliett, *American Musicians*, p. 370.

6. Naming the principals (or my informant) would violate a confidence.

7. John Coltrane, *My Favorite Things* (Atlantic 1361). For whatever it may be worth, my conclusion is that Jones's complaints on this score are fully justified.

8. To hear these differences, compare the performances by the Coltrane group in which Billy Higgins played, "Exotica" and "One and Four" (on John Coltrane and Lee Morgan, *The Best of Birdland*, vol. 1, Roulette 52094), with their counterparts in which Elvin Jones was the drummer, "Body and Soul" (on *Coltrane's Sound*, Atlantic 1419) and "Mr. Day" (on *Coltrane Plays the Blues*, Atlantic 1382), respectively; it is surely a misfortune for Coltrane scholars that the former selections (with Higgins) are more often than not out of print.

Note, incidentally, that in the course of constituting his quartet, Coltrane tried out two drummers who had formerly been with Sonny Rollins, Pete La Roca and Elvin Jones (each of whom plays with Rollins on his recording *A Night at the Village Vanguard*, Blue Note 1581) as well as a drummer (Billy Higgins) and a bassist (Jimmy Garrison) who had come to him from the group of Ornette Coleman. If this fact leads one to suspect that Coltrane was a student of the two saxophone innovators who came the closest to being his peers, the suspicion is, I believe, well founded. Indeed, Coltrane was widely compared to both Rollins and Coleman, beginning in the latter half of the 1950s with the former, who shot to national prominence earliest of the three, then continuing to an almost equal degree with the latter during the early 1960s. The interest, moreover, was mutual, as is readily apparent from a comparison of the accompanists with whom each of the three saxophonists chose to record.

Toward the end of the 1950s, both Rollins and Coltrane often recorded with Miles Davis's "rhythm section"—that is, pianist Red Garland, bassist Paul Chambers, drummer Philly Joe Jones—or one of its myriad spin-offs (Coltrane, of course, was a quondam member of the Davis group during this period and Rollins also worked with Davis on a few occasions). On *Tenor Madness* (Prestige 7047, recorded 1956), Rollins used all three musicians, in addition to incorporating Coltrane on the title selection—the only known recording of a Rollins-Coltrane duet. Coltrane made a pair of albums with Garland and Chambers (Art Taylor substituting for Philly Joe Jones on drums), *Traneing In* (Prestige 7123; recorded 1957) and *Soultrane* (Prestige 7142; recorded 1958), and a third with a different variant of this trio (Chambers, Jones, and pianist Kenny Drew replacing Red Garland) for a sextet recording, *Blue Train* (Blue Note 1577).

Rollins and Coltrane each also called upon the services of pianist Tommy Flanagan, the former on his 1956 work *Saxophone Colossus* (Prestige 7079), the latter on *Giant Steps* (Atlantic 1311; 1959). Likewise for a second pianist, Wynton Kelly, who played on *Sonny Rollins* (Blue Note 1542; 1957 or 1958) and, in 1959, when both he and Coltrane were members of Miles Davis's group, on *Coltrane Jazz* (Atlantic 1354).

When Ornette Coleman's arrival in New York caused a tremendous stir in jazz circles at the start of the 1960s, the two tenor saxophonists were evidently drawn to some of his ideas. Thus, Coltrane in mid-1960 was co-leader with Coleman's chief associate, trumpeter Don Cherry, on a recording on which two other Coleman colleagues, bassist Charlie Haden and drummer Ed Blackwell, also played; their repertoire numbered three compositions by Coleman, one by Cherry and one by pianist Thelonious Monk (John Coltrane and Don Cherry, *The Avant-Garde*, Atlantic 1451). Subsequently, when Sonny Rollins emerged from one of his sporadic retirements, for several months he led and recorded with a trio that included Don Cherry and another former Coleman drummer whom we have already encountered, Billy Higgins; see *Our Man in Jazz* (RCA Victor 2612; 1963).

Finally, to complete the circle, during the second half of the 1960s Rollins and Coleman both made albums using Coltrane's accompanists Elvin Jones and Jimmy Garrison; see Rollins's album, *East Broadway Run Down* (Impulse 9121) and Coleman's two albums, *New York Is Now* (Blue Note 84287) and *Love Call* (Blue Note 84356).

In all, an impressive amount of interaction among these three saxophone masters, even if by proxy.

9. See the extended discussion in the preceding chapter on the importance of the soprano saxophone in catalyzing Coltrane's development of his new style.

10. See the following John Coltrane recordings: for "Countdown," "Naima," "Syeeda's Song Flute" and one version of "Giant Steps," *Giant Steps* (Atlantic 1311); for a second version of "Giant Steps," *Alternate Takes* (Atlantic 1668); for "Like Sonny," *Coltrane Jazz* (Atlantic 1354); for "Satellite," *Coltrane's Sound* (Atlantic 1419); for the selections performed with Don Cherry, *The Avant-Garde* (cited in full in note 8).

11. See the following John Coltrane recordings, some of which I cited in full in the previous note: for "Fifth House," *Coltrane Jazz;* for "Liberia" and "Satellite," *Coltrane's Sound;* for "26-2," *The Coltrane Legacy* (Atlantic 1553).

12. See the following John Coltrane recordings, some of which I cited in full in the previous two notes: for "Body and Soul," "Central Park West," "Equinox" and "Satellite," *Coltrane's Sound;* for "Mr. Day" and "Mr. Knight," *Coltrane Plays the Blues* (Atlantic 1382); for "26-2," *The Coltrane Legacy;* for "But Not for Me," "My Favorite Things" and "Summertime," *My Favorite Things* (Atlantic 1361); for "Impressions," *Impressions* (Impulse 42) and *Afro Blue Impressions* (Pablo Live 2620 101).

13. Coltrane's comments are in the interview in chapter 13; the ellipsis is in the original. One can sample Elvin Jones's playing prior to his joining the Coltrane quartet, for example, on Miles Davis, *Collector's Items* (Prestige 24022; selections dating from 1955), and Sonny Rollins, *A Night at the Village Vanguard* (Blue Note 1581; late 1957 or early 1958).

14. McCoy Tyner and Stanley Dance, "Tyner Talk," *down beat*, October 24, 1963, p. 19. Jimmy Garrison, the bassist who had the longest tenure (five years) in any of the Coltrane groups, concurred in McCoy Tyner's description of the ethos Coltrane created: "John had confidence in the men he had with him, and that gives you confidence in return. You say to yourself, well, if a fellow like John Coltrane thinks you can do it, then you can do it, and you put out a little bit more and find that you really can do it. . . . John's an amazing man. He feels that he was called to do what he's doing, and that's something—to realize your purpose on this earth. And it's a marvel being with him, because some of it rubs off on you— you stop thinking superficially, and it comes through in the things you're trying to do musically." Quoted in Don Heckman, "Jimmy Garrison: After Coltrane," *down beat*, March 9, 1967, p. 18 (repunctuated from the original).

15. Only some of the groups led by Cecil Taylor have come anywhere near equaling the intensity and cohesion of the interplay of which the Coltrane quartet was capable. As for the subject of this chapter, Elvin Jones, after leaving Coltrane's employ, he would never

again enjoy the constant stimulus and challenge of playing in a setting in which the quality of musical interaction was so consistently
high. Perhaps for that reason, his work since the mid-1960s did not
ever attain quite the same brilliance it had during his years with
Coltrane.

16. Given the topic of this chapter, I hope I may be forgiven a few
more words on the matter of drum solos. Of all the instruments in
the conventional jazz ensemble, the drum set is the least suitable
for solo improvisation. At the disposal of the contemporary jazz
drummer are, typically, a snare drum, two or three tom-toms, a bass
drum and an assortment of cymbals. One can alter the sounds these
instruments produce in a variety of ways: by using timpani mal-
lets or wire brushes (or, as was the custom of Los Angeles drummer
Frank Butler, by playing on the drum with the fingers); by releasing
the snare attachment from the snare drum; by striking the rim and
the head of the drum simultaneously (a "rim shot"); by raising the
pitch of a drum through applying pressure on the drumhead with
one end of a stick, the other hand or elbow; by opening or closing
the high-hat cymbals (which are mounted, parallel to the floor, on
a stand and controlled by a foot-operated pedal); by tapping with
sticks on the rims and shells of the drums, the cymbal stands, and
so forth.

For all this profusion of effects and colors, however, the simple
truth is that the drummer does not possess so much as a single instrument capable of producing a discrete, identifiable note—a fact
that makes the notion of "melodic drumming" a commendable
fantasy for the most part, even though that it has been common
practice to speak of "melodic" drummers ever since such bebop percussionists as Kenny Clarke and Max Roach first appeared in the
1940s. (The term still turns up in jazz textbooks, incidentally.) One
can elicit melody, harmony and rhythm from a piano or guitar; a
brass or reed instrument—or even a bass violin—has the capacity
for at least some combination of rhythmic and melodic expression.
But only by the loosest use of language can one refer to a "melodic"
drum solo. Lacking the ability to play true melodies, the drummer
is the one performer most in need of support from the rest of the
ensemble. Nonetheless, in a perfect instance of logic being stood

on its head, that selfsame drummer is also the only performer who normally has to solo completely unaccompanied (even a bass soloist can have the backing of piano and/or guitar and drums if he or she so desires). As the creation of anything very elaborate in the way of a melodic line is clearly beyond the scope of the instrument itself, and as there generally are no other performers standing by to keep the music going if the drummer pauses for a moment to create some variety, no wonder most drummers simply succumb to temptation and pack their solos with an unrelenting fusillade of rolls and single strokes. Only a relative handful have developed the restraint necessary to compose statements displaying a higher order of musical imagination, whence the assortment of percussion pyrotechnics the typical jazz drummer unleashes during an extended solo. In contrast to these solos, however, the practice of "trading fours" or "eights"—four- or eight-measure exchanges between the drums and the other instruments—can often yield fascinating results. But with a change in quantity comes a change in quality: where a drum solo of eight measures can be wonderfully musical and imaginative, one of eight (or eighteen!) choruses all too often degenerates into little more than an assault on the listeners' patience.

17. The polyrhythmic nature of African music, as Gunther Schuller points out in *Early Jazz: Its Roots and Musical Development* (New York: Oxford University Press, 1968), pp. 11–16, is such that the musicians, singers, clappers, and others, in an ensemble will produce rhythms in which: (1) there is an assortment of time signatures (4/4, 3/4, 5/4, 3/8, 2/4) played or sung simultaneously; (2) the measure lines of the different performers or groups of performers (sections) do not normally coincide; and (3) the meter in which any given component of the ensemble (cantor, chorus, drummer, bell player) performs is not constant but may vary from one measure to the next. Polyrhythm to an African person, in other words, involves a great deal more complexity than the mere superimposition of rhythms— that is, the juxtaposition of two or more rhythms against each other, but within a fixed framework determined by coincident measure lines—that people of European descent usually have in mind when they employ that term.

Owing to the European-dominated social setting in which it

developed, African-American polyrhythm has taken the simpler form of rhythmic superimposition. A common example is the three-against-two pattern frequently employed in a so-called jazz waltz (see, for example, the third variant in example 8 to this section, below). Stripped to the barest essentials, this pattern can be notated:

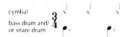

I treat the subject of the Afro-American approach to African polyrhythms at much greater length in the concluding part of this chapter.

18. On the African polyrhythmic roots of swing, see Schuller, *Early Jazz*, pp. 6–26; his suggested derivation of the ensemble style of New Orleans jazz from African musical practices is on pp. 11–23. See also the discussion of African elements in African-American jazz in chapter 7 of Frank Kofsky, *Black Music, White Business: Illuminating the History and Political Economy of Jazz* (New York: Pathfinder Press, 1997).

19. "Although," he adds, "it later came to be used as foreground material in the so-called riff tunes of the Swing Era." *Ibid.*, p. 48; see also pp. 47–50.

20. In *Jazz: Its Evolution and Essence*, trans. David Noakes (New York: Grove Press, 1956), p. 215; see also pp. 213–17. This moving away during the swing years from the European concept of a heavily accented "downbeat" (first beat of a measure) toward what Schuller calls the "democratization" of the pulse (*Early Jazz*, pp. 15–16, 25–26 and *passim*), as represented by the production of the "four equal beats," again suggests the retention on a folk level of African musical predispositions. But as Hodeir correctly indicates (*Jazz: Its Evolution and Essence*, pp. 210–15), it required increased technical facility before this predisposition could be expressed in practice. To generalize from this, it would appear that the more proficient black jazz musicians become in the use of European instruments, the more resolutely they employ their expertise to express an essentially African cultural heritage. Thus Charles Keil provocatively comments: "In every instance" in which a new Afro-American musical style has been created, "the new music has

been an amalgamation of increased musical knowledge (technically speaking) and a reemphasis of the most basic Afro-American resources"; hence, for example, "Elvin Jones and the other percussion virtuosos of contemporary jazz [have,] in attempting to create a maximum of swing . . . inevitably worked toward the crossed triplet rhythms of West Africa." *Urban Blues* (Chicago: University of Chicago Press, 1966), pp. 43, 45. In chapter 7 of *Black Music, White Business,* I attempt to identify the concrete mechanisms that explain the observations that Schuller, Hodeir, Keil, and others, have made in this regard.

21. The examples, it probably goes without saying, are most useful when heard with the recording from which I transcribed them. "One O'Clock Jump," in an electronically reprocessed reissue of the original, is on Count Basie, *The Best of Count Basie* (Decca DXSB-7170). A further comment regarding notation. It is conventional to write the figures of Example 2 using eighth notes rather than the triplet eighth-notes I have employed, with the understanding that such eighth notes are to be given a "jazz interpretation" (that is, played as if they were eighth-note triplets). It seems to me, however, that what one gains in convenience from using eighth notes instead of eighth-note triplets one loses in precision. In any event, with the conventional notation, Example 2-a would become

and so on.

22. *Jazz: Its Evolution and Essence,* p. 218; see also pp. 217–23.

23. To Elvin Jones, "it didn't seem . . . that the four-four beat on the bass drum was necessary. What was needed was *flow* of rhythm all over the set." Jones quoted in Balliett, *American Musicians,* p. 370.

24. The very word "bebop" is probably an onomatopoetic rendering of a (relatively high pitched) snare-drum accent on the beat, followed immediately by an accent on the (low-pitched) bass drum:

Jazz musicians, like their African counterparts (especially drummers), habitually use such onomatopoeia to indicate how certain figures should be phrased.

25. I again refer the reader to Gunther Schuller's treatment of African polyrhythms in relation to Afro-American jazz, *Early Jazz,* pp. 6–26, *passim,* for additional details.

26. Hodeir, *Jazz: Its Evolution and Essence,* pp. 198–204; Schuller, *Early Jazz,* pp. 6–10.

27. Although it is, by convention, often written as a dotted-eighth- and sixteenth-note figure,

to play it as such at most tempos would result in such a stiff and choppy feeling that the swing would be destroyed.

28. On the album *Coltrane Plays the Blues* (Atlantic 1382).

29. Even at that, I would hate to have to wager my life that the transcription (or the "sticking" pattern above the ride-cymbal line) is absolutely correct. In any event, here as elsewhere, the serious student of Jones's style should use the examples in conjunction with the recordings for the former to be of greatest value.

30. John Coltrane, *Coltrane's Sound* (Atlantic 1419).

31. On *Coltrane "Live" at the Village Vanguard* (Impulse 10).

32. On the album of that name, Atlantic 1361; recorded October 1960.

33. "Out of This World" is on the album *Coltrane* (Impulse 21), recorded in June 1962.

34. To play such a rim shot, which produces a loud clicking sound, the drummer places the bead (thin end) of the drumstick on the drumhead and, while keeping that end of the stick in contact with the head, strikes the rim with the other.

35. Such as: playing double strokes where single strokes appear in Example 11, interchanging tom-tom and Latin-rim-shot strokes, and so forth.

36. If so, this would be another instance of the correctness of Charles Keil's point that "in every instance" in which a new Afro-American musical style has been created, "the new music has been

an amalgamation of increased musical knowledge (technically speaking) and a reemphasis of the most basic Afro-American resources"; *Urban Blues*, p. 43. In advancing this observation, Keil had in mind "Elvin Jones and the other percussion virtuosos of contemporary jazz" (p. 45), but perhaps Coltrane's predilection for polyrhythm illustrates the phenomenon even more dramatically.

37. See, for example, *Coltrane Live at the Village Vanguard Again!* (Impulse 9124, recorded May 28, 1966) and *John Coltrane Live in Japan* (MCA Records and GRP Records, GRD–4–102, recorded July 22, 1966).

38. *Ascension* occupies both sides of the recording of the same name (Impulse 95); A.B. Spellman quotes Archie Shepp in the notes.

11

Elvin Jones: an interview

Attentive readers of this interview may notice that Elvin Jones appears to be of two minds on the question of his evolution as an artist. Although at one point he denies "thinking anything about style" and maintains that he "just reacted to whatever [he] heard," subsequently he seems to reverse himself. "I've always had a definite feeling about the way that drums should sound with different instruments," he remarks, "I've always had that idea in my mind as to the way I would play if given the opportunity." He also recalls that, in response to some advice from his pianist brother Hank Jones, he "played a little louder and made it come out more." "That's an overall feeling that I like to have when I am playing, to make the rhythmic sound blend with the harmonic," he adds by way of conclusion.

All of which makes it clear that—in contrast to his comment that "a style just seems to develop"—a great deal of thought went into the formation of Jones's mature approach to the drums. Indeed, how could it be otherwise? Nine times out of ten, we can recognize his playing on a (well-made) recording almost from the moment we hear him apply drumstick to drumhead or cymbal. To establish such an unmistakable musical identity is not so extraordinary for a saxophonist, a trumpeter, a pianist—even a bassist. Only a very few drummers in the history of jazz, however, have managed the feat. You can be sure that they did not do it by inadvertence.

KOFSKY: The first time I ever heard you on a record was with Sonny Rollins on *A Night at the Village Vanguard*. Had you recorded before that?

JONES: Yes, I believe so. I think I had.[1]

KOFSKY: Compared to your playing with Sonny Rollins on that record, you sounded quite different the next time I heard you, which was on John Coltrane's album, *My Favorite Things*.[2] At the time you were with Rollins, were you prepared to play the same way you did later with Coltrane, or is that a style that you worked out after you joined the Coltrane group?

JONES: Well, nothing was contrived about it. When I made that record with Sonny, I had just finished playing with J.J. Johnson. I had been relieved of my position with the band and had been in Europe all that summer. I just happened to walk into the Vanguard the day of the recording and Sonny asked me if I'd play. It happened just like that. It wasn't that I was trying to maintain any kind of style, or anything like that.

KOFSKY: What did you do after that record? I didn't hear much of you until all of a sudden you popped up with John Coltrane and seemed to be playing in a way that was totally different from anyone else.

JONES: There were a lot of things after that. I played with Sweets Edison and Tyree Glenn; I tried to keep moving and keep active musically. And as I said before, I wasn't thinking anything about style. It was just a reaction to what was going on. However, a style just seems to develop and I just reacted to whatever I heard; that's my style, I suppose.

KOFSKY: The reason I'm going at the matter in this way is because I felt that the way of sensing time that came in with the Coltrane quartet was different from anything I had ever heard before. I'm wondering where the roots of it lay—whether it was something that was in your head all along, or something in John's, or something that came out of the interaction of three or four of you in that group?

JONES: Well, all of that could be true. But then, as far as I am concerned, I've always had a definite feeling about the way that drums should sound with different instruments, depending on their instrumentation. And I've always had that idea in my mind as to the way I would play if given the opportunity, and so on.

KOFSKY: In particular, the things I noticed were figures played with your left hand—to me, it sounded like a triple-meter feeling that nobody else had. Was that something that you'd been doing all along, but it just emerged more strongly with John?

JONES: Possibly I'd been doing it all along, because when you hear a certain sound—whenever, say, the tenor [saxophone] plays—I hear that kind of rhythm. Also, my brother Hank told me to make my sound more definite, make it louder. You see, he made a few remarks about what I was doing in my left hand and wanted to know what it was that I was playing before, so I just played a little louder and made it come out more. That's an overall feeling that I like to have when I am playing, to make the rhythmic sound blend with the harmonic.

KOFSKY: How did it come about that you joined Coltrane's band? Had you talked with John for a long time?

JONES: No. When John started that group, he mentioned to Tommy Flanagan, who was working with him at that time, that he wanted to see me. They were at the time rehearsing some things. John was living on 103rd Street, I think, and I finally got around to going up to visit him, and he said, "Oh, I've already got a drummer," so that was that. You know, I liked John very much and had experience playing with him and with Miles [Davis] in Philadelphia, and a few other times when he was with Miles, and I just loved the way he played. Let's not get nostalgic about it, but he was just very, very good—an excellent musician, a real artist, I think. I won't say everything that happened to me came from my association with him, but. . . . Anyway, I was staying at a friend of mine's house, on 9th Street and 4th Avenue, and John walked in there one day, flew in from California, and said, "Do you want to join the band? Do you want to come out to San Francisco with us?"

And I thought at the time that he just wanted me to join because I could drive, and he was tired of driving! So I said, no, I don't want to go to San Francisco.[3] He said they were going from there to Denver and he said, I'll meet you in Denver. We went out and went up to Birdland—I think Dizzy [Gillespie] was working there at the time—and Dizzy asked me to go with him and I said, "Well, I'm going to go with Coltrane." I did, and I met him, got the ticket and everything, took a plane to Denver and met him in Denver. Then I was with him.

KOFSKY: Was McCoy Tyner already in the band?

JONES: McCoy was in the band and I think they had Billy Higgins playing drums, and Steve Davis on bass—McCoy, Steve, and Billy.

KOFSKY: Were they playing "My Favorite Things" then?

JONES: Oh, yes, yes. They had a rehearsal at this club . . . and I said I don't want to play—I want to hear what you're doing, so I can learn it. So they had a rehearsal, and when I heard what they were playing, I knew what to do. I didn't want to make the trip in vain and so it evolved in that way.

There are a lot of things I could leave out or put in, but I don't want to make it anything more than it was or anything less. That's just the way it happened.

KOFSKY: Then you had played "My Favorite Things" with the group for quite a while before cutting that record? It wasn't the case that you played it for the first time in the studio?

JONES: No, no, nothing like that. They had been playing it before I joined the band and I must have played it at least 300 or 400 times before I recorded it.

KOFSKY: That's very interesting, because to me the drums are so poorly recorded that one can hardly hear what you are doing, and I had thought that perhaps there was some problem in the group. But it wasn't that way at all.

JONES: No, I think it's probably just an engineer's problem, because most of the time the engineers don't cater to sidemen, at least while recording in the studio.

KOFSKY: It also seems to be an Atlantic Records characteristic in general that the drums are hard to hear and that the bass is somewhat over-recorded.

JONES: I suppose that could be true, but that's something I wouldn't be in a position to say.[4]

KOFSKY: Had you had any experience playing with Mc-Coy Tyner before that band?

JONES: No, I didn't. I saw McCoy when he was with Benny Golson and Art Farmer in the Jazztet and I heard him play and thought that it was, you know—he's a good piano player, and that's all. My reaction to listening to him was, "Very good."

KOFSKY: Can you remember what your impressions were after you joined the band and heard what he was doing in that group?

JONES: Yes. I thought that at times he would rush the tempo a little bit—he played so fast that on some of the runs that he would make the thirty-second notes into sixty-fourths.

I asked him about it, and told him to just slow down a little bit and it would be kind of more definite.

KOFSKY: To an outsider, though, it certainly appeared that you worked very closely with him in his particular way of phrasing.

JONES: Yes, well, his conception of things is different from a lot of piano players'.

KOFSKY: Different from almost anyone's, really.

JONES: He has a very unique style of playing that—well, you just don't hear it in anyone else. Just McCoy Tyner. Most people, I don't think, are willing to sacrifice that much of their time and life to devote to the things they believe in, in order to get to that level of performance. He practices constantly and studies constantly, and thinks about it constantly. That's the way that whole band was, that whole group. It was more of an honor, you know? No kind of applause that could be given would mean more to me than just having been with them and been around and been involved in what we were doing at the time. It's one of the greatest things that ever happened in my life, as far as I am concerned.

KOFSKY: I don't want to put you on the spot or rake up any unpleasant experiences, but that prompts me to wonder, then, how you happened to leave the group?

JONES: Well, I don't think I want to talk about it any more. I've already talked about it and I believe I've said everything that I wanted to say. It wasn't anything personal. I just don't want to, like you say, rake up old things. . . . don't think it's necessary or even needed at this time.

KOFSKY: The only reason I asked is that a lot of people were very emotionally attached to that particular group and were puzzled when you and McCoy were no longer together with John, and wondered why it happened.

JONES: There was a complete understanding—we were so close as people and as human beings could be, at the time. There was an understanding that we all had with each other, that when the time came, anybody could go. There was no commitment there. There was just a gentlemen's agreement to stay together; and as gentlemen agree, we agreed that we could part, and that's the way it happened.

KOFSKY: Did you find, during that period, that your idea of time and pulse was changing as a result of that group—that you were beginning to hear the time being kept a different way? For instance, when Charlie Parker and Dizzy Gillespie were playing in the 1940s, they were doing something different with the time—they played 4/4 a different way than the big swing bands had. Did you feel that that same thing was happening in the Coltrane group—that you were finding different ways of keeping 4/4 time, not to mention 6/8?

JONES: I didn't feel it in that concept. I knew it was happening, but I just didn't feel it—hindsight, that's what it is. I didn't feel it that way.

KOFSKY: You weren't aware of it, then, at the time.

JONES: Well, I was aware that things were happening, and I was aware of what we were doing—very, very much aware. But I didn't think of it in that way, that's all.

KOFSKY: What's your feeling now, in retrospect? Do you feel that that was a new way of sensing time and playing?

JONES: No.

KOFSKY: You don't think so?

JONES: No. I just think there's another way of listening. I think that right now, it's the listener who is being informed; I don't think it's the artist at all.

KOFSKY: When you yourself were developing as a drummer, were there any other drummers who appealed to you particularly and on whom you might at one point or another have modeled yourself?

JONES: There were a lot of them. Just about every drummer that was playing anywhere or played with anybody, I had a great deal of deep respect for and a burning desire to listen to, just to find out what they were doing. That was my way—I've always felt like that and still do.

KOFSKY: What about Roy Haynes?

JONES: Roy Haynes—he's one of my heroes.

KOFSKY: Didn't he play with the Coltrane group on a number of occasions?

JONES: Yes, I had the flu one time and the band had to go to Rochester, I believe it was, and Roy—I was just laid up for three days and I couldn't make it—and Roy filled in. He took over and nobody missed me.

KOFSKY: Well, I wouldn't say that! But I know that he also played with the Coltrane group one year [1963] at the Newport Jazz Festival, and that there's a recording of that performance.[5] Did you ever have a chance to hear him with John's group?

JONES: No, I didn't. Yes, I did, too, you know. I came back from the hospital one time and he was playing at Birdland and I did hear him play one set, and then he saw me and threw the sticks at me. He said, "Go on, play with your band!" Roy's a nice guy. He's a beautiful person.

KOFSKY: Do you find the time to hear many of the young drummers today?

JONES: Well, I hear as many as I can. It's not possible to hear everybody, but as many as I can, I listen to. I can't name all of them, but there's Louis Hayes and Roy Brooks. That's two, and I could—I think that, really, they have absorbed the essence of what is really prevailing right now.

KOFSKY: Do you ever hear your ideas coming back to you in the playing of younger drummers, and if so, how does that strike you?

JONES: If I do hear my ideas, I can only reflect that maybe, that it's just something that was manifested within me from what I heard before. I think that music is evolutionary and the things that we're doing and the things that everybody is doing—well, to put it in a cliché, there's nothing new under the sun; it's just a matter of rediscovering and using the things that are already being done in other parts of the world and in other areas of endeavor.

KOFSKY: From time to time, John had other people in the group—Eric Dolphy before he died, and, I believe, Archie Shepp played with the group sometimes. And didn't Albert Ayler also sit in?

JONES: Yes.

KOFSKY: And, of course, Pharoah Sanders. I'm curious to know if you formed any impression of these younger saxophonists, if there were any who appealed to you particularly, or what your views on their styles of playing are?

JONES: Well, a lot of them, a lot of the young saxophonists that I heard, I felt at the time—I am only saying this is what I thought when I heard them—that they were more or less copying what John was doing. And also that they were imposing on him, and on all of us, as a matter of fact.

KOFSKY: In what sense?

JONES: Well, if anybody jumps on the bandstand and wants to play until he exhausts everything that he's got in his mind, in addition to what we're already doing, it is a hardship, I believe, and it's not very respectful of people you profess to admire.

KOFSKY: Have you kept up with the careers of any of those players subsequently?

JONES: I don't keep up with anybody's career, because I just don't.

KOFSKY: What I mean to say is, have you heard them and listened to their records, and do you have any opinion on the younger musicians now?

JONES: I would like to do that. You know, it's just recently that I have been able to acquire a record player. Before that, it was impossible for me to listen to anybody's record, for a long period of time.

KOFSKY: If you haven't listened to many jazz records, I suppose it goes without saying that you haven't listened to many rock records either.

JONES: I don't know—I've listened to some. . . .

KOFSKY: The reason I asked is because most of the rock drummers whom I've heard seem to be very much influenced by what you play, and if you ask them, it almost invariably comes down to the fact that they like Coltrane and, like most jazz drummers, they listen to Elvin Jones.

JONES: No, I wasn't really that aware of it. I read the magazines and I talk to musicians and I see a lot of people. They play with this and that band and they come to see me when I am playing, and I automatically assume that if they didn't like the music, they wouldn't come in there to spend their money. But I've never been really concerned about it or thought much about it. I don't have time. I am busy thinking about what I'm doing, I need all the time that I have to devote to what I believe. If other people have that much admiration for the things that I'm doing, then I feel very humble and very grateful to think that they are, and it just makes me feel that I'm not all that wrong in what I believe.

KOFSKY: When you say that, I wonder if you think there have been people who felt that you were playing incorrectly?

JONES: No, I don't. I think there were a lot of people—including me, because I didn't really understand everything that I was doing, and so I am sure that other people feel this more strongly than I would. But I think it's more of a lack of understanding in general, and in me too. I am trying to find, through the process of elimination, I suppose, like any scientist would try to work on a project, what is right and what is wrong and try to—musically, you have to make up your mind and you don't have time to wait for the results. You experiment and do it right away, make your selection, and it's almost immediate or simultaneous with the other things that are going on, so far as the rhythmic patterns are concerned.

KOFSKY: You seem familiar with the structure of scientific experiments. Do you have any background in science?

JONES: No, not really.

KOFSKY: But it sounds as though you have a good grasp of the theoretical approach.

JONES: Well, I think that music is a science, and religion is a science, and just about everything—I look at things, I suppose, in that way. I don't know why. I am not academically acclimated to that kind of thought.

KOFSKY: May I ask you why your groups are usually organized without a piano? Have you tried pianists and found that they didn't work out?

JONES: Well, I tried piano players and they don't—there aren't that many, I don't think, that were available at the time.

KOFSKY: Had you thought about McCoy Tyner, or wasn't he available?

JONES: Not available. As I said, there weren't that many good unemployed piano players available at the particular time when I was fortunate enough to have a job and would have been able to hire them.[6]

KOFSKY: Now that you have had a group of your own for a while and it doesn't have a piano in it, what are your feelings on that score?

JONES: We feel that, as a group, we have compensated for not having the piano. We have made albums as a trio and we intend to make more.[7] We've made a movie sound track, too.

KOFSKY: How did that come about?

JONES: I was chosen to be a director of the movie, to be a musical director, to at least oversee the score, to play and to perform the score. We did it with the trio and with our repertoire that we have. The name of the movie is *The Long Stripe*, it's about a couple who get involved in worldly things. The guy is a painter and his wife is a writer. She had written a textbook about some medical subject, and she was asked to write a book about sex; they said, "You did this so well, you ought to be able to do that." So her publisher tells her, and it starts off like that. She gets involved with some lesbians and he also—their whole lives, in other words, are disrupted by this new venture. There are a lot of different characters built into their lives, and it sort of distorts their lives. Finally, I think this is left hanging in the air, as far as the story's concerned. There's a lot of humor in it, too. Eventually, they get back to where they began, with a little more knowledge of the world and with a little better understanding of themselves and that's what it's about.

KOFSKY: I'd like to ask you on what record you think your sound comes out best, or what is the record on which you've played that you like best, if there is one?

JONES: I think it's the one called *Puttin' It Together*.[8] You know, that's where more interest was placed on what I was actually doing when it was produced. That's one time I think that everything I really tried to do so far as the dynamics, et cetera, has been brought to the forefront. So when we play it back, you hear exactly what has been played. That's what I believe is a real recording, and that's what it's supposed to be. That's what it should be when reproduced.

You know, earlier, we were talking about engineers recording jazz groups. I think more attention should be paid to the sidemen there, because, after all, it should be realized that it is the group that is playing and it is the group that the people who are going to buy the album are interested in, and not just the leader. This is one of the problems in the recording industry that I think is very easy to correct, what with all the very expensive and very elaborate equipment. There can very easily be an improvement and that obstacle very easily overcome.

KOFSKY: There's just one other thing that pops into my mind, after spending an afternoon watching you teaching, and that is to ask you if you have any general advice for young drummers. Because, as I've mentioned, many young drummers do look up to you as somewhat of a model and they are very influenced by what you do and, I suppose, by what you say.

JONES: It's very difficult to give a mass lesson, but I think that anybody who has any aspirations for drumming should try to examine their reasons for wanting to do it, and if they finally decide that they want to be a drummer, then they should realize that the drum is just as important as any other instrument and to act accordingly—to use the philosophy of artistry.

KOFSKY: Why did you decide to become a drummer?

JONES: Well, that's all I ever wanted to do. I've always liked the sound of the drums; its rhythm and those sounds make me feel good and I just like to do it because I like to hear it. I like to hear it done well; that's why I wanted to be a drummer. You have to like to, and you have to want to, and you have to love it.

NOTES

1. Sonny Rollins, *A Night at the Village Vanguard* (Blue Note 18511). Earlier, in 1955, Jones recorded, for example, with a group that included bassist Charles Mingus and trumpeter Miles Davis; see Miles Davis, *Collector's Items* (Prestige 24022).

2. John Coltrane, *My Favorite Things* (Atlantic 1361).

3. My recollection—for whatever it may be worth—is that Jones had already joined the Coltrane quartet at the time it appeared at the Jazz Workshop in San Francisco.

4. A most diplomatic response that burns no bridges. In view of the number of recordings that Jones, both as a leader in his own right and as a member of the Coltrane quartet, made for Atlantic Records, one has to wonder who would be in a better "position to say."

5. John Coltrane, *Selflessness* (Impulse 9161).

6. Perhaps it was also the case that Jones—who said a few moments earlier that it was only "just recently" that he had "been able to acquire a record player"—was not earning enough to pay any of the pianists he might have liked to hire their asking salaries.

7. The other two members of the trio Jones referred to here and in subsequent paragraphs were the late Joe Farrell, saxophones, flutes, and piccolo, and the late Jimmy Garrison, bass.

8. Elvin Jones, *Puttin' It Together* (Blue Note 84282), recorded with Farrell and Garrison.

12

McCoy Tyner: an interview

I recorded this interview with McCoy Tyner, one of a series seeking to probe the relationship between black nationalism and the new music of the jazz avant-garde, in New York City on August 16, 1966. The questions I put to Tyner were in the main the same as those I asked all the musicians I interviewed, but there were some that I designed specifically with him in mind as well.

For six years, the piano artistry of McCoy Tyner was a mainstay in the groups led by John Coltrane, a period during which his approach to the instrument became almost as influential and pervasive among younger musicians as was that of Coltrane himself. Though primarily, of course, a jazz musician—a designation that Tyner and his peers often call into question*—elements of Tyner's highly personal style

---

* I realize that many black musicians dislike the word "jazz" because of what they consider its pejorative connotations, but no one as yet has devised a better term, and I have therefore used it throughout.

can be heard across the entire spectrum of contemporary popular music.

Particularly during the early part of this interview, Tyner was somewhat diffident or hesitant in answering questions on such controversial topics as black nationalism, radical politics, and the like. We can best understand such caution as the product of bitter experience. Unlike white rock musicians, who are free to speak, write, and sing about virtually any subject in language of their own choosing without fear of penalty, black jazz artists enjoy no such license. As I brought out earlier (especially in chapter 1), there have been and are now several uncompromising, radical critics of the status quo among jazz musicians, including Max Roach, Charles Mingus and, later, Cecil Taylor, Bill Dixon, and Archie Shepp, to mention only the best known. Significantly, however, few of them work with any regularity in the nightclubs, festivals, and concert tours where jazz is usually performed, and their commercial recordings during the 1960s—if any—appeared only with great rarity.

Hence the majority of black jazz musicians find survival difficult enough with two strikes—their color and their art, in a country hostile to both—against them; they are not so bent on self-destruction as to add a third in the form of radical politics, least of all in conversations with a white interlocutor. Typically, the black jazz musician can expect to sweat out a too-brief existence—witness the lives of Charlie Parker, Fats Navarro, John Coltrane, Eric Dolphy, Albert Ayler, and innumerable others—playing a series of underpaid, over-exploited "gigs" in dank and dingy "clubs." In view of these facts, it is hard to object if a jazz artist chooses to operate on the maxim that discretion is the better part of valor. I trust these considerations will explain whatever reserve the reader may detect in certain of McCoy Tyner's replies to my questions.

In addition to those replies, I have also incorporated in

what follows some excerpts from an interview with Tyner that appeared in the *Black Scholar* in 1970.[1] I chose to do so because many of the questions in this second interview closely resemble those I asked—a likeness that, as I will explain, may not be entirely due to chance—and therefore the pianist's answers shed additional light on some of the topics I raised with him. The circumstances of this second interview, to the extent I know them, are these. Well over a year before my interview with Tyner appeared in the first edition of this book, I submitted a transcript of it to *Black Scholar.* I was only mildly disappointed when, after several months had elapsed, I received a rejection note from that journal; I was considerably more dismayed to discover shortly thereafter, however, that having turned down my interview with Tyner, *Black Scholar* had then procured one of its own, using questions very similar to mine in the bargain. Coincidence? I leave it to the reader to judge. In any event, Tyner seems somewhat less guarded in this second interview. Because it goes over much of the same terrain as my own—and because I cannot, I confess, entirely rid myself of a certain proprietary attitude toward it—I have thought it useful to include some excerpts from it here. To distinguish between the two interviews, material from the second is printed in italics.

KOFSKY: Do you think the phrase "new black music" is an accurate title for some of the newer styles that are being played today in jazz?

TYNER: That's a very difficult question. I guess maybe to some this may be an accurate description of what they're doing. But I don't know whether you could—I really couldn't speak for them on that particular . . .

KOFSKY: I think you should speak for yourself.

TYNER: It's not an accurate title. It's really hard to say; still, I can't be specific on that point, because some individuals feel

---

that what they're doing is—that this title is more appropriate to what they're doing, because of the fact that they are more or less nationalistically geared.

KOFSKY: What about for what you're doing? Do you see it as accurate for yourself?

TYNER: Not necessarily. No, not necessarily. Number one, I don't like to categorize myself or my music in any respect, because I feel that music, number one, is universal; and that, at least the way I feel, is that I'm motivated by different aspects of life. I'm not motivated mainly by . . .

KOFSKY: Political considerations?

TYNER: Yes, necessarily politically motivated.

KOFSKY: When we spoke of this earlier, you said that it was true that society did influence the music, but that you didn't want to concentrate exclusively on that. Do you still think that it is true that there is a relationship between the society and the music?

TYNER: I think there is an indirect relationship, yes.

KOFSKY: Would you talk about the relationship?

TYNER: Well, I feel it's like anything else. I mean that if you're living in a society . . . that this music has been influenced by the environment, by the things that people have gone through. To me, this is how this music, one of the reasons why the music emerged, because of the fact that the society had imposed certain things upon people and this was an outlet.

KOFSKY: Restrictions?

TYNER: Restrictions or certain pressures, and people—the black people in particular—used it as a form of expressing themselves. So I believe that society does have an effect on the music.

To me, this is our system of music, the Afro-American system of music. This is the African system of music. . . . A lot of these expressions—jazz, avant-garde—came about because of our environment. As musicians began to think more about our cultural heritage, they began to refer to it more and more as black music. But it's always been the music of black musicians. It is an extension of the whole body of black experience.[2]

KOFSKY: Do you ever find that the response of an audience to your music is different according to the race of the audience? That is, that a black audience might respond differently than a white audience? Have you ever noticed that about your own music?

TYNER: That's a very difficult question to answer. It all depends on where you're playing; and it's really hard, because sometimes you find you can't really categorize audiences, because sometimes you get a good audience one place one set. It varies from set to set; you can't really tell.

KOFSKY: So there's no generalization that would apply, say, 60 percent of the time?

TYNER: Right, right—it's really difficult. . . .

KOFSKY: Malcolm X's autobiography reveals that he was a jazz lover and a close friend of many jazz musicians. Do you think that this is just an accident, or that there is some deeper significance about this—that this says something about the nature of jazz and the nature of Malcolm X?

TYNER: Well, I believe that there is something related there, because Malcolm came out of the ghetto, was a product of the ghetto, as I feel the music is a product of the ghetto. So I feel that it is only natural that he would have a close feeling, you know, to the music, because it is something that was just part of him, because it's a part of the ghetto. I believe that both of them, that they're one and the same.

KOFSKY: And his ideas also came out of the ghetto then, would you say?

TYNER: Yes, basically, I think they did.

KOFSKY: Would you ever consider dedicating a composition to Malcolm?

TYNER: I might consider that.

I accepted a different faith, Islam. I got exposed to it as I got older and it appealed to my sense of logic. The first I heard of it was when I was about 16 years old. I think the first thing I heard was Elijah's (Muhammad) [sic] thing. A lot of musicians were looking into it. I also saw Malcolm X about this time; he was just a minister then. But it was something I hadn't heard before. Some of it I couldn't quite rationalize, but there was a lot of it that made sense. I eventually found out what the true concepts of Islam were. My wife was already involved in it. . . .[3]

KOFSKY: Would you ever consider dedicating a composition to *anyone*? Political, musical, social—any public figure that would be known by everybody?

TYNER: Possibly, yes; possibly.

KOFSKY: But you can't think of anyone right offhand?

TYNER: No, not right offhand, no.

KOFSKY: So your reluctance to talk about jazz and the social questions doesn't come about because you see these social questions as unrelated, but simply because you would rather focus on the music?

TYNER: I feel that for me, as a musician, this is the primary thing—the music. If you want to, let's say, dedicate some time to discussing social problems, I feel that it's a different category, even though it's all related, but it's still a different category, it's a different subject.

. . . You can look back and see who have been the innovators [in jazz], who have been the creators. You'll see all innovation is directly related to black people. Music speaks for the times and for the people. That's the function of music all through history. . . . You ever noticed the sunflower? It draws its energy from the sun. Where there is enough sun, it will grow. This music, even though it's universal, moves only as far as black people move in this country. All the political, social and cultural developments we experience here influence this music. . . .[4]

KOFSKY: Do musicians spend time discussing such social questions?

TYNER: I don't think they spend any more time than anybody else who's involved in the social problems.

KOFSKY: Well, it's been said that they don't spend any time at all.

TYNER: [*Laughter.*] Well, I don't think they do specifically. I mean, just like if you're socializing, or if you're playing together, occasionally something pops up in the news, you might discuss it. It's only natural, it's like anybody else. But to just set aside an appointed time to discuss—

KOFSKY: No, I don't mean—

TYNER: It's just haphazardly, like any other general subject.

KOFSKY: What I'm trying to establish is whether or not musicians are *interested* in these questions.

TYNER: Well, I think they *are*. I think they're interested, just like any other citizen would be interested in social problems.

KOFSKY: In general, do they see the music as related to these problems?

TYNER: I feel that, being that the problem is directly related to them, that they may feel an inner urge or inner feeling to maybe write or express themselves, express this problem through their music, sometimes. Occasionally, a person may dedicate a number to something that has happened. I think that this type approach has been incorporated years ago. Guys used to write about social problems, what happened in society, so it's really nothing new.

KOFSKY: You don't disapprove?

TYNER: No, I don't disapprove of that, no.

KOFSKY: Some musicians have said that jazz comes out of conditions of poverty and oppression and *is* opposed to those conditions of poverty and oppression. Would you agree?

TYNER: I think it has a lot to do with it, I think that has

a lot to do with it. I think that has a great deal to do with it. I really do. But I think, also, I think it probably would have happened maybe naturally. I think that it happened to be a vehicle to express the suffering that the black man had incurred in this country; but I think that maybe, that being that the uniting of the two cultures, I think if it had just taken place under any other circumstance, maybe it might have happened. Maybe with not as much meaning—I don't know; it's really hard to say. But I think that it's really an amalgamation of the two cultures—the African and the European culture.

You see, the blues originally came from Africa. The blues is really based on a five-note scale which is African, or Eastern and Middle-Eastern. It didn't start here [in the United States]. It was just black people's concept of music before they came here and it was like a chant. . . . We were the originators of the music. This music, the blues, is based on African music. There's some talk about the American or European influence on our music, but again, the five-note scale is African. Africa is the mother of civilization and all else is, obviously, based on that.[5]

KOFSKY: Leaving aside the fact that you're a musician, do you, as an individual, have any opinions about the situation in Vietnam and the United States's activities there?

TYNER: I'm not really that familiar with the situation there, but I've heard. . . . To tell you the truth, if it's what I suspect, if it's some sort of suppression or it's some sort of injustice going on there, then I feel that, that it should be ended. That's the way I look at it; but I'm not really that familiar with the problems of Vietnam to really comment on it.

KOFSKY: What is your general opinion of working conditions for jazz musicians? Do you feel that jazz musicians are treated, on the whole, as artists deserve to be treated?

TYNER: No, they're not.

KOFSKY: Why?

TYNER: That's a very difficult question. I think that jazz music, if you want to use that term, jazz—I don't particularly care for it, but it's an accepted word and I use it because I have so much respect for the music, that I feel that the word really. . . . But, getting off that, I think that jazz is really not given the proper exposure, and it's really not exposed in the true light of what it really is. This is the way I look at it; and consequently I think that we suffer, because people get the wrong idea about what it's all about. And I think that sometimes deliberately it seems as though the music doesn't get the proper exposure—it's not being exposed right or properly. It gets sort of a minimum amount of exposure—not enough, I don't feel.

KOFSKY: Could this be connected with the fact that many of the musicians are themselves black?

TYNER: Possibly, possibly. I believe that, to a degree, I really do. Because, I mean, that's like in any other field, any other thing, especially. I believe that being that black musicians seemingly have been the innovators in this particular field, that's another thing that I think keeps it at a certain level.

KOFSKY: You mean white people find it difficult to accept the fact that black people could make valid artistic innovations?

TYNER: I wouldn't say as a whole, white people, but I think that there is a good majority, probably because of the way society points to the black as inferior, in many, many ways. So I guess it's very difficult for white people to accept that.

KOFSKY: Just as in the history textbooks you don't read that there were three black men who crossed the Delaware with Washington.[6]

TYNER: Right, right. That's what I'm saying.

KOFSKY: Do you think in jazz white musicians get better treatment than blacks, on the whole?

TYNER: In jazz? Well, to tell you the truth, I really couldn't be conclusive on that, but one thing I do feel: that being that society is the way it is, and white supremacy seems to be a dominant thing, it's only natural that a white musician, under certain circumstances, would get better treatment.

KOFSKY: So when you have a fellowship to give, you give it to Don Ellis instead of Cecil Taylor?

TYNER: Maybe in some cases that would happen.

KOFSKY: It *has* happened.

TYNER: In most cases, that would happen.

KOFSKY: What I'm interested in is the general rule.

TYNER: Yeah, in most cases, right.

KOFSKY: Do you have any idea about how conditions could be improved for jazz musicians?

TYNER: Like I said, exposure has a lot to do with it—the right kind of exposure. But like I say, jazz doesn't get the exposure that rock and roll gets, and I really can't understand it, in a sense—in a way I can and in a way I can't. I think it's unjust, because we don't get the same amount of exposure that the other art forms get, as far as the radio medium is concerned and television medium. And the image that's being painted of the jazz musicians is a very degrading one. So we can go back to the old reason, if you want.

Being involved in this form of music is difficult because we don't have popular support. The media have alienated black people from this form of music. This is unfortunate because what we're doing is an extension of the blues; I feel it's an extension of traditional black music. It's even more unfortunate because the lack of the black community's support makes us vulnerable to people who are not really interested in the art, but only in how much money they can make.

For some reason, our records aren't being released as often as we feel they should be. So, by lack of exposure, those who control the industry are holding jazz back. When music is released right away, it's fresh and it has a strong effect. They don't worry about it selling that much because they don't promote it that much. But I'm sure it would sell more than you could imagine if it got started.[7] It sells enough to keep them from going into the hole, as it is.

But they really don't want this music to move out. I think what they're trying to do is mix jazz and "rock." Rock is supposed to weaken the jazz and blues market. That's why it's way out there. . . . It's a racial thing because "rock music" is predominantly white music. We live in a racist society and we've got to evaluate this in those terms, too.[8]

KOFSKY: It all comes back to slavery.

TYNER: Yes, and keeping the black man at a certain level.

KOFSKY: Because how else could you keep them slaves? And how else could you convince the white people that it was a good idea to keep them that way?

TYNER: That's right.

KOFSKY: What do you think about attempts like that of the Jazz Composers Guild to organize jazz musicians to better their circumstances?

TYNER: I think that it's a very good—I think it's very good.

KOFSKY: What about Cecil Taylor's idea of a boycott of all recording companies, night clubs, promoters?[9]

TYNER: I think that would be very difficult. Especially if you want to survive. It's very hard as it is, you know. But I think that jazz musicians can do a little more to better their condition by doing some things together, it's only natural. But I don't think they should completely boycott. . . .

KOFSKY: Just as a technique for getting better wages?

TYNER: Well, that might. . . . Well, when I mean boycott, I mean boycott completely, or indefinitely. But I think maybe if that was tried, it might be successful.

KOFSKY: Do the musicians who play in some of the newer styles look to Africa and Asia for their musical inspiration?

TYNER: I know I do. I do.

KOFSKY: Is there any particular reason why you do?

TYNER: I have a lot of personal reasons. I think mainly because of my religious convictions—I'm orthodox Muslim. But I think that has a lot to do with my leaning. And not just because of that, I think because a lot of musicians are realizing that this is where the roots of the music really come from, as far as this music is concerned.

KOFSKY: Rather than Europe?

TYNER: Yeah, yeah, know what I mean? But I think that mostly black musicians feel that they can better relate to Africa. . . . I'm not speaking for all, but I mean there's a great number of them.

KOFSKY: Do you think that group improvisation is becoming more important in the newer styles?

TYNER: I think so.

KOFSKY: Can you think of any reason why it should be becoming more prevalent at this particular time?

TYNER: All I can say is that there's something that is a different approach. I think anything different—I think a lot of musicians are seeking to explore new areas and I think that this is a new area, a different style of playing. Now years ago, I think they used to play like that; it's nothing new.

KOFSKY: Yes, a couple of generations ago.

TYNER: It's a different concept now—it's a sort of conglomeration of what has happened before and what's happening now.* I believe that all of it is related, the whole scope.

KOFSKY: Another kind of new music that started a while back but never caught on was Third Stream Music, an attempted fusion between the jazz and European traditions. Why do you think it didn't win more of a following among the musicians?

TYNER: I really couldn't say for sure why it didn't catch on,

---

* As I noted at length in chapter 10.

but I found out from my observation over the last years—
at least my participation in the art form—that seemingly if
there isn't enough of the roots there to really identify the
music for what it is, it seemed very difficult to reach the average person, the average listener to the music. I feel that
this element definitely has to be present in order to even
approach the majority of the listeners, anyway, to jazz. Not
that one should compromise, but I think that this element
is very important and distinguishes jazz from other forms
of music.

KOFSKY: We were talking earlier about African and Asian
music being important, and it seems as though this might
have some bearing on the case, too. Because if musicians are
going to look to Africa and Asia for their musical inspiration,
perhaps they're not going to be as interested in Third Stream
Music, which really is going in another direction.

TYNER: Yeah, I guess so. But quite naturally you're going
to find musicians who are going to delve into areas similar
to the Third Stream area. I couldn't say what they're going
to come up with; but this is the way I feel—I feel that's the
way I'm looking towards, in the direction of Africa.

KOFSKY: But the young black musicians, most of them do
not seem to be very interested in Third Stream. They seem
to be much more interested in Africa and Asia.

TYNER: Right, right, sure; that's true.

KOFSKY: Here's another question on musical developments
that maybe you can help me solve: I notice that many of the
newer groups do not use the piano, and even in cases where
there is a piano, oftentimes the piano is silent when a brass
or reed soloist plays. I noticed, for example, that when you
were with John Coltrane, he had you lay out in some parts
of his solos. Why do you think that is? Why do you think
this tendency to de-emphasize the piano, or to give it another role in the music, is emerging?

TYNER: Well, one thing is the practical end of it. I used to try to play the length of his [Coltrane's] solo. He brought it to my attention first; but after I thought about it, I realized that it didn't make sense to play the length of the solo, because, after all, the horn player is familiar with the structure of the tune, whatever you're playing. And it's not really important for the piano to play the entire length of a person's solo. I feel that it's there purely for color and support; but I feel that a musician, a soloist, shouldn't have to depend upon the piano being there. You see what I mean? Not only that, it gives him more of an area harmonically, melodically, to work. It doesn't restrict him, in other words.

KOFSKY: That's what I was thinking.

TYNER: In some areas, when a person reaches a peak in their solo, they might want to move into different areas, and there may come a time when I'm moving maybe into the area that may not be simultaneous to the area that they're moving into.

KOFSKY: Particularly so if he's going to play notes that aren't really on the piano, or overtones, or shrieks, or squeals. How are you going to reconcile that with what the piano is playing?

TYNER: Yeah, that's true. And then at times it may, at times—well, actually it's really left up to, to what's happening at the time. Maybe a piano would sound good at that particular point, but it all depends on what's happening at the time.

KOFSKY: How was that determined in John's group? Was it that he asked you to lay out, or you just decided to lay out?

TYNER: No, it was just decided at a certain point.

KOFSKY: Certain writers and critics have charged that the new music in jazz lacks form, lacks structure, and so on and so forth. What do you think about those charges?

TYNER: I really can't say that they're valid altogether, although I can say this: that at times it's very hard to comprehend the structure of most of the newer attempts by some of the groups. Of course, my way of doing it wouldn't be quite as . . . well, it would be sort of different from a lot of other groups. You know, I have a way of approaching a thing—free-form, or whatever you want to call it—and it wouldn't be quite as "free" as some of the other groups, if you want to use that term.

KOFSKY: Is this inherent in the nature of the piano, or just something of your own choice?

TYNER: What do you mean, my approach?

KOFSKY: I mean, do you see it being dictated by the piano, or do you see it being simply as a matter of your own choice?

TYNER: I think it's a matter of my own choice, I don't think it's dictated by the piano necessarily, no.

KOFSKY: Why do you think so much of the new music has met with hostility on the part of many critics?

TYNER: I really couldn't say.

KOFSKY: Remember, there was a time when John's group especially was given a roasting, back in 1961–62?

TYNER: I think mainly because, in the function of being a critic, one doesn't like to feel that he's misinformed or— well, that's just like anything else, anything new that comes along quite naturally is going to meet some sort of rivalry from certain elements. I guess that's like anything else—a change. And some people might accept it, some might reject it. But in this particular position, where they have to speak with some sort of authority, they don't want to be at a disadvantage if something new comes along.

KOFSKY: Do you think there's anything social here, in the sense that most of these critics are white and many of them are middle-aged, and many of the musicians are young and black, and in some cases have radical political ideas?

TYNER: I think in most of the cases—I mean, I can't speak for all, because I know that there are some probably that are men of integrity—but I believe that there is an element of dishonesty among the critics. I couldn't say that with proof, but there's certain things that seem to point in that direction. They seem to be biased, biased in points.

KOFSKY: Well, if you want some proof, here are two quick examples. First of all, for the last two years in a row, there have been people who voted for albums in the *down beat* Critics Poll for which they wrote the notes. One of these "critics" is Ira Gitler, who was one of the writers who attacked John's group most viciously in that period—and he voted for *two* recordings whose notes he had written![10]

TYNER: [*Laughter.*] Yeah, I know what you mean. You see, that's the problem—it becomes a job.

KOFSKY: It *is* a job.

TYNER: The guy has a position; his interest in the art might be minimal; it might not be that much.

KOFSKY: At some point he becomes more interested in keeping himself alive.

TYNER: Right.

KOFSKY: And he may have to do that by something that isn't criticism at all, such as writing album notes, which isn't in the least criticism.

TYNER: No, it isn't. And not only that, sometimes I think that it can do harm at certain points.

KOFSKY: Another example is that of Leonard Feather, who wrote the liner notes for Eric Dolphy's memorial album on Vee Jay Records after giving Eric such unfavorable reviews when he was with John.

TYNER: Yeah, that's the thing. See, that's what I'm talking about. That's something—I can't accept that. And I mean, after the man [Dolphy] dies, put him in the [*down beat*] Hall of Fame—that's ridiculous!

KOFSKY: The same people who put him in poverty—

TYNER: That's what I mean, see, he couldn't work, he couldn't work in this country.[11]

KOFSKY: One other example. Speaking of working, I don't

know if you read *down beat*, but some time ago there was a very laudatory review by Dan Morgenstern of a concert by Cecil Taylor, which finished by saying that this man Taylor was a genius and needed many more opportunities to perform music for an audience. But what he didn't say was that he, Dan Morgenstern, as New York editor of *down beat*, had been responsible for drawing up the list of artists who participated in the [1966] Jazz in the Garden series at the Museum of Modern Art [*Laughter*]. And he *didn't* have Cecil Taylor in that list.[12] So that's what really annoys me—that's why I don't even like to call myself a critic, because when you say "critic," one thinks of those people.

TYNER: Not only that, it's very hard, you see, in an art form to really set yourself up as an authority.

KOFSKY: The only genuine authorities are the musicians.

TYNER: Yes, you really can't do that. You have to accept whatever is here for whatever it's worth. You can only speak from a personal point.

KOFSKY: Ultimately, it comes down to whether or not other musicians are going to pay attention to what you're doing.

TYNER: Yeah, that's about it.

KOFSKY: As an artist, do you feel that you have any responsibility to educate your audience, besides in the music?

TYNER: Not necessarily. I feel that, really, the only way that I can communicate with them—besides now and then talking—is musically. That's about the only way I can do it. Because I don't believe that if you explain the thing to a person, that doesn't mean that they're going to better their musical taste. They have to be exposed to it, listen to it, and see what they can absorb; that's about all that I can say.

KOFSKY: To you, who are the most influential artists playing the music? And how did you arrive at your decision?

TYNER: Well, I don't know. That's another difficult question, although I feel that Ornette Coleman and John Coltrane have been tremendous influences.

KOFSKY: Four quick biographical questions. Where were you born and where were you raised; and how old are you; and what's your educational background?

TYNER: I was born in Philadelphia, Pennsylvania, was raised there, and I'm twenty-seven years old, and, well, I had elementary, you know, I had a little harmony theory at Granoff Music School, and I studied privately, first of all— at the age of thirteen I started, and I studied privately for a while with a teacher. I had about two or three teachers during that time, and I studied about four years. After that I went on my own from what I learned. That's about the size of that. I think that most of the things I learned really was through practical experience, applying myself. I think that's the best.

KOFSKY: That leads me to ask you another question, if you don't mind—namely, I'm curious to know how much of what you're doing now in music you were doing before you joined John Coltrane's group. It occurs to me that perhaps your style was very similar when you were playing with the Jazztet, but people just weren't aware of it, because you weren't with a group that got as much attention as John's groups do.

TYNER: Yeah, that's true. I don't feel—that's like John, when I first met him, I felt like what he's doing now is the same thing he was doing years ago when I met him. I mean it just wasn't as developed as it is now.

KOFSKY: Nor was it as relatively accepted as it is now.

TYNER: Yeah, that's true.

KOFSKY: That's the end of my list of prepared questions, do you have anything else that you'd like to say?

TYNER: Well, all I can say is that I hope that people will at least listen more closely to us musically and not be so conclusive on certain things, musically, without remaining open-minded. I feel that, not that everything that happens is valid, because everything that a person does doesn't mean that it's right. But it has some purpose. . . .

[We continued to talk after I turned off the tape recorder, and as some of this dialogue was relevant to Tyner's earlier remarks, I tried to capture as much of it as possible.]

KOFSKY: You were saying while the recorder was off. . . .

TYNER: I was just saying, like about the Black Power thing, I feel that a lot of people have gotten a wrong concept about that. I'm pretty sure that all that the black Americans want is the same thing as the whites. They seized this phrase as a means to convey emotionally what they mean—what they mean by what they've been demanding, actually.

KOFSKY: Whites never had to talk about white power, because they had it all the time.

TYNER: Yeah, that's true. So I believe it's very significant in this situation.

KOFSKY: You know, in the 1940s, what happened was that a tremendous gap opened up between the new musicians of that day and the public. And most of the critics didn't really do anything to help; in many cases, they made the situation worse.

TYNER: Here is what I can't understand: why, when I spoke to you earlier about labels, I realize that things have to be identified, as a means just to identify. But at times these labels can hamper an individual or they can be very harmful, in a sense. It all depends on how they are being used and what they mean, you know what I mean?

KOFSKY: Like the phrase "the New Black Music"?

TYNER: Yes. Well, I was saying, like they used it when Bird [Charlie Parker] was alive, they had certain words for them—"anti-social," and what have you.

KOFSKY: That's right. In the case of the "New Black Music," I think one can use it in a very simple descriptive sense, just the way you did, to mean that the *innovators* almost always are black.

TYNER: Yeah, right.

KOFSKY: If you just say *that*, I don't see how anybody can take offense. But then the matter gets distorted, it gets out of perspective, it becomes another "Black Power" issue. People start screaming that you're a racist, you're talking about "black supremacy," and so on.

TYNER: Yeah, that's the way it's defined, that's true.

KOFSKY: There's a lot of distortion around [*Laughter*], and nobody is very happy about it except the distorters.

TYNER: Yeah, that's true.

NOTES

1. Al McFarlane, "*The Black Scholar* Interviews: McCoy Tyner," *Black Scholar*, II:2 (October 1970), pp. 40–46.

2. *Ibid.*, pp. 40–41.

3. *Ibid.*, p. 42.

4. *Ibid.*, pp. 40–41.

5. *Ibid.*

6. See Herbert Aptheker, *Essays in the History of the American Negro* (2nd. ed.; New York: International Publishers, 1964), p. 105.

7. A point I argue at considerable length in chapter 4 of *Black Music, White Business: Illuminating the History and Political Economy of Jazz* (New York: Pathfinder Press, 1997).

8. McFarlane, *op. cit.*, pp. 45–46.

9. For a discussion of the Jazz Composers Guild, see chapter 7. Cecil Taylor's proposal for a boycott by black musicians of white business institutions is in the (partial) transcript of a panel discussion among Taylor, Archie Shepp, Rahsaan Roland Kirk, and others, "Point of Contact," in *down beat Music '66*, ed. Don DeMicheal (Chicago: Maher Publications, 1966), p. 19.

10. In the 1965 International Critics Poll, David A. Himmelstein voted in the Record of the Year category for an album he had annotated, Booker Ervin, *The Freedom Book* (Prestige 7295); see "How They Voted," *down beat*, August 12, 1965, p. 14. The following year

Ira Gitler voted in the same category for Jaki Byard, *Live!* (Prestige 7419), and Booker Ervin, *The Space Book* (Prestige 7386), the notes for both of which he, as a frequent employee of Prestige Records, had written; see "How They Voted," *down beat*, August 25, 1966, p. 40. See also the discussion of the critics in chapters 2 and 3 and the extensive analysis in chapter 8 of the critical assault on John Coltrane's music during the early 1960s.

11. See the notes by Leonard Feather to *The Eric Dolphy Memorial Album* (Vee Jay 2503). In chapter 8 I explore the possibility that the hostility white critics unleashed against Eric Dolphy contributed to his premature death (see note 42 especially); John Coltrane also discusses this idea in the interview in the next chapter. Subsequently, Feather also wrote commentary for recordings by former Coltrane drummer Elvin Jones, Coltrane's widow and collaborator, pianist Alice McLeod Coltrane, Coltrane's fellow innovator Ornette Coleman and, not least—McCoy Tyner; the details are in chapter 3, note 11.

12. For Morgenstern's review of Cecil Taylor, see "Caught in the Act," *down beat*, July 28, 1966, p. 24; Morgenstern's role in selecting artists for the Jazz in the Garden series of concerts at the Museum of Modern Art is documented in the "News" feature of *down beat* of the same date, p. 10, and in the issue of October 10, 1966, p. 9. I also examine this incident at greater length in chapter 3.

13

John Coltrane: an interview

A. Some thoughts on John Coltrane

Above and beyond the music itself, one of the things that has always made the jazz environment so intriguing (as I hope has by now become clear) is its propensity to mirror in microcosm all the convolutions and complexities of the turbulent "racial" cauldron that boils, bubbles, and from time to time even bursts into flames in a society obsessed with ethnic color lines.

But perhaps "mirror" in the previous paragraph is not quite the correct word, for as we have seen, one can often discern social trends in the hothouse jazz environment long before the general public becomes aware of them. Thus, serious students of events in jazz could not have been wholly astonished when, in 1966, Stokley Carmichael's cry of "Black Power" first rent the air.[1] After all, the disputes and debates that Carmichael's political gesture unleashed had for several years—certainly since the early 1960s—been a more-or-less-constant feature of the far narrower world of jazz.

And with much the same results, I might add. Just as white liberals started to defect from the campaign for black liberation when it swerved from its original civil-rights orientation toward a more nationalist stance, so, too, did prominent white writers and business executives react with implacable hostility to the various manifestations of black nationalism in jazz. Ultimately, like their counterparts in the civil-rights movement, these whites turned their back on jazz—or, at any rate, on the most innovative black jazz artists—and sought refuge in places where they would not have to confront the growing movement toward black radicalism in music and/or politics.[2]

The key figure in provoking this split—in weeding out the musically militant sheep from the liberal lambs, if you will—was John Coltrane. Politically, Coltrane was not a black nationalist, at least not in any overt sense.* Nonetheless, there were aspects of black nationalism that genuinely intrigued or attracted him. Malcolm X, Coltrane said in response to my question, was "a man I had to see," and, having duly seen him, Coltrane affirmed that he was "quite impressed."[3]

Be that as it may, Coltrane never fully immersed himself in the heady and swirling currents of the political black nationalism of the 1960s—that simply was not his style. If he had, no doubt the conservative white anti-nationalist forces would have had an easier time of it. For as we have witnessed repeatedly in these pages, jazz musicians who have the habit of thinking and writing and speaking in unabashedly nationalist and/or radical terms—Charles Mingus and Max Roach at first, later followed by Cecil Taylor, Bill Dixon, Archie Shepp, and others—have reaped ostracism, vilification

---

* Nor have I ever claimed that he was, although this minor inconvenience has not for a moment stopped those writers who reject my views from attempting to attribute that position to me and then—in a classic straw-man maneuver—proceeding to "refute" it.

and isolation for their pains. Several times already I have pointed out that during the 1960s such artists only rarely enjoyed the opportunity to play in concerts and festivals and perform in the recording studio—a state of affairs unlikely to be the outcome of mere coincidence.[4]

Although it did overlap to some degree with black nationalism, Coltrane's philosophical outlook gravitated in the direction of what, for want of a better phrase, I think it fair to describe with the phrase "cosmic mysticism." When, for instance, I mentioned the name coined by Amiri Baraka (LeRoi Jones) for the avant-garde jazz of the 1960s, the new black music, Coltrane's response was to state, "When I know a man's sound, well, to me, that's him, that's this man. . . . Labels, I don't bother with."*[5]

Still, his mysticism clearly possessed strong social implications. "Music," he asserted, "is an instrument . . . that can create change in the thinking of the people." Jazz—a term that Coltrane himself rejected—he considered "an expression of higher ideals. . . . So therefore, brotherhood is there; and I believe with brotherhood, there would be no poverty . . . there would be no war." Expanding on these ideas, Coltrane added that he wanted

> to be a force for real good. In other words, I know that there are bad forces, forces out here that bring suffering to others and misery to the world, but I want to be the opposite, I want to be a force which is truly for good.

Likewise, having reflected on the treatment accorded black jazz artists in the United States, he no longer found playing in jazz nightclubs congenial: "It doesn't make sense, man, to have somebody drop a glass, or somebody ask for

---

* At other times, however, as I will bring out momentarily, Coltrane would, if pressed, refer to his music as "classical."

some money, right in the middle of Jimmy Garrison's [bass] solo.[6] Accordingly, he applauded the efforts of musicians to "work out their own problems in this area" through "self-help." Of the Jazz Composers Guild, one of the earliest efforts in this direction, he said: "I *do* think that was a good idea; I really do, and I don't think it's dead."[7] "The music is rising, in my estimation," he told me, and the corollary was that the so-called jazz club did not offer a proper setting for a dedicated artist. Some remarks about his music he made in an interview six weeks earlier (portions of which appear following my interview with him) throw additional light on his thinking in this regard:

> The term "classical music," in my opinion, means the music of a country that is played by the composers and musicians of the country, as opposed to the music that the people dance to or sing, the popular music. So in other words, there are classical musics all over the world—different types of classical music. So if you want to name [Coltrane's music] anything, you could name it a "classical music."[8]

These things—the reluctance to perform in nightclubs, the interest in musicians' self help through organizations like the Jazz Composers Guild, the desire to have his music perceived as "classical," and his concomitant unhappiness with the word "jazz" to describe it—all these indicate both Coltrane's conviction that jazz innovators—the overwhelming majority, of whom, of course, were black—have never obtained even a fraction of the artistic recognition they deserve as well as his intention to do whatever lay within his power to alter this state of affairs.

There were moments, moreover, when Coltrane also seemed to be aware, although perhaps only tacitly, that the music he and the other jazz revolutionaries were evolving posed an implicit challenge to the class biases and other limitations of the European concert-hall approach to art music. I have already commented (in chapters 7 and 8) on the fact that the titles to many of Coltrane's compositions drew their inspiration from what was then called the Third World; that, as a token of the mutual esteem in which he and Ravi Shankar held each other, John and Alice Coltrane named one of their sons after the Indian sitar master; and that, a year before his death, Coltrane was planning "to make a trip to Africa, to gather whatever I can find, particularly the musical sources."

What these instances illustrate is the non-European—and, perhaps, in some senses even the counter-European—direction of Coltrane's music during the 1960s, despite the fact that the saxophonist was not given to issuing defiant political manifestos dramatically declaring his intent. Manifestos or no, it was, in reality, just these tendencies that precipitated the Great Schism and convulsed the world of jazz during the 1960s. On the one hand, Coltrane's ardent young black followers discovered in his work—rightly so, I believe— the clearest possible expression of the African-American mentality in the second half of the twentieth century: the quintessential distillation, conceivably, of what it meant to be black in that time and place.[*] On the other, the same aspect of his art that black people celebrated exuberantly led the bulk of the white-business Establishment, and its spokesmen among the critics (including even some of his former supporters, such as Ira Gitler), to turn their withering assaults upon him, condemning his playing with the scornful epithet, "anti-jazz." If and when history ever renders a full

---

[*] I hope it is obvious that I am in no way maintaining that Coltrane's appeal was confined to blacks alone. On the contrary, as I pointed out in chapter 8 and will reemphasize below, Coltrane served as a model for white youth as well.

accounting of this period, I suspect the final verdict will be that this response represents the nadir in what has generally been a decades-long tale of white incomprehension or outright rejection of black musical art.

With the objectivity that the passage of time makes possible, already it is evident that the dominant white critics, who had sentimental attachments to the music of the bebop era and who had become accustomed to reigning as the arbiters of jazz orthodoxy, were enormously ill at ease with the undisguised emotions, fervid evangelicalism, and spiritual exaltation—with the thoroughly *black* nature, in short—of a typical Coltrane performance. To this day, the bulk of these writers continue to show themselves incapable of digesting the jazz revolution fomented by Coltrane, his soulmates, and his followers.[9] Many have simply renounced their former allegiance to jazz and departed in search of greater rewards elsewhere.[10]

Be that as it may, the extent of Coltrane's influence on young musicians has only increased during the three decades since his death. Even the first wave of rock musicians—beginning in the mid-1960s with the Byrds, the Jefferson Airplane, the Grateful Dead, and Frank Zappa (Mothers of Invention), and continuing thereafter with Jimi Hendrix, Chicago, and Santana later that decade—were not immune to his appeal.[11] But, naturally, it is among jazz artists that Coltrane's innovations have had the broadest and most profound impact. One indication of this impact is the ubiquitousness of the soprano saxophone in jazz after the 1960s, having been rescued by Coltrane from the near-total obscurity in which it languished following the death of Sidney Bechet.[12] Another, the details of which I leave for the notes, is the frequency with which other artists have recorded either his compositions or compositions dedicated to him. To the best of my knowledge, individual pieces and/or albums offered in tribute to Coltrane's memory are far more numerous than those honoring any other one individual, be he or she black, brown, yellow, white, political agitator, musician, intellectual, or what have you.[13]

Of greater interest than a recital of the various kinds of evidence demonstrating the breadth of Coltrane's influence on younger jazz musicians, however, is the question of accounting for it. We can, I believe, understand Coltrane's charismatic effect on subsequent generations of black musicians partly in musical terms, partly in extra-musical ones.

The musical ones first, because they are more concrete and, therefore, easiest to grasp. Here I propose to conduct what the Germans describe as a "thought-experiment." Let us take an imaginary journey into the past, back to the opening years of the 1960s. At that point, nearly two decades after the bebop revolution first threw the jazz world into turmoil, the conventional way of improvising in jazz, by constructing a solo over the foundation of a fixed and regularly recurring sequence of chords, had turned utterly stale, predictable, and unchallenging for the music's most creative spirits. Though some (notably, Ornette Coleman) had tried, no one as yet had succeeded in breaking the impasse. The question still remained: where do we go from here?

It was that question that Coltrane faced squarely and, in my opinion, did more to answer than any other single artist. Initially, as we saw in chapter 8, he himself had thought along traditional, if nonetheless extremely demanding, bebop lines: more chords, and more complex clusters of chords, might serve to restore to bebop the adventurousness it possessed during its heyday. Coltrane, typically, did not shrink from the recognition that this first attempt had failed. Instead, cutting his losses, he embarked upon a series of forays that took him in a number of different directions. Finally, after a period of the most intense searching that he would repeat more than once in his career, he evolved what would become the backbone of his new style. Always open to fresh ideas from every quarter—the breadth of his musical interests appears to be at least as great as that of any jazz musician before or since—Coltrane drew from wildly disparate sources in synthesizing this style: from Miles Davis (with whom, of course, he had played for most of the second half of the 1950s) he borrowed the idea of basing an improvisation on a mode or scale; from Ornette Coleman he took a diffuse but exhilarating concept of "free" melodic invention that gave an improviser latitude beyond what even modes offered; from the work of saxophonist and flutist Yusef Lateef he was prompted to draw upon Mid-eastern melodies and sonorities; from Indian raga, as exemplified in the performances of Ravi Shankar, he absorbed lessons in how a soloist might play fifteen or twenty minutes (or longer) without any loss of intensity or creativity. As a result of mulling over these different approaches to improvisation, Coltrane ultimately was led to conclude that to overcome the stagnation engulfing jazz by the late 1950s, he would have to do away with rigid chord cycles as a framework for improvisation, replacing them with nothing more than a set of modes or scales, a time-signature and tempo, and a chorus-length of a predetermined number of measures. Often, moreover, especially toward the end of his life, he went even further, dispensing with the practice of constructing an improvisation by stitching together a series of chorus-length statements for a more open-ended approach.

Indeed, even at the outset in mid-1960, Coltrane and McCoy Tyner (and Eric Dolphy, when he performed as part of the group) already had begun improvising solos whose duration was not tied to the number of measures in a chorus. It was in "My Favorite Things," not surprisingly, that Coltrane initially took this step. As we have already seen in chapter 9, "My Favorite Things" was not only the vehicle for Coltrane's debut with the soprano saxophone, but it was also the first piece in the repertoire of his newly formed quartet in which the improvisation was based on scales rather than chord sequences and a chorus of fixed length. "The way the song is constructed," he explained, "it's divided into parts. We play both parts. There's a minor and a major part. We improvise in the minor, and we improvise in the major modes," with the length of each of these two solos left "entirely up to the artist—his choice."[14] Coltrane's later work veered even more strongly in this direction, especially his most radical composition, *Ascension* (1965).[15] Here, sections in which the soloist plays with near-total freedom from constraints of tonality and measure lines alternate with sections of dense collective improvisation by the entire group of two trumpets, five saxophones, piano, two basses, and drums. In these latter passages, as I suggested in chapter 10, Coltrane most likely was making another attempt to develop a fully polyrhythmic music, a goal that exerted an unmistakable fascination over him throughout the final years of his life.

At the same time, however, Coltrane never completely relinquished songs based on a fixed-length chorus. Among the best-known cases in point are his modal composition "Impressions" and "I Want to Talk About You," both 32-measure pieces in the AABA form, and the "Pursuance" section of *A Love Supreme*, a 12-measure blues in a minor key.[16] It was as if, having moved well beyond chord-and-chorus-based improvisation, Coltrane could now return to this form and recapture some of the enjoyment he had once found in creating within its boundaries. Secure in the knowledge that his new approach(es) had rescued him from the paralysis of bebop at the end of the 1950s, he could simply take earlier styles on their own terms—he no longer had to try to wring from them a revolutionary content they did not and could not possess. Having attained the summit, one can then look back and delight in the view.

Coltrane's breakthrough in 1960, in summary, was simple in content, but revolutionary in effect. I argued earlier (in chapters 9 and 10) that the great achievement at this point in his career was to develop a synthesis of the techniques of melodic invention and extended improvisation of Indian raga with the cross-rhythmic patterns of African percussion and the traditional jazz device of the riff. We can grasp the nature of this profound innovation most readily, perhaps, by comparing his approach to that of a raga. Like a raga, a representative Coltrane improvisation—any recorded version of "My Favorite Things" will illustrate the point—is based on a set of scales or modes (Coltrane seems to have used the two terms interchangeably); his composition "Impressions," constructed on the Dorian mode (essentially a D-minor scale) offers another good example in this regard. Underlying the scale is the tonic note, or in raga, the drone. The supporting instruments—*tabla* drums and *tamboura* (drone instrument) in raga; piano, bass, and drums in jazz— serve to establish both the tonality and scale (drone and raga), as well as to supply a constant rhythmic counterpoint over which the soloist weaves an improvised melody.

So much Coltrane's music and raga have in common. What sets them apart is the greater variety of sounds that the instruments of jazz can produce, and especially the vast amount of sonic *power* these instruments can unleash.[17] Liberated from the domination of one cycle of chords endlessly repeated, Coltrane put this new freedom to superb effect by introducing into music some of the most indescribably evocative—and quintessentially *human*—sounds ever created on any instrument. The possibilities the saxophonist thus opened were virtually unlimited—and, it must be said, he made the most of them. With the introduction of electronic instruments into popular music, the sensation of being surrounded and sometimes even overpowered by exploding waves of sound became a familiar one. In point of fact, however, well before heavily amplified rock music burst onto the scene, Coltrane and his associates—in particular Elvin Jones, as Coltrane's comments in the following interview attest—had demonstrated their ability to whip audiences to peak after peak of emotional fervor, until a final crescendo left listeners drained and gasping for breath: an hour-long performance, often of only one or two pieces, that seemed to have lasted days.

Such was the almost-superhuman intensity that the Coltrane group could bring to bear. For those willing to submerge themselves beneath the billowing layers of sound, the results were almost always ecstatic. Others, as we have witnessed, lacked the desire or the capacity to be swept to the heights; they were, in many cases, the ones who became dogmatic musical and/or social reactionaries, denouncing in bitterest vitriol Coltrane's "anti-jazz"; or else, as I have remarked earlier, they simply abandoned jazz altogether.

It was at this point that the extra-musical aspects of Coltrane's career began to acquire greater significance, as Coltrane increasingly took on the stature of a combination guru and culture-hero (much to his own bemusement, if he was even aware of the phenomenon, one can be certain). It is true that, initially, Coltrane's towering reputation stemmed from the innovations that revivified jazz after 1960; much of his influence on musicians and listeners alike will always reflect his artistic inventions and the devastating force with which he implemented them.

That, however, is only part of the story. For in the course of consummating the changes he began, the saxophonist gradually assumed the proportions of a symbol larger than life. Symbol of what, you may ask? Of the present-day musical artist who—to paraphrase Edgard Varèse (and to borrow one of the late Frank Zappa's favorite aphorisms)—refuses to die? To be sure. Of the vital energies of a historically oppressed black community? Undoubtedly that, too.

But conceivably above all else, we can read Coltrane's career as an object lesson in uncompromising honesty, total devotion to the creation of art as he, the artist, perceived it, regardless of what adversities he might face as a consequence. This facet of the man is difficult to convey to those who never had the privilege of seeing him perform. Some of his recordings, though, especially those made in the presence of audiences, can at least suggest why, even before his untimely death, Coltrane was the object of veneration on the part of many. Take, for instance, the first recorded performance of "Chasin' the Trane" (so named, incidentally, by the recording engineer, not the composer) that I discussed in chapter 9 in connection with Albert Ayler's work. Here, Coltrane reworked a few simple blues figures uninterruptedly for a full sixteen minutes, with only bass and drums by way of support—a tour de force that in terms of sheer vigor and passion eclipses almost everything else in recorded jazz.[18]

Performances of this intensity—too infrequently captured on record, alas[19]—were the rule rather than the exception with Coltrane. His popularity was certainly sizable enough to have allowed him to get by, as many another artist in a similar situation has chosen to do, with an endless series of minutely different variations on themes of proven appeal. That course would have required a much smaller expenditure of his talents and energies—but it was not for him. The standards by which Coltrane measured himself were always the highest; giving less than full measure was an idea that I strenuously doubt he ever entertained—or for that matter, even *could* entertain.

As part of what he required of himself, Coltrane never ceased exploring new musical vistas. In the months before his death in July 1967, he developed the habit of keeping a flute in his bedroom, so that after he had exhausted himself playing the saxophones, he could "go there [when] I'm tired and . . . lay down and practice"—a small but representative index of the supreme dedication he brought to his art.

Another, as we saw earlier, was his willingness to take

under his wing the youngest and most iconoclastic black musicians, especially (but not only) saxophonists, to whom he evidently felt particularly close. Coltrane interceded with Impulse Records, where he was under contract for the last half-dozen years of his life, to have the company record such avant-garde pioneers as Albert Ayler, Pharoah Sanders, Archie Shepp, and Marion Brown.[20] On several occasions, as I noted in chapter 9, he asked to have Ayler's group included on the same concert bill as his own.[21] Coltrane's generosity even extended to the point of using his group to spotlight some of these younger saxophonists—starting with Eric Dolphy, then Archie Shepp, and finally Pharoah Sanders—heedless of the additional expenses that would have to come out of his own pocket or of the possibility that he might be upstaged in his own group by a musician more than ten years his junior. Such magnanimity and absence of self-regard are rare in any walk of life; coming in the extremely competitive jazz milieu—where underemployment is an ever-present fact of life[22]—they were unprecedented. Coupled with his resolute determination to push his music beyond what he had already perfected, and his constant, unfeigned humility, such attributes made Coltrane appear a Christ-like personification of incorruptible integrity and the quest for truth in a society that defines artistic merit in terms of box-office receipts and record-sales figures.

At this point, it may be fitting to introduce a personal note to supplement what I have been relating in somewhat abstract terms. Although I am not at all a religious person, I revered John Coltrane in some respects as one would a saint. I could never have written these words when he was alive—if nothing else, it would have been too embarrassing for him had he read them. But as he is gone, there is no reason now for biting my tongue. I feel, moreover, that such an acknowledgment is the smallest gesture of gratitude I can offer for the beauty he brought into my life.

My veneration for John and my devotion to his music began, I believe, in the winter of 1957–1958, when I first heard him on Miles Davis's *'Round About Midnight* recording. I was immediately thrilled by his sound. Although familiarity is supposed to lead to contempt, the process worked just in reverse with my fondness for Coltrane's playing: the more I heard, the greater the attraction. If I ever doubted the proposition, I could consistently rely on the unquenchable affirmation one hears on his recordings (to say nothing of his appearances in the flesh) to convince me that life was indeed worth the effort.

Meeting John did nothing to tarnish his appeal for me, as sometimes happens with one whose work you have admired from a distance, but only enhanced it. I will not pretend I knew him extremely well. I introduced myself to him at San Francisco's Jazz Workshop shortly after he formed the quartet—it would have to have been in 1960—during his first West Coast engagement as a leader in his own right. The members of the Students for Racial Equality at the University of California had delegated me to ask him if he would perform a benefit concert whose proceeds would go to the Student Nonviolent Coordinating Committee (SNCC). Although he readily consented—both he and McCoy Tyner appeared eager to support the cause, as I recall—the concert itself never took place: the then-chancellor of the university, Clark Kerr, denied our group permission to raise funds on campus for the use of an off-campus organization—even though, prior to that time, fraternities and sororities regularly had access to university facilities for precisely such purposes. In any event, with the possibility of our being able to get money into the hands of SNCC thus blocked, there was not much point in continuing with plans for the concert.[23] Still, it had been exhilarating for me, as the liaison with John Coltrane, to carry on even those few fragmentary and truncated conversations we had in the cubbyhole that passed for a dressing room in the rear of the Jazz Workshop.

I did my best to keep up the acquaintanceship in the years that followed. I moved to Los Angeles in 1961, and whenever Coltrane appeared there—which was not anywhere near as often as I would have liked—I made it a point to seek him out and exchange a few words. Poor man! How I later came to regret robbing him of those precious minutes he liked to use for catnapping during intermissions.

In the summer of 1966 I was able (thanks to a small grant from the Louis A. Rabinowitz Foundation) to arrange for a two-week stay in New York to interview the musicians involved in the Jazz Revolution. The name that topped my list, of course, was that of John Coltrane. In spite of his crowded schedule (and what I now suppose was his ill health), he acceded to my request and—to my great delight—allowed me the privilege of putting my questions to him.

The circumstances of that interview (on August 18, 1966) may help explain the affection I felt for John and why the closer one got to the man, the more one loved and respected him. There was, to begin with, no earthly reason why he should have consented to submit to my questions, especially as it involved a certain amount of inconvenience for him. Merely to meet me at the Deer Park station of the Long Island Railroad, he had to drive some thirty or forty minutes from his home. Then, as there would be no time for us to return to his home for the interview if I planned to be on the last train to Manhattan that day, he sat with me in his station wagon for over an hour, sweltering in the August heat and humidity while we tape-recorded an interview in the parking lot of a local supermarket (part of our conversation on the tape proceeds to an accompaniment of vigorously rattled shopping carts!). After we had finished and John had driven me back to the station, over my protestations he insisted on waiting with me on the sun-scorched platform until the next train to New York arrived. As we were sitting and conversing, John asked me about my political philosophy—a logical sequel to our earlier dialogue about changing the world for the better. He was thoughtful and attentive when I told him I was a socialist, and I tried as best I could, given my agitated state, to explain why. And then the train came.

This, however, was not the last of John's kindnesses. The next day I had a telephone call from Pharoah Sanders, who said that John had told him I was searching for him—as indeed I had been, with complete futility, ever since my arrival in New York—to interview. As a result, we arranged an appointment for that purpose, owing to the continuing good offices of John Coltrane.

Why did John Coltrane go so far out of his way to assist someone as uninfluential as myself? I can only speculate that, whatever reservations he may have had about my political ideas, he was convinced of my sincerity in working for a radical improvement in the human condition, and for that reason, if I am not mistaken, he put himself at my disposal.[24] To say that his actions touched me would be an enormous understatement.[25] But by then I appreciated that John Coltrane was unlike other people: his humility seemed to grow in proportion to his greatness, and I believe him the most truly modest soul I have ever met. It was this characteristic combination of modesty and human warmth that overwhelmed me in talking to John and lent an additional dimension to my feeling for his music.

In the 1964 election, I wrote in the names of Malcolm X and John Coltrane for president and vice president, respectively. I mention this matter now only because I have mused about it often since. Then, I made that choice because John Coltrane and Malcolm X were to my mind the two greatest living Americans. Later, however, it occurred to me to wonder if there isn't some more-basic connection between them as well. I believe there is.

Although John Coltrane, as I remarked above, was not

someone who viewed the world primarily in political terms, whereas Malcolm X—who died at almost the identical age as Coltrane only two years before him—was deeply committed to political activism, a certain parallel nonetheless unites them. The very fact that the musician and the agitator (a term of praise in my lexicon) alike became folk-heroes to younger black-nationalist radicals (and not a few whites as well) suggests that profound similarities may lie concealed beneath undeniable, but perhaps superficial, differences. Both men, after all, perceived a fundamental reality about this country—the reality that you could know only if you were black and had worked your way up through the tangled, fetid jungle of jazz clubs, dance halls, bars, narcotics, alcohol, gangsters, and so on. Both had the strength of character that prevented them from being trapped and destroyed in this environment. Instead, both were later able to *use* what they had learned in an effort to show us not just the necessity for creating a world without ghettos of any sort, but also how to set about doing it, by employing to the maximum our human potentialities—our reason and our emotions—to reconstruct society on a just, compassionate, and harmonious basis. Clearly, Malcolm X would have had no difficulty in agreeing with Coltrane's wish "to be a force which is truly for good."

Neither John Coltrane nor Malcolm X, to continue exploring the parallel, was ever content with a static description of a world they sought to change. Rather, both of them, each in his unique way, exhorted their followers to break out of accustomed modes of thinking and reacting—and, moreover, they showed themselves willing to lead the way by challenging all the dogmas of the Conventional Wisdom, even when that meant subjecting their own most cherished assumptions, concepts, and attitudes to relentless scrutiny. If any of these proved inadequate or outmoded, so much the worse for them: once their shortcomings were revealed, out they went, like yesterday's newspapers. Each man, finally, could have assured himself a life of relative comfort and well-being merely by making a few seemingly minor concessions, yet neither was willing to accept such a mess of pottage if that meant curtailing his right to seek out and proclaim higher truths.

Such was the compulsive honesty of these two titans that made Malcolm X and John Coltrane the charismatic figures they were. If sometimes they worried, as anyone would, that their single-minded dedication jeopardized material security, health, and even physical safety, the hesitations were always momentary, the decisions to forge ahead unalterable. It is an irony of which only history is capable that precisely their most admirable qualities ultimately cost these two their lives. Cut down in their prime—their work far from finished, their best years surely still to come—it is safe to say that no end to their influence is remotely in sight.

If we are ever to construct the kind of humane society for which both John Coltrane and Malcolm X stood—a goal that looks little closer now than it did thirty years ago, I regret to say—we will need every last morsel of wisdom and decency they bequeathed us. To deserve their legacy, we have no choice but to be as fiercely skeptical of what we have been conditioned to accept unquestioningly, as rigorously demanding of ourselves, as they were. If, somehow, we can manage to take that first step, we will indeed have begun to absorb the best of what they tried to teach us.

B. An interview with John Coltrane

KOFSKY: The first thing I want to ask you about is a story that somebody told me the first night I came here. The people I was staying with have a friend, a young lady, and she was downtown at one of Malcolm X's speeches—and lo and behold, who should plop down on the seat next to her but John Coltrane [*laughter*]. Right away, that whetted my

JOHN COLTRANE: AN INTERVIEW / 503

curiosity, and I wanted to know how many times you had seen him, what you thought of him, and so forth.

COLTRANE: That was the only time.

KOFSKY: Were you impressed by him?

COLTRANE: Definitely. That was the only time. I thought I had to see the man, you know. I was living downtown, I was in the hotel, I saw the posters, and I realized that he was going to be over there, so I said, well, I'm going over there and see this cat, because I had never seen him. I was quite impressed.

KOFSKY: That was one of his last speeches, wasn't it?

COLTRANE: Well, it was toward the end of his career.

KOFSKY: Some musicians have said that there's a relationship between some of Malcolm's ideas and the music, especially the new music. Do you think there's anything in that?

COLTRANE: Well, I think that music, being an expression of the human heart, or of the human being itself, does express just what *is* happening. I feel it expresses the whole thing—the whole of human experience at the particular time that it is being expressed.

KOFSKY: What do you think about the phrase, the "new black music," as a description of some of the newer styles in jazz?

COLTRANE: Phrases, I don't know. They don't mean much to me, because usually I don't make the phrases, so I don't react too much. It makes no difference to me one way or the other what it's called.

KOFSKY: If you did make the phrases, could you think of one?

COLTRANE: I don't think there's a phrase for it that I could make.[26]

KOFSKY: The people who use that phrase argue that jazz is particularly closely related to the black community and it's an expression of what's happening there. That's why I asked you about your reaction to Malcolm X.

COLTRANE: Well, I think it's up to the individual musician, call it what you may, for any reason you may. Myself, I recognize the artist. I recognize an individual when I see his contribution; and when I know a man's sound, well, to me that's him, that's this man. That's the way I look at it. Labels, I don't bother with.

KOFSKY: But it does seem to be a fact that most of the *changes* in the music—the innovations—have come from black musicians.

COLTRANE: Yes, well, this is how it is.

KOFSKY: Have you ever noticed—as you've played all over the United States and in all kinds of circumstances— have you ever noticed that the reaction of an audience varies or changes if it's a black audience or a white audience or a mixed audience? Have you ever noticed that the racial composition of the audience seems to determine how the people respond?

COLTRANE: Well, sometimes, yes, and sometimes, no.

KOFSKY: Any examples?

COLTRANE: Sometimes it might appear to be one; you might say—well, it's hard to say, man. Sometimes people like it or don't like it, no matter what color they are.

KOFSKY: You don't have any preferences yourself about what kind of an audience you play for?

COLTRANE: Well, to me, it doesn't matter. I only hope that whoever is out there listening, they enjoy it; and if they're not enjoying it, I'd rather they not be there.

KOFSKY: If people do enjoy the music, how would you like them to demonstrate it? Do you like an audience that's perfectly still and unresponsive, or do you like an audience that reacts more visibly to the music?

COLTRANE: Well, I guess I like an audience that does show what they feel; to respond.

KOFSKY: I remember when you played at the Jazz Workshop in San Francisco, you sometimes got that kind of an audience, which you didn't get when you played at Shelly's Manne-Hole in Los Angeles, and it seemed to me that that had some effect on the music.

COLTRANE: Yes, because it seems to me that the audience, in listening, is in an act of participation, you know. And when you know that somebody is maybe moved the same way you are, to such a degree or approaching the degree, it's just like having another member in the group.

KOFSKY: Is that what happened at the *Ascension* recording session?[27] The people who were there—did they get that involved?

COLTRANE: I don't know. I was so doggone busy; I was worried to death. I couldn't really enjoy the date. If it hadn't been a date, then I would have really enjoyed it. You know, I was trying to get the time and everything, and I was busy. I hope they felt something. To hear the record, I enjoyed it; I enjoyed all of the individual contributions.

KOFSKY: What do you think, then, about playing concerts? Does that seem to inhibit the interaction between yourself, your group, and the audience?

COLTRANE: Well, on concerts, the only thing that bugs me might be a hall with poor acoustics, where we can't quite get the unit sound. But as far as the audience goes, it's about the same.

KOFSKY: Another reason I asked you about Malcolm was because I've interviewed a number of musicians and the consensus seems to be that the younger musicians talk about the political issues and social issues that Malcolm talked about when they're with each other. And some of them say that they try to express this in the music. Do you find in your own groups or among musicians you're friendly with that these issues are important and that you do talk about them?

COLTRANE: Oh, they're definitely important; and as I said, the issues are *part* of what *is* at this time. So naturally, as musicians, we express whatever is.

KOFSKY: Do you make a *conscious* attempt to express these things?

COLTRANE: Well, I tell you for myself, I make a conscious attempt, I think I can truthfully say that in music I make or I have *tried* to make a conscious attempt to change what I've found, in music. In other words, I've tried to say, "Well, *this* I feel, could be better, in my opinion, so I will try to do this to make it better." This is what I feel that we feel in any situation that we find in our lives, when there's something we think could be better, we must make an effort to try and make it better. So it's the same socially, musically, politically, and in any department of our lives.

KOFSKY: Most of the musicians I have talked to are very concerned about changing society and they do see their music as an instrument by which society can be changed.

COLTRANE: Well, I think so. I think music is an instrument. It can create the initial thought patterns that can change the thinking of the people.

KOFSKY: In particular, some of the people have said that jazz is opposed to poverty, to suffering, and to oppression; and therefore, that jazz is opposed to what the United States is doing in Vietnam. Do you have any comments on that subject?

COLTRANE: On the Vietnam situation?

KOFSKY: Well, you can divide it into two parts. The first part was whether you think jazz is opposed to poverty and suffering and oppression, and the second part is whether you think, if so, jazz is therefore opposed to the United States's involvement in Vietnam?

COLTRANE: In my opinion I would say yes, because jazz— if you want to call it that; we'll talk about that later—to me, it is an expression of music; and this music is an expression of higher ideals, to me. So therefore, brotherhood is there; and I believe with brotherhood, there would be no poverty.

And also, with brotherhood, there would be no war.

KOFSKY: That also seems to be what most of the musicians feel. David Izenson [a bassist who often played with Ornette Coleman during the mid-1960s], for example, said almost the same thing when I talked with him. He said, "Well, we're saying in our music we want a society without classes, without these frictions, without the waste, and without the warfare."

Would you care to comment on working conditions for "jazz" musicians? Do you think that jazz artists are treated as they deserve to be, and if not, can you see any reason why they wouldn't be?

COLTRANE: I don't know. It's according to the individual. Well, you find many times that a man may feel that the situation is all right with him, where another man might say, that situation is no good for you. So it's a matter of a man knowing himself, just what he wants, and that way, it's according to his values. If he doesn't mind a certain sort of treatment, I'm sure he can find it somewhere. If he does mind it, then he doesn't have to put up with it. In my opinion, at this stage of the game, I don't care too much for playing clubs, particularly. Now there was a time when it felt all right to play clubs, because with my music, I felt I had to play a lot to work it out, you see. But now I don't think that that was absolutely where it was at; but I had to find it out myself. It is a matter of being able to be at home and be able to go into yourself. In other words, I don't feel the situation in clubs is ideal for me.

KOFSKY: What is it about clubs that you don't like?

COLTRANE: Well, actually, we don't play the set forty-minute kind of thing anymore, and it's difficult to always do this kind of thing now. The music, changing as it is, there are a lot of times when it doesn't make sense, man, to have somebody drop a glass, or somebody ask for some money right in the middle of Jimmy Garrison's solo. Do you know what I mean?

KOFSKY: I know *exactly*.

COLTRANE: And these kind of things are calling for some other kind of presentation.

KOFSKY: In other words, these really are artists who are playing, yet they're really not being treated as artists, but as an extension of the cash register.

COLTRANE: Yes, I think the music is rising, in my estimation, it's rising into something else, and so we'll have to find this kind of place to be played in.

KOFSKY: Why do you think conditions have been so bad for producing art by the musicians? What do you think causes these poor conditions that you've spoken of?

COLTRANE: Well, I don't know; I don't really know how it came about. Because I do know there was one time when the musicians played more dances, and they used to play theaters and all; and this took away one element, you know, but still it was hard work. I remember some of those one-nighters, it was pretty difficult.

But it just seems that the music has been directed by businessmen, I would suppose, who know how to arrange the making of a dollar, and so forth. And maybe often the artist hasn't really taken the time himself to figure out just what he wants. Or if he does feel it should be in some other way. I think these are the things which are being thought about more now.

KOFSKY: Do you think the fact that almost all of the original jazz musicians were black men and have continued to be throughout the generations, do you think this has encouraged the businessmen to take advantage of them and to treat their art with this contempt—ringing up of the cash register in the middle of a bass solo?

COLTRANE: Well, I don't know.

KOFSKY: Most of the owners, I've noticed, are white.

COLTRANE: Well, it could be, Frank, it could be.

KOFSKY: How do you think conditions are going to be improved for the musicians?

COLTRANE: There has to be a lot of self-help, I believe. They have to work out their own problems in this area.

KOFSKY: You mean, for example, what the Jazz Composers Guild was trying to do?[28]

COLTRANE: Yes, I *do* think that was a good idea, I really do, and I don't think it's dead. It was just something that couldn't be born at that time, but I still think it's a good idea.

KOFSKY: This is true in the history of all kinds of organizations—they're not always successful the first time. But I think it's inevitable that musicians are going to try to organize to protect themselves.

COLTRANE: Yes.

KOFSKY: For example, I was at the Five Spot Monday night, and I figure that there are about a hundred tables in there; and with two people at a table, it comes to about $7.50 a set, at three drinks a set. That means the owner's making $750, say, a set and he has five sets. And I know the musicians for that night aren't getting anywhere *near* five times $750, or even two times $750. So actually it turns out that these businessmen are not only damaging the art, but they're even keeping people away.

COLTRANE: Yes, it's putting them up tight, lots of people, man. I feel so *bad* sometimes about people coming to the club and I can't play long enough for them, because, you know, they're hustling you. They come to hear you play and you get up, you have to play a little bit, then split. Something has to be done about it.

KOFSKY: Do the musicians who play in the newer styles look to Africa and Asia for some of their musical inspiration?

COLTRANE: I think so; I think they look all over. And inside.

KOFSKY: Do they look some places more than others? I heard you, for example, talking about making a trip to Africa, to gather musical sources. Is that the idea?

COLTRANE: Well, I intend to make a trip to Africa to gather whatever I can find, particularly the musical sources.

KOFSKY: Do you think that the musicians are more interested in Africa and Asia than in Europe, as far as the music goes?

COLTRANE: Well, the musicians have been exposed to Europe, you see. So it's the other parts that they haven't been exposed to. Speaking for myself, at least, I'm trying to have a rounded education.

KOFSKY: Is that the significance of those rhythmic instruments that you've incorporated into your group—to give it a sort of Middle Eastern or African flavor?

COLTRANE: Maybe so; it's just something I feel.

KOFSKY: Why do you think that the interest in Africa and Asia is growing at this particular time?

COLTRANE: Well, it's just time for this to come about, that's all. It's a thing of the times.

KOFSKY: Bill Dixon suggested to me that it might have something to do with the fact that many African nations became independent in the 1950s and changed the way Negroes in this country looked at themselves—it made them more aware of their African heritage and made them more interested in going back and looking for it. Do you think there's anything to that line of thought?

COLTRANE: Yes, yes, that's part of it.

KOFSKY: Another question along the same lines: it seems that group improvisation is growing in importance—for example, what you do with Pharoah [Sanders] when you're playing simultaneously. And also, of course, *Ascension*. Do you think that this is a new trend now, or if not a new trend, do you think this is growing in importance now?

COLTRANE: Well, maybe. It seems to be happening at this time; I don't know how long it's going to last.

KOFSKY: Why do you think that's taking place now?

COLTRANE: I don't know *why*; it just *is*, that's all.

KOFSKY: But it is there—I'm not making something up when I say that?

COLTRANE: No, no, I feel it, it's there, but I don't know why.

KOFSKY: And another question about the new music: I've noticed that a lot of the new groups are piano-less; or even in your case, where you have a piano, sometimes you'll have the piano lay out [not play] during a solo, or during parts of a solo. Why is this coming about at this particular time? Why the desire to de-emphasize the piano or to give it another kind of role in the group?

COLTRANE: I still use the piano, and I haven't reached the point where I feel I don't need it. I might, but . . . maybe it's because—well, when you're not playing on a given [harmonic] progression, you don't really need it to state these things. And it would get in your way to have somebody going in another direction and you trying to go in this, there it would be better for you not to have it.

KOFSKY: It seems that the direction the brass and reeds are going in, too, is to get away from the twelve-tone scale—to play notes that really aren't on the piano: the high-pitched notes, the shrieks and screams. I don't know what words you use to describe those sounds, but I think you know what I mean: sounds that were considered "wrong"—well, still are considered wrong by some people.

Now if you play those notes that really aren't on the pianos and you have the piano there stating notes, do you feel that this produces some kind of a clash that you'd rather avoid?

COLTRANE: I suppose that's the way some men feel about it. As I say, I still use the piano. I haven't reached the point, yet, where the piano is a drag to me. The only thing is, I don't, we don't *follow* what the piano does any more, because we all move in our own directions. I like it for a backdrop, you know, for its sound.

KOFSKY: You do have the piano, though, lay out for a fairly large part of the time.

COLTRANE: Well, I always instruct the piano players that whenever they wish they can just lay out and let it go on as it is. Because after a while, lots of times, the pianists, well, they get tired. If you can't think of anything else to play— stroll!

KOFSKY: When I talked to you some years ago in Los Angeles and asked if you would ever consider adding another brass or reed instrument to your group, you said probably the thing you would do is, if you added anything, you would add drums [*laughter*]. Did you have in mind then these kind of things that. . . ?

COLTRANE: I don't even know, man, but I guess so. I still feel so strongly about drums, I really do. I feel very strongly about these drums. I experimented in it, but we didn't have too much success. I believe it would have worked, but Elvin and McCoy couldn't hold it; it was time for them to go.

KOFSKY: It doesn't necessarily have to be two drums. It could be drums and another rhythm instrument. That's really what I was referring to.

COLTRANE: I think so, too. It could come in different forms, shapes; I just don't know how to do it, though.

KOFSKY: After all, the things that you're using in the group now—shakers, bells, maracas—are rhythm instruments, too. Not all rhythm instruments are drums.

COLTRANE: Oh, that's true.

KOFSKY: That's what I meant, when I asked you if that's what you had in mind.

COLTRANE: Yes.

KOFSKY: Speaking of Elvin and McCoy reminds me of something Sun Ra said,[29] and I'll repeat it. Let me make it clear that I don't put any faith in it, but as he said it, and he told me to tell you, I'll pass it along. He said that you hired [drummer] Rashied Ali as a means of driving Elvin and Mc-

Coy out of the band, because you didn't want them in the band in the first place, and that was your way of doing it. Do you want to respond to that?

COLTRANE: No, I don't. I was trying to do something. . . . There was a thing I wanted to do in music, see, and I figured I could do *two* things: I could have a band that played like the way we used to play, and a band that was going in the direction that the one I have now is going in—I could combine these two, with these two concepts going. And it could have been done.

KOFSKY: Yes. Sun Ra is quite bitter, and claims that you've stolen all of your ideas from him, and in fact that everybody has stolen all of his ideas from him.

COLTRANE: There may be something to that. I've heard him and I know that he's doing some of the things that I've wanted to do.

KOFSKY: How do you feel about having another saxophonist in your group? Do you feel that it in any way competes with you or that it enhances what you're doing?

COLTRANE: Well, it helps me. It helps me stay alive sometimes, because physically, man, the pace I've been leading has been so hard and I've gained so much weight, that sometimes it's been a little hard physically. I feel that I like to have somebody there in case I can't get that strength. I like to have that strength in that band, somewhere. And Pharoah is very strong in spirit and will, see, and these are the things that I like to have up there.

KOFSKY: Do you feel that spurs you on, the presence especially of a man as powerful as Pharoah?

COLTRANE: Yes, all the time, there's always got to be somebody with a lot of power. In the old band, Elvin had this power. I always have to have somebody there with it, you know? Rashied has it, but it hasn't quite unfolded completely; all he needs to do is play.

KOFSKY: That was my impression, too, that he really was

feeling his way ahead in the music and didn't have the confidence Elvin had. But then, of course, look how long Elvin was with you before—

COLTRANE: He was there, Elvin was there for a couple of years—although Elvin was ready from the first time I heard him, you know, I could hear the genius there—but he had to start playing steadily, steadily, every night. . . . With Miles [Davis], it took me around two and a half years, I think, before it started developing, taking the shape that it was going to take.

KOFSKY: That's what's so tragic about the situation of the younger musicians now: they don't have that opportunity to play together.

COLTRANE: Yes, it certainly needs to be done. It should be happening all the time and the men would develop sooner.

KOFSKY: Have you listened to many of the other younger saxophonists besides Pharoah?

COLTRANE: Yes, Albert Ayler, first. I've listened very closely to him. He's something else.

KOFSKY: Could you see any relationship between what you are doing and what he is doing? In other words, do you think he has developed out of some of your ideas?

COLTRANE: Not necessarily; I think what he's doing, it seems to be moving music into even higher frequencies. Maybe where I left off, maybe where he started, or something.

KOFSKY: Well, in a sense, that's what I meant.

COLTRANE: Yes. Not to say that he would copy this and that, but just that he filled an area that it seems I hadn't gotten to.

KOFSKY: It seems to me that your solo on "Chasin' the Trane,"[30] that Albert developed some of the ideas that you had introduced there, that he had expressed some of them in his own way, and that this was one of the points from which he had begun. Had you ever thought of it in that light?

COLTRANE: No, I hadn't.

KOFSKY: Did you ever listen to that selection much?

COLTRANE: Only at the time it came out. I used to listen to it and wonder what happened to me.

KOFSKY: What do you mean?

COLTRANE: Well, it's a sort of surprising thing to hear this back, because—I don't know, it came back another way. It was a little longer than I thought it was and it had a fairly good amount of intensity in it, which I hadn't quite gotten into a recording before.

KOFSKY: You were pleased with it?

COLTRANE: To a degree, not that I could sit there with it and love it forever.

KOFSKY: Well, no, you'd never be pleased with anything that you did for longer than a week!

COLTRANE: I realized that I'd have to do that or better, you see, and then I. . . .

KOFSKY: I think it's a remarkable record and I also think you ought to go back and listen to it.

COLTRANE: Maybe so.

KOFSKY: Because I don't see any saxophonist now who isn't playing something that you haven't at least sketched out before. But maybe you would rather not think about that.

COLTRANE: No, because like it's a big reservoir that we all dip out of. And a lot of times, you'll find that a lot of those things. . . . I listened to John Gilmore [a saxophonist in Sun Ra's Arkestra] kind of closely before I made "Chasin' the Trane," too. So some of those things on there are really direct influences of listening to this cat, you see. But then I don't know who he'd been listening to, so. . . .

KOFSKY: After "Chasin' the Trane," and then *Impressions* came out, you had a kind of change of pace, you remember? You did the album with Duke Ellington and *Ballads*, and the album with [singer] Johnny Hartman. Whose idea were these albums? Were they yours, or Bob Thiele's?[31]

COLTRANE: Well, I tell you, I had some trouble at that time.

I did a foolish thing. I got dissatisfied with my mouthpiece and I had some work done on this thing, and instead of making it better, it ruined it. It really discouraged me a little bit, because there were certain aspects of playing—that certain fast thing that I was reaching for—that I couldn't get because I had damaged this thing, so I just had to curtail it. Actually, I never found another [mouthpiece], but after so much of this laying around and making these kind of things, I said, "Well, what the hell, I might as well go ahead and do the best I can." But at that moment, it was so vivid in my mind—the difference in what I was getting on the horn— it was so vivid that I couldn't do it. Because as soon as I did, I'd hear it, and it just discouraged me. But after a year or so passed, well, I'd forgotten.

KOFSKY: That's funny, because I think I know your music as thoroughly as any non-musician, yet that wouldn't have been apparent to me.

COLTRANE: That's a funny thing. That's one of the mysteries. And to me, as soon as I put that horn in my mouth, I could hear it. It feels, you know. . . . I just stopped and went into other things.

KOFSKY: The reason I asked that was because I recall that was the time you had Eric [Dolphy] in and out of the group.

COLTRANE: Yes.

KOFSKY: And there was a whole wave of really hostile criticism.

COLTRANE: Yes, and all of this was at the same time, so you see how it was. I needed all the strength I could have at that time; and maybe some of these things might have caused me to feel, "Hell, man, I can't get what I want out of this mouthpiece, so I'll work on it."

KOFSKY: You think this might have undermined your self-confidence?

COLTRANE: It could have, it certainly could have.

KOFSKY: Why do you think there's been all this hostility

to the new music, especially in your case?

COLTRANE: Oh, man, I never could figure it out! I couldn't even venture to answer it now. Because as I told them then, I just felt that they didn't understand.

KOFSKY: Do you think they were making as conscientious and thorough an attempt to understand as they could have?

COLTRANE: At the time I didn't feel they were, because I did offer them, in an article in *down beat*, that if any of you men were interested in trying to understand, let's get together and let's talk about it, you know? I thought if they were really genuinely interested or felt there was something here, that instead of just condemning what you don't know about, if you want to discuss it, let's talk about it. But no one ever came forth, so I don't think they wanted to know what I had to say about it [*laughter*].[32]

KOFSKY: I think it frightened them. Bill Dixon and I talked about this, too, at great length, and he said: "Well, these guys, it's taken them years to pick out 'I Got Rhythm' on the piano, and now the new music comes along and undermines their entire career," which is built around understanding things based on those chord patterns.

COLTRANE: Yes, I dug it like that too. I said, "Well, this could be a real drag to a cat if he figures this is something that he won't be able to cope with and he won't be able to write about." If he can't write about it, he can't make a living at this. And then I realized that, so I quieted down. I wouldn't allow myself to become too hostile in return. Although there was a time I kind of froze up on those people at *down beat*. I felt that there was something there that wasn't—I felt that they were letting their weakness direct their actions, which I didn't feel they should have. The test was for me. They could do what they wanted to do. The thing was for me to remain firm in what I was doing. That was a funny period in my life, because I went through quite a few changes, you know, like home life—everything, man, I just went through so many . . . everything I was doing.

KOFSKY: The perfect wrong time to hit you.

COLTRANE: Everything I was doing was like that, it was a hell of a test for me, and coming out of it, it was just like I always said, man: when you go through these crises and you come out of them, you're definitely stronger, in a great sense.

KOFSKY: Did the reaction of Impulse to these adverse criticisms have anything to do with those records that we talked about?

COLTRANE: The ballads and that?

KOFSKY: Yes.

COLTRANE: Well, I don't know. I think Impulse was interested in having what they might call a balanced sort of thing, a diversified sort of catalog, and I find nothing wrong with this myself. You see, I like—in fact most of the songs that I even write now, the ones that I even consider songs, are ballads. So there's something there, that—I mean, I really love these things.

And these ballads that came out were definitely ones which I felt at this time. I chose them; it seemed to be something that was laying around in my mind—from my youth, or somewhere—and I just had to do them. They came at this time, when the confidence in what I was doing on the horn had flagged, it seemed to be the time to clean that out. And Johnny Hartman—a man that I had stuck up in my mind somewhere—I just felt something about him, I don't know what it was. I liked his sound, I thought there was something there I had to hear, so I looked him up and did that album. Really, I don't regret doing those things at all.

The only thing I regret was not having kept that same attitude, which was: I'm going to do, no matter what. That was the attitude in the beginning, but as I say, there were a whole lot of reasons why these things happened.[33]

KOFSKY: Do you think that learning how to play the soprano saxophone changed your style?

COLTRANE: Definitely, definitely. It certainly did.

KOFSKY: How so? Could you spell it out?

COLTRANE: Well, the soprano, by being this small instrument, I found that playing the lowest note on it was like playing one of the middle notes on the tenor. So therefore, after I got so that my embouchure would allow me to make the upper notes, I found that I would play *all over* this instrument. On tenor, I hadn't always played all over it, because I was playing certain ideas which just went in certain ranges, octaves. But by playing on the soprano and becoming accustomed to playing from that low B-flat on up, it soon got so that when I went to the tenor, I found myself doing the same thing. It caused the change or the willingness to change and just try to play as much of the instrument as possible.

KOFSKY: Did it give you new rhythmic ideas, too?

COLTRANE: I think so, I think so. A new shape came out of this thing, and patterns—the way the patterns would fall.

KOFSKY: It seemed to me that after you started playing the soprano, and particularly after "My Favorite Things," that you started projecting the same kind of a pulse on the tenor that hadn't been there in your work before.

COLTRANE: I think that's quite possible. In fact, the patterns started—the patterns were one of the things I started getting dissatisfied with on the tenor mouthpiece,[*] because the sound of the soprano was actually so much closer to me in my ear. There's something about the presence of that sound, that to me—I didn't want to admit it, but to me it would seem like it was better than the tenor; I liked it more. I didn't want to admit this damn thing, because I said the tenor's my horn, it is my favorite. But this soprano, maybe

---

[*] See chapter 9 for an analysis of the growing importance of patterns in Coltrane's style.

it's just the fact that it's a higher instrument, it started pulling my conception.

KOFSKY: How do you feel about the two instruments now?

COLTRANE: Well, the tenor is the power horn, definitely; but soprano, there's still something there in just the voice of it that's really beautiful, something that I really like.

KOFSKY: Do you regard the soprano saxophone as an extension of the tenor?

COLTRANE: Well, at first I did, but now it's another voice, it's another sound.

KOFSKY: Did you ever use the two saxophones on the same piece, as you did on "Spiritual"?[34]

COLTRANE: I think that's the only time I've done that. Sometimes in clubs, if I feel good, I might do something like this—start on one and end on another—but I think that's the only one on record.

KOFSKY: What prompted Pharoah to take up the alto saxophone? Was that to get away from two tenors?

COLTRANE: I don't know. This is something he wanted to do, and about the same time I decided I wanted to get one, so we both got one.

KOFSKY: I haven't heard you play the alto. Do you play it much?

COLTRANE: I played it in Japan. I played it in 'Frisco a little bit, but I've had a little trouble with the intonation of it. It's a Japanese make, it's a new thing they're trying out, so they gave us these horns to try, and mine has to be adjusted at certain point where it's not quite in tune, so I don't play it, but I like it.[35]

KOFSKY: I saw a picture of you with a *flute*! Are you playing that, too, now?

COLTRANE: I'm learning.

KOFSKY: You're always learning, aren't you?

COLTRANE: I hope so. Always trying to learn.

KOFSKY: I looked at all of the various critics' poll for two years in a row, and both years, this year and last year, I noticed that European critics are much more in favor of the new music than the Americans. Almost 50 percent or 60 percent of them voted for new musicians, whereas only about a quarter of the Americans did. Is this what you found in Europe? Or in general, have you found outside the United States that your music is more favorably received by the critics—the power structure, shall we say—than in the U.S.?

COLTRANE: I'd say in the new music—and when I say new music, I mean most of the younger musicians that are starting out—I know that they definitely have found a quicker acceptance in Europe than they have here. When I started, it was a little different, because I started through Miles Davis, who was an accepted musician, and they got used to me here in the States. Now when they first heard me with Miles here, they did not like it.

KOFSKY: I remember.

COLTRANE: So it's just one of those things: everything that they haven't heard yet and that's a little different, they are going to reject it at first. But the time will roll around, the time when they will like it. Now, by being here with Miles and running around the country with him, they heard more of me here, and consequently they began to accept it before they did in Europe, because they hadn't heard me in Europe. When we went to Europe the first time, it was a shock to them there. They booed me and everything in Paris, because they just weren't with it. But now I find, the last time I was in Europe, it seems that the new music—they've really opened up. They can hear it there better than they do here.

KOFSKY: I think that part of this may be because what's happening in the new music is analogous to what's happened in painting, say, and sculpture and literature, and the people who appreciate jazz in Europe are much more aware of this. What do you think?

COLTRANE: Well, I don't know.

KOFSKY: In Europe, jazz is regarded as a serious art, whereas here, it's regarded as, well. . . .

COLTRANE: Whatever it is.

KOFSKY: As part of the nightclub business. Otherwise, you couldn't have a magazine like *down beat*.

I know Albert [Ayler] is going back to Europe, and I know that there are many of the younger musicians who want to get away from the United States because they just don't feel there's any hope for them here.

Do you remember Third Stream Music, what was called Third Stream Music?

COLTRANE: Yes.

KOFSKY: Did you ever feel much of an urge to play that kind of music?

COLTRANE: No.

KOFSKY: Why do you think it didn't catch on with the musicians? Was there anything about it that suggests why it was never popular with them?

COLTRANE: I think it was an attempt to create something, I think, more with labels, you see, than true evolution.

KOFSKY: You mean, it didn't evolve naturally out of the desires of the musicians?

COLTRANE: Maybe it did; I can't say that. It was an attempt to do something, and evolution is about trying, too. But there's something in evolution—it just happens when it's ready, but this thing wasn't really where it was coming from. What was it—an attempt to blend, to wed two musics? That's what it really was.

KOFSKY: You said, talking about saxophone players, that there was a common reservoir that everybody dipped into. Maybe here there wasn't enough of that reservoir for the musicians to dip in to.

COLTRANE: Well, I just think it wasn't time. It was an attempt to do something at a time when it wasn't time for this to happen, and therefore it wasn't lasting. But there may have been some things that came out of this that have been beneficial in promoting the final change, which is coming. So nothing is really wasted, although it might appear to fail or not succeed the way that men would have desired it to.

KOFSKY: Even the mistakes can be instructive if you try to use them.

Do you make any attempt, or do you feel that you should make any attempt, to educate your audience in ways that aren't strictly musical. That is, it's obvious that you want your audience to understand what you're doing *musically*. But do you feel that you want them to understand other things, too, and that you have some kind of responsibility for this?

COLTRANE: Sure, I feel this, and this is one of the things I am concerned about now. I just don't know how to go about this. I want to find out just how I should do it. I think it's going to have to be very subtle; you can't ram philosophies down anybody's throat, and the music is enough! That's philosophy. I think the best thing I can do at this time is to try to get myself in shape and know myself. If I can do that, then I'll just play, you see, and leave it at that. I believe that will do it, if I really can get to myself and be just as I feel I should be and play it. And I think they'll get it, because music goes a long way—it can influence.

KOFSKY: That's how I got interested in those things I was talking about earlier, such as Malcolm X, and so on. I might not have come to it, or come to it as fast, if it hadn't been for the music. That was my first introduction to something beyond my own horizons, something that would make me think about the world I was living in.

COLTRANE: Yes. That's what I'm sure of, man, I'm really sure of this thing. As I say, there are things which, as far as spirituality is concerned—which is very important to me at this time—I've got to grow through certain phases of this

to other understanding and more consciousness and awareness of just what it is that I'm supposed to understand about
it; and I'm sure others will be part of the music. To me, you
know, I feel I want to be a force for good.

KOFSKY: And the music too?

COLTRANE: Everywhere. You know, I want to be a force for
real good. In other words, I know that there are bad forces,
forces put here that bring suffering to others and misery
to the world, but I want to be the force which is truly for
good.

KOFSKY: I don't have any more of my prepared questions
to ask you—or my improvised questions to ask you [laugh-
ter]. I had many questions that are specifically related just to
you; many of those questions about music I don't ask other
musicians. But I've always had a very special interest in your
work, so I took this opportunity, as I don't know when I'll
ever get the chance to get your words down on tape again.

Do you have anything else that you'd like to say here?

COLTRANE: I think we just about covered it, I believe, just
about covered it.

[As John drove me back to the station, the tape recorder
continued running while we talked. After some humorous
exchanges, the conversation turned to the proper function
of a jazz writer or critic.]

KOFSKY: If you can't play the music, and if you're going
to write about it, you have, I think, an obligation to do it as
conscientiously as possible.

COLTRANE: Yes, I believe it, man.

KOFSKY: And always when it's a question of your opinion
versus the musician's opinion, to give the benefit of the doubt
to the musician, because he knows the music *far* better than
you'll ever know it. In other words, you have to be humble.
A lot of writers aren't humble—they get arrogant because
they think they have some kind of power.

COLTRANE: Well, that's one of the main causes of this arrogance—the idea of power. Then you lose your true power, which is to be part of all, and the only way you can be part of all is to understand it. And when there's something you don't understand, you have to go humbly to it. You don't go to school and sit down and say, "I know what you're getting ready to teach me." You sit there and you learn. You open your mind. You absorb. But you have to be quiet, you have to be still to do all of this.

KOFSKY: That's what so annoyed me about all the things the critics were saying about you in 1961 and '62.

COLTRANE: Oh, that was terrible. I couldn't *believe* it, you know, it just seemed so preposterous. It was so *ridiculous*, man, that's what bugs me. It was absolutely ridiculous, because they made it appear that we didn't even know the first thing about music—the first thing. And there we were really trying to push things off.

KOFSKY: Because nothing ever stands still.

COLTRANE: Eric [Dolphy], man, as sweet as this cat was and the musician that he was—it hurt me to see him get hurt in this thing.

KOFSKY: Do you think that this possibly contributed to the fact that he died so young?

COLTRANE: I don't know, but Eric was a strong cat. Nobody knows what caused it. The way he passed, there was a mystery about it.

KOFSKY: I didn't mean that it was directly the cause, but—

COLTRANE: Indirectly?

KOFSKY: Yes.

COLTRANE: Yes. The whole scene, man. He couldn't work. . . .

KOFSKY: That's what I meant, really.

COLTRANE: He always seemed to be a very cheerful young man, so I don't think that would put him . . . I don't *think* so, because he had an outlook on life which was very, very good—optimistic, and he had this sort of thing, friendliness, you know, a real friend to everyone. He was the type of man who could be as much a friend to a guy he'd just met today as he was to one he'd known for ten years. This kind of person, I don't think it would really hurt him to the point where he would do something to hurt himself consciously or unconsciously.

KOFSKY: Yes. That friendliness was one of the things that has impressed me about the musicians here. I really didn't expect to be greeted with open arms, because I am an outsider, after all. And yet I have been amazed constantly by how eager the musicians were to cooperate when they decided that I was sincere and that this wasn't a joke or a swindle or something of that nature.

COLTRANE: I think all we need is sincerity, empathy. . . .

I think I want to get closer to town. Maybe there's something I can do in music. Get a place, a little room to play in. I don't want a loft, but maybe there's something I can get to play in, just some place to be able to work in.

KOFSKY: Where do you play at home?

COLTRANE: Anywhere. There's a room over the garage that I'm getting fixed now and I think it's going to be my practice room. You never know. Sometimes you build a little room and it ends up [that] you're still going in the toilet. I hope I like it, but. . . . I keep a horn on the piano and I have a horn in my bedroom—a flute usually back there, because when I go there I'm tired and I lay down and practice.

KOFSKY: About how many hours a day do you play?

COLTRANE: Not too much at this time. I find that it's only when something is trying to come through that I really practice. And then I don't even know how many hours—it's all day, on and off. But at this time there's nothing coming out now.

KOFSKY: I was very surprised to hear of you practicing at all, because I just couldn't conceive of what you could find to practice! But I know it isn't like that.

COLTRANE: I *need* to practice. It's just that I want something to practice, and I'm trying to find out what it is that I want, an area that I want to get into.

C. Afterword: an interview in Japan

John Coltrane took his group to Japan during the summer of 1966, and while there he recorded a short interview that, according to Bob Thiele, was played over Japanese commercial radio stations to advertise his appearances—something that, of course, never happened in the United States. In any event, on listening to the interview, I was struck by the similarity between his answers to some of the questions put to him by the Japanese interviewer and those he gave to questions (on, for example, the U.S. war in Southeast Asia) that I asked him six weeks later. Given that certain unscrupulous souls have tried to argue that in the preceding interview I somehow "forced" Coltrane to express an opposition to war as well as his other social concerns—an assertion implicitly insulting to the man's memory—his answers here are particularly instructive.[36] They should serve to establish once for all both the nature of Coltrane's beliefs about human suffering in general and the U.S. war in Southeast Asia in particular and the fact that, to him, discussion of such issues was anything but irrelevant to his music.

INTERVIEWER: Many jazzmen are said to be influenced by classical music. What about you?

COLTRANE: I may be wrong on this, but the term "classical music," in my opinion, means the music of a country that is played by the composers and musicians of the country, more or less, as opposed to the music that the people dance to or sing, the popular music. So in other words, there are different types of classical musics all over the world—different types of classical music. I don't know if I'm correct on this, but that's the way I feel about it.

As far as types of music, if you ask me what *we* are playing, to go beyond what I've said already, I feel it is a music of the individual contributors. And if you wanted to name it anything, you could name it a "classical music."

INTERVIEWER: Have you ever studied classical music?

COLTRANE: Nothing but the type that I'm trying to play.

INTERVIEWER: There are people who think your music is too difficult to understand, too avant-garde. How do you answer people who say they cannot understand your music?

COLTRANE: I've heard that comment; I don't feel like there's an answer to it. I think that either the person will understand with time, upon repeated listenings, or some things he will never understand. You know, that's the way it is. There are many things in life we don't understand, but we go on with life anyway.

INTERVIEWER: How do you spend your leisure time away from music?

COLTRANE: I haven't had much leisure time in the last fifteen years, and when I get any, I'm usually so tired I just go somewhere and lay around for two weeks—if I can *get* two weeks! And most of the time my mind's still on music anyway.

INTERVIEWER: What are your feelings on the Vietnamese war?

COLTRANE: The Vietnamese war? Well, I dislike war—period. So therefore, as far as I'm concerned, it should stop, it should have already been stopped. And any other war. Now as far as the issues behind it, I don't understand them well enough to tell you how this should be brought about; I only know that it should stop.

INTERVIEWER: What are your feelings about religion?

COLTRANE: As I told the young man, the student who asked me if I was a Christian, I couldn't answer this. I don't talk much, you know, but you've got me talking, man—for hours I've been talking, and I'm not a talker. But I thought about this question after I had answered it as best I could [at a previous press conference], and I thought that what I didn't tell him was what I really wanted to. He felt that I was a Christian. I am, by birth—that is, my mother was and my father was, and so forth, and my early teachings were of the Christian faith. Now, as I look out upon the world—and this has always been a thing with me—I feel that all men know the truth, you see? I've always felt that even though a man was not a Christian, he still had to know the truth some way. Or if he was a Christian, he could know the truth—or he could *not*. It's according to whether he knew the truth, and the truth doesn't have any name on it. Each man has to find this for himself, I think.

INTERVIEWER: What is your goal for the future?

COLTRANE: I tell you, I believe that men ought to grow themselves into the fullest, the best that they can be. At least this is what I want to do, this is my belief—that I am supposed to grow to the best good that I can get to. As I'm going there, becoming this, if I ever become, this will just come out of the horn. So whatever that's going to be, that's what it will be. I'm not so much interested in trying to say what it's going to be—I don't know. I just know that good can only bring good. . . .

NOTES

1. Carmichael was then at the head of the Student Non-Violent Coordinating Committee (SNCC), which was conducting a variety of protests against racism and segregation in the South.

2. It would be hard to find a better exemplar of this trend than one Saul Levine, who was in 1970 the president and general manager of KBCA, an "all-jazz" FM radio station. Levine, said by the author of an article about him to be "eminently qualified in his views on the jazz idiom," left no doubt about his perspective on the

new black music: "There was a long period of time, covering many years, when the kids [!] wouldn't go near a jazz club," because jazz had "been derailed for the last half-dozen years" by those who, like "John Coltrane[,] went from a very, very listenable musician to this avant-garde thing. It drove people away." Fortunately, however, now that Coltrane was no longer around to make such mischief, "things are getting better." See Carl LaFong, "Notes from the Jazz Underground," *Record World,* January 24, 1970, p. 18.

3. Given Malcolm X's close relationship to the jazz world, as I recount in chapter 14, the admiration may have been reciprocal.

4. Archie Shepp, of course, did have a spate of recording and festival engagements during the late 1960s, but primarily because of John Coltrane's intercession in his behalf.

5. All of Coltrane's words that I quote in this section are, unless indicated to the contrary in the text or notes, from the interview later in this chapter. LeRoi Jones used the phrase "new black music" in, for example, his notes to *The New Wave in Jazz* (Impulse 90), an anthology with selections by Coltrane, Albert Ayler, Archie Shepp, and others.

6. As actually occurred during one of Coltrane's last engagements at New York's Village Vanguard; the moment is preserved on record, approximately three minutes and 20 seconds from the start of Garrison's solo on "My Favorite Things," side one of John Coltrane, *John Coltrane Live at the Village Vanguard Again!* (Impulse 9124). Coltrane may well have had this incident in mind during our conversation, as he had recorded at the Village Vanguard only a few weeks earlier and the album was then in the final stages of production.

7. See the discussion of the Jazz Composers Guild in chapters 6 and 8.

8. "The Tokyo Interview—1966," in the notes to John Coltrane, *John Coltrane Live in Japan* (MCA Records and GRP Records, GRD–4–102), p. 6. A transcript of this interview given me in the late 1960s by Bob Thiele, Coltrane's producer at Impulse Records, differs in some significant respects from that in "The Tokyo Interview," and I have drawn on both versions.

9. Thus, Ira Gitler, a representative specimen: "Coltrane may be

searching for new avenues of expression, but if it is going to take this form . . . then it should be confined to the woodshed [that is, to practice in private]"; review of Coltrane *"Live" at the Village Vanguard* (Impulse 10) in *down beat,* April 26, 1962. It bears noting that, in this music in particular, there is little opportunity to "rehearse"— assuming that is the appropriate term—except in public because, as Coltrane explains in the interview that follows, the nature of a performance depends in part on the interaction between artists and audience: "It seems to me that the audience, in listening, there is an act of participation going on there, you know. And when you know that somebody is maybe moved to such a degree or approaching the degree, it's just like having another member in the group." Human ingenuity has yet to devise a way of reproducing this phenomenon in the privacy of a musician's home.

10. As did *down beat,* in large part, during the 1970s; see chapter 2 for more on this topic.

11. For an extended consideration of Coltrane's influence on rock, see chapter 9 of the first edition of *Black Nationalism and the Revolution in Music* (New York: Pathfinder, 1970).

12. In making this assertion, I intend no slight to Steve Lacy, the one contemporary jazz artist who was playing the soprano saxophone before Coltrane. With all due respect to Lacy, however, his example was hardly so compelling as to inspire the legion of followers that Coltrane commanded.

13. A complete list would fill pages. Suffice it that within the first five years following his death, the following musicians, among others, recorded selections or entire albums paying explicit homage to Coltrane: The Art Ensemble of Chicago, *Phase One* (Prestige 10064); Albert Ayler, *Albert Ayler in Greenwich Village* (Impulse 9155); Gary Bartz, *Taifa* (Milestone 9031) and *Uhuru* (Milestone 9032), "humbly dedicated, respectively, to the memories of Malcolm X and John Coltrane" (Bartz's statement on the album cover of *Taifa*); Doug Carn, *Infant Eyes* (Black Jazz 3); Alice Coltrane, *A Monastic Trio* (Impulse 9156), "dedicated to the mystic, Ohnedaruth, known as John Coltrane during the period from September 23, 1926[,] to July 17, 1967," and *Journey to Satchidinanda* (Impulse 9023); Elvin Jones, *Dear John C.* (Impulse 88); Rahsaan Roland Kirk, *Volunteered*

Slavery (Atlantic 1534); Pharoah Sanders, *Pharoah Sanders Live at The East* (Impulse 9227); Archie Shepp, *Archie Shepp Live at the Donaueschingen Music Festival* (Saba 15148); McCoy Tyner, *Tender Moments* (Blue Note 84275) and *Extensions* (Blue Note LA–006–F); Michael White, *Spirit Dance* (Impulse 9215).

14. Quoted in Don DeMicheal, "John Coltrane and Eric Dolphy Answer the Jazz Critics"—note the title—*down beat,* April 12, 1962, p. 21. For the most readily available versions of "My Favorite Things," see the album of that name on the Atlantic label (Atlantic 1361), recorded in the studio in 1960; *Afro Blue Impressions* (Pablo Live 2620 101), recorded in 1961 or 1962; *Selflessness* (Impulse 9161), recorded at the 1963 Newport Jazz Festival with Roy Haynes substituting for Elvin Jones; *Coltrane Live at the Village Vanguard Again!* (Impulse 9124) and *John Coltrane Live in Japan* (MCA Records and GRP Records, GRD–4–102) recorded in 1966 with Pharoah Sanders, Alice Coltrane, Jimmy Garrison and Rashied Ali.

15. This composition occupies both sides of the recording of the same name (Impulse 95).

16. "Impressions" is on the album with that title (Impulse 42) and also on *Afro Blue Impressions* (cited in note 14), both recorded in the early 1960s. There are performances of "I Want to Talk About You" from the same period on *Coltrane Live at Birdland* (Impulse 50), *Selflessness* and *Afro Blue Impressions* (both cited in note 14). "Pursuance" is on *A Love Supreme* (Impulse 77); other Coltrane blues pieces recorded on location (that is, before audiences) include "Chasin' the Trane" and "Cousin Mary," *Afro Blue Impressions;* "Traneing In," a 44-measure composition with an AABA form, in which the A section is a 12-measure blues, *"Bye Bye Blackbird": John Coltrane* (Pablo Live 2308–227); "Mr. P.C. [Paul Chambers]," *The Paris Concert* (Pablo Live 2308 217) and *The European Tour* (Pablo Live 2308–222).

17. These differences arise from the facts that, first, each jazz instrument can be played louder than its raga counterpart; second, the jazz percussionist has instruments—snare drum, high-hat and ride cymbals, bass drums—that his opposite number does not.

18. "Chasin' the Trane" is on John Coltrane, *Coltrane "Live" at the Village Vanguard* (Impulse 10); the information on titling this

composition is in Frank Kofsky, "The New Wave: Bob Thiele Talks to Frank Kofsky about John Coltrane," *Coda*, May 1968, p. 3.

19. Then again, it may be asking too much of technology that it reproduce the full might of the Coltrane group in the throes of creation. In any event, it is the on-location recordings—the "Live" series on Impulse and all of the volumes on Pablo Live, as well as several releases on a variety of small European and U.S. labels—that come closest to conveying the reality of a Coltrane performance.

20. Kofsky, "The New Wave," pp. 6, 8.

21. Frank Kofsky, "An Interview with Albert and Donald Ayler," *Jazz*, September 1968, pp. 22–24 *passim*.

22. The effect of underemployment on the lives and art of jazz musicians is a topic I consider at greater length in *Black Music, White Business: Illuminating the History and Political Economy of Jazz* (New York: Pathfinder Press, 1997).

23. Later, the Free Speech Movement was able to mobilize the Berkeley campus around this issue, but in 1961, indifference to the question far outweighed concern.

24. Some thirty years after the fact, bassist Arthur Davis—to whom I am most indebted for this information—confirms that such was in fact the case.

25. Especially so when I later learned that John, whom A.B. Spellman accurately describes as one "of the three most important jazz musicians of the [1960s] decade," had chosen, for whatever reasons, "not [to be] included" as a subject in that author's book "because he did not want to be." See Spellman, *Four Lives in the Bebop Business* (New York: Pantheon, 1966), p. xi. Both of Spellman's other two choices, Cecil Taylor and Ornette Coleman, did consent to his request for interviews.

26. But see Coltrane's comments on this subject in the afterword to this chapter.

27. John Coltrane, *Ascension* (Impulse 95).

28. There is a discussion of the Jazz Composers Guild in chapter 7.

29. In an interview that I tape-recorded in New York City, August 9, 1966.

30. On John Coltrane, *Coltrane "Live" at the Village Vanguard.* See chapter 9 on the relationship between Coltrane and Albert Ayler and the importance of "Chasin' the Trane" in it.

31. The albums in question are John Coltrane, *Impressions* (Impulse 42); *Duke Ellington and John Coltrane* (Impulse 30); John Coltrane, *Ballads* (Impulse 32); *John Coltrane and Johnny Hartman* (Impulse 40). As I explain below in note 33, it was at the behest of Bob Thiele, then the director of artists and repertoire (A & R) for Impulse Records, that Coltrane temporarily swerved from the style he had unveiled on "Chasin' the Trane," "Impressions" (on the album of the same name, cited above) and "Out of this World" (on *Coltrane*, Impulse 21).

32. The article Coltrane referred to is Don DeMicheal, "John Coltrane and Eric Dolphy Answer the Jazz Critics," pp. 20–23 (cited in full in note 14). In introducing the remarks of Coltrane and Dolphy, DeMicheal wrote: "Coltrane felt" that, in order to "answer his critics adequately . . . he would have to meet them and discuss what has been said [note the passive construction] so that he could see just what they mean" (p. 23). I document some of the venomous hostility directed against Coltrane during this period in chapter 8.

33. Bob Thiele, who presided over the operations of Impulse Records (a subsidiary of ABC Records), confirms that it was he who urged Coltrane to record the *Ballads, Duke Ellington and John Coltrane,* and *John Coltrane and Johnny Hartman* albums, all of which he produced between late September 1962 and early March 1963. "After you've been in the record business for years and years," he explains, "you're always concerned about the commercial aspects . . . You're always concerned with how well the record will sell." The destructive campaign jazz critics were waging against Coltrane during the early 1960s disturbed Thiele: "I think he [Coltrane] was less affected by the reviews than I was . . . I don't think they really affected what he was doing [in his public appearances]." With respect to the aforementioned recordings, Thiele states: "Yes, they were all my ideas and John accepted them. . . . *Ballads* was really my idea to try and educate more listeners." "Here I was working for a record company and concerned about how well our records would sell, and we have a critic [Ira Gitler] who comes along and says, 'John Col-

trane's records are windy, flat and need editing, *et cetera,*' or whatever he said. I have done my best to forget what he ever said, but at the time he registered, and I figured we had better go in and see if we can get John to do some melodic things, do some standard tunes . . . [S]o in a way, it was my idea, through Ira Gitler, if you get the message." Quoted in Kofsky, "The New Wave," p. 4.

34. Coltrane's composition "Spiritual" is on his recording *Coltrane "Live" at the Village Vanguard* (Impulse 10).

35. Coltrane's original instrument was the alto saxophone.

36. See "The Tokyo Interview," pp. 6, 8–9 (cited in full in note 8). There are some discrepancies between the transcript of this interview given me by Bob Thiele and that in "The Tokyo Interview"; I have tried to reconcile them as best I can while remaining faithful to John Coltrane's style of speaking.

Part 5

Malcolm X

14

Black revolution and black music:
the thought of Malcolm X

A. Malcolm X and black music

*I'm saying that essentially there is no difference, as
long as you're black, where you come from; that the
thing that unites us is the sameness in the oppression
that we have undergone at the hands of the white man,
no matter where we are from. That's one of the things
that binds us.*

—CECIL TAYLOR[1]

*Some of us are more bitter about the way things are going.
We are only an extension of that entire civil rights–Black
Muslims–black nationalist movement that is taking place
in America. That is fundamental to our music.*

—ARCHIE SHEPP[2]

There was a time—and not so long ago, at that—when
one could not begin a book on jazz without an obligatory

attempt at defining it. There definitions almost invariably were worth little, however, for what they had in common was their complete disregard for the dialectical principle that it is impossible to formulate any static definition that will encompass something so dynamic as jazz (or art, or even life itself) and yet exclude without exception everything else. In recognition of that principle, I do not feel in the least compelled to provide such a definition, but for those who find them reassuring, I submit that we can hardly improve on the one proposed by Archie Shepp. Jazz is, he contends,

> one of the most meaningful social, aesthetic contributions to America. It is . . . [a] profound contribution to America—it is antiwar; it is opposed to [the U.S. war in] Vietnam; it is for Cuba; it is for the liberation of all people. That is the nature of jazz. . . . Why is that so? Because jazz is a music itself born out of oppression, born out of the enslavement of my people. It is precisely that.[3]

I like to think that this book is informed by the point of view that Shepp, with his customary force and eloquence, here advances, which is one reason why I have chosen to conclude it with an essay on Malcolm X. For as Shepp explains in a passage at the head of this chapter, the innovations in black music during the 1960s were "only an extension of that entire civil rights–Black Muslim–black nationalist movement . . . taking place in America. That is fundamental to music." Thus, it is hardly fanciful to suggest that both Malcolm X and this new music not only were products of the discontent and frustrations, the desperation and the rebelliousness, of the northern ghettoes especially, but both gave voice to those sentiments with unmatched clarity and eloquence. The oratory of Martin Luther King, so redolent of the South, may well have been the most sonorous and elevated this country has produced in the twentieth century—but it was in the clipped and staccato tones of Malcolm X, with their relentless machine-gun delivery, that one hears the same electrifying urgency and intensity of John Coltrane's diamond-hard sound.

In any case, in interviewing African-American jazz artists during the 1960s, I consistently found that Malcolm X, as a one-person distillation of the black-nationalist movement, was the single non-musician to whom the greatest number of musicians, including some whites, would dedicate a composition (assuming they dedicated one to anybody at all). Indeed, Archie Shepp's poem, "Malcolm, Malcolm—Semper Malcolm"—printed on the jacket of his *Fire Music* recording—was among the earliest efforts by an African-American artist to commemorate the assassinated leader. It would hardly be the last, however, for the memory of Malcolm X continued to serve as an inspiration to members of Shepp's generation and those who followed. It was Malcolm X's words that came the closest to articulating their hopes and aspirations, their fears and frustrations. As Shepp put it in explaining the name of his poem,

I call it "Malcolm Forever" because of my belief in his immortality. I mean, he was killed, but the significance of what he was will continue and grow. . . . Malcolm knew what it is to be faceless in America and to be sick and tired of that feeling. And he knew the pride of black, that négritude which was bigger than Malcolm himself. There'll be other Malcolms.[4]

Without exaggeration, moreover, it does appear that there is a remarkable parallel between the curve of Malcolm X's personal history—his evolution from narcotics, numbers, and ghetto racketeering in general to become (in actor Ossie Davis's words) the "shining prince" of black nationalism—and the history of jazz itself during recent decades. Where

African-American musicians of Charlie Parker's generation were all too often driven into the quicksand trap of heroin addiction and/or alcoholism, younger black artists have been able to renounce narcotics and alcohol for more humanizing activity, often including political commitment. In that sense, jazz, as a social phenomenon, has taken much the same course as that marked out by Malcolm X.

If young black jazz musicians of the 1960s and 1970s were pulled toward Malcolm X, it is no less true that he was always attracted to jazz as one expression—perhaps *the* expression—of the soul of his people. This point has been overlooked or denied outright by some of those who have written about him, but he himself left the matter in no doubt. In his address to the founding meeting of the Organization of Afro-American Unity (OAAU) on June 28, 1964—an occasion that must have had enormous importance for him— he made a point of drawing an analogy between the black musician's ability to improvise and the ability of the black person, "in an atmosphere of complete freedom where he has the right, the leeway, to bring out of himself all of that dormant, hidden talent that has been there for so long," to devise new political and social forms:

> And in that atmosphere, brothers and sisters, you'd be surprised what will come out of the bosom of this black man. I've seen it happen. I've seen black musicians when they'd be jamming at a jam session with white musicians—a whole lot of difference. The white musician can jam if he's got some sheet music in front of him. He can jam on something that's he's heard jammed before. But that black musician, he picks up his horn and starts blowing some sounds that he never thought of before. He improvises, he creates, it comes from within. It's his soul; it's that soul music. *It's the only area on the American scene where the black man has been free to create*

[my emphasis]. And he has mastered it. He has shown that he can come up with something that nobody ever thought of on his horn.*

It is tempting to speculate on whether this paean to the creative powers of black musicians was inspired by the presence of jazz artists in Malcolm X's audience. We know from the interview in Chapter 13, for instance, that John Coltrane was in attendance at one of this great agitator's last speeches. Be that as it may, it is undeniable from the foregoing that Malcolm X had a high regard for—indeed, appears to have identified with—the African-American musician. So much so, in fact, that he held up the black musician as a model of resourcefulness and ingenuity for the African-American liberation movement. The black person, he asserted, could "likewise . . . do the same thing" as the black musician

if given intellectual independence. He can come up with a philosophy that nobody has heard of yet. He can invent a society, a social system, an economic system, a political system, that is different from anything that exists or has ever existed anywhere on this earth. He will improvise; he'll bring it from within himself. And this is what you and I want.

---

* To make my own position completely clear: I do *not* believe that there is any such difference as Malcolm X claimed to be able to discern between the improvisatory abilities of black and white musicians as a whole; to paraphrase what he said elsewhere about marriage across the color line, races do not improvise—only individuals do. Before rushing to pass judgment on Malcolm X's words, however, we should keep in mind his *purpose:* not to narrate the history of jazz, but to exhort his followers to action. In that cause, a bit of harmless oratorical license is surely forgivable. I might add for good measure that anyone who thinks my point of view is identical with the one Malcolm X voiced here simply has not understood this book's theses.

You and I want to create an organization that will give us so much power we can sit down and do as we please. Once we sit down and think as we please, speak as we please, and do as we please, we will show people what pleases us. And what pleases us won't always please them. So you've got to get some power before you can be yourself. Do you understand that? Once you get power and you be yourself, why, you're gone—you've got it and gone. You create a new society and make some heaven right here on this earth.[5]

In view of both Malcolm X's symbolic significance for the innovators of the jazz revolution of the 1960s and his own undisguised identification with the black jazz artist, it strikes me as fitting to close this volume with an essay that seeks to bring out why the power of his example, in Archie Shepp's phrase, "will continue and grow."

B. The evolution of a revolutionary

After his death if not before, Malcolm X's figure has become larger than life itself. Even among those friendly to him, his biography is being subtly rewritten and rearranged to symbolize the archetypical odyssey of a latter-day black-nationalist Ulysses. From these stylized treatments of Malcolm's history we learn of the death of his father, an unyielding disciple of Marcus Garvey, at the hands of a group of white racist assassins; later, institutionalized white bigotry destroys the young Malcolm's family and, in the person of a cruel and boorish grammar school teacher, frustrates the boy's hopes for a legal career. The Little family (Little was Malcolm's original surname) is thus shattered on the altar of white supremacy—the mother goes into a mental institution, the children are disposed of hither and yon—and the nationalist pedigree is transmitted intact from father to son. The latter, it is implied, then vows vengeance on white society for its crimes against black humanity.

This is the stereotype. Undoubtedly, a considerable amount of it *is* true. Yet there is an irritating distortion in the picture: we recognize the subject, but the likeness is not entirely convincing.

That matter of hatred of whites, for example. The New Mythology (which one can find in any number of *favorable* appraisals of the *Autobiography*) depicts the antipathy of Malcolm toward whites as having been forged out of the crucible of his boyhood experiences. The truth of the matter, however, is nowhere near that simple. Though many of Malcolm's earliest contacts with whites were unpleasant, this was, by his own account, far from universally the case. He described members of the white family that ran the reform school where he was sent as a boy as "good people" who "probably meant well" (though their attitude toward him was one of "kindly condescension").[6] Significantly, his first mistress was not black but white—ample evidence of the young Malcolm's underlying ambivalence regarding the color line. "Now at that time," he later recalled, "in any black ghetto in America, to have a white woman who wasn't a known, common whore was—for the average black man, at least—a status symbol of the first order."[7] To the sixteen-year-old Malcolm, the lure of that "status symbol" was overwhelming.

That whatever youthful resentments and hostilities Malcolm harbored remained particular and were not translated into a universal animus needs to be emphasized for a variety of reasons. For one thing, it sheds considerable light on Malcolm's intellectual development. Of even greater significance, it illustrates that anti-white sensibilities among black nationalists operate to supply a unifying *ideology* transcending the experience of any single individual. Hence to read Malcolm's evolution, as some have, as the inevitable consequence of his boyhood rebuffs is profoundly in error—otherwise, there would be tens of millions of proclaimed black nationalists in this country. In point of fact, however, black nationalism is much more than a response to white outrages (although it is, of course, that, too). In the hands of such a gifted exponent as Malcolm X, black nationalism is a sophisticated and pervasive political ideology based on a generalized understanding of the history of black people in the United States. As such, therefore, the "hatred" of whites that is one of its central tenets is of primarily symbolic importance and has very little to do with attitudes toward any particular white individual. Marxists especially should have little difficulty in comprehending this notion; from their own practice it should be familiar to them as the analogous sentiment of class solidarity.*

Malcolm X himself left no room for debate on this question. "When we Muslims had talked about 'the devil white man,'" he explains at one point, "he had been relatively abstract, someone we Muslims rarely came into contact with. . . ."[8] A standard passage in many of his speeches dealt with the issue in the same vein:

Unless we call one white man, by name, a "devil," we are not speaking of any *individual* white man. We are

---

* Precisely because this generalized anti-white outlook did (and does) serve as a kind of ideological cement among black nationalists, it is extremely silly to argue—as have some less-than-fair-minded polemicists—that to call attention to the socialist content in Malcolm X's last speeches, as I do below, is tantamount to claiming that he was about to affiliate with this or that white-radical group. Clearly, Malcolm's stock in the black community would have plummeted to zero had he ever indicated the slightest intention of joining *any* white or even mixed organization, political, social, religious, intellectual, cultural, or what have you. Certainly he knew as much, and it is hard to imagine that there was anyone so obtuse as not to recognize this elementary fact of political life at the time.

speaking of the *collective* white man's *historical* record. We are speaking of the collective white man's cruelties, and evils, and greeds, that have seen him *act* like a devil toward the non-white man. Any intelligent, honest, objective person cannot fail to realize that this white man's slave trade, and his subsequent devilish actions, are directly *responsible* for not only the *presence* of this black man in America, but also for the *condition* in which we find this black man here. . . .[9]

For that matter, it is a reasonable presumption that had Malcolm's characterization of the white man as a devil been personal rather than ideological, his repudiation of racist dogmas would never have taken place following his open rupture with Elijah Muhammad. But even before that schism, he had given evidence of the ideological nature of his "hatred" for whites. Alex Haley, who transcribed and organized the *Autobiography*, observed that he

saw Malcolm X too many times exhilarated in after-lecture give-and-take with predominantly white student bodies at colleges and universities to ever believe that he nurtured at his core any blanket white-hatred. "The young whites, and blacks, too, are the only hope that America has," he said to me once.[10]

This point has to be hammered upon repeatedly. There have been all too many whites of good will—including, regrettably, not a few ostensible radicals—inclined to condemn black-nationalist teachings about whites as some sort of "reverse" fascism or racism.* Such a simplistic interpretation

---

* Much as white jazz critics have accused black-nationalist musicians of practicing "Crow Jim" by discriminating against their white counterparts, a topic I treat in chapter 2 and elsewhere above. Along this

is no more tenable than the romanticized New Mythology that postulates a direct and inexorable progression from oppressed black youth to militant nationalist spokesman. Would that the growth of revolutionary sentiment were so automatic!

As long as we are correcting misconceptions, moreover, we need to address Malcolm X's decision to become a follower of Elijah Muhammad. With a certain unimaginative uniformity, reviewers of the *Autobiography*, confronted with this question, have tended to throw up their hands and rush to consult William James's *Varieties of Religious Experience*.[11] There is no denying that James's insights can help us understand Malcolm's "conversion" to the Nation of Islam (Black Muslims). But to concede this leaves much unsaid. The excerpts from James that the reviewers have deployed are all decidedly ahistorical; they fail to elucidate why this particular black man, Malcolm Little, at this particular time and place, chose the faith he did (not to mention the reasons why he later broke with his spiritual mentor). For if, as has been claimed, Malcolm was psychologically prepared for his conversion by the events of his first year in prison, it is undeniable that he was altogether beyond the reach of the orthodox Christian faith—in fact, other inmates were so awed by the vehemence with which he cursed God and the Bible (his "favorite targets") that they took to calling him "Satan."

---

line, I recall being one of about 50 whites out of a total audience of about 1,200 at a speech by Malcolm X in Los Angeles in 1963, shortly after the March on Washington. Although I cannot pretend that my companions and I were received with open arms—and why should we have been?—there was never the slightest danger to our precious white skins. Let all those inclined to easy equations of black nationalism with genuine "hate groups" such as the Ku Klux Klan and the Aryan Brotherhood speculate on the probable results had we been a similar number of blacks who dared to attend a gathering of one of *those* organizations!

Obviously, something more was at work within Malcolm than a previously frustrated religious impulse.

At bottom, the cause for Malcolm's conversion is not obscure: his insatiable curiosity and desire to improve himself simply could not be suppressed. While still on "the street," he had rapidly distinguished himself by his ability as a hustler; imprisoned, he turned—even prior to his exposure to the doctrines of Elijah Muhammad—to correspondence courses in English and Latin (the latter because of a desire to learn about word derivations). James, in discussing the phenomenon of conversion, cites the maxim, "Man's extremity is God's opportunity." But Malcolm had already reached and overcome *his* extremity without any assistance from Allah. By the time of his first encounter with Elijah Muhammad, he was moving ahead on the road to recovery.

What Elijah *did* do for Malcolm was to provide him with three things that hastened the process of recovery and guaranteed its success. The first of these was the promise of early release. The brother to whom he was closest had written him, "Malcolm, don't eat any more pork, and don't smoke any more cigarettes. I'll show you how to get out of prison."[12] It was this promise that secured Malcolm's allegiance in the crucial first phase of conversion. The second of Elijah's gifts to Malcolm was enhanced self-esteem. By adhering to Muhammad's injunctions, particularly the prohibition on pork, Malcolm at once drew attention to himself as a convict, and a Negro, who was somehow different from the rest. The psychological dividends from this were as therapeutic as they were gratifying. "It made me feel good to see that my not eating [pork] had especially startled the white convicts."[13]

But probably the most important thing that Elijah Muhammad accomplished was to inspire Malcolm to impose a systematic discipline on himself, both with respect to his intellectual life and his overt behavior. The consequences of this decision can hardly be overestimated, for it restructured Malcolm's entire existence. The nationalistic doctrines of Muhammad not only furnished Malcolm with a coherent worldview that put his entire previous life in perspective, but it also enabled him to pursue his studies with a fixed end constantly in mind: to discover the truth about black people and their enslavement by whites. "Once I heard [from Muhammad] of the 'glorious history of the black man,'" Malcolm told Alex Haley, "I took special pains to hunt in the [prison] library for books that would inform me on details about black history."[14] Related to this program of study was Malcolm's desire to become more literate so as to hold up his end of the correspondence with Muhammad. At the time of his conversion, Malcolm "couldn't even write in a straight line."[15] Without a formal guide, Malcolm was at first at a loss how to proceed. Finally, he began by transcribing a dictionary: "In my slow, painstaking, ragged handwriting, I copied into my tablet everything printed on that first page, down to the punctuation marks."[16]

Like many other prison inmates who became celebrated after their release, Malcolm used his confinement to broaden his political education. (One thinks especially of another notable agitator, Eugene Debs. Where Debs had gone to prison a trade unionist and emerged a socialist, Malcolm went in a hustler and came out a nationalist.) From the time his reading comprehension began to improve "until I left that prison, in every free moment I had, if I was not reading in the library, I was reading on my bunk. You couldn't have gotten me out of books with a wedge."[17] In this way Malcolm familiarized himself with the storehouse of the world's knowledge, from Socrates to W.E.B. Du Bois, from Gregor Mendel to Mahatma Gandhi, from Herodotus to the anthropologist Louis S.B. Leakey, from Spinoza and Kant to Schopenhauer and Nietzsche. Curiously enough, by imprisoning him, white society performed one of its few services for Malcolm; his own conclusion was that "up to then, I never had been so truly free in my life."[18] He walked out of the prison gates not only a free man, but an educated and (by virtue of frequent prison debates) a ferociously articulate one as well.

The remaining events in Malcolm X's biography—his rapid rise within the Muslim hierarchy, his simultaneous catapulting to international fame as a result of frequent television appearances, the silencing by Muhammad following Malcolm's "chickens coming home to roost" comment on the Kennedy assassination, the subsequent break with Muhammad, and the formation of a rival black-nationalist organization—are too well known to need rehearsal here. *Interpretation* of these facts, in contrast, is still a matter for some dispute. Can we, for example, really accept the verdict of those who contend that Muslim recruiting efforts "came to a halt" when Malcolm first started appearing in television debates, and that Muhammad's subsequent censure of his chief lieutenant took place solely because Malcolm had been neglecting his organizational responsibilities to concentrate on "explaining [the Muslims] to people who didn't give a damn about them, but only wanted to assess how deeply they should be feared"?[19] I think not. Although such a judgment sounds plausible—and perhaps to some even "militant"—there are a number of considerations, inconvenient for the writer but essential for our assessment, that it omits.

To begin with, although it is quite likely that Elijah Muhammad was envious of the reputation which Malcolm X had achieved from his frequent public appearances—*and* from his organizing prowess within the black ghettos—we can scarcely construe this resentment as valid evidence that Malcolm gave short shrift to his Muslim duties. For even if some of Malcolm's speaking engagements were in front of predominantly white audiences, the bulk of his radio and television commitments—as the anti-nationalist Black Establishment wistfully acknowledged in retrospect[20]—aided the Muslims in disseminating their doctrines in a way that their own limited activities never could have done. Nor did Malcolm slacken his organizing efforts in order to maintain his speaking schedule. On the contrary, as he himself related, in testimony yet to be contravened:

> I couldn't have asked Allah to bless my efforts any more than he had. Islam in New York City [Malcolm's jurisdiction] was growing faster than anywhere in America. From the one tiny mosque to which Mr. Muhammad had originally sent me, I had now built three of the nation's most powerful and aggressive mosques. . . . And on a national basis, I had either directly established, or I had helped to establish, most of the one hundred or more mosques in the fifty states. I was crisscrossing North America sometimes as often as four times a week. Often, what sleep I got was caught in the jet planes.[21]

Everything points to the conclusion that when Muhammad lost Malcolm, he lost the most capable executive, as well as the most commanding emissary to the public, the Muslims possessed—a man who personally had overseen the meteoric rise of the Nation of Islam from an obscure sect to a domestic organization perhaps as dreaded as any other in the eyes of the U.S. ruling class.

Second, the notion that the parting of the ways between prophet and disciple came about because of the disciple's malfeasance takes no notice of Malcolm X's own version of the events; in particular, it writes off as unimportant or irrelevant his mounting dissatisfaction with Elijah Muhammad's policy of having the Muslims abstain from all participation in the Afro-American liberation movement. Yet far more than Muhammad's reputed unhappiness with Malcolm's

ministerial performance, the real issues provoking the split
revolved around Malcolm's personal conviction that

> our Nation of Islam could be an even greater force in the
> American black man's overall struggle—if we engaged
> in more *action*. By that I mean I thought privately that
> we should have amended or relaxed our general non-
> engagement policy. I felt that, wherever black people com-
> mitted themselves, in the Little Rocks and Birminghams
> . . . militantly disciplined Muslims should also be there—
> for all the world to see, and respect, and discuss.
>
> It could be heard increasingly in the Negro commu-
> nities: "Those Muslims *talk* tough, but they never *do*
> anything. . . ."[22]

It was this desire of Malcolm to give the Nation of Islam
an actual, as opposed to a merely rhetorical, involvement in
the day-to-day battles of black people which, when combined
with his pronounced distaste for the limousine-and-mansion
opulence in which Muhammad's plentiful brood had begun
to loll, made the schism unavoidable.

After all of this has been said about Malcolm X, we are
still left with the question of the larger significance of his
life, especially with regard to the whirlwind chain of events
that filled his last fifteen months following the attempted
silencing by Muhammad. I am afraid that on this question
the *Autobiography*, generally invaluable for the insight it
affords into Malcolm X and the environment from which he
sprang,[23] is of only limited assistance. In making this point,
I am not at all disparaging the work. At the same time, however, one must recognize its deficiencies as well as its assets,
and a sizable shortcoming is that, almost of necessity, the
Autobiography concentrates on the private rather than the
public Malcolm X. The likeness that peers forth from its
pages is, consequently, in some respects two-dimensional;

an integral aspect of the man's personality and career has been truncated.

These omissions might not have proven serious had Malcolm lived to work out and enunciate his vision for the future of black nationalism. As it is, however, the assassin's guns denied him the necessary time, with the result that conclusions about the direction of Malcolm's politics at the moment of his death must always remain tentative.

Be that as it may, thanks to an excellent collection of speeches (admirably edited by George Breitman) from a watershed period in Malcolm X's life, we have something much more substantial to go on than mere speculation.[24] Not that Malcolm's speeches set forth every detail of his political philosophy with absolute clarity, for that is not—and could not be—the case. Given the workhorse schedule of his final months and the absence of much opportunity for sustained reflection, one expects that here and there an occasional solecism, murky generalization, or even self-contradiction will crop up. But such minor lapses occur in the rhetoric of any one who speaks extemporaneously with the frequency that Malcolm X did during those hectic days; they are utterly inconsequential with respect to the overall tenor of his thinking—a tenor that even the most casual reader of these addresses can scarcely fail to recognize.

The simplest way to describe this tendency is with the phrase *revolutionary socialist internationalism*. For some it may come as a shock that Malcolm was moving in the direction of socialist internationalism; these skeptics are best advised to read the speeches and judge for themselves. To any informed and reasonably open-minded person, however, the conclusion will be obvious—even if, for the writers of the popular (and liberal) press, it is a mystery hidden behind the legendary seven veils. At any rate, it is undeniable that weeks before assassins' bullets cruelly cut him down in mid-flight, Malcolm X already had proclaimed his conviction that socialism was superior to capitalism.[25]

It is instructive in this respect to consider a few representative excerpts from Malcolm X's speeches that illustrate his revolutionary socialist internationalism. First of all, then, the question of *revolution*. Even prior to his break with the Nation of Islam, Malcolm X had expressed his conviction that no solution for the oppression and subjugation of black peoples in this country could be found short of social revolution. Indeed, social revolution was, for him, the quintessence of black nationalism. In an address to the Northern Negro Leadership Conference in Detroit in November 1963, he put the matter succinctly: "If you're afraid of black nationalism, you're afraid of revolution. And if you love revolution, you love black nationalism."[26] When he referred to revolution, furthermore, he did not invoke the word loosely, in the style of advertising copywriters. But here—let him tell the tale in his own words:

> The white man knows what a revolution is. He knows that the black revolution is world-wide in scope and in nature. The black revolution is sweeping Asia, is sweeping Africa, is rearing its head in Latin America. The Cuban Revolution—that's a revolution. They overturned the system. . . .
>
> Revolution is bloody, revolution is hostile, revolution knows no compromise, revolution overturns and destroys everything that gets in its way. . . . Whoever heard of a revolution where they lock arms . . . singing "We Shall Overcome"? You don't do any singing, you're too busy swinging. . . .[27]

Similar passages leap to one's eye on virtually every page of this book. But was Malcolm X calling for *socialist* revolution? Although the fact continues for the most part to be a well-kept secret, an honest and objective answer—one based on the weight of the available evidence—has to be in the affirmative. Replying to a question at the Militant Labor Forum, for example, Malcolm stated his view that

> all of the countries that are emerging today from under the shackles of colonialism are turning toward socialism. I don't think it's an accident. Most of the countries that were colonial powers were capitalist countries, and the last bulwark of capitalism today is [the United States]. . . .

"You can't have capitalism," he concluded on this occasion, "without racism."[28]

That was in May 1964. By the end of the year Malcolm X had become less guarded in his endorsement of the socialist path: socialism was no longer a topic to be debated in front of white radicals *downtown;* it now demanded discussion in front of all-black audiences *uptown* as well. "You don't find any capitalist countries [in Asia] too much nowadays," Malcolm explained to a meeting of his followers at Harlem's Audubon Ballroom:

> Almost every one of the countries that has gotten independence has devised some kind of socialist system, and this is no accident. This is another reason why I say that you and I here in America . . . before [we] start trying to be incorporated, or integrated, or disintegrated, into this capitalistic system, should look over there and find out what are the people who have gotten their freedom adopting to provide themselves with better housing and better education and better food and better clothing.
>
> None of them are adopting the capitalistic system because they realize they can't. You can't operate a capitalistic system unless you are vulturistic; you have to have someone else's blood to suck to be a capitalist. . . . So, when we look at the African continent, when we look

at the trouble that's going on between East and West, we find that the nations in Africa are developing socialist systems to solve their problems.[29]

That Malcolm X's commitment to socialism had become an open and avowed one in the six months between May and December 1964 was due to the observations he made during his pilgrimage to Mecca and subsequent travels throughout Africa. Although some have seen fit to claim that his pilgrimage was "a tragic diversion" having "no real relevance to the streets of Harlem,"[30] just the opposite appears to be true: the experiences of his travels broadened his political perspective, causing him to view Afro-American liberation in a dramatically different light than he had before the rift with the Muslims.

Besides impelling him to study and, finally, to adopt socialism as his goal, the African tour furnished Malcolm with a keen understanding of modern imperialism. In the same address from which I have already excerpted his remarks on socialism, Malcolm offered his black audience a cogent exposition on the workings of the imperialist system. Stressing the need of the capitalist economies for the markets and cheap raw materials of the developing world "in order to survive," he assured his listeners that without these things, capitalism in Europe and the United States "wouldn't be worth two cents." It followed, therefore, that in order to preserve "free access" to the vital markets and raw materials of the preindustrial countries,

European nations in the past have kept the nations in Latin America and in Africa and in Asia from becoming industrial powers. They keep the machinery and the ability to produce and manufacture limited to Europe and limited to America. Then this puts America and the Europeans in a position to control the economy of all other nations and keep them living at a low standard.

The solution to this problem, from the standpoint of the less-developed nations, was to root out all forms of imperialism and neocolonialism and embark on a program of planned socialist industrialization. "The people," Malcolm continued, in his typically vivid imagery,

> are beginning to see that. The Africans see it, the Latin Americans see it, the Asians see it. So when you hear them talking about freedom, they're not talking about a cup of coffee with a cracker. No, they're talking about getting in a position to feed themselves and clothe themselves and make these other things that, when you have them, make life worth living. So this is the way you and I have to understand the world revolution that's taking place right now.[31]

Could one ask for a more compact and luminous summary?

From what I have said above, it should come as no revelation that Malcolm X's revolutionary socialism was predicated on united action of all the wretched of the earth to overcome their common imperialist foe. Like the conversion to socialism, he worked out this idea as a result of coming into contact with the forces of revolution in the developing countries (once more demonstrating the shortsightedness of the notion that Malcolm's travel in Africa was "a tragic diversion"). This principle—solidarity of the world's revolutionary forces—was behind his attempt to utilize the United Nations as a forum for embarrassing the U.S. ruling class. Other times, at his most blunt, he might laconically state, "If your power base is only here, you can forget it."[32] Regardless of the specific formulation, however, his premise was always that

> you can't understand what is going on in Mississippi if you don't understand what is going on in the Congo. . . .

They're both the same. The same interests are at stake. The same sides are drawn up, the same schemes are at work in the Congo that are at work in Mississippi.[33]

But perhaps the most telling versions of this thesis were the ones Malcolm X pronounced in the month immediately preceding his death. In January 1965, for instance, when questioned by a television interviewer about the possibility of an "Armageddon in the United States by 1984," Malcolm replied:

I believe that there will ultimately be a clash between the oppressed and those that do the oppressing. I believe that there will be a clash between those who want freedom, justice, and equality for everyone and those who want to continue the systems of exploitation. I believe that there will be that kind of clash, but I don't think that it will be based upon the color of the skin, as Elijah Muhammad had taught it.[34]

Three short days before his tragic murder, during an address at Columbia University on "The Black Revolution and its Effect Upon the Negroes of the Western Hemisphere," Malcolm returned to the same theme:

We are living in an era of revolution, and the revolt of the American Negro is part of the rebellion against the oppression and colonialism which has characterized this era. . . .
It is incorrect to classify the revolt of the Negro as simply a racial conflict of black against white, or as a purely American problem. Rather, we are today seeing a global rebellion of the oppressed against the oppressor, the exploited against the exploiter.[35]

It was this global rebellion that persuaded Malcolm that the African-American liberation movement had no choice but to merge with like-minded anti-imperialist and revolutionary movements in Africa, Asia, and Latin America in a united campaign against their common enemy. Once black people in the United States came to the realization that they were actually part of a revolutionary *majority* and not an isolated minority, they could join the battle for freedom with renewed intensity and confidence of ultimate victory.[36]

Alas for all concerned, Malcolm X was cut down almost before these words had ceased to ring in the air. But who is to say that it was not these very views that made his continued existence unbearable to the U.S. ruling class or one of its agencies?*

At the moment of his death, Malcolm X was, in my opinion, the preeminent American political figure of our time and verging on becoming the foremost spokesman for revolutionary socialism this country has yet produced. As great as is our grief at his slaying, we must recall that his voice never sounded for himself alone; it cried out as well for those mute legions—the "faceless in America," Archie Shepp termed them—whose aspirations and goals, resentments and frustrations, would otherwise have gone unuttered. He was, thus, in a very precise sense, in the vanguard of his people. In light of that, we need to keep in mind that where the vanguard leads, there, too, the remaining columns yet may march.

NOTES

1. Quoted in the (partial) transcript of a panel discussion among Taylor, Archie Shepp, Rahsaan Roland Kirk, and others, "Point of

---

* If the administrations of John F. Kennedy and Lyndon B. Johnson were capable of having the Central Intelligence Agency attempt the assassination of a foreign head of state—namely, Fidel Castro—why should we expect them to scruple at having a mere black rabble-rouser in this country put to death?

Contact," in *down beat Music '66,* ed. Don DeMicheal (Chicago: Maher Publications, 1966), p. 111.

2. Quoted in *ibid.,* p. 29.

3. Quoted in *ibid.,* p. 20.

4. Shepp's poem appears on the inside cover of *Fire Music* (Impulse 86); his comments on the poem are quoted in the notes to the recording. When I did an impressionistic survey of the titles of jazz recordings in the 1970s, I found that John Coltrane (as I said in the preceding chapter) had more compositions and/or albums dedicated to his memory than did any other person; Malcolm X shared second place with Angela Davis. That jazz musicians regard Coltrane and Malcolm X in similarly heroic terms indicates, as I argue in this and previous chapters, a connection or parallel between them. Many black writers such as Stephen Henderson agree. Henderson writes: "What Coltrane signifies for black people because of the breadth of his vision and the incredible energy behind his spiritual quest, Malcolm X signifies in another way—not as musician, but simply and profoundly as black man, as Black Experience, and that experience in the process of discovering itself, of celebrating itself." See "Survival Motion: A Study of the Black Writer and the Black Revolution in America," in Henderson and Mercer Cook, eds., *The Militant Black Writer: In Africa and the United States* (Madison: University of Wisconsin Press, 1969), p. 110.

5. All quotations are from *By Any Means Necessary,* ed. George Breitman (New York: Pathfinder, 1970, 1992), pp. 91–92 [2010 printing].

6. *The Autobiography of Malcolm X* (with the assistance of Alex Haley), Grove Press, New York, 1965, pp. 26–27.

7. *Ibid.,* p. 68

8. *Ibid.,* pp. 242–43.

9. *Ibid.,* p. 269.

10. *Ibid.,* p. 404.

11. William James, *Varieties of Religious Experience: A Study of Human Nature* (New York: Modern Library, 1929).

12. Quoted in *Autobiography,* p. 156.

13. *Ibid.,* p. 157.

14. *Ibid.*

15. *Ibid.*, p. 173.

16. *Ibid.*

17. *Ibid.*, p. 174.

18. *Ibid.*

19. Truman Nelson, "Delinquent's Progress," a review of *The Autobiography of Malcolm X* in *The Nation*, November 8, 1965, p. 337.

20. See, for example, *Autobiography*, p. 240.

21. *Ibid.*, p. 294.

22. *Ibid.*, p. 293.

23. As I pointed out earlier—and as the epigraph from Archie Shepp further suggests—the same milieu that gave rise to Malcolm X also produced the most vital forms of contemporaneous jazz. The *Autobiography* reveals that Malcolm was an intimate friend of many of Harlem's leading jazz figures of the 1940s and '50s. There has, incidentally, been a good deal of nonsense written about the supposed relationship between black nationalism and jazz. Thus, I.F. Stone, reviewing the *Autobiography* and *Malcolm X Speaks* ("The Pilgrimage of Malcolm X," *The New York Review of Books*, November 11, 1965, p. 4), follows the lead of E.U. Essien-Udom in maintaining that the Muslims—and by extension, all black nationalists—turn up their noses at jazz; see for instance, Essien-Udom, *Black Nationalism: A Search for an Identity in America* (Chicago: University of Chicago Press, 1962), p. 119. From this, Stone infers that the Muslims described by Essien-Udom were inadvertently displaying their ostensible "self-hatred." The real situation is nowhere near that clear-cut. In the program that I described in a content note above, Malcolm X's appearance came after forty-five minutes of jazz by the organ trio of Richard ("Groove") Holmes. Malcolm himself, moreover, made explicit reference to the music in his opening comments, remarking that he had been in the back of the auditorium "patting my foot" while Holmes was playing. Does this sound like the repudiation of African-American culture that Stone and many others would have us believe characterizes the nationalists?

24. Malcolm X, *Malcolm X Speaks: Selected Speeches and State-*

ments, ed. George Breitman (New York: Pathfinder Press, 1965, 1989); see also the companion volume, Malcolm X, *By Any Means Necessary,* cited above in note 5, as well as Breitman's own study, *The Last Year of Malcolm X: The Evolution of a Revolutionary* (New York, Pathfinder Press, 1967).

25. Let me reiterate that, as I sought to explain above, I emphatically do not mean by this paragraph that Malcolm X was considering an affiliation with any white radical or socialist organization. While on the subject, moreover, I may add as well that although this essay does not pretend to be a review of the voluminous material on Malcolm X that has emerged since his death, I have attempted to keep abreast of this literature, and I see nothing within it that leads me to conclude my account of Malcolm X's thinking during the final months of his life is in any significant respect mistaken.

26. *Malcolm X Speaks,* p. 23 [2009 printing].

27. *Ibid.,* p. 22.

28. *Ibid.,* p. 91.

29. *Ibid.,* pp. 148–49.

30. Nelson, "Delinquent's Progress," p. 338.

31. *Malcolm X Speaks,* pp. 156–57.

32. *Ibid.,* p. 158.

33. *Ibid.,* p. 153–154.

34. *Ibid.,* p. 256.

35. *Ibid.,* p. 256–57.

36. Some have professed to see a contradiction between Malcolm X's black nationalism and his socialist internationalism. If, their argument runs, he remained a black nationalist until the end of his life, then he could not have become an internationalist. If, in contrast, he became a convert to internationalism, then he must have forsaken black nationalism. I hope no one takes such semantic sleight of hand and nonsensical debaters' tricks with any seriousness. It is a commonplace that nationalist freedom-fighters in, say, Vietnam, South Africa, and Central America not only fully sympathized with each other's liberation struggles, but also understood that, directly or indirectly, they were all fighting the same foe. Here, for example, is how the Guatemalan revolutionary leader Yon Sosa

expressed the interconnectedness of his struggle with that of the Vietnamese: "The war in Vietnam may be a determining factor. If the United States loses there or withdraws, the victory of socialist revolutions in Latin America could come much sooner." Quoted in Frank Kofsky, "Vietnam and Social Revolution," *Monthly Review*, March 1967, p. 34.

Index

Index of songs and albums

CULTURE AND POLITICS

ART AND REVOLUTION
Writings on Literature, Politics, and Culture

Leon Trotsky

One of the outstanding revolutionary leaders of the 20th century examines the place and aesthetic autonomy of art, literature, and artistic expression in the struggle for a new, socialist society. $22

SOCIALISM AND MAN IN CUBA

Ernesto Che Guevara, Fidel Castro

"Man truly reaches his full human condition when he produces without being compelled by physical necessity to sell himself as a commodity." $7. Also in Spanish, French, Farsi, and Greek.

BLACK MUSIC, WHITE BUSINESS
Illuminating the History and Political Economy of Jazz

Frank Kofsky

Probes the economic and social conflicts between the artistry of Black musicians and the control by largely white-owned businesses of jazz distribution—the recording companies, booking agencies, festivals, clubs, and magazines. $17

THEIR MORALS AND OURS
The Class Foundations of Moral Practice

Leon Trotsky

Participating in the revolutionary workers movement "with open eyes and an intense will—only this can give the highest moral satisfaction to a thinking being," Trotsky writes. He explains how morality is rooted in the interests of contending social classes. With a reply by the pragmatist philosopher John Dewey and a Marxist response to Dewey by George Novack. $15. Also in Spanish.

The US rulers have begun

Three books for today's spreading and deepening debate among working people looking for a way forward in face of capitalism's global economic and social calamity and wars.

The Clintons' Anti-Working-Class Record
Why Washington Fears Working People

Jack Barnes

Hillary Clinton contemptuously called workers who refused to vote for her irredeemable "deplorables."

Winner Donald Trump tries to divide and weaken the working class—demagogically targeting Mexicans, Muslims, unionists, women, and others—while lining the bosses' pockets.

This book documents the profit-driven course over the last quarter century of the party of capital, Democrat and Republican alike. It explains the awakening anger and wide-ranging discussion among working people seeking to understand and resist the capitalists' assaults.

$10. Also in Spanish.

to fear the working class

Are They Rich Because They're Smart?

Class, Privilege, and Learning under Capitalism

Jack Barnes

Barnes explains the sharpening class inequalities in the US and takes apart self-serving rationalizations by layers of well-paid professionals that their intelligence and schooling equip them to "regulate" the lives of working people, who don't know our own best interests.

$10. Also in Spanish, French, and Farsi.

Is Socialist Revolution in the US Possible?

A Necessary Debate Among Working People

Mary-Alice Waters

An unhesitating "Yes"—that's the answer by Waters. Possible—but not inevitable. That depends on us. Fighting for a society only working people can create, it's our own capacities we will discover as we cast off the false image of ourselves promoted by those who profit from the exploitation of our labor.

$10. Also in Spanish and French.

The class struggle

50 Years of Covert Operations in the US
Washington's political police and the American working class
Larry Seigle, Farrell Dobbs, Steve Clark
Traces the decades-long fight by class-conscious workers against efforts to expand presidential powers and build the "national security" state essential to maintaining capitalist rule.
$12. Also in Spanish and Farsi.

"It's the Poor Who Face the Savagery of the US 'Justice' System"
The Cuban Five talk about their lives within the US working class
In a 2015 interview, five Cuban revolutionaries framed up by the US government and imprisoned for 16 years talk about their lives as part of the US working class. And prospects for Cuba's socialist revolution today. Includes 24 pages of photos.
$15. Also in Spanish and Farsi.

Malcolm X Talks to Young People
"The young generation of whites, Blacks, browns, whatever else there is—you're living at a time of revolution," Malcolm said in December 1964. "And I for one will join in with anyone, I don't care what color you are, as long as you want to change this miserable condition that exists on this earth." Four talks and an interview given to young people in the last months of Malcolm's life.
$15. Also in Spanish, French, Farsi, and Greek.

in the United States

Teamster Politics
Farrell Dobbs

A central leader of the battles records how Minneapolis Teamster Local 544 combatted FBI and other government frame-ups in the 1930s; organized the unemployed; mobilized labor opposition to US imperialism's entry into World War II; and fought to lead labor and its allies on an independent working-class political course.
$19. Also in Spanish.

Capitalism's Long Hot Winter Has Begun
Jack Barnes

Published as the storm clouds of the 2008 financial crisis were forming, Barnes explains that today's global capitalist crisis is but the opening stage of decades of economic, financial, and social convulsions and class battles. Class-conscious workers, he writes, confront this historic turning point for imperialism with confidence, drawing satisfaction from being "in their face" as we chart a revolutionary course to take power. In *New International* no. 12.
$16. Also in Spanish, French, Farsi, Arabic, and Greek.

Puerto Rico: Independence Is a Necessity
Rafael Cancel Miranda

One of the five Puerto Rican Nationalists imprisoned by Washington for more than 25 years and released in 1979 speaks out on the brutal reality of US colonial domination, the campaign to free Puerto Rican political prisoners, the example of Cuba's socialist revolution, and the ongoing struggle for independence.
$6. Also in Spanish and Farsi.

African freedom struggle

 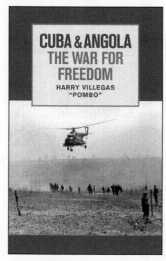

How Far We Slaves Have Come!
SOUTH AFRICA AND CUBA IN TODAY'S WORLD

Nelson Mandela, Fidel Castro

Speaking together in Cuba in 1991, Mandela and Castro
discuss the place in the history of Africa of the victory
by Cuban, Angolan, and Namibian combatants over the
US-backed South African army that had invaded Angola.
Cuba's internationalist volunteers, said Mandela, made an
"unparalleled contribution to African independence, freedom,
and justice."
$10. Also in Spanish and Farsi.

Cuba and Angola: The War for Freedom

Harry Villegas ("Pombo")

The story of Cuba's unparalleled contribution to the fight to
free Africa from the scourge of apartheid. And how, in the
doing, Cuba's socialist revolution was strengthened.
$10. Also in Spanish.

Women's Liberation and the African Freedom Struggle

Thomas Sankara

"There is no true social revolution without the liberation of
women," explains the leader of the 1983–87 revolution in the
West African country of Burkina Faso.
$8. Also in Spanish, French, and Farsi.

Thomas Sankara Speaks

THE BURKINA FASO REVOLUTION 1983–87

In 1983 the peasants and workers of Burkina Faso established a popular revolutionary government and began to combat the colonial legacy of hunger, illiteracy, and economic backwardness. Thomas Sankara, who led that struggle, explains the example set for Africa and the world.
$24. Also in French.

In Defense of Socialism

FOUR SPEECHES ON THE 30TH ANNIVERSARY OF THE CUBAN REVOLUTION, 1988–89

Fidel Castro

Castro describes the decisive place of volunteer Cuban fighters in the final stage of the war in Angola against invading forces of South Africa's apartheid regime. Not only is economic and social progress possible without capitalism's dog-eat-dog competition, the Cuban leader says, but socialism is humanity's only way forward.
$15. Also in Greek.

Che Guevara Talks to Young People

Guevara challenges youth of Cuba and the world to study, to work, to become disciplined. To join the front lines of struggles, small and large. To politicize themselves and the work of their organizations. To become a different kind of human being as they strive together with working people of all lands to transform the world.
$15. Also in Spanish and Greek.

Nelson Mandela Speaks

FORGING A DEMOCRATIC, NONRACIAL SOUTH AFRICA

Speeches from 1990–93 recounting the struggle that put an end to apartheid and opened the fight for a deep-going political and social transformation in South Africa.
$25

www.pathfinderpress.com

WOMEN'S LIBERATION AND SOCIALISM

Cosmetics, Fashions, and the Exploitation of Women
Joseph Hansen, Evelyn Reed, Mary-Alice Waters

How big business plays on women's second-class status and economic insecurities to market cosmetics and rake in profits. And how the entry of millions of women into the workforce has irreversibly changed relations between women and men—for the better.

$15. Also in Spanish and Farsi.

Woman's Evolution
From Matriarchal Clan to Patriarchal Family
Evelyn Reed

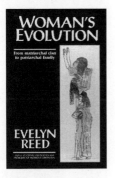

Assesses women's leading and still largely unknown contributions to the development of human civilization and refutes the myth that women have always been subordinate to men. "Certain to become a classic text in women's history."—*Publishers Weekly*.

$32. Also in Farsi.

Abortion Is a Woman's Right!
Pat Grogan, Evelyn Reed

Why abortion rights are central not only to the fight for the full emancipation of women, but to forging a united and fighting labor movement.

$6. Also in Spanish.

Communist Continuity and the Fight for Women's Liberation
Documents of the Socialist Workers Party 1971–86

How did the oppression of women begin? Who benefits? What social forces have the power to end women's second-class status? 3 volumes, edited with preface by Mary-Alice Waters.

$30

EXPAND YOUR REVOLUTIONARY LIBRARY

The Communist Manifesto
KARL MARX AND FREDERICK ENGELS

Why communism is not a set of pre-conceived principles but the line of march of the working class toward power, "springing from an existing class struggle, a historical movement going on under our very eyes." The founding document of the modern revolutionary workers movement. $5. Also in Spanish, French, Farsi, and Arabic.

The Jewish Question
A Marxist Interpretation
ABRAM LEON

Traces the historical rationalizations of anti-Semitism to the fact that, in the centuries preceding the domination of industrial capitalism, Jews emerged as a "people-class" of merchants, moneylenders, and traders. Leon explains why the propertied rulers incite renewed Jew-hatred in the epoch of capitalism's decline. $25

Fighting Racism in World War II
From the pages of the Militant

An account of struggles against racist discrimination in US war industries, the armed forces, and society as a whole from 1939 to 1945, taken from the pages of the socialist newsweekly, the *Militant.* These struggles helped lay the basis for the proletarian-based civil rights movement that followed. $25

U.S. Imperialism
Has Lost the Cold War
JACK BARNES

Contrary to imperialist expectations with the collapse of regimes claiming to be communist across Eastern Europe and the USSR, the Cuban Revolution did not follow suit. Cuban working people and their leadership have continued to show the world what "socialist revolution" means. In *New International* no. 11. $16. Also in Spanish, French, Farsi, and Greek.

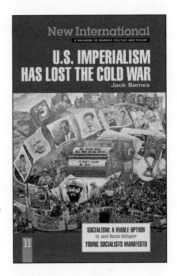

Lenin's Final Fight
Speeches and Writings, 1922–23
V.I. LENIN

In 1922 and 1923, V.I. Lenin, central leader of the world's first socialist revolution, waged what was to be his last political battle. At stake was whether that revolution, and the international movement it led, would remain on the proletarian course that had brought workers and peasants to power in October 1917. $20. Also in Spanish and Greek.

The Revolution Betrayed
What Is the Soviet Union
and Where Is It Going?
LEON TROTSKY

In 1917 workers and peasants of Russia were the motor force for one of the deepest revolutions in history. Yet within ten years a political counterrevolution by a privileged social layer whose chief spokesperson was Joseph Stalin was being consolidated. The classic study of the Soviet workers state and its degeneration. $20. Also in Spanish, Farsi, and Greek.